The ClojureScript Playbook

The Grand ClojureScript Hotel: 10 Floors of Interactive Fun

Nicolas Modrzyk

Apress®

The ClojureScript Playbook: The Grand ClojureScript Hotel: 10 Floors of Interactive Fun

Nicolas Modrzyk
Tokyo, Japan

ISBN-13 (pbk): 979-8-8688-2878-2 ISBN-13 (electronic): 979-8-8688-2879-9
https://doi.org/10.1007/979-8-8688-2879-9

Managing Director, Apress Media LLC: Welmoed Spahr
Acquisitions Editor: James Robinson-Prior
Editorial Assistant: Gryffin Winkler

Cover designed by eStudioCalamar

Cover image from jplenio on pixabay (pixabay.com)

Distributed to the book trade worldwide by Springer Science+Business Media New York, 1 New York Plaza, New York, NY 10004. Phone 1-800-SPRINGER, fax (201) 348-4505, e-mail orders-ny@springer-sbm.com, or visit www.springeronline.com. Apress Media, LLC is a Delaware LLC and the sole member (owner) is Springer Science + Business Media Finance Inc (SSBM Finance Inc). SSBM Finance Inc is a **Delaware** corporation.

For information on translations, please e-mail booktranslations@springernature.com; for reprint, paperback, or audio rights, please e-mail bookpermissions@springernature.com.

Apress titles may be purchased in bulk for academic, corporate, or promotional use. eBook versions and licenses are also available for most titles. For more information, reference our Print and eBook Bulk Sales web page at http://www.apress.com/bulk-sales.

Any source code or other supplementary material referenced by the author in this book is available to readers on GitHub. For more detailed information, please visit https://www.apress.com/gp/services/source-code.

If disposing of this product, please recycle the paper

To my new reader.

If you go to the roof of this hotel and look up, you can see exactly where we are going.

Table of Contents

About the Author

Nicolas Modrzyk is a veteran technologist, author, and CTO based in Tokyo, with more than two decades of international experience spanning Asia, Europe, and the United States. Throughout his career, he has led complex technology initiatives at the intersection of software engineering, architecture, innovation, and business transformation, helping organizations turn ambitious ideas into elegant and scalable systems.

A long-time advocate of expressive programming and thoughtful software design, Nicolas has authored numerous books on Clojure, functional programming, and modern software craftsmanship. His work emphasizes clarity, creativity, and the belief that technology should not only solve problems but also inspire better ways of thinking. Blending deep technical expertise with an artistic mindset, he is known for approaching software as both engineering and composition—where structure, rhythm, and simplicity matter as much as performance.

Beyond the world of technology, Nicolas draws inspiration from music, improvisation, and creative expression. Whether through guitar textures, saxophone lines, or late-night deep jazz sessions, his artistic influences continue to shape his vision of leadership, design, and innovation.

About the Technical Reviewer

Shantanu Kumar is a software engineer and architect based in Bangalore, India, with decades of experience building enterprise and distributed systems. He has a strong interest in performance, scalability, and pragmatic software design and has worked across a wide range of technologies in production environments. An active member of the Clojure community, he has delivered talks at conferences such as Functional Conf and IN/Clojure. Shantanu is also the author of *Clojure High Performance Programming* (1st and 2nd editions, Packt) and an open-source contributor, most recently building PluMCP, a low dependency Model Context Protocol (MCP) SDK for Java and JavaScript runtimes, based on Clojure/ClojureScript, to integrate business systems with AI agents.

Acknowledgments

Building a ten-floor hotel in the middle of a rushing world is not a project you can complete alone. I owe my deepest gratitude to those who helped lay the foundation, provided the quiet, and kept me grounded along the way.

To Abirami, Divya, Gryffin, and the entire team at Apress: thank you for supporting this out-of-the-ordinary project and for believing in its architecture.

To everyone at Karabiner Software: thank you for doing great work alongside me and for giving me the midnight hours to burn the midnight oil.

To my soccer circle: thank you for teaching me that without a proper team spirit, it is far too easy to break.

To my music circle—the ones I sing for and the ones I go listening to: thank you for bringing the melody of freedom to every single floor.

To my family—the close ones, the faraway ones, and the ones who have already left the hotel: thank you for always wanting to understand what it is I am writing about.

And, finally, to my two resilient daughters: thank you for always doing your best in style. You are the best thing I have ever helped build.

Reader Level and Prerequisites

Grand ClojureScript Hotel: 10 Floors of Interactive Fun

Target Experience Level

The book targets intermediate developers—designed to be fun and accessible for someone who already programs but is new to ClojureScript (or Clojure). A complete beginner will struggle; an experienced developer curious about functional front-end programming will have a blast.

Profile	Experience Level
Sweet spot	Developer with 1–3 years of JS/web experience, curious about Clojure/FP
Will manage	Seasoned Clojure/Java developer with no front-end experience
Will struggle	Complete programming novice

The difficulty ramps deliberately—Chapters 1–4 are approachable; Chapters 8–10 (WebGL, neural nets, Mobile apps) require real confidence with both ClojureScript and the underlying JS ecosystem.

Prerequisites

Required (Must-Have)

- **Basic programming fluency**: Variables, loops, functions, data structures.
- **Some JavaScript or web exposure**: Understanding of HTML, the DOM, and events; you don't need to be an expert, but "what is a browser?" must not be a mystery.
- **Comfort with the command line**: Running `npm` and `npx`, navigating directories.

Strongly Recommended (Will Save Frustration)

- **Clojure/ClojureScript basics**: Parentheses, `defn`, `let`, `atom`, vectors/maps; even one afternoon with clojurescript.org helps enormously.
- **Basic React/component thinking**: Especially for Chapters 4–6 (Reagent, re-frame, charting).
- **Familiarity with `npm`/Node.js**: The toolchain is `shadow-cljs` + npm, so knowing what `package.json` is matters.

Bonus (Unlocks the Advanced Floors)

- **Canvas/WebGL basics**: For Chapters 2, 7, and 8 (animations, PixiJS, Three.js)
- **Basic ML/linear algebra concepts**: For Chapter 9 (backpropagation, weights, loss functions)
- **Mobile Devices Experience**: For Chapter 10 (mobile deployment, simulators)

Floor-by-Floor Difficulty

Chapter	Topic	Difficulty
Ch 1	Getting Started—Pong, Unit Converter	1/5
Ch 2	Canvas Sketches and Animations	2/5
Ch 3	Generative Art with Quil	2/5
Ch 4	Reactive UIs with Reagent and Toolkits	2/5
Ch 5	Standalone Mini-Apps (Re-frame, GitHub Explorer)	3/5
Ch 6	Data Visualization and Charts	2/5
Ch 7	Audio and Video Processing	3/5
Ch 8	Graphics Engines and Games (PixiJS, Three.js)	4/5
Ch 9	Neural Networks and Visualizations	4/5
Ch 10	Mobile and Wellness Apps with Mobile Devices	5/5

The book is structured so readers can **check in at any floor**—you don't need to read linearly if you already have the background for a given chapter.

Total projects: 46 ClojureScript examples across ten chapters, all building and warning-free as of the latest release.

Introduction

Introduction: A Room of Your Own, Ten Floors Up

We live in an age of acceleration.

Algorithms hum through our decisions before we've finished making them. Language models draft our emails, summarize our meetings, and answer questions we haven't yet thought to ask. The world, it seems, has grown faster than our ability to simply be in it.

And yet—the lobby door swings open.

You step inside.

This book is an invitation to check in.

Not to escape the age of artificial intelligence (AI)—that would be both futile and dishonest—but to find, within it, a place of deliberate stillness. A ten-floor hotel where each landing offers something the algorithm cannot: the unhurried texture of a lived moment, the particular light through a particular window at a particular hour, the weight of a key in your hand.

Hotels have always been liminal places. They belong to everyone and no one. In a hotel room, you are briefly released from the accumulated architecture of your own life—your routines, your role, your name on the mailbox. You are, for a night or a week, a stranger in a generous country. And in that strangeness, something loosens.

You remember how to look.

There are ten floors here, and they are not organized by price or prestige. They rise, instead, the way a mind rises through a long afternoon of thought—from the grounded and the sensory, up through the reflective and the luminous, toward something that does not quite have a name yet. Each floor is a different register of rest: the rest that comes from silence, from beauty, from conversation, from solitude, from wonder.

The rooms are real. The stories that fill them are real. The people who passed through—travelers, dreamers, the quietly extraordinary—left something behind, the way travelers always do. A book dog-eared to a page. An observation about the rain. A question that outlasted their stay.

In an era when intelligence is being distributed across machines at a scale no single mind can comprehend, there is something quietly radical about a place built for human presence. A hotel does not optimize. It accommodates. It makes space for you to arrive—tired, curious, unfinished—and asks nothing more than that you stay awhile.

This book is that place.

In a world that never stops generating, this is your permission to pause. To ascend—not toward productivity or optimization, but toward yourself.

Welcome.

CHAPTER 1

Building Pong in ClojureScript: A Late-Night Tutorial

> "Pong is where it all began. Two paddles, one ball, and the birth of an industry."

The Concept

If you weren't around in 1972, here's what you missed: Pong was the game that kicked off the video game industry. Two paddles, one ball, pure arcade magic. Atari released it, and suddenly everyone wanted to play electronic ping-pong. It's the "Hello, World" of game development, simple enough to understand in an evening, deep enough to teach you the fundamentals.

What makes Pong elegant from a functional programming perspective is that it's a perfect state machine. At any moment, the entire game can be described by a handful of numbers: ball position, ball velocity, paddle position, and score. There are no hidden variables, no complex object hierarchies, no tangled dependencies. Just data transforming predictably over time.

The original Pong was built with discrete logic chips, literally hardware that computed the next state from the current state. In a way, those engineers were doing functional programming before the term was even popular. Each frame was a pure transformation: given the current positions and velocities, calculate the next positions and velocities. Collision? Invert the velocity. Miss? Reset the state.

This is why Pong is such a natural fit for ClojureScript and functional programming. We're not fighting against the paradigm; we're embracing it. Our game loop will be

N. Modrzyk, *The ClojureScript Playbook*, https://doi.org/10.1007/979-8-8688-2879-9_1

a series of pure functions, each taking the world as it is and returning the world as it should be. No mutations, no surprises, just elegant transformations flowing through a pipeline.

We're building a single-player variant. You control a paddle at the bottom of the screen, trying to keep the ball in play. Miss the ball? Game over. Hit it? Score points. Simple, satisfying, and perfect for learning ClojureScript.

This is the first floor of our journey through ClojureScript. Before moving to higher floors with more sophisticated patterns and deeper abstractions, we need to master the basics. And there's no better place to start than with Pong, a simple and timeless game that teaches the fundamentals.

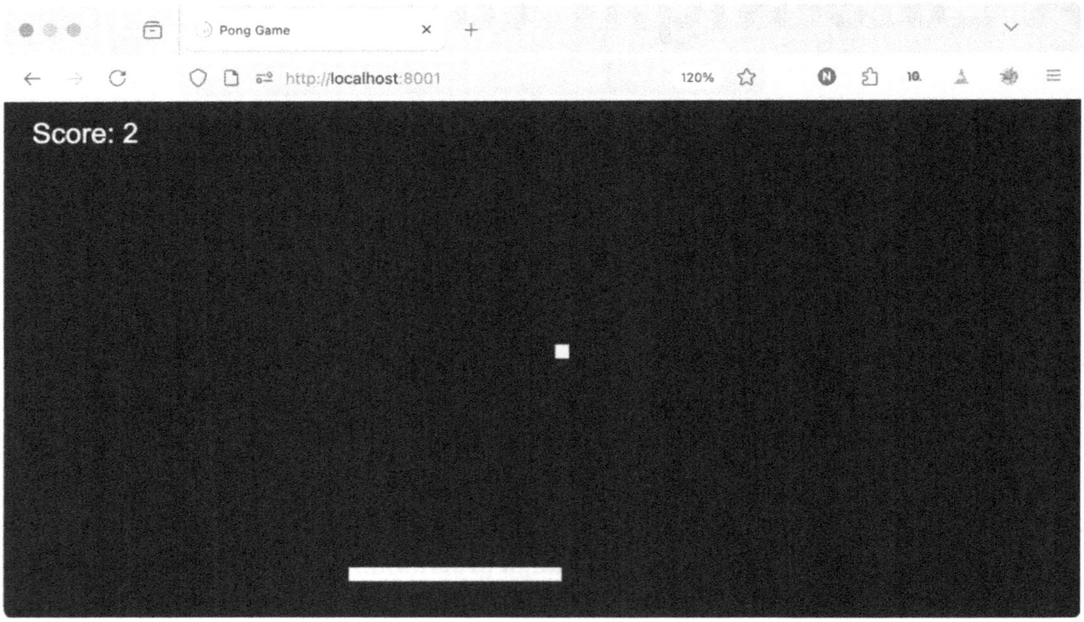

***Figure 1-1.** The classic Pong game interface with paddle and ball rendered on an HTML5 canvas*

The Foundation

Before we draw a single pixel, we need to set up the project. A ClojureScript project relies on configuration files that tell our tools what we need and how to build it.

Here's how the pieces fit together, from code to running game.

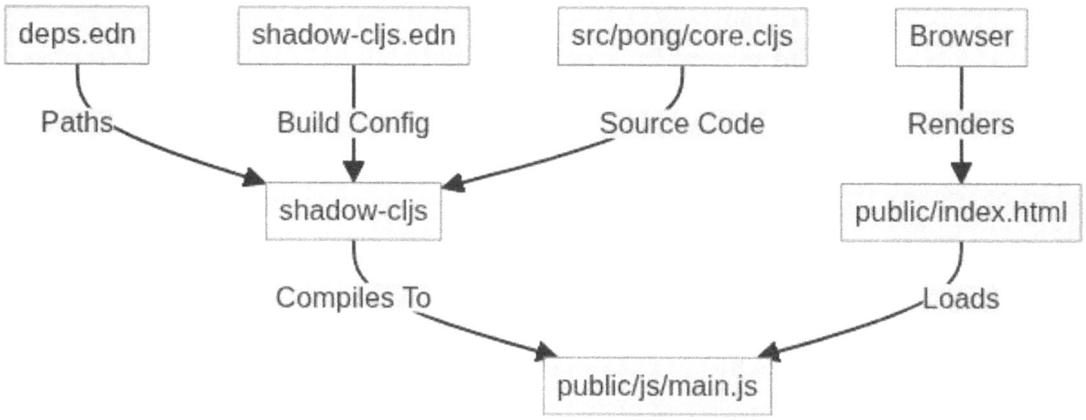

Figure 1-2. *Project architecture showing how shadow-cljs compiles ClojureScript source code into browser-ready JavaScript*

We begin with `deps.edn`. For this project, we are keeping it delightfully minimal. We simply tell the tools where our source code lives.

Listing 1-1. Minimal deps.edn configuration file specifying source code and resource directories for the ClojureScript project

```
{:paths ["src" "resources"]}
```

The `:paths` key points to a vector of directories. Clojure will look for `.clj` and `.cljs` files inside `src` and `resources`. It's the equivalent of setting your `CLASSPATH` in Java, but more readable.

Next is `shadow-cljs.edn`, which tells the compiler where to find our source code ("src"), where to output the compiled JavaScript ("public/js"), and which function to call when the application starts (`pong.core/init`).

We also configure a development server on port 8001, allowing us to see changes instantly.

Listing 1-2. shadow-cljs.edn build configuration defining development server, output directory, and application entry point

```
{:dev-http     {8001 "public"}
 ;:deps true
 :source-paths ["src"]
 :builds {:app {:target :browser
        :output-dir "public/js"
```

```
                :asset-path "/js"
                :modules {:main {:entries [pong.core] :init-fn pong.core/
                init}}}}}
```

The :builds map is where the heavy lifting happens. We define a build named :app targeting the :browser. The :modules section bundles our code starting at pong.core. The :init-fn tells the compiler to call pong.core/init automatically when the script loads, starting our application.

To start the development server, run this command. It tells shadow-cljs to watch our :app build and recompile whenever we change a file.

Listing 1-3. Command to start shadow-cljs watch mode for live code reloading during development

```
npx shadow-cljs watch app
```

Finally, we need an HTML file. The public/index.html provides the canvas element where our game will live. We keep the styling minimal and inline: a dark background and a centered canvas.

Listing 1-4. HTML5 canvas container with inline styling and JavaScript bundle loading for the Pong game

```
<!DOCTYPE html>
<html lang="en">
<head>
  <meta charset="UTF-8">
  <title>Pong Game</title>
  <style>
    body { margin: 0; }
    #app { width: 400px; height: 100%; position: relative; }
    #game-canvas { width: 100%; height: 100%; background-color: black; }
  </style>
</head>
<body>
  <canvas id="game-canvas" width="800" height="400"></canvas>
  <script src="js/main.js"></script>
</body>
```

The `<canvas>` tag is the key player here. It provides a raw bitmap surface that we can draw on using JavaScript (and by extension, ClojureScript). The `width` and `height` attributes set the internal resolution, while CSS controls how big it appears on screen. We load `main.js` at the end to ensure the DOM exists before our code runs.

Game State and Setup

Let's look at `src/pong/core.cljs`.

In functional programming, we separate data from behavior. Before writing functions to move the ball, we define what a "ball" actually is using simple, immutable data structures.

We start with constants for physics parameters. Then we define our `game-state` atom, which holds the entire game state: ball position, score, paddle location, and canvas dimensions.

The functions `layout!`, `center!`, and `reset-game!` handle initialization, ensuring everything is in the right place before the game starts.

Here's the setup code.

Listing 1-5. Game physics constants defining ball size, paddle dimensions, movement speed, and collision parameters

```
(ns pong.core)

(def ball-size 10)        ;; ball size
(def paddle-width 150)      ;; paddle width
(def paddle-height 10)       ;; paddle height
(def paddle-offset 40) ;; distance from bottom
(def paddle-step 20)    ;; keyboard movement speed
(def speed-increase-interval 5) ;; hits before speed increase
(def speed-multiplier 1.2) ;; speed increase factor
(def angle-sensitivity 25) ;; paddle hit position effect on angle
(def max-horizontal-speed 12) ;; maximum ball horizontal velocity
```

We use `def` to bind names to values. These are our constants, avoiding magic numbers in our code.

Next, we define some helper functions and our application state. `defn` creates functions. Notice `get-element`: it uses ClojureScript's interop syntax (`.getElementById js/document id`) to call the native JavaScript method.

Listing 1-6. Utility functions and game state atom definition with immutable data structure for ball, paddle, and canvas properties

```
(defn get-element
  "Get a DOM element by its ID."
  [id]
  (.getElementById js/document id))

(defn clamp
  "Restrict a value v to be within the range [lo, hi]."
  [v lo hi]
  (-> v (max lo) (min hi)))

(defonce animation-frame-id (atom nil))
(defonce game-state
         (atom {:running? false :score 0 :hits 0
                :ball   {:x 0 :y 0 :vx 4 :vy 4}
                :paddle {:x 0}
                :canvas {:el nil :ctx nil :w 800 :h 600}}))
```

The `game-state` is wrapped in an `atom`. In Clojure, data is immutable by default. To manage change, we need a mutable container. An atom provides safe, synchronous mutation. `defonce` ensures that when we hot-reload code during development, we don't wipe out the current game state.

Next, we adapt to the screen. `layout!` handles high-DPI screens (like Retina displays) for crisp rendering.

Listing 1-7. Canvas layout function handling high-DPI screen scaling with device pixel ratio calculation and state updates

```
(defn layout!
  "Update the canvas dimensions and context based on the window size and
  device pixel ratio."
  []
```

```
  (let [canvas   (get-element "game-canvas")
        context (.getContext canvas "2d")
        dpr (or js/window.devicePixelRatio 1)
        width   (max 1 (.-clientWidth canvas))
        height   (max 1 (.-clientHeight canvas))]
    (set! (.-width canvas) (* width dpr))
    (set! (.-height canvas) (* height dpr))
    (.setTransform context dpr 0 0 dpr 0 0)
    (swap! game-state #(-> %
                 (assoc-in [:canvas :el] canvas)
                 (assoc-in [:canvas :ctx] context)
                 (assoc-in [:canvas :w] width)
                 (assoc-in [:canvas :h] height)))))
```

The exclamation mark in `layout!` is a convention indicating "this function has side effects." We use `swap!` to update atoms. It takes the atom and a function that transforms the current value into the new value.

To reset the board, we separate concerns into `center!` and `reset-game!`.

`center!` calculates the middle of the canvas and places the ball and paddle there. It reads the current width and height from the state, ensuring elements stay centered even if the window is resized.

Listing 1-8. Center function positioning ball and paddle at canvas midpoint using functional state transformation

```
(defn center!
  "Center the paddle and ball in the game canvas."
  []
  (swap! game-state (fn [state]
              (let [width (get-in state [:canvas :w]) height (get-in state
              [:canvas :h])]
                (-> state
                  (assoc-in [:paddle :x] (clamp (- (/ width 2) (/ paddle-
                  width 2)) 0 (- width paddle-width)))
                  (assoc-in [:ball :x] (/ width 2))
                  (assoc-in [:ball :y] (/ height 2)))))))
```

reset-game! handles the game state: it stops the game loop (:running? false), zeros the score and hits, and resets the ball's velocity. Notice it calls center! at the end, composing our helper functions.

Listing 1-9. Reset game function restoring initial values for score, hits, and ball velocity while calling center positioning

```
(defn reset-game!
  "Reset the game state to initial values."
  []
  (swap! game-state #(-> %
                (assoc :running? false :score 0 :hits 0)
                (assoc-in [:ball :vx] 4)
                (assoc-in [:ball :vy] 4)))
  (center!))
```

Finally, start-game! kicks things off by setting the :running? flag to true.

Listing 1-10. Start game function centering elements and setting running flag to begin game loop execution

```
(defn start-game!
  "Start the game loop."
  []
  (center!)
  (swap! game-state assoc :running? true :score 0 :hits 0))
```

The Physics Engine

With our world established, we can now breathe life into it. Game physics, at this scale, is simply the art of transforming numbers.

We break movement down into small, composable behaviors. move-ball is the simplest: it just adds velocity to position. bounce-walls checks boundaries and inverts velocity if necessary. bounce-paddle is more nuanced; it calculates where the ball struck the paddle to apply a satisfying "spin" (horizontal deflection) and increases the difficulty as the game progresses.

This state transformation pipeline is the core of our engine. Notice that these functions are pure—they take a state map and return a new state map. They change nothing in the outside world.

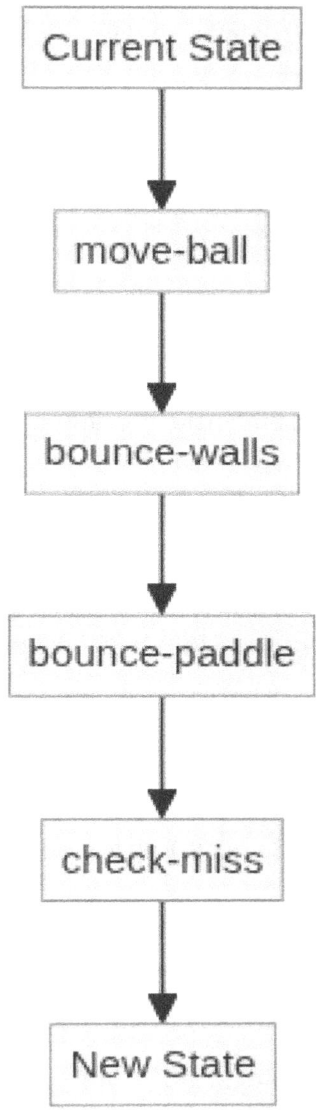

Figure 1-3. *The physics pipeline transforming game state through movement, collision detection, and scoring logic*

Here is the implementation of our physics engine. We'll build it piece by piece. First, `move-ball` is the simplest: it just adds velocity to position.

Listing 1-11. Ball movement function calculating new position by adding velocity vectors to current coordinates

```
(defn move-ball
  "Update the ball's position based on its velocity."
  [state]
  (let [{:keys [x y vx vy]} (:ball state)]
    (-> state
        (assoc-in [:ball :x] (+ x vx))
        (assoc-in [:ball :y] (+ y vy)))))
```

We use destructuring `{:keys [x y vx vy]}` to pull values out of the `:ball` map. It's concise and readable. The `->` macro threads the state through the two `assoc-in` updates, making the coordinate update clear.

Next, `bounce-walls` keeps the ball inside the arena.

Listing 1-12. Wall collision detection with velocity inversion using cond-> threading macro for clean conditional updates

```
(defn bounce-walls
  "Bounce the ball off the left, right, and top walls."
  [state]
  (let [width (get-in state [:canvas :w])
        {:keys [x y]} (:ball state)
        hit-left? (< x 0)
        hit-right? (> (+ x ball-size) width)
        hit-top? (< y 0)]
    (cond-> state
      (or hit-left? hit-right?) (update-in [:ball :vx] -)
      hit-top? (update-in [:ball :vy] -))))
```

`cond->` is a gem of the Clojure language. It conditionally threads the state. "If we hit the left or right wall, update velocity-x with negation (`-`). If we hit the top, update velocity-y." It allows us to express complex branching logic as a flat, linear pipeline.

Now for the complex part: `bounce-paddle`. This function calculates where the ball struck the paddle to apply a satisfying "spin" (horizontal deflection) and increases the difficulty as the game progresses.

Listing 1-13. Paddle collision with angular deflection calculation and progressive difficulty through periodic speed increases

```
(defn bounce-paddle
  "Bounce the ball off the paddle and update score/hits."
  [state]
  (let [height (get-in state [:canvas :h])
        paddle-x (get-in state [:paddle :x])
        paddle-y (- height paddle-offset)
        {:keys [x y vx]} (:ball state)
        hit-paddle? (and (>= (+ y ball-size) paddle-y)
                         (< x (+ paddle-x paddle-width))
                         (> (+ x ball-size) paddle-x))]
    (if hit-paddle?
      (let [hits (inc (:hits state))
            center-x (+ paddle-x (/ paddle-width 2))
            rel (- (+ x (/ ball-size 2)) center-x)
            speed-up? (zero? (mod hits speed-increase-interval))
            speed-factor (if speed-up? speed-multiplier 1)]
        (-> state
            (update :score inc)
            (assoc :hits hits)
            (update-in [:ball :vy] (fn [v] (* -1 v speed-factor)))
            (update-in [:ball :vx] (fn [v] (clamp (+ v (/ rel angle-
            sensitivity))
                                                (- max-horizontal-speed)
                                                max-horizontal-
                                                speed)))))
      state)))
```

This function shows the power of `let`. We define all our intermediate calculations (hit detection, center position, relative impact) up front, making the final state transformation clean and obvious. We are calculating `vx` based on where the ball hits the paddle—giving the player control over the angle.

Finally, we need to know if the player lost.

Listing 1-14. Miss detection function stopping the game when the ball passes bottom boundary below paddle reach

```
(defn check-miss
  "Check if the ball missed the paddle and end the game if so."
  [state]
  (let [height (get-in state [:canvas :h])
        y (get-in state [:ball :y])]
    (if (> y height)
      (assoc state :running? false)
      state)))
```

The Game Loop and Rendering

We have our setup and our physics rules. Now we need the engine that drives them.

The `update-game!` function is the conductor. It orchestrates the flow of data through our physics pipeline. It retrieves the current state, checks if the game is running, and, if so, threads the state through movement and collision checks. Crucially, it ends by calling `draw!`.

The `draw!` function is our bridge back to the visual world. It is the only place where we allow ourselves to be "impure," issuing side-effecting commands to the HTML5 canvas to paint the rectangle of the paddle, the square of the ball, and the text of the score.

Listing 1-15. Canvas rendering function drawing paddle, ball, score text, and start prompt using HTML5 Canvas 2D API

```
(defn draw!
  "Render the game state to the canvas."
  []
  (let [state          @game-state
        {:keys [ctx w h]} (get-in state [:canvas])
        {:keys [x y]}     (:ball state)
        paddle-x         (get-in state [:paddle :x])
        running?   (:running? state)
        score      (:score state)]
```

```
  (.clearRect ctx 0 0 w h)
  (set! (.-fillStyle ctx) "#fff")
  (.fillRect ctx paddle-x (- h paddle-offset) paddle-width paddle-height)
  (when running? (.fillRect ctx x y ball-size ball-size))
  (set! (.-font ctx) "20px Arial")
  (.fillText ctx (str "Score: " score) 20 30)
  (when-not running?
    (set! (.-font ctx) "28px Arial")
    (.fillText ctx "Click or Space to start" (- (/ w 2) 140) (/ h 2)))))
```

We start by dereferencing the atom (`@game-state`) to get an immutable snapshot of the world. Then, we use standard JavaScript Canvas API methods via interop: `clearRect` to wipe the screen, `fillStyle` to set the color, and `fillRect` to draw shapes. The `!` at the end of the function name is a community convention—a warning sign that says, "This function changes the world."

Next, we have the conductor of our orchestra: `update-game!`. It retrieves the current state, checks if the game is running, and, if so, threads the state through our physics pipeline. Crucially, it ends by calling `draw!`.

Listing 1-16. Frame update orchestrator threading game state through physics transformation pipeline before rendering

```
(defn update-game!
  "Update the game state for a single frame."
  []
  (swap! game-state
         (fn [state]
           (if-not (:running? state)
             state
             (-> state
                 move-ball
                 bounce-walls
                 bounce-paddle
                 check-miss))))
  (draw!))
```

This function is the assembly line I mentioned earlier. `swap!` applies our transformation function to the atom. Notice how clean the logic is inside: just a `cond->` or `->` pipeline. It's pure data transformation.

Finally, we need a heartbeat. `game-loop!` keeps the game alive by requesting the next animation frame from the browser.

Listing 1-17. Recursive game loop using requestAnimationFrame for browser-synchronized 60 fps update cycle

```
(defn game-loop!
  "The main game loop, driven by requestAnimationFrame."
  []
  (update-game!)
  (reset! animation-frame-id (js/requestAnimationFrame game-loop!)))
```

This is a recursive function, but it's asynchronous. `js/requestAnimationFrame` tells the browser, "When you are ready to paint the next frame—usually in about 16 milliseconds—call this function again." This ensures our game creates smooth motion without hogging the CPU.

Here is the heartbeat of our application visualized.

Figure 1-4. *The game loop heartbeat driven by requestAnimationFrame for smooth 60 fps animation*

Interaction and Initialization

A game is nothing without a player. We need to listen to the whispers of the outside world—mouse movements and key presses—and translate them into changes in our internal state.

The `move-paddle!` function handles explicit commands (like arrow keys). It reads the canvas width to prevent the paddle from disappearing off the edge.

Listing 1-18. Paddle movement function with boundary clamping preventing paddle from leaving canvas bounds

```
(defn move-paddle!
  "Move the paddle by dx."
  [dx]
  (let [width (get-in @game-state [:canvas :w])]
    (swap! game-state update-in [:paddle :x] #(clamp (+ % dx) 0 (- width
    paddle-width))))
  (draw!))
```

To support mouse control, we need to translate the pointer's position on the screen to its position on the canvas. `getBoundingClientRect` gives us the canvas's position relative to the viewport, allowing us to calculate the correct offset.

Listing 1-19. Mouse event handler converting screen coordinates to canvas space for paddle tracking

```
(defn on-mouse-move
  "Handle mouse move events to control the paddle."
  [e]
  (let [rect (.getBoundingClientRect (get-in @game-state [:canvas :el]))
        width    (get-in @game-state [:canvas :w])
        mouse-x   (- (.-clientX e) (.-left rect))]
    (swap! game-state assoc-in [:paddle :x] (clamp (- mouse-x (/ paddle-
    width 2)) 0 (- width paddle-width)))))
```

Keyboard input is simpler. We just listen for key strings. `ArrowLeft` and `ArrowRight` move the paddle; the spacebar acts as our "Insert Coin" button to start the game.

Listing 1-20. Keyboard event handler using case expression for arrow key paddle control and spacebar game start

```
(defn on-key
  "Handle keyboard events."
  [e]
  (case (.-key e)
    "ArrowLeft"  (move-paddle! (- paddle-step))
```

```
    "ArrowRight" (move-paddle! paddle-step)
    " "          (when-not (:running? @game-state) (start-game!))
    nil))
```

We wrap everything up in `start!`. This function acts as the bridge between the browser environment and our game logic.

Listing 1-21. Event listener registration for window resize, keyboard, mouse, and click interactions with game loop initialization

```
(defn start!
  "Initialize event listeners and start the game loop."
  []
  (when-not @animation-frame-id (reset! animation-frame-id (js/
  requestAnimationFrame game-loop!)))
  (.addEventListener js/window "resize" (fn [_] (layout!) (when-not
  (:running? @game-state) (center!)) (draw!)))
  (.addEventListener js/document "keydown" on-key)
  (.addEventListener js/document "mousemove" on-mouse-move)
  (.addEventListener js/document "click" (fn [_] (when-not (:running?
  @game-state) (start-game!)))))
```

This function is a masterclass in JavaScript interop, which is ClojureScript's superpower.

- `js/window` and `js/document` refer to the global JavaScript objects you know and love.
- `.addEventListener` (note the leading dot) calls a method on those objects. The syntax is `(.methodName object arg1 arg2)`.
- `js/requestAnimationFrame` accesses a global function.

We aren't wrapping these native APIs; we are calling them directly. This means we have the full power of the browser at our fingertips, with zero overhead.

Finally, we expose an `init` function. This is the entry point we referenced way back in our `shadow-cljs.edn` file. It is the big bang that sets our universe in motion. The `^:export` metadata is critical—it tells the compiler to preserve this name so it can be called from JavaScript.

Listing 1-22. Application entry point with export metadata orchestrating layout, reset, rendering, and event listener setup

```
(defn ^:export init
  "Initialize the game."
  []
  (layout!)
  (reset-game!)
  (draw!)
  (start!))
```

Exercises: Expand Your Game

Now that you've built Pong, here are some exercises to enhance it. Each one builds on what you've learned and introduces new challenges.

Exercise 1: Color the World

Difficulty: Easy **Concepts**: State management, drawing

Right now, everything is white on black. Let's add some personality:

1. Add a `:color` field to the ball in your game state (maybe `"#00ff00"` for green?).
2. Add a `:paddle-color` to the state.
3. Modify the `draw!` function to use these colors.
4. **Bonus**: Change the ball color every time it hits the paddle (cycle through an array of colors).

Hint You'll need to modify `game-state` and update the `(set! (.-fillStyle ctx) ...)` lines in `draw!`.

Exercise 2: The Countdown

Difficulty: Medium **Concepts**: State transitions, time-based logic

Add a 3-2-1 countdown before the game starts:

1. Add a `:countdown` field to your game state (starts at 3).
2. Modify `start-game!` to set `:countdown 3` instead of immediately setting `:running? true`.
3. In `update-game!`, if `:countdown` is greater than 0, decrement it every 60 frames (roughly 1 second).
4. When countdown reaches 0, set `:running? true`.
5. Update `draw!` to display the countdown number in the center.

Hint You might need a frame counter, `(mod frame-count 60)`, to track seconds.

Exercise 3: Power-Up Paradise

Difficulty: Hard **Concepts**: Game mechanics, collision detection, randomness

Add power-ups that randomly appear and modify gameplay:

1. Add a `:powerup` field to game state with `{:x :y :type}` (types: `:wide-paddle`, `:slow-ball`, `:extra-points`).
2. Spawn a power-up every 10 hits at a random x position.
3. Detect collision between paddle and power-up.
4. Apply effects:
    - `:wide-paddle`: Double `paddle-width` for 5 seconds.
    - `:slow-ball`: Halve ball velocity for 5 seconds.
    - `:extra-points`: Next hit is worth 10 points.
5. Draw power-ups as small rectangles with different colors.

Hint Use `(js/Math.random)` for random positions. Track effect duration with a timer in state.

Exercise 4: Sound Effects

Difficulty: Medium **Concepts**: Side effects, JavaScript interop, audio

Add sound effects to make it feel like a real arcade game:

1. Find or create three sound files: `ping.mp3` (paddle hit), `wall.mp3` (wall bounce), `miss.mp3` (game over).
2. Create audio elements in your HTML or load them via JavaScript.
3. Add a `play-sound!` function that takes a sound name.
4. Call `play-sound!` at appropriate moments in your game logic.
5. **Bonus**: Add background music that starts/stops with the game.

Hint Use the HTML5 Audio API, `(.play (.getElementById js/document "ping-sound"))`, or create audio elements on the fly, `(doto (js/Audio. "ping.mp3") .play)`.

Final challenge: Combine all four exercises! Imagine a Pong game with colors, countdowns, power-ups, and sound. That's how you go from a simple tutorial to a real game.

Remember: Start small, test often, and keep your functions pure. The functional way is the sustainable way.

Summary

Before you move on, pause for a second and think about `game-state`. Not what's in it—*why* it's there. The entire game—ball position, score, running flag, canvas reference—lives in one atom. Nothing is scattered across global variables or hidden inside objects. That's not accidental; it's the whole point. When you can look at a single data structure and understand the complete state of your program, debugging becomes obvious and testing becomes possible.

The second thing worth sitting with is the game loop. `update-game!` doesn't know anything about time or rendering—it just takes state and returns state. `draw!` doesn't know anything about physics—it just reads state and paints. `game-loop!` knows nothing about either; it just schedules the next frame. You could swap `draw!` for a different renderer and the game logic wouldn't notice. That separation is what makes functional code worth writing.

The exercises are there if you want to push further. The power-up one in particular will test whether you really understood how to extend the state without breaking anything that already works.

The code is yours now. Break it intentionally and fix it. That's the fastest way to learn.

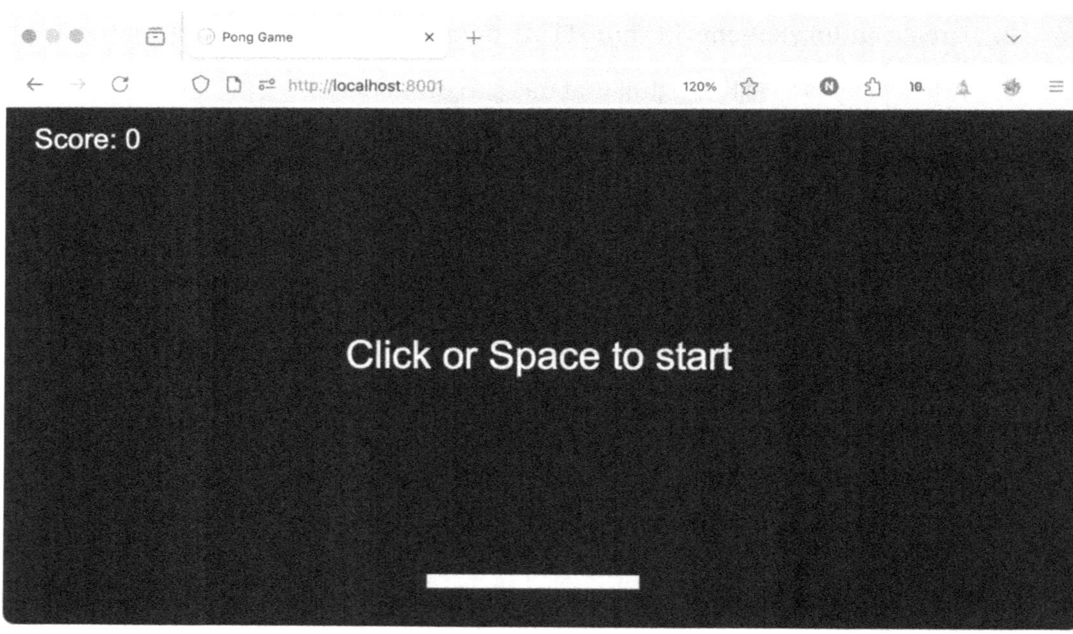

Figure 1-5. *The running Pong game showing score display and game over state*

Intermission

You've built a game. You've wrestled with animation loops, collision detection, and the relentless heartbeat of `requestAnimationFrame`. You've seen how ClojureScript handles *continuous* state transformation—60 times per second, every second, until the player misses.

But not all applications live in constant motion. Some sit quietly, waiting. They don't transform state until asked. They respond to events, not to time.

The arcade was loud and energetic. Now let's walk down the hall to the lounge—still on the first floor, still learning the fundamentals, but with a different rhythm entirely.

In the arcade, we built something that *runs*. In the lounge, we'll build something that *reacts*.

Building a Unit Converter in ClojureScript: A Practical Journey

"Simple tools, done well, are the unsung heroes of the web."

The Concept

A Unit Converter is one of those practical web tools everyone needs. Converting miles to kilometers, Celsius to Fahrenheit, pounds to grams. It's straightforward but teaches important concepts: data transformation, component composition, and reactive UI.

Unlike Pong, this isn't about game loops or animation. It's about handling real-world forms and user input in ClojureScript.

Still on the first floor, we've moved from the energetic arcade to a quieter space. We're building a different kind of application, one that reacts to user input rather than running continuously.

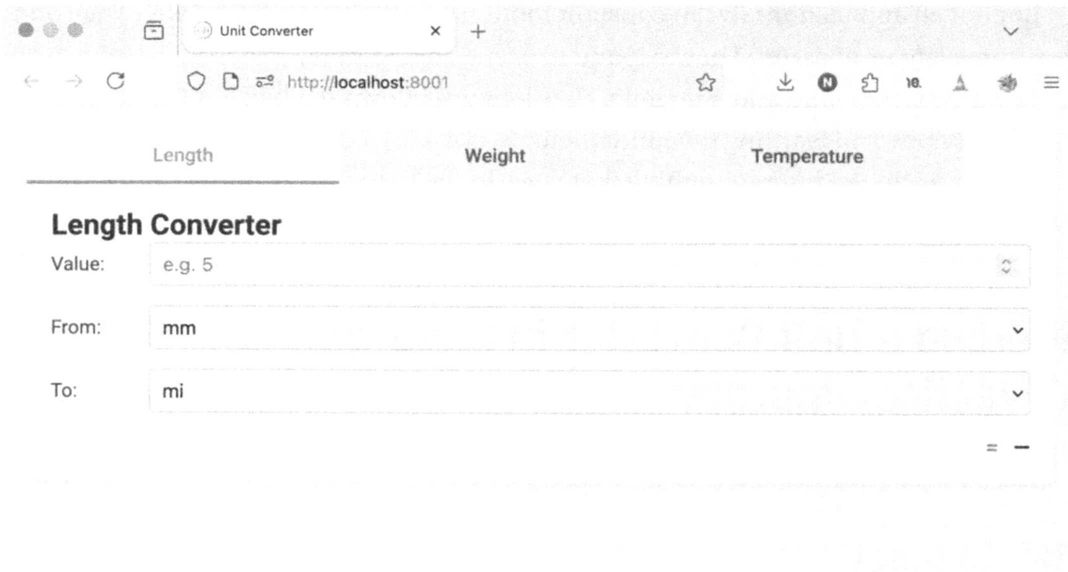

***Figure 1-6.** The Unit Converter application interface with tabbed navigation for different conversion types*

The Architecture

In the arcade, we had a game loop driving pixels across the screen. Here, the architecture is reactive, not continuous. Nothing moves until you interact with it.

The system responds to your input instantly and gracefully. No polling, no waiting. Just clean cause and effect.

Here's how it works.

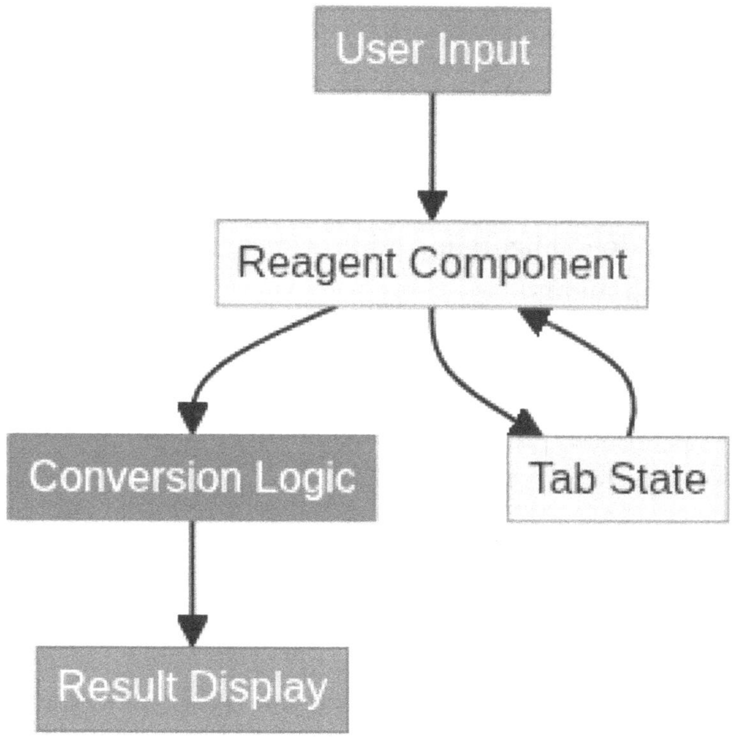

Figure 1-7. *The reactive data flow in the Unit Converter showing how user input triggers component updates*

The flow is simple:

1. User enters a value and selects units.
2. Reagent components react to changes.
3. Pure conversion functions transform the data.
4. Results update automatically.

No game loop. No animation frames. Just reactive data flow.

This is a different kind of elegance than Pong. Where Pong was about continuous motion, this is about instantaneous response. Where Pong transformed state 60 times per second, this transforms state only when needed. It's the difference between a river and a spring—both are water, both flow, but in fundamentally different ways.

The Foundation: Configuration and Setup

Just as we did with Pong, we begin with the foundation. But this time, we have an additional dependency: Reagent, ClojureScript's elegant wrapper around React.

Our `deps.edn` declares both ClojureScript itself and Reagent.

Listing 1-23. deps.edn configuration adding Reagent dependency for reactive React-based UI components

```
{:paths ["src" "resources"],
 :deps
 {org.clojure/clojurescript #:mvn{:version "1.12.42"},
  reagent/reagent #:mvn{:version "2.0.1"}},
 :aliases
 {:shadow-cljs
  {:extra-deps #:thheller{shadow-cljs #:mvn{:version "3.3.5"}},
   :main-opts ["-m" "shadow.cljs.devtools.cli"]}}}
```

Notice the `:deps` map now includes Reagent. This is our gateway to React's virtual DOM and reactive rendering, all wrapped in ClojureScript's functional embrace.

The `shadow-cljs.edn` configuration is similar to Pong's but with a crucial difference—we're now working with multiple namespaces.

Listing 1-24. shadow-cljs.edn build configuration with React development mode and multi-namespace entry points

```
{:source-paths ["src"]
 :dependencies [[reagent/reagent "2.0.1"]]
 :dev-http     {8001 "public"}
 :builds
 {:app
  {:target     :browser
   :output-dir "public/js"
   :asset-path "/js"
   :compiler-options {:external-config {:react {:development true}}}
   :modules    {:main {:init-fn unit-converter.ui/init
                       :entries [unit-converter.ui unit-converter.
                       core]}}}}}
```

The `:init-fn` points to `unit-converter.ui/init`, and we explicitly list both namespaces in `:entries`. This tells shadow-cljs to compile both our core logic and our UI components.

Our HTML is refreshingly simple.

Listing 1-25. HTML template with external stylesheet and Reagent mounting point div

```
<!DOCTYPE html>
<html lang="en">
<head>
    <meta charset="UTF-8"/>
    <title>Unit Converter</title>
    <link rel="stylesheet" href="styles.css"/>
</head>
<body>
<div id="app"></div>
<script src="js/main.js"></script>
</body>
</html>
```

Notice the `<link>` tag for `styles.css`. Unlike Pong, which used inline styles, this application has enough CSS to warrant a separate file. The `#app` div is our mounting point—the place where Reagent will inject our entire application.

To start the development server, we use the same command as before.

Listing 1-26. Development server command for hot-reloading ClojureScript compilation

```
npx shadow-cljs watch app
```

With the foundation laid, we can now turn our attention to the heart of the matter: the data.

The Data: Conversion Factors

> "All science is either physics or stamp collecting."
>
> —Ernest Rutherford

Let's start with the science. Every unit can be expressed as a factor of a base unit. For length, we use meters. For weight, kilograms.

Listing 1-27. Length conversion factors map with meters as base unit for imperial and metric measurements

```
(def length-factors
 {"m"  1.0, "km" 1000.0, "cm" 0.01, "mm" 0.001,
  "mi" 1609.344, "yd" 0.9144, "ft" 0.3048,
  "in" 0.0254, "nm" 1.852e+3})
```

This is beautiful in its simplicity. Each unit is a multiplier relative to meters:

- 1 kilometer = 1000 meters
- 1 centimeter = 0.01 meters
- 1 mile = 1609.344 meters

Here's the complete picture.

Table 1-1. *Common length units and their conversion factors relative to meter (base unit)*

Unit	Symbol	Factor (to meters)	Historical Note
Meter	m	1.0	Originally 1/10,000,000 of the distance from equator to pole
Kilometer	km	1000.0	From the Greek *chilioi* (thousand)
Centimeter	cm	0.01	The width of a standard fingernail
Millimeter	mm	0.001	A logic of thousands, minimizing decimals
Mile	mi	1609.344	*Mille passus*: 1,000 double paces of a Roman soldier
Yard	yd	0.9144	Legend says it was the girdle size of an Anglo-Saxon king
Foot	ft	0.3048	Historically, the length of a human foot (often the King's)
Inch	in	0.0254	The width of a man's thumb, or three barleycorns end-to-end
Nautical Mile	nm	1852.0	Exactly one minute of latitude along a meridian

The insight: By storing everything as factors, conversion becomes trivial. Converting from A to B is just `value × (factor_A / factor_B)`.

The Core: Pure Conversion Logic

Listing 1-28. Generic conversion function using factor ratio calculation with NaN validation guard

```
(defn convert [value from to factors]
 (if (and value (not (js/isNaN value)))
  (* value (/ (factors from) (factors to)))
  nil))
```

This is the heart of the application. Let's break it down:

1. **Guard clause**: Check if the value exists and is a number.
2. **Conversion**: Multiply the value by the ratio of factors.
3. **Nil safety**: Return `nil` if the input is invalid.

Example: Converting 5 kilometers to miles

Listing 1-29. Example conversion calculation showing 5 kilometers to miles using factor ratio math

```
(convert 5 "km" "mi" length-factors)
;; => (* 5 (/ 1000.0 1609.344))
;; => (* 5 0.621371)
;; => 3.106855
```

The beauty? This function works for *any* unit system. Length, weight, volume—just pass different factors. It's a perfect example of abstraction: we've captured the *pattern* of conversion, not just a specific instance of it.

We also have weight factors, following the same principle.

Listing 1-30. Weight conversion factors map with kilograms as base unit including imperial and metric units

```
(def weight-factors
 {"kg" 1.0, "g"  0.001, "mg" 0.000001,
  "lb" 0.45359237, "oz" 0.0283495231,
  "st" 6.35029318, "t"  1000.0})
```

Here, kilograms are our base unit—defined purely by physics constants now, though for a long time it was a platinum-iridium cylinder locked in a vault in Paris.

Table 1-2. *Common weight units and their conversion factors relative to kilogram (base unit)*

Unit	Symbol	Factor (to kg)	Historical Note
Kilogram	kg	1.0	The base unit, now defined by the Planck constant
Gram	g	0.001	Originally the weight of 1 cm^3 of water at melting point
Milligram	mg	0.000001	A thousandth of a gram, for the finest precision
Pound	lb	0.45359237	The Roman *libra*, hence the symbol "lb"
Ounce	oz	0.0283495231	1/16th of a pound (originally 1/12th in Rome)
Stone	st	6.35029318	14 lbs; literally based on a standard stone for weighing wool
Tonne	t	1000.0	From the *tun*, a large wine cask

The pattern repeats, elegant and consistent, bridging ancient trade with modern physics.

Temperature: The Exception

> "Temperature is different. Temperature is special. Temperature doesn't play by the rules."

Unlike length or weight, temperature conversions aren't simple multiplications. They involve offsets and different zero points.

Listing 1-31. Temperature conversion function with explicit formulas for Celsius, Fahrenheit, and Kelvin scale transformations

```
(defn convert-temp [value from to]
 (when value
  (let [v (js/parseFloat value)]
   (cond
    (= from to) v
    (and (= from "C") (= to "F")) (+ (* v 1.8) 32)
    (and (= from "F") (= to "C")) (* (- v 32) 0.5555556)
    (and (= from "C") (= to "K")) (+ v 273.15)
    (and (= from "K") (= to "C")) (- v 273.15)
    (and (= from "F") (= to "K")) (+ (* (- v 32) 0.5555556) 273.15)
    (and (= from "K") (= to "F")) (+ (* (- v 273.15) 1.8) 32)))))
```

Here's the conversion matrix.

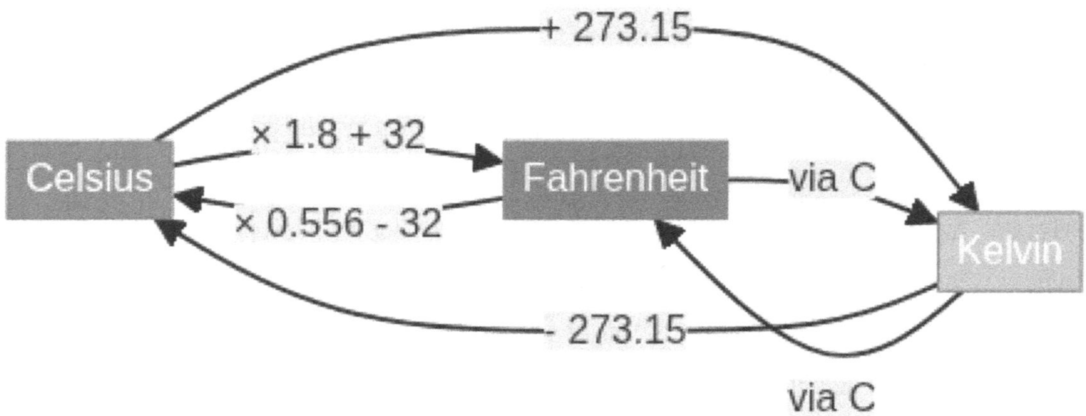

Figure 1-8. *Temperature conversion relationships between Celsius, Fahrenheit, and Kelvin scales*

Why the complexity? Because history is messy:

- **Celsius**: Anders Celsius originally defined 0 as boiling and 100 as freezing (yes, backwards!) before it was flipped.
- **Fahrenheit**: Daniel Fahrenheit used a brine solution for 0°F and his estimation of human body temperature for ~96°F.
- **Kelvin**: Lord Kelvin wanted a scale where 0 was truly *zero*—the absence of all thermal energy (absolute zero).

The scales have different intervals and starting points.

This is one of those cases where a lookup table won't work. We need explicit formulas. Sometimes, the real world refuses to be simplified, and we must meet it on its own terms.

With our conversion logic complete, we now have everything we need to transform data. But data transformation alone doesn't make an application. We need a way for users to interact with our functions, to see the results, to *feel* the conversions happening. We need a user interface.

Reagent: Reactive Components

"The best reaction is no reaction at all—until it's needed."

Now we enter the world of Reagent, and it deserves a proper introduction.

What is Reagent? It's ClojureScript's elegant wrapper around React, Facebook's UI library that revolutionized web development in 2013. But Reagent isn't just a thin wrapper—it's a *reimagining* of React through a functional lens.

Where React uses JavaScript classes and hooks, Reagent uses **atoms** and **pure functions**. Where React requires you to think about component lifecycles, Reagent lets you think about **data flow**. It's the difference between managing a machine and tending a garden—both require care, but one feels more natural.

The philosophy: In Reagent, your UI is a *function of your state*. Change the state, and the UI updates automatically. No manual DOM manipulation. No imperative updates. Just declare what you want, and Reagent handles the rest.

The magic: Reagent's atoms are *reactive*. When you change an atom's value, any component that reads that atom automatically re-renders. It's like having a staff that anticipates your needs—you don't ask for updates, they simply happen.

If you're coming from React, this will feel familiar but more refined. If you're new to reactive UI programming, prepare to have your mind gently expanded.

The Converter Component: Full Implementation

Let's look at the complete converter component and understand every piece.

Listing 1-32. Reagent converter component with reactive atoms and Hiccup syntax for form inputs and unit selectors

```
(defn converter [title units convert-fn decimals id-prefix]
 (let [val  (r/atom "")
       from (r/atom (first units))
       to   (r/atom (second units))]
  (fn []
   (let [num (js/parseFloat @val)
         result (convert-fn num @from @to)]
```

```
[:div.tab-content {:id (str "content-" id-prefix)}
 [:h2 title]
 [:div.form-row
  [:label {:for (str id-prefix "-value")} "Value:"]
  [:input {:type "number"
           :id (str id-prefix "-value")
           :placeholder "e.g. 5"
           :value @val
           :on-change #(reset! val (.. % -target -value))}]]
 [:div.form-row
  [:label {:for (str id-prefix "-from")} "From:"]
  [:select {:id (str id-prefix "-from")
            :value @from
            :on-change #(reset! from (.. % -target -value))}
   (for [u units] ^{:key u} [:option {:value u} u])]]
 [:div.form-row
  [:label {:for (str id-prefix "-to")} "To:"]
  [:select {:id (str id-prefix "-to")
            :value @to
            :on-change #(reset! to (.. % -target -value))}
   (for [u units] ^{:key u} [:option {:value u} u])]]
 [:div.result-row
  " " [:span {:id (str id-prefix "-result")}
       (uc/format-result result decimals)]]]))))
```

Key concepts:

1. **Atoms for state**: `(r/atom "")` creates reactive state. When it changes, the component re-renders.
2. **Dereferencing**: `@val` reads the current value of an atom.
3. **Hiccup syntax**: `[:div.tab-content ...]` is Reagent's way of writing HTML. It's just vectors and maps.
4. **Component factory**: The outer function runs once, creating the atoms. The inner function runs on every render.

Understanding the Two-Function Pattern

This is crucial. The component has **two functions**:

```
(defn converter [title units convert-fn decimals id-prefix]  ; ← Outer
                                                               function
 (let [val  (r/atom "")                                       ; ← Runs ONCE
       from (r/atom (first units))
       to   (r/atom (second units))]
  (fn []                                                       ; ← Inner
                                                                 function
   (let [num (js/parseFloat @val)                             ; ← Runs on
                                                               EVERY render
         result (convert-fn num @from @to)]
    [:div.tab-content ...]))))
```

Why two functions?

- **Outer function**: Creates the component instance and initializes local state (atoms). Runs once when the component is mounted.
- **Inner function**: The actual render function. Runs every time state changes.

This pattern prevents recreating atoms on every render, which would lose state.

Event Handling: The JavaScript Interop

Look at this event handler.

Listing 1-33. Event handler example using JavaScript interop thread-through macro for input value extraction

```
:on-change #(reset! val (.. % -target -value))
```

Let's decode it:

1. `#(...)`: Anonymous function shorthand. `%` is the argument (the event object).
2. `..`: The thread-through macro for JavaScript property access.
3. `-target`: Access the `target` property (the input element).

4. `-value`: Access the `value` property (the input's current value).

5. `reset!`: Set the atom to a new value.

This is equivalent to JavaScript:

```
(e) => val = e.target.value
```

But with Reagent, setting the atom automatically triggers a re-render! Here's the component lifecycle.

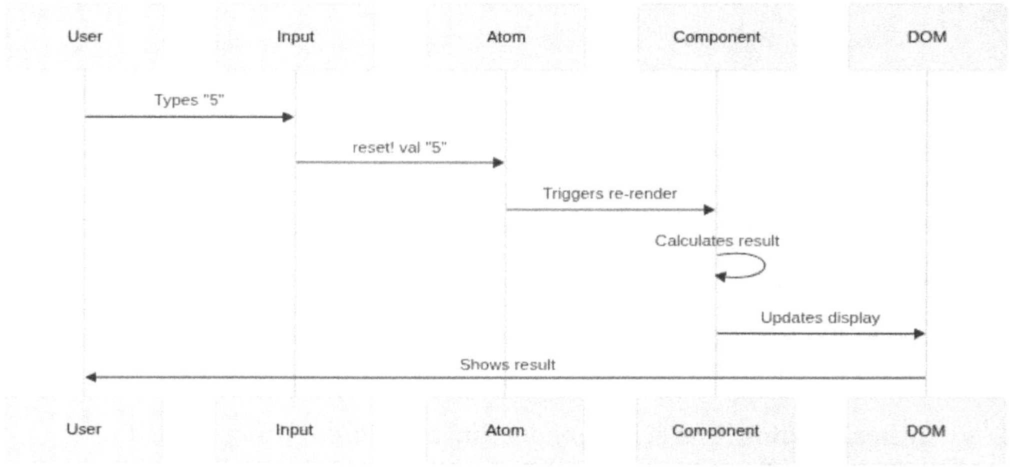

Figure 1-9. *The component lifecycle showing how user input flows through atoms to trigger DOM updates*

This is the magic of reactive programming. The user doesn't trigger a "calculate" button. They don't submit a form. They simply type, and the world responds. It feels instantaneous because it *is* instantaneous—there's no delay, no loading, no waiting. Just pure, immediate feedback.

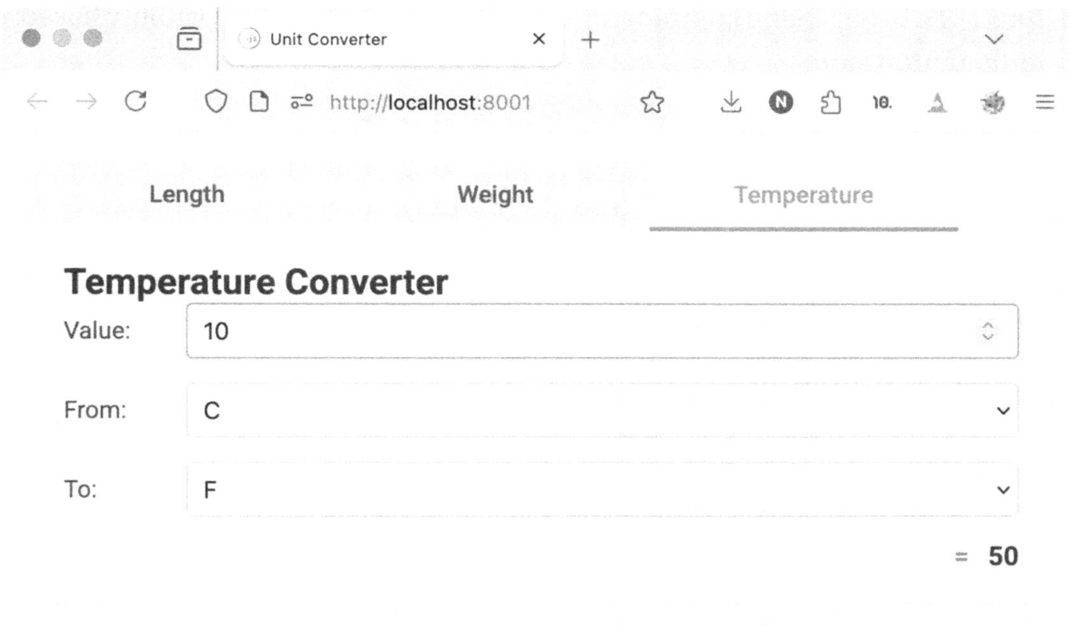

Figure 1-10. *The completed Unit Converter showing real-time conversion calculations*

The Tab System: CSS Tricks

One of the clever parts of this app is the tab system. No JavaScript state management—just CSS and radio buttons.

Listing 1-34. Radio button tab navigation markup with Hiccup syntax for CSS-based state management

```
[:input {:type "radio" :name "tabs" :id "tab-length" :defaultChecked true}]
[:label.tab-label {:for "tab-length"} "Length"]

[:input {:type "radio" :name "tabs" :id "tab-weight"}]
[:label.tab-label {:for "tab-weight"} "Weight"]

[:input {:type "radio" :name "tabs" :id "tab-temp"}]
[:label.tab-label {:for "tab-temp"} "Temperature"]
```

The CSS does the heavy lifting.

Listing 1-35. CSS sibling combinator rules toggling tab content visibility based on radio button state

```
#tab-length:checked ~ #content-length { display: block; }
#tab-weight:checked ~ #content-weight { display: block; }
#tab-temp:checked   ~ #content-temp   { display: block; }
```

The magic: When a radio button is checked, CSS shows the corresponding content. No state management needed. The browser handles it all.

How the CSS Selector Works

Let's break down `#tab-length:checked ~ #content-length`:

- `#tab-length`: Select the element with id "tab-length."
- `:checked`: Pseudo-class that matches when the radio is checked.
- `~`: General sibling combinator (selects siblings that come after).
- `#content-length`: The content div to show.

So this reads: "When the radio button with id 'tab-length' is checked, find its sibling with id 'content-length' and apply these styles."

The structure:

```
.tab-container
├── input#tab-length (radio)
├── label (for tab-length)
├── input#tab-weight (radio)
├── label (for tab-weight)
├── input#tab-temp (radio)
├── label (for tab-temp)
├── div#content-length (hidden by default)
├── div#content-weight (hidden by default)
└── div#content-temp (hidden by default)
```

All elements are siblings, so the ~ combinator can reach from the radio buttons to the content divs.

This is a beautiful example of using the platform. We didn't need to write JavaScript to manage tab state. We didn't need a state machine or a reducer. We just used HTML radio buttons and CSS selectors, and the browser did the rest. Sometimes, the best code is the code you don't write.

Component Composition

The final app assembles like this.

Listing 1-36. Tab container component composing radio buttons and three converter instances with different parameters

```
(defn tabs []
 [:div.tab-container
  ;; Radio inputs and labels
  [:input {:type "radio" :name "tabs" :id "tab-length"
  :defaultChecked true}]
  [:label.tab-label {:for "tab-length"} "Length"]
  ;; ... More tabs ...

  ;; Tab content
  [converter "Length Converter" (keys length-factors)
   #(convert %1 %2 %3 length-factors) 6 "length"]

  [converter "Weight Converter" (keys weight-factors)
   #(convert %1 %2 %3 weight-factors) 6 "weight"]

  [converter "Temperature Converter" temp-units
   convert-temp 2 "temp"]])
```

Notice how we reuse the `converter` component three times, just with different parameters:

- Different titles
- Different unit lists
- Different conversion functions
- Different decimal precision

This is composition. Build one component well, then reuse it everywhere. This is the Unix philosophy applied to UI: small, focused components that do one thing well, composed together to create something greater than the sum of their parts.

Formatting Results

Listing 1-37. Result formatting function handling nil values and whole numbers with dynamic decimal precision

```
(defn format-result [x decimals]
 (if (nil? x)
  "_"
  (if (== (js/Math.floor x) x)
   (str x)
   (.toFixed x decimals))))
```

Small function, big impact:

- If the result is nil, show an em dash (—).
- If it's a whole number, show it without decimals.
- Otherwise, format to the specified decimal places.

User experience detail: Nobody wants to see "5.000000" when "5" would do. This function makes the output clean and professional.

The Double Equals Trick

Notice (== (js/Math.floor x) x)? This checks if a number is a whole number:

```
(js/Math.floor 5.0)   ;; => 5
(== 5 5.0)            ;; => true (whole number!)

(js/Math.floor 5.7)   ;; => 5
(== 5 5.7)            ;; => false (has decimals)
```

Why == instead of =? In ClojureScript

- = is for value equality (works on any types).
- == is for numeric equality (faster, numbers only).

Since we know `x` is a number, == is the right choice.

Application Initialization

Finally, let's see how everything comes together.

Listing 1-38. Application initialization with Reagent 2.0 API creating persistent root and rendering tabs component

```
(defonce root (rdc/create-root (.getElementById js/document "app")))

(defn ^:export init []
 (rdc/render root [tabs]))
```

This initialization uses Reagent 2.0's recommended approach:

1. **`defonce root`**: Creates the React root once and reuses it across hot reloads. The `defonce` ensures it's only created on first load.
2. **`rdc/create-root`**: Reagent 2.0's function to create a root container for the React tree. This replaces the older `render-root` function.
3. **`^:export`**: Metadata that tells the ClojureScript compiler to preserve this function name in the compiled JavaScript. Without it, the name would be mangled and we couldn't call it from HTML.
4. **`rdc/render`**: Renders the component into the previously created root. Takes two arguments:
    - `root`: The root container created above
    - `[tabs]`: The component to render (in Hiccup format)
5. **JavaScript interop**: `(.getElementById js/document "app")` calls `document.getElementById("app")` in JavaScript.

The HTML side is simple:

```
<div id="app"></div>
<script src="js/main.js"></script>
```

When the JavaScript loads, it calls `init()`, which renders our entire app into the `#app` div.

And just like that, we have a working application. Type a number, select units, and watch the conversion happen in real time. No page refreshes, no form submissions, no waiting. Just pure, reactive data flow.

The Big Picture: Thinking in Components

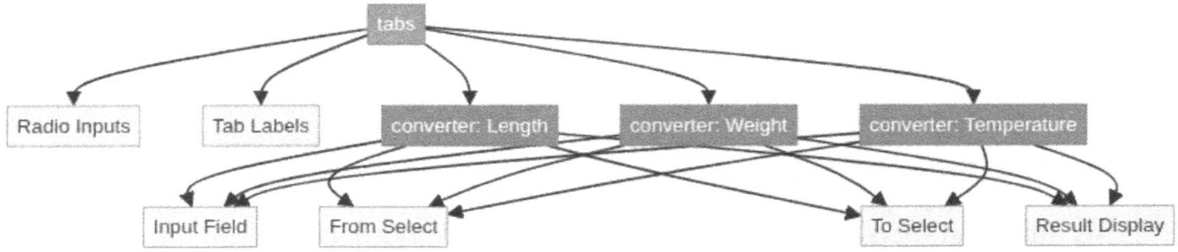

Figure 1-11. *Component composition tree showing how the tabs component reuses the converter component for each category*

Here's what we've learned:

1. **Separation of concerns**: Conversion logic lives in `core.cljs` and UI in `ui.cljs`.
2. **Pure functions**: `convert` and `convert-temp` have no side effects. Same inputs = same outputs.
3. **Reactive state**: Reagent atoms automatically trigger re-renders when they change.
4. **Component reuse**: One `converter` component serves three different use cases.
5. **CSS for state**: Sometimes the simplest solution is to let CSS handle it.

Comparing Approaches: Pong vs. Converter

Let's see how these two apps differ.

Table 1-3. *Architectural comparison between the Pong game and Unit Converter applications*

Aspect	Pong	Unit Converter
State Management	Single atom with game state	Multiple atoms per component
Update Cycle	Animation loop (60 fps)	Event driven (user input)
Side Effects	Canvas drawing	DOM updates (handled by React)
Data Flow	Continuous transformation	Reactive computation
Complexity	Physics simulation	Data transformation
Testing	Hard (timing dependent)	Easy (pure functions)

The lesson: Different problems need different architectures. Pong needed a game loop. The converter needs reactive components. Choose your tools wisely.

Both approaches are valid. Both are functional. Both embrace immutability and pure functions. But they solve different problems in different ways. This is the power of ClojureScript—it doesn't force you into a single paradigm. It gives you the tools and lets you choose the right one for the job.

Epilogue

Here's a question worth sitting with before you move on: do you understand why the `convert` function is only four lines?

It could be longer. You could write a `convert-km-to-miles` function and a `convert-kg-to-pounds` function, one for every pair you'll ever need. Lots of projects do exactly that. But our `convert` function doesn't know about kilometers or pounds or any unit specifically—it just knows about ratios. Feed it any two units whose factors you've measured against a shared base, and it works. That's not a trick; it's what abstraction actually means.

If that clicked, you're ready for the next floor. If it felt a little fuzzy, go back to `convert-temp`. Temperature is the counterexample—the function where that same abstraction *breaks down* because Celsius and Fahrenheit have different zero points, not just different scales. Seeing why the elegant version fails for temperature is just as valuable as seeing why it works for length.

Pong and the converter look nothing alike. One runs 60 times a second whether you touch it or not; the other sits quietly until you type. But open both files side by side and look for what's the same: an atom holding all the state, pure functions doing all the thinking, a thin UI layer that's barely there. That pattern is what you're actually learning. The Pong ball and the kilometer sign are just excuses to practice it.

Ready to level up? Here are some challenges to enhance your Unit Converter.

Exercise 1: Add Volume Conversions

Difficulty: Easy **Concepts**: Data structures, component reuse

Add a fourth tab for volume conversions:

1. Create a `volume-factors` map in `core.cljs` with units like
   - Liters (L): base unit (1.0)
   - Milliliters (mL): 0.001
   - Gallons (gal): 3.78541
   - Fluid ounces (fl oz): 0.0295735
   - Cups (cup): 0.236588
2. Add a new tab in `ui.cljs` for volume.
3. Reuse the existing `converter` component.

Hint You'll need to add the radio button, label, and converter component. The conversion logic already works—just pass the new factors!

Exercise 2: Swap Button

Difficulty: Medium **Concepts**: State manipulation, event handlers

Add a "⇄" button that swaps the "from" and "to" units:

1. Add a button between the two select dropdowns.
2. Create an `on-click` handler that swaps the values of `@from` and `@to`.
3. Style it nicely with CSS (maybe a circular button with an icon?).

Hint You'll need to swap both atoms simultaneously. Something like:

```
(let [temp @from]
  (reset! from @to)
  (reset! to temp))
```

Exercise 3: Conversion History

Difficulty: Hard **Concepts**: State management, data structures, rendering lists

Add a history panel that shows the last five conversions:

1. Add a `history` atom at the top level (outside the converter component).
2. When a conversion is calculated, add an entry to history with
   - Input value
   - From unit
   - To unit
   - Result
   - Timestamp
3. Display the history below the converter in a nice list.
4. Add a "Clear History" button.

Hint Use `(swap! history conj new-entry)` to add entries and `(take 5 history)` to limit the size.

Exercise 4: Custom Unit Builder

Difficulty: Expert **Concepts**: Dynamic data, form handling, local storage

Let users define their own custom units:

1. Add a “Custom Units” section where users can
   - Enter a unit name (e.g., “football field”)
   - Enter its factor relative to the base unit (e.g., 91.44 meters)
   - Save it to the conversion factors
2. Store custom units in browser localStorage so they persist.
3. Allow users to delete custom units.
4. Show custom units in a different color in the dropdown.

Hint You’ll need to: - Make `length-factors` an atom instead of a def - Use `js/localStorage.setItem` and `js/localStorage.getItem` - Parse JSON to/from localStorage

---

Final challenge: Combine Exercises 2, 3, and 4! Imagine a converter with swap buttons, conversion history, and custom units. That’s a production-ready tool.

Remember: Start with the data structures. Get the logic working in the REPL. Then build the UI around it. The functional way is the sustainable way.

CHAPTER 2

Pulsating Tiles: The Art of Animated Decomposition

"A picture broken into a thousand dancing pieces is poetry in motion."

The Concept

We've moved up to the second floor, where we explore canvas manipulation, image decomposition, and parametric animation. We're building something at the intersection of art and mathematics: a system that takes an image and breaks it into hundreds of tiny tiles, each pulsating with its own rhythm, creating wave patterns that respond to your mouse.

This is different from Pong's collision detection or the Unit Converter's forms. This is about visual transformation, taking static data (an image) and making it dance.

The technique has deep roots. In the 1960s, artists like Bridget Riley pioneered "Op Art" with geometric optical illusions. In the 1980s, demo scene programmers created plasma effects and tunnel animations. Today, creative coders use similar techniques in installations, visualizers, and generative art.

We're building three iterations:

1. **Random pulsation**: Each tile dances to its own beat.
2. **Wave patterns**: Horizontal waves and radial circles.
3. **Interactive waves**: Animation responds to mouse position.

N. Modrzyk, *The ClojureScript Playbook*, https://doi.org/10.1007/979-8-8688-2879-9_2

By the end, you'll understand image decomposition, sine wave animation, and interactive visual effects using pure functions and immutable data.

Figure 2-1. *The Pulsating Tiles gallery interface showing animated image decomposition effects*

The Architecture

Here's what we're building.

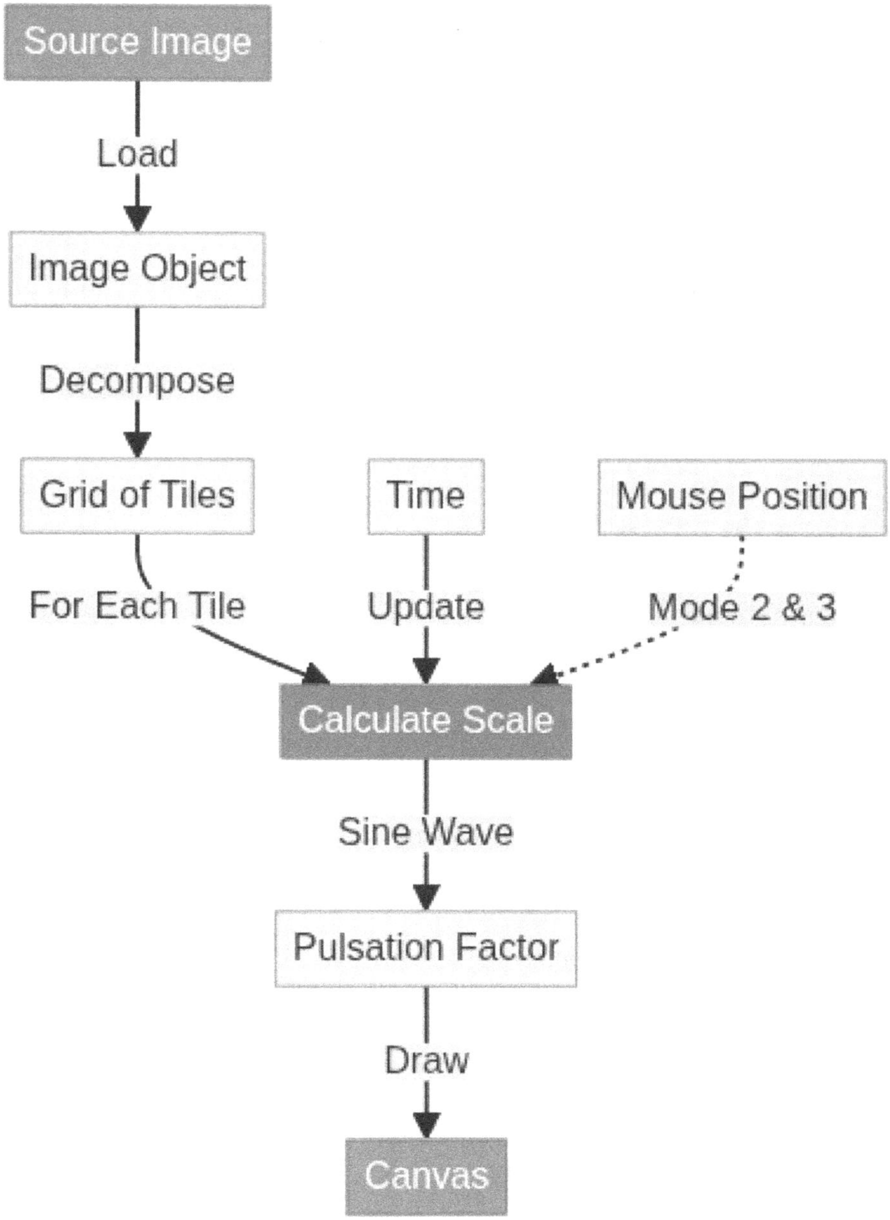

Figure 2-2. *Architecture diagram showing the image decomposition pipeline from source to animated canvas tiles*

The flow:

1. Load an image (in our case, a Hokusai painting).
2. Divide it into a grid of small square tiles.
3. For each tile, calculate a pulsation scale based on time and position.
4. Draw each tile at its calculated size 5. Repeat 60 times per second.

This is data-driven animation. We're not moving pixels around; we're transforming how we sample the source image. Each tile is a window into the original, scaled by a mathematical function.

The Foundation: Project Setup

Our `deps.edn` is minimal—just ClojureScript.

Listing 2-1. Minimal deps.edn configuration for canvas-based animation project without React dependencies

```
{:paths ["src" "resources"],
 :deps #:org.clojure{clojurescript #:mvn{:version "1.12.42"}},
 :aliases
 {:shadow-cljs
  {:extra-deps #:thheller{shadow-cljs #:mvn{:version "3.3.5"}},
   :main-opts ["-m" "shadow.cljs.devtools.cli"]}}}
```

The `shadow-cljs.edn` configuration points to our namespace.

Listing 2-2. shadow-cljs.edn build targeting browser with direct canvas manipulation entry point

```
{:source-paths ["src"]
 :dependencies []
 :dev-http     {8001 "public"}
 :builds
 {:app
  {:target     :browser
```

```
:output-dir "public/js"
:asset-path "/js"
:compiler-options {:external-config {:react {:development true}}}
:modules    {:main {:entries [small-tiles.core] :init-fn small-tiles.
core/init}}}}}
```

Notice we're targeting `:browser` again, but this time there's no Reagent. We're going back to raw canvas manipulation—direct, immediate, and fast.

Our HTML is sparse.

Listing 2-3. Fullscreen HTML canvas with overflow hidden for immersive animation experience

```
<!DOCTYPE html>
<html lang="en">
<head>
    <meta charset="UTF-8" />
    <title>Pulsating Small tiles</title>
</head>
<body style="margin:0; padding:0; overflow:hidden;">
<canvas id="my-canvas"></canvas>
<script src="js/main.js"></script>
</body>
</html>
```

The `overflow:hidden` ensures no scrollbars appear. The canvas will fill the entire viewport, creating an immersive experience.

To start development, see below.

Listing 2-4. Development watch command for live canvas animation development

```
npx shadow-cljs watch app
```

With our foundation laid, let's build the first iteration.

Iteration 1: Random Pulsation

The Image and Canvas Setup

We begin by grabbing references to our canvas and loading an image.

Listing 2-5. Canvas context and image loading setup using Google Closure DOM utilities

```
(ns small-tiles.e01
 (:require [goog.dom :as gdom]))

(def canvas (gdom/getElement "my-canvas"))
(def ctx (.getContext canvas "2d"))

(def img (js/Image.))
(set! (.-src img) "Katsushikahokusaipaint.webp")
```

Key concepts:

- `goog.dom/getElement` is Google Closure's DOM helper (similar to `document.getElementById`).
- `.getContext canvas "2d"` gets the 2D rendering context for drawing.
- `js/Image.` creates a new JavaScript image object.
- `set!` mutates the image's `src` property to start loading.

The image loads asynchronously. We need to wait for it before we can work with it.

Defining Our Grid

Listing 2-6. Tile size constant and reactive atom for storing grid metadata

```
(def tile-size 24)

(defonce squares (atom []))
```

Each tile will be 24×24 pixels. Why 24? It's small enough to create a dense grid, large enough to see detail, and divisible by many numbers (making calculations clean).

The `squares` atom will hold our tile metadata. Each entry will be a map describing one tile's position and animation phase.

Initializing the Grid

When the image loads, we need to

1. Resize the canvas to match the image
2. Calculate how many tiles fit
3. Store metadata for each tile

Listing 2-7. Grid initialization function dividing image into tiles with randomized animation phases

```
(defn init-squares! []
 (let [w (.-width img)
       h (.-height img)]
  ;; Resize canvas to match image
  (set! (.-width canvas) w)
  (set! (.-height canvas) h)

  ;; Build grid of tiles
  (let [xs (range 0 w tile-size)
        ys (range 0 h tile-size)]
   (reset! squares
           (for [sy ys
                 sx xs]
            {:sx    sx
             :sy    sy
             :phase (* 2 Math/PI (rand))})))))

(.addEventListener img "load" init-squares!)
```

Breaking it down:

1. **`(.-width img)`**: JavaScript interop to read the image's natural width
2. **`(range 0 w tile-size)`**: Creates a sequence `[0, 24, 48, 72, ...]` up to `w`
3. **`for` comprehension**: Nested loops creating a map for each (x, y) position
4. **`:phase`**: A random value between 0 and 2π—this ensures tiles don't all pulsate in unison

The result? If our image is 720×480, we get 30×20 = 600 tiles, each with its own random phase.

The Animation Loop: Making It Breathe

Now comes the magic—the animation loop that makes our tiles pulsate.

Listing 2-8. Animation loop with sine wave pulsation calculating scale and centered drawing for each tile

```
(defn draw-frame [timestamp]
 (let [t (/ timestamp 1000.0)
       base-scale 0.6
       amplitude 0.4
       two-pi (* 2 Math/PI)]

  ;; Clear canvas
  (.clearRect ctx 0 0 (.-width canvas) (.-height canvas))

  ;; Draw each tile
  (doseq [{:keys [sx sy phase]} @squares]
   (let [scale (+ base-scale
                  (* amplitude
                     (js/Math.sin (+ (* two-pi t) phase))))
         dw (* tile-size scale)
         dh dw
```

```
        center-x (+ sx (* 0.5 tile-size))
        center-y (+ sy (* 0.5 tile-size))
        dx (- center-x (* 0.5 dw))
        dy (- center-y (* 0.5 dh))]

    (.drawImage ctx img
              sx sy                       ; source x, y
              tile-size tile-size         ; source width, height
              dx dy                       ; destination x, y
              dw dh)))                    ; destination width, height

  ;; Request next frame
  (js/requestAnimationFrame draw-frame)))
```

This function is the heart of the animation. Let's dissect it.

Time and Scale

```
(let [t (/ timestamp 1000.0)
      base-scale 0.6
      amplitude 0.4]
  ...)
```

- `timestamp` comes from `requestAnimationFrame` in milliseconds.
- We convert to seconds for cleaner math.
- `base-scale 0.6` means tiles are 60% of their original size on average.
- `amplitude 0.4` means they oscillate between 20% (0.6 - 0.4) and 100% (0.6 + 0.4).

The Sine Wave

```
(let [scale (+ base-scale
               (* amplitude
                  (js/Math.sin (+ (* two-pi t) phase))))]
  ...)
```

This is **parametric animation** at its finest:

- `sin(2πt + phase)` oscillates between -1 and +1.
- Multiply by `amplitude` to get oscillation between -0.4 and +0.4.
- Add `base-scale` to shift the range to 0.2 to 1.0.
- Each tile has a different `phase`, so they're out of sync.

The math: If `t = 0` and `phase = 0`, then `sin(0) = 0`, so `scale = 0.6`. As time advances, the sine wave cycles, making the scale grow and shrink smoothly.

Centered Scaling

```
(let [center-x (+ sx (* 0.5 tile-size))
      center-y (+ sy (* 0.5 tile-size))
      dx (- center-x (* 0.5 dw))
      dy (- center-y (* 0.5 dh))]
  ...)
```

We want tiles to scale from their center, not their top-left corner. So

1. Calculate the tile's center point.
2. Calculate the destination width/height (`dw`, `dh`).
3. Offset the draw position so the center stays fixed.

Without this, tiles would appear to slide around as they scale.

The Draw Call

```
(.drawImage ctx img
            sx sy                   ; source x, y
            tile-size tile-size     ; source width, height
            dx dy                   ; destination x, y
            dw dh)                  ; destination width, height
```

This is the nine-parameter version of `drawImage`:

- **Source rectangle**: `(sx, sy, tile-size, tile-size)`—which part of the image to sample
- **Destination rectangle**: `(dx, dy, dw, dh)`—where and how big to draw it

We're sampling a fixed 24×24 square from the image and drawing it at a variable size on the canvas. This is how we create the pulsation effect—the source never changes, only the destination size.

Starting the Animation

Listing 2-9. Exported initialization function kickstarting requestAnimationFrame loop

```
(defn ^:export init []
 (js/requestAnimationFrame draw-frame))
```

The `^:export` metadata ensures this function name survives compilation. When the page loads, `init` is called, which kicks off the animation loop.

The result: Hundreds of tiles, each pulsating at its own rhythm, creating a shimmering, organic effect. The image is recognizable but alive, breathing with mathematical precision.

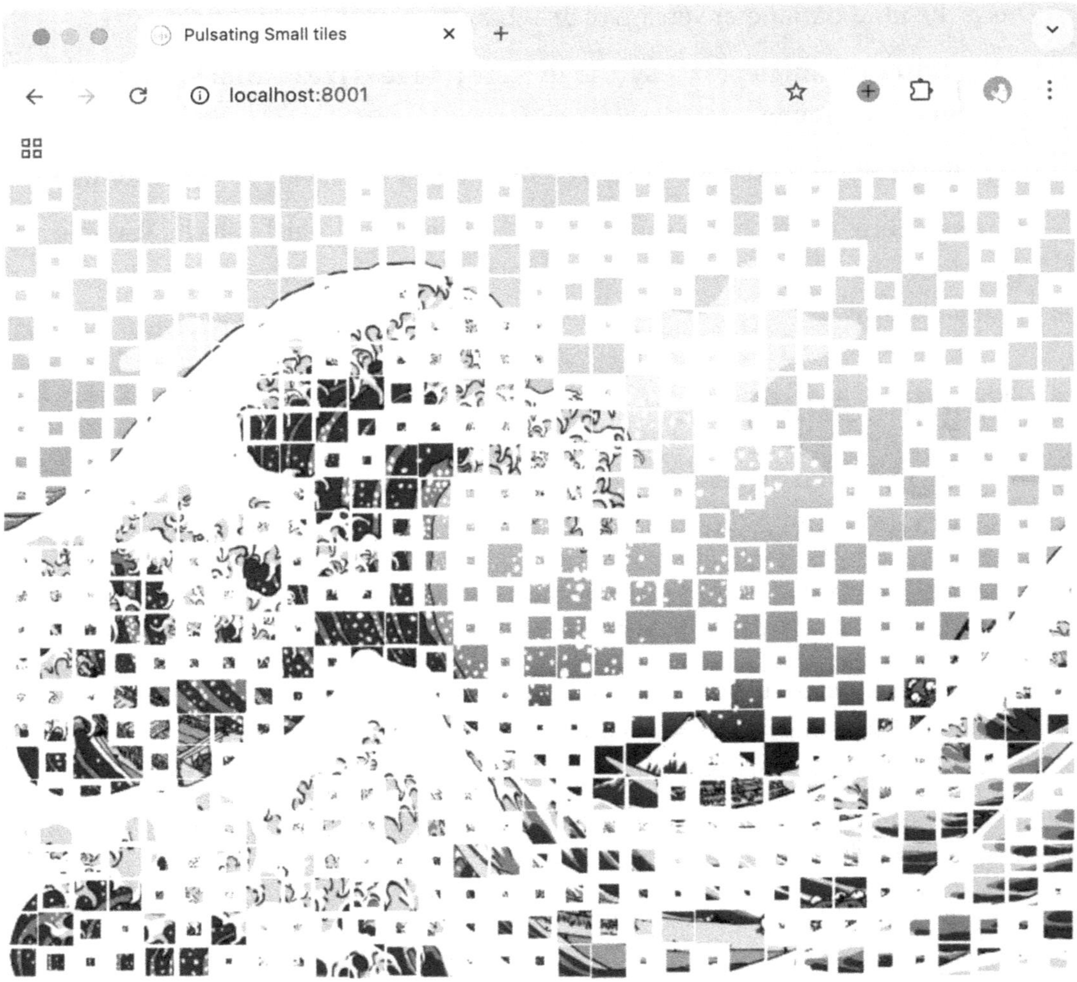

Figure 2-3. *Random pulsation effect with each tile dancing to its own rhythm*

Iteration 2: Wave Patterns

Random pulsation is mesmerizing, but what if we want *structure*? What if we want waves that sweep across the image or ripples that emanate from the center?

This is where we introduce **modes**—different mathematical functions that create different visual patterns.

Adding Mode State

Listing 2-10. Mode atom for switching between different animation pattern algorithms

```
(defonce mode (atom 0))
;; 0 = random phases, 1 = horizontal wave, 2 = radial circles
```

We'll randomly pick a mode when the image loads, giving us variety each time we refresh.

Enhanced Tile Metadata

Now each tile needs more information.

Listing 2-11. Enhanced grid initialization with precomputed wave phases and normalized distances for structured patterns

```
(defn init-squares! []
 (let [w      (.-width img)
       h      (.-height img)
       cols   (Math/floor (/ w tile-size))
       rows   (Math/floor (/ h tile-size))
       cx     (/ w 2.0)             ; image center x
       cy     (/ h 2.0)             ; image center y
       max-d  (Math/sqrt (+ (Math/pow cx 2)
                            (Math/pow cy 2)))]

  (set! (.-width  canvas) w)
  (set! (.-height canvas) h)

  (reset! mode (js/Math.floor (* 3 (js/Math.random))))

  (reset! squares
         (for [row (range rows)
               col (range cols)]
          (let [sx         (* col tile-size)
                sy         (* row tile-size)
```

```
                center-x   (+ sx (/ tile-size 2.0))
                center-y   (+ sy (/ tile-size 2.0))
                dx         (- center-x cx)
                dy         (- center-y cy)
                dist       (Math/sqrt (+ (* dx dx) (* dy dy)))
                dist-norm  (/ dist max-d)
                phase      (* 2 Math/PI (js/Math.random))
                phase-wave (* 2 Math/PI (/ col (dec cols)))]
           {:sx          sx
            :sy          sy
            :phase       phase
            :phase-wave  phase-wave
            :dist-norm   dist-norm})))))
```

New fields:

- **`:phase-wave`**: A static phase based on column index (0 to 2π across the width)
- **`:dist-norm`**: Normalized distance from the image center (0 at center, 1 at corners)

These precomputed values let us create structured patterns without recalculating distances every frame.

Mode-Based Scale Calculation

Listing 2-12. Mode-based animation loop using case expression for random, horizontal wave, and radial circle patterns

```
(defn draw-frame [timestamp]
 (let [t           (/ timestamp 1000.0)
       base-scale 0.6
       amplitude  0.4
       two-pi     (* 2 Math/PI)
       current-mode @mode]

  (.clearRect ctx 0 0 (.-width canvas) (.-height canvas))
```

```
(doseq [{:keys [sx sy phase phase-wave dist-norm]} @squares]
 (let [scale
       (case current-mode

        ;; Mode 0: Random phase (same as before)
        0 (let [θ (+ (* two-pi t) phase)]
           (+ base-scale (* amplitude (js/Math.sin θ))))

        ;; Mode 1: Horizontal wave
        1 (let [θ (+ (* two-pi t) phase-wave)]
           (+ base-scale (* amplitude (js/Math.sin θ))))

        ;; Mode 2: Radial circles
        2 (let [θ (* two-pi (- t dist-norm))]
           (+ base-scale (* amplitude (js/Math.sin θ))))

        ;; Default fallback
        (+ base-scale (* amplitude (js/Math.sin (* two-pi t)))))

       ;; ... Rest of drawing code ...
       ]))))
```

Mode 1: Horizontal Wave

```
(let [θ (+ (* two-pi t) phase-wave)]
  (+ base-scale (* amplitude (js/Math.sin θ))))
```

Since `phase-wave` is based on column index, tiles in the same column have the same phase. As time advances, a wave appears to sweep horizontally across the image.

Mode 2: Radial Circles

```
(let [θ (* two-pi (- t dist-norm))]
  (+ base-scale (* amplitude (js/Math.sin θ))))
```

Here, `dist-norm` acts as a time offset. Tiles at the same distance from the center pulsate together, creating concentric rings that expand outward.

The beauty: Same drawing code, same tile data, but three completely different visual effects—all controlled by a single parameter. This is the power of parametric design.

Iteration 3: Interactive Waves

The final evolution: Making the animation respond to the mouse. Instead of fixed wave patterns, the waves emanate from wherever your cursor is.

Fullscreen Canvas

First, we make the canvas fill the entire viewport.

Listing 2-13. Fullscreen canvas setup with viewport dimensions and CSS positioning using doto macro

```
(defn canvas-dimensions []
  {:width (.-innerWidth js/window)
   :height (.-innerHeight js/window)})

(defn resize-canvas! [{:keys [width height]}]
  (set! (.-width canvas) width)
  (set! (.-height canvas) height)

  ;; Set CSS to make canvas truly cover the viewport
  (doto (.-style canvas)
    (aset "position" "fixed")
    (aset "top" "0px")
    (aset "left" "0px")
    (aset "width" "100%")
    (aset "height" "100%")))
```

The doto macro is elegant—it threads `(.-style canvas)` through multiple aset calls, setting CSS properties imperatively but concisely.

Image-to-Canvas Mapping

Here's where it gets interesting. The canvas is now viewport sized, but the image has its own dimensions. We need to map screen coordinates to image coordinates.

Listing 2-14. Scale factor calculation mapping screen coordinates to image coordinates for different aspect ratios

```
(defn calculate-scale-factors [canvas-dims img-dims]
  {:scale-x (/ (:width img-dims) (:width canvas-dims))
   :scale-y (/ (:height img-dims) (:height canvas-dims))})
```

If the canvas is 1920×1080 and the image is 960×540, then `scale-x = 0.5` and `scale-y = 0.5`. Every screen pixel maps to 0.5 image pixels.

Enhanced Tile Creation

Listing 2-15. Tile creation function with separate screen and source coordinates for canvas-to-image mapping

```
(defn create-tile [row col scale-factors]
  (let [{:keys [scale-x scale-y]} scale-factors
        screen-x (* col tile-size)
        screen-y (* row tile-size)
        center-x (+ screen-x (/ tile-size 2.0))
        center-y (+ screen-y (/ tile-size 2.0))
        source-x (* screen-x scale-x)
        source-y (* screen-y scale-y)
        source-width (* tile-size scale-x)
        source-height (* tile-size scale-y)
        random-phase (* two-pi (js/Math.random))]
    {:screen-x screen-x
     :screen-y screen-y
     :center-x center-x
     :center-y center-y
     :source-x source-x
     :source-y source-y
     :source-width source-width
     :source-height source-height
     :phase random-phase}))
```

Each tile now stores

- **Screen coordinates**: Where to draw on the canvas
- **Source coordinates**: Where to sample from the image
- **Center point**: For centered scaling
- **Phase**: For randomized animation

This separation of concerns makes the code crystal clear.

Mouse Tracking

Listing 2-16. Mouse position tracking with canvas-relative coordinate conversion using getBoundingClientRect

```
(defonce mouse-position (atom [0 0]))

(defn handle-mouse-move! [event]
  (let [rect (.getBoundingClientRect canvas)
        mouse-x (- (.-clientX event) (.-left rect))
        mouse-y (- (.-clientY event) (.-top rect))]
    (reset! mouse-position [mouse-x mouse-y])))

(.addEventListener canvas "mousemove" handle-mouse-move!)
```

`getBoundingClientRect` gives us the canvas's position on the page. We subtract that from the mouse's client coordinates to get canvas-relative coordinates.

Interactive Pulsation Functions

Mode 1: Horizontal Wave from Mouse

Listing 2-17. Horizontal wave scale calculation using tile distance from mouse x-position for interactive wave effects

```
(defn calculate-horizontal-wave-scale [time center-x mouse-x canvas-width]
  (let [dx (- center-x mouse-x)
        normalized-x (/ dx canvas-width)
        theta (+ (* two-pi time) (* two-pi normalized-x))]
    (+ base-scale (* amplitude (js/Math.sin theta)))))
```

The wave phase is now based on the tile's distance from the mouse's x-position. Move the mouse left and right, and the wave follows.

Mode 2: Radial Circles from Mouse

Listing 2-18. Radial circle scale calculation creating ripple effects emanating from mouse position

```
(defn calculate-radial-scale [time center-x center-y mouse-x mouse-y max-
distance]
  (let [dx (- center-x mouse-x)
        dy (- center-y mouse-y)
        distance (js/Math.sqrt (+ (* dx dx) (* dy dy)))
        distance-normalized (/ distance max-distance)
        theta (* two-pi (- time distance-normalized))]
    (+ base-scale (* amplitude (js/Math.sin theta)))))
```

Ripples emanate from the mouse position. Move the mouse, and the epicenter moves with it.

Unified Scale Calculation

Listing 2-19. Unified scale calculation dispatcher using case expression to delegate to mode-specific pure functions

```
(defn calculate-tile-scale [mode time tile mouse-pos canvas-dims]
  (let [{:keys [center-x center-y phase]} tile
        {:keys [width]} canvas-dims
        [mouse-x mouse-y] mouse-pos
        max-distance (diagonal-distance canvas-dims)]
    (case mode
      0 (calculate-random-phase-scale time phase)
      1 (calculate-horizontal-wave-scale time center-x mouse-x width)
      2 (calculate-radial-scale time center-x center-y mouse-x mouse-y max-
      distance)
      (+ base-scale (* amplitude (js/Math.sin (* two-pi time)))))))
```

This is **functional composition** at its best. Each mode has its own pure function. The main calculation delegates to the appropriate function based on mode. Clean, testable, extensible.

The Drawing Pipeline

Listing 2-20. Simplified animation orchestration reading state atoms and delegating to pure drawing functions

```
(defn draw-frame [timestamp]
  (let [time-seconds (/ timestamp 1000.0)
        mode @pulsation-mode
        mouse-pos @mouse-position
        canvas-dims (canvas-dimensions)]

    (clear-canvas! canvas-dims)
    (draw-all-tiles! mode time-seconds mouse-pos canvas-dims)
    (js/requestAnimationFrame draw-frame)))
```

The animation loop is now beautifully simple:

1. Get current state (time, mode, mouse position, canvas size).
2. Clear the canvas.
3. Draw all tiles with their calculated scales.
4. Request the next frame.

All the complexity is hidden in pure functions. The loop itself is just orchestration.

The Big Picture: Functional Animation

Let's step back and appreciate the architecture.

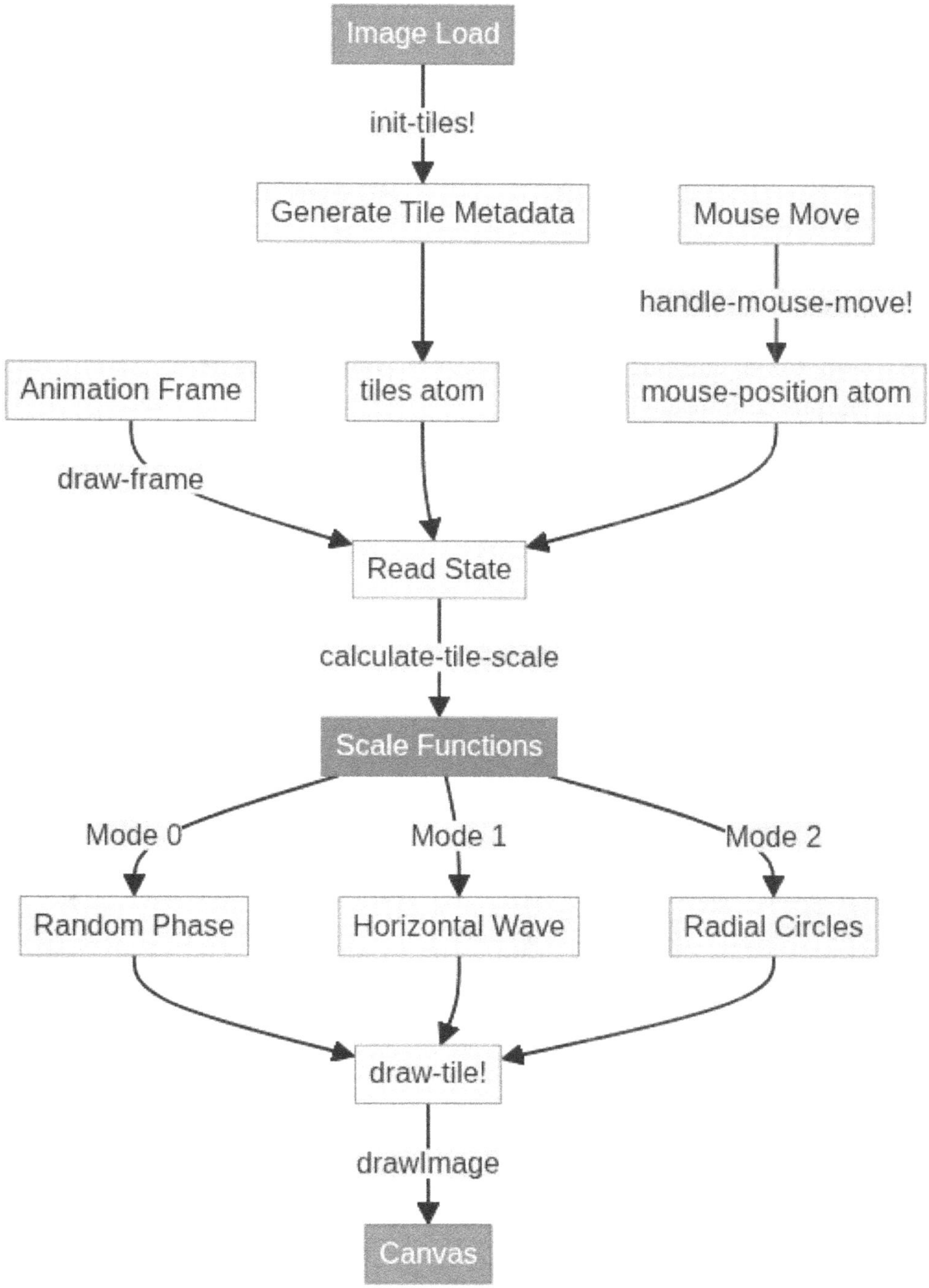

Figure 2-4. *Functional animation architecture showing the flow from image load through scale calculation to canvas rendering*

Key principles:

1. **Immutable data**: Tile metadata never changes after initialization.
2. **Pure functions**: Scale calculations have no side effects.
3. **Atoms for state**: Mouse position and mode are mutable containers.
4. **Separation of concerns**: Drawing, calculation, and state management are distinct.
5. **Functional composition**: Complex behavior emerges from simple, composable functions.

This is the second-floor lesson: **data transformation at scale**. We're not just converting units or bouncing a ball. We're transforming hundreds of data points every frame, creating emergent visual complexity from simple mathematical rules.

Comparing Floors

Let's see how the second floor builds on the first.

Table 2-1. *Comparison of animation approaches between first and second floor projects*

Aspect	First Floor	Second Floor
Data Volume	Single ball, single paddle	Hundreds of tiles
Animation	Physics simulation	Parametric sine waves
Interactivity	Keyboard/mouse control	Mouse-driven wave patterns
Rendering	Simple shapes	Image decomposition
Complexity	Collision detection	Coordinate mapping
Pattern	Game loop	Visual transformation

The lesson: As we ascend, the problems get more complex, but the tools remain the same. Pure functions, immutable data, atoms for state. The patterns scale.

Exercises: Expand Your Gallery

Ready to experiment? Here are some challenges.

Exercise 1: Color Tinting

Difficulty: Medium **Concepts**: Canvas compositing, color manipulation

Add a color tint that changes over time:

1. Before drawing each tile, set `ctx.globalCompositeOperation` to `"multiply"` or `"screen"`.
2. Set `ctx.fillStyle` to a color calculated from time: `hsl(${time * 30 % 360}, 70%, 50%)`.
3. Fill a rectangle over the tile after drawing it.
4. Reset `globalCompositeOperation` to `"source-over"`.

Hint: This creates a color wash effect that cycles through the spectrum.

Exercise 2: Variable Tile Sizes

Difficulty: Hard **Concepts**: Dynamic grid generation, responsive design

Make tile size vary based on image brightness:

1. After the image loads, create a temporary canvas.
2. Draw the image to it and use `getImageData` to read pixel colors.
3. For each tile, calculate average brightness.
4. Store brightness in tile metadata.
5. Multiply the scale factor by `(1 + brightness * 0.5)` so bright areas pulsate more.

Hint You'll need to sample the image data before creating tiles.

Exercise 3: Multiple Images

Difficulty: Medium **Concepts**: State management, image loading

Allow switching between multiple images:

1. Create an array of image URLs.
2. Load all images on startup.
3. Add keyboard listener for number keys (1–5).
4. When a key is pressed, reinitialize tiles with the new image.
5. Smoothly transition by fading out the old canvas and fading in the new.

Hint Use `ctx.globalAlpha` for fading effects.

Exercise 4: Sound Reactivity

Difficulty: Expert **Concepts**: Web Audio API, frequency analysis

Make the animation react to music:

1. Use the Web Audio API to capture microphone input or load an audio file.
2. Create an `AnalyserNode` to get frequency data.
3. In the animation loop, read frequency data into an array.
4. Map frequency bins to tile rows (bass at bottom, treble at top).
5. Multiply the scale factor by the frequency amplitude.

Hint `analyser.getByteFrequencyData(dataArray)` gives you the spectrum.

Final challenge: Combine all four! Imagine color-tinted, variably sized tiles reacting to music across multiple images. That's a full audio-visual installation.

Wrapping Up

One thing I want to make sure landed before you move on: the sine wave formula. `(+ base-scale (* amplitude (sin (+ (* 2π t) phase))))`. If you read that and it immediately makes sense—great. If it still feels like magic, slow down. The `phase` per tile is the only thing separating "they all pulse together" from "each one does its own thing." Change all phases to zero and run it; then change them back. That one experiment will make the whole formula concrete.

The second thing is: why do we precompute `dist-norm` and `phase-wave` and store them in the tile data, instead of recalculating them every frame? Think about it. We do hundreds of tiles, 60 times a second. Anything that doesn't depend on the current timestamp should be calculated once. The tile metadata isn't just bookkeeping—it's performance. And in ClojureScript, where data is immutable and pure, there's no penalty for holding pre-computed values indefinitely.

Move your mouse over the canvas one more time. Watch the ripples chase the cursor. That's not a special effect—it's the same sine function with a different phase offset. Everything here is one equation, applied differently.

Motion.js and SVG Animation: The Art of Orchestrated Movement

> "The best animations don't just move—they tell a story, one frame at a time."

The Concept

Still on the second floor, we're exploring a different kind of animation: choreographed sequences. We're building an animated tic-tac-toe grid that draws itself. Lines appear with spring physics. Circles trace themselves. Rectangles materialize with perfect timing. It's a performance, a carefully orchestrated sequence of movements.

This introduces declarative animation. Instead of manually calculating positions every frame (like we did with Pong and the Pulsating Tiles), we declare what we want to happen, and a library handles the details. We're moving from imperative ("move this pixel here") to declarative ("animate this element to this state").

We're using Motion.js (formerly Framer Motion), a modern animation library that brings physics-based animations to the web. It understands spring dynamics, easing curves, and orchestration, the same principles that make iOS animations feel smooth.

This is also our first deep dive into JavaScript interop at scale. We're integrating an entire external library, mapping its JavaScript API to ClojureScript idioms, and combining it with Reagent's component model.

By the end, you'll understand

- How to integrate npm packages into ClojureScript
- How to use JavaScript libraries idiomatically
- How to create declarative animations with Motion.js
- How to orchestrate complex sequences
- How to combine Reagent components with external animation libraries

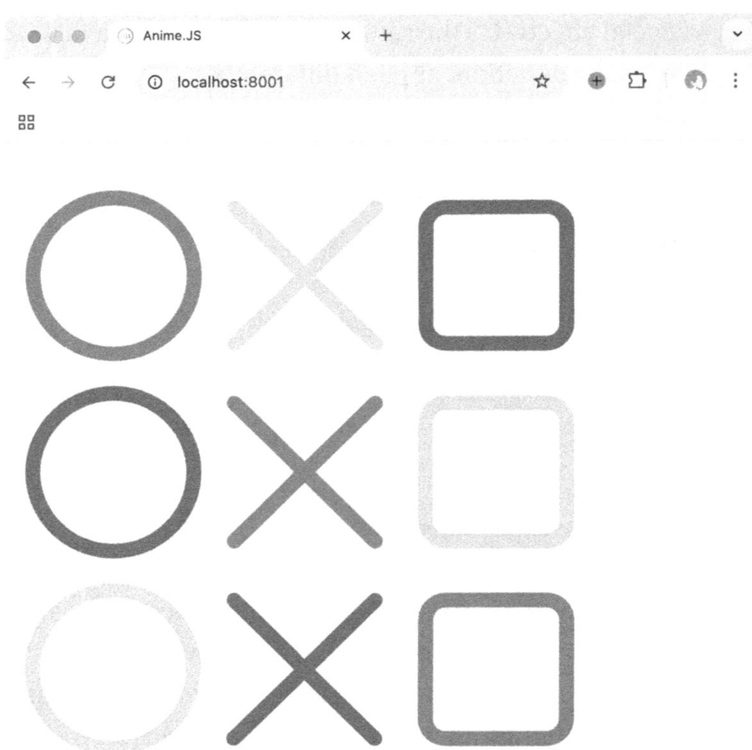

Figure 2-5. *The Motion.js theater interface showing choreographed SVG animation*

The Architecture: Declarative Animation

Let's understand the flow.

Below is the key difference from our previous projects:

- **Pong**: We controlled the animation loop explicitly.
- **Pulsating Tiles**: We calculated every frame's state manually.
- **Motion.js**: We declare the start and end states; the library handles interpolation.

This is **inversion of control**. We're not driving the animation; we're describing it.

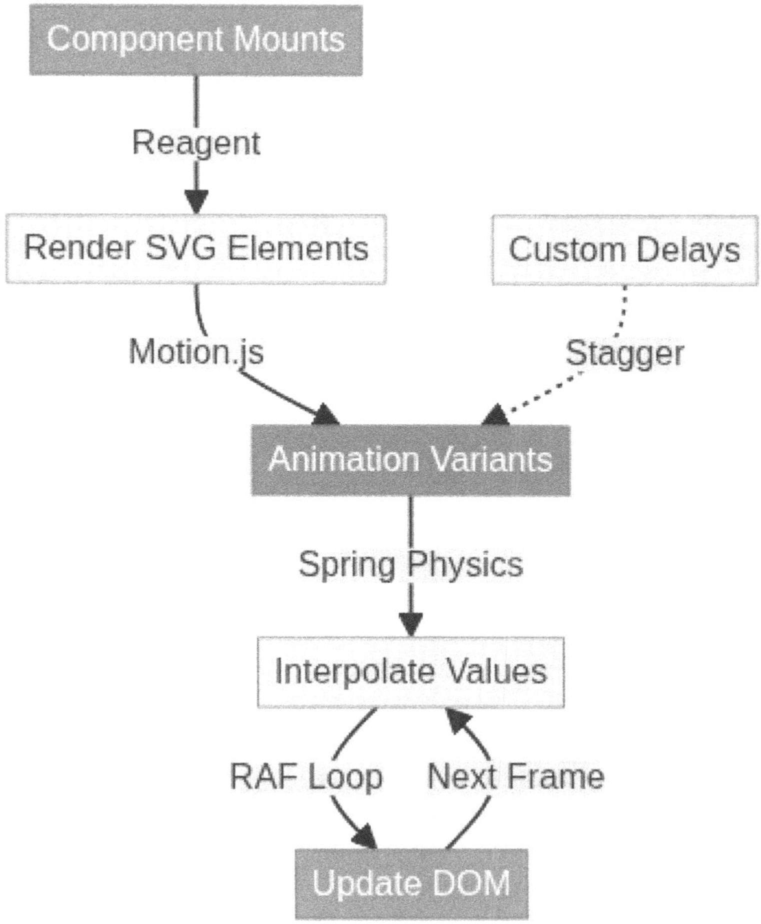

***Figure 2-6.** Declarative animation architecture showing how Motion.js interpolates between variant states*

The Foundation: npm Integration

For the first time, we're using an external JavaScript library from npm. Let's see how ClojureScript handles this.

Package Dependencies

Our package.json declares the JavaScript dependencies.

Listing 2-21. package.json declaring Motion.js and React dependencies for npm package management

```
{
  "name": "pyjama-rts",
  "version": "0.0.1",
  "private": true,
  "devDependencies": {
    "shadow-cljs": "3.3.5"
  },
  "dependencies": {
    "@emotion/is-prop-valid": "^1.3.1",
    "motion": "^12.4.10",
    "react": "^19.2.4",
    "react-dom": "^19.2.4"
  }
}
```

Key points:

- `motion`: The animation library (version 12.4.10)
- `react` and `react-dom`: Required by Motion.js (and Reagent)
- `@emotion/is-prop-valid`: A utility library Motion.js uses internally

When you run `npm install`, these packages are downloaded to `node_modules/`. Shadow-cljs automatically makes them available to your ClojureScript code.

ClojureScript Dependencies

Our `deps.edn` includes Reagent.

Listing 2-22. deps.edn with Reagent for bridging ClojureScript and React-based animation libraries

```
{:paths ["src" "resources"],
 :deps
 {org.clojure/clojurescript #:mvn{:version "1.12.42"},
  reagent/reagent #:mvn{:version "2.0.1"}},
 :aliases
 {:shadow-cljs
  {:extra-deps #:thheller{shadow-cljs #:mvn{:version "3.3.5"}},
   :main-opts  ["-m" "shadow.cljs.devtools.cli"]}}}
```

Reagent is our bridge between ClojureScript and React. Motion.js is built for React, so Reagent lets us use it naturally.

Shadow-cljs Configuration

Listing 2-23. shadow-cljs.edn with explicit npm-deps for React version compatibility

```
{:source-paths ["src"]
 :dependencies [[reagent/reagent "2.0.1"]]
 :dev-http     {8001 "public"}
 :builds
 {:app
  {:target     :browser
   :output-dir "public/js"
   :asset-path "/js"
   :npm-deps   {react     "19.2.4"
                react-dom "19.2.4"}
   :modules    {:main {:init-fn abstract-art.core/init}}}}}
```

The `:npm-deps` section explicitly specifies React versions. This ensures compatibility between Reagent and Motion.js.

HTML Setup

Listing 2-24. Minimal HTML with Reagent mounting point for declarative animation demo

```
<!DOCTYPE html>
<html lang="en">
<head>
    <meta charset="UTF-8">
    <title>Motion.js Animation</title>
</head>
<body>
<div id="app"></div>
<script src="js/main.js"></script>
</body>
</html>
```

Simple and clean. The #app div is our mounting point, just like in the Unit Converter. To start development, see below.

Listing 2-25. Development workflow installing npm dependencies before starting ClojureScript watch mode

```
npm install
npx shadow-cljs watch app
```

The `npm install` step is new—it downloads the JavaScript dependencies before we start the ClojureScript compiler.

JavaScript Interop: Importing Motion.js

Here's where ClojureScript's JavaScript interop shines. We can import npm packages directly.

Listing 2-26. Namespace declaration importing Motion.js React client module for SVG animation

```
(ns react.path-drawing
  "More evolved example, using SVG animation via MotionJS."
  (:require
    ["motion/react-client" :as motion]))
```

Breaking it down:

- `["motion/react-client" :as motion]`: Import the `motion/react-client` module.
- The string `"motion/react-client"` tells Shadow-cljs to look in `node_modules/motion/`.
- `:as motion` binds it to the name `motion` in our namespace.

Now we can use Motion.js components like `motion/svg`, `motion/circle`, `motion/line`, etc.

Alternative: Direct Function Import

For simpler cases, you can import specific functions.

Listing 2-27. Alternative import syntax using refer for selective function importation from Motion.js

```
(ns js.core
  "Integration with the MotionJS library. Super simple example"
  (:require
    ["motion" :refer [animate]]
    [reagent.core :as r]))
```

Here, `["motion" :refer [animate]]` imports just the `animate` function. This is like JavaScript's

```
import { animate } from 'motion';
```

Simple Example: Animated Box

Let's start with the simplest possible animation—a box that slides in and fades up.

Listing 2-28. Reagent class component with lifecycle hook triggering Motion.js animate function on mount

```
(defn animated-box []
  (r/create-class
    {:component-did-mount
     (fn [this]
       (animate (js/document.querySelector "#box")
                #js {:x 500 :opacity 1}
                #js {:duration 3}))

     :reagent-render
     (fn []
       [:div {:id    "box"
              :style {:width      "100px"
                      :height     "100px"
                      :background "blue"
                      :opacity    0}}])}))
```

Understanding the code:

Reagent Class Components

Listing 2-29. Reagent class component pattern with lifecycle method map for mounting and rendering

```
(r/create-class
  {:component-did-mount (fn [this] ...)
   :reagent-render (fn [] ...)})
```

This is Reagent's way of creating components with lifecycle methods. It's similar to React class components:

- `:component-did-mount`: Called once, after the component is added to the DOM
- `:reagent-render`: Returns the Hiccup to render

We need `:component-did-mount` because we want to start the animation *after* the DOM element exists.

⚠ Important: Reagent 2.0 Change

In Reagent 2.0+ (which uses React 18), lifecycle methods **must** accept the component instance as their first parameter, even if you don't use it. This is a breaking change from Reagent 1.x:

```
;; ✗ Reagent 1.x (no longer works in 2.0)
:component-did-mount (fn [] ...)
;; ✓ Reagent 2.0+ (required)
:component-did-mount (fn [this] ...)
```

The same applies to all lifecycle methods:

- `:component-did-mount (fn [this] ...)`
- `:component-did-update (fn [this old-argv] ...)`
- `:component-will-unmount (fn [this] ...)`

Even if you don't need to access the component instance (like in our simple animation example), you must still accept the `this` parameter. This ensures compatibility with React 18's stricter requirements.

The Animate Function

Listing 2-30. Motion.js animate function call with target selector, final state object, and transition options

```
(animate (js/document.querySelector "#box")
         #js {:x 500 :opacity 1}
         #js {:duration 3})
```

Motion.js's `animate` function takes three arguments:

1. **Target**: A DOM element (or selector)
2. **To**: The final state (an object with properties to animate)
3. **Options**: Animation configuration (duration, easing, etc.)

The `#js` reader literal:

`#js {:x 500 :opacity 1}` converts a ClojureScript map to a JavaScript object. This is crucial—JavaScript libraries expect JavaScript objects, not ClojureScript maps.

- ClojureScript: `{:x 500 :opacity 1}`
- JavaScript: `{x: 500, opacity: 1}`

The `#js` prefix does this conversion at compile time.

Initial State

Listing 2-31. Initial box element with zero opacity before Motion.js animation applies transforms

```
[:div {:id    "box"
       :style {:width      "100px"
               :height     "100px"
               :background "blue"
               :opacity    0}}]
```

The box starts at `opacity: 0` (invisible) and at its default position (x = 0). The animation moves it to `x: 500` and `opacity: 1` over 3 seconds.

The result: A blue box slides in from the left while fading in. Simple, but it demonstrates the core concept: declare the end state, and Motion.js handles the interpolation.

Advanced Example: SVG Path Drawing

Now for the main event—a tic-tac-toe grid that draws itself with choreographed timing.

Animation Variants

Listing 2-32. Animation variants definition using staggered delays and spring physics for pathLength drawing effect

```
(def draw
  (clj->js
    {:hidden  {:pathLength 0 :opacity 0}
     :visible (fn [i]
               (let [delay (* i 0.5)]
                 (clj->js
                   {:pathLength 1
                    :opacity    1
                    :transition {:pathLength {:delay delay :type "spring"
                    :duration 1.5 :bounce 0}
                                 :opacity    {:delay delay :duration
                                 0.01}}})))}))
```

This is **variant-based animation**—a powerful Motion.js pattern. **Breaking it down**:

1. **`:hidden` state**: `pathLength: 0, opacity: 0` (invisible, not drawn)
2. **`:visible` state**: A function that takes an index `i` and returns the final state

The `:visible` function is clever.

Listing 2-33. Delay calculation function multiplying element index by 0.5 seconds for sequential staggered appearance

```
(fn [i]
  (let [delay (* i 0.5)]
    ...))
```

Each element can have a different delay based on its index. If `i = 1`, delay is 0.5 seconds. If `i = 2`, delay is 1 second. This creates a **staggered animation**—elements appear one after another.

Transition Configuration

Listing 2-34. Transition configuration map with per-property spring physics and timing parameters

```
:transition {:pathLength {:delay delay :type "spring" :duration 1.5 :bounce 0}
             :opacity    {:delay delay :duration 0.01}}
```

Each property can have its own transition:

- **`pathLength`**: Uses spring physics (`type: "spring"`) with 1.5-second duration and no bounce
- **`opacity`**: Instant transition (0.01 seconds)—we want it to appear immediately when the path starts drawing

Spring physics: Instead of linear interpolation, spring animations simulate physical springs. They overshoot slightly, then settle—creating more natural, organic motion.

Style Definitions

Listing 2-35. Shared SVG style definition for round-capped strokes with transparent fill

```
(def shape-style
  {:strokeWidth   15
   :strokeLinecap "round"
   :fill          "transparent"})
```

SVG (scalable vector graphics) strokes with round caps look smooth and hand-drawn. `fill: transparent` means we only see the outline, not a filled shape.

The SVG Component

Listing 2-36. Motion.js SVG component with declarative initial and animate states triggering automatic transitions

```
(defn PathDrawing []
  [:> motion/svg {:width   600
                  :height  600
                  :viewBox "0 0 600 600"
                  :initial "hidden"
                  :animate "visible"
                  :style   image-style}
   ;; ... Shapes ...
   ])
```

Key attributes:

- **`:>`**: Reagent's syntax for using React components directly (Motion.js components are React components)
- **`motion/svg`**: A Motion.js-enhanced SVG element
- **`:initial "hidden"`**: Start in the "hidden" variant
- **`:animate "visible"`**: Animate to the "visible" variant

When the component mounts, Motion.js automatically animates from `:initial` to `:animate`.

Drawing a Circle

Listing 2-37. Motion.js circle component with custom delay parameter for orchestrated appearance timing

```
[:> motion/circle {:className "circle-path"
                   :cx        100 :cy 100 :r 80
                   :stroke    "#ff0088"
```

```
             :variants  draw
             :custom    1
             :style     shape-style}]
```

Attributes:

- **`cx, cy, r`**: SVG circle attributes (center x, center y, radius)
- **`stroke`**: Color of the outline
- **`variants`**: The `draw` variants object we defined earlier
- **`custom 1`**: Passed to the `:visible` function as `i` (so delay = 1 × 0.5 = 0.5 seconds)
- **`style`**: Our shared style object

Drawing Lines (Tic-Tac-Toe X)

Listing 2-38. Motion.js line components forming tic-tac-toe X with sequential custom delay values creating diagonal drawing effect

```
[:> motion/line {:x1       220 :y1 30 :x2 360 :y2 170
                 :stroke   "#4ff0b7"
                 :variants draw
                 :custom   2
                 :style    shape-style}]
[:> motion/line {:x1       220 :y1 170 :x2 360 :y2 30
                 :stroke   "#4ff0b7"
                 :variants draw
                 :custom   2.5
                 :style    shape-style}]
```

Two lines form an “X”. Notice the following:

- **First line**: `custom 2` (delay = 1 second)
- **Second line**: `custom 2.5` (delay = 1.25 seconds)

The second line starts slightly after the first, creating a natural drawing sequence.

Drawing Rectangles

Listing 2-39. Motion.js rectangle with rounded corners and staggered animation via custom index value

```
[:> motion/rect {:width    140 :height 140
                 :x        410 :y 30 :rx 20
                 :stroke   "#0d63f8"
                 :variants draw
                 :custom   3
                 :style    shape-style}]
```

The `:rx 20` attribute gives the rectangle rounded corners (radius = 20).

The Complete Grid

The full component renders a 3×3 grid:

```
[O] [X] [□]
[O] [X] [□]
[O] [X] [□]
```

Each shape has a different `custom` value (1, 2, 2.5, 3, 3.5, 4, 4.5, 5), creating a cascading animation that flows down the grid.

The Magic of pathLength

The `pathLength` property is SVG-specific and incredibly powerful:

- `pathLength: 0`: The path is not drawn at all.
- `pathLength: 1`: The path is fully drawn.
- `pathLength: 0.5`: The path is half drawn.

Motion.js animates this value from 0 to 1, creating the illusion of the path being drawn in real-time. Combined with spring physics, it looks like an invisible hand is sketching the shapes.

This is a classic SVG animation technique, but Motion.js makes it trivial to implement.

Orchestration and Timing

Let's visualize the timing:

```
Time (seconds):
0.0  ─────────────────────────────────────────────────────────
0.5  [Circle 1 starts]
1.0  [Circle 2 starts] [Line 1 starts]
1.25                   [Line 2 starts]
1.5  [Circle 3 starts]                [Rect 1 starts]
2.0                    [Line 3 starts]
2.25                   [Line 4 starts]
2.5                                    [Rect 2 starts]
3.0                    [Line 5 starts]
3.25                   [Line 6 starts]
3.5                                    [Rect 3 starts]
```

Each element starts at a precise time, creating a choreographed sequence. This is **orchestration**—coordinating multiple animations to create a cohesive whole.

Comparing Animation Approaches

Let's see how this differs from our previous work.

Table 2-2. *Comparison of animation control approaches across Pong, Pulsating Tiles, and Motion.js*

Aspect	Pong	Pulsating Tiles	Motion.js
Control	Manual RAF loop	Manual RAF loop	Declarative
Calculation	Physics formulas	Sine wave math	Spring physics (built-in)
State	Explicit (atoms)	Explicit (atoms)	Implicit (library managed)
Timing	Frame by frame	Frame by frame	Declarative (delays, durations)
Complexity	High (we do everything)	Medium (math heavy)	Low (library handles it)
Flexibility	Total control	Total control	Constrained by library API

The trade-off: Motion.js is easier and more declarative, but we have less control. For complex physics simulations (like Pong), manual control is better. For choreographed UI animations, declarative libraries shine.

The Integration Pattern

This project demonstrates a powerful pattern: **ClojureScript as the orchestrator, JavaScript libraries as the workers**.

We write our application logic in ClojureScript, use Reagent for component structure, and delegate animation to Motion.js. Each layer does what it does best.

This is **composition over inheritance**, **separation of concerns**, and **leveraging the ecosystem**—all functional programming principles applied to the JavaScript world.

Figure 2-7. *Integration pattern showing ClojureScript orchestrating JavaScript libraries through Reagent*

Exercises: Expand Your Theater

Ready to choreograph your own animations?

Exercise 1: Reverse Animation

Difficulty: Easy **Concepts**: State management, animation control

Add a button that reverses the animation:

1. Add a Reagent atom to track animation state: `(defonce anim-state (r/atom "visible"))`.
2. Add a button that toggles between `"visible"` and `"hidden"`.
3. Change the `:animate` prop to read from `@anim-state`.
4. Watch the shapes draw and undraw.

Hint Motion.js automatically animates between any state changes.

Exercise 2: Interactive Delays

Difficulty: Medium **Concepts**: Dynamic variants, user input

Let the user control the stagger delay:

1. Add a range slider (HTML `<input type="range">`).
2. Store the delay multiplier in an atom.
3. Modify the `draw` variants function to use `(* i @delay-multiplier)`.
4. Watch the animation speed up or slow down.

Hint You'll need to recreate the variants object when the delay changes.

Exercise 3: Draw on Hover

Difficulty: Medium **Concepts**: Event handlers, conditional animation

Make shapes draw only when you hover over them:

1. Add `:whileHover` prop to each shape: `:whileHover {:pathLength 1 :opacity 1}`.
2. Set `:initial` to `{:pathLength 0 :opacity 0}`.
3. Remove the `:animate` prop.
4. Hover over shapes to draw them individually.

Hint Motion.js has built-in hover detection.

Exercise 4: Signature Animation

Difficulty: Hard **Concepts**: SVG paths, custom animations

Create an animated signature:

1. Use a tool like Figma or Illustrator to create an SVG path of your signature.
2. Extract the `<path d="...">` data.

3. Create a `motion/path` component with the path data.
4. Animate `pathLength` from 0 to 1 with spring physics.
5. Add a "Sign" button that triggers the animation.

Hint Use `strokeDasharray` and `strokeDashoffset` for more control over path drawing.

Final challenge: Create a full animated logo reveal—multiple shapes, colors, and timing, all orchestrated into a 5-second sequence. Export it as a video using browser screen recording.

Wrapping Up

Watch the tic-tac-toe grid draw itself one more time. Notice where the spring settles—that slight deceleration at the end, the way it doesn't quite stop cleanly but eases in. That's not in your code. You declared `type: "spring"` and Motion.js took it from there. That's the whole trade-off on this page, right there in that settling curve.

Here's the honest check: did you feel the loss of control, or did you feel relieved? If you felt relieved, declarative animation is your natural mode. If something nagged at you—"but how does it *actually* do that?"—then keep that instinct. Pulsating Tiles is the answer; that chapter shows what's underneath.

The `#js` literal is worth understanding properly before you move on. `#js {:x 500 :opacity 1}` looks small, but it's doing something culturally important: acknowledging that Motion.js speaks JavaScript, not ClojureScript, and you need to hand it an object it recognizes. Every time you cross that library boundary, you'll face this choice. Get comfortable with it now, because the next floors cross it constantly.

The second floor is done. You know how to move pixels manually and how to let a library move them for you. That's not a small thing.

CHAPTER 3

Abstract Art with Quil: Dancing Shapes

"Art is not what you see, but what you make others see."

—Edgar Degas

Welcome to the Third Floor

The elevator doors open, and you step into an artist's studio. Canvases line the walls, but these aren't static paintings—they're alive, constantly regenerating, never the same twice.

Welcome to the third floor: **generative art**. This entire floor is dedicated to one powerful library: **Quil** (pronounced "quill"), ClojureScript's wrapper around Processing, the legendary creative coding framework that's been used by artists, designers, and educators for over two decades.

This floor is different from the ones below. We're not building utilities or games. We're creating **art**—visual experiences that exist purely for their aesthetic value. But don't mistake simplicity for lack of depth. Generative art teaches you about randomness, emergence, and the beauty that arises when you let code make creative decisions.

We're starting with **abstract art**—colorful shapes that float, morph, and dance across the screen. It's simple enough to understand in minutes, deep enough to explore for hours.

N. Modrzyk, *The ClojureScript Playbook*, https://doi.org/10.1007/979-8-8688-2879-9_3

What Is Quil?

Quil is ClojureScript's gateway to Processing, a framework originally created in 2001 at MIT Media Lab to make programming accessible to artists and designers. Processing pioneered the idea that code could be a creative medium, not just a tool.

Quil brings Processing's philosophy to ClojureScript:

- **Immediate visual feedback**: See your changes instantly.
- **Simple drawing primitives**: Circles, rectangles, lines—the building blocks of visual art.
- **Functional middleware**: Manage state the ClojureScript way.
- **Cross-platform**: Run in the browser via HTML5 Canvas.

The philosophy: Lower the barrier between thought and creation. If you can imagine it, you can sketch it.

The Architecture: Sketch Lifecycle

Quil applications are called "sketches"—a nod to their artistic origins. Every sketch follows a lifecycle.

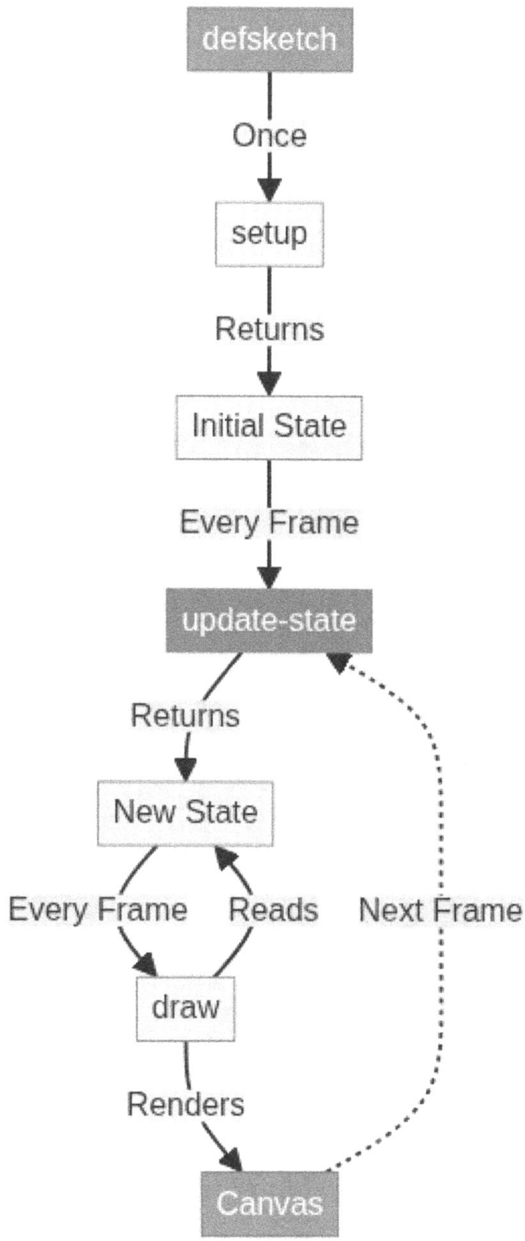

Figure 3-1. *Quil sketch lifecycle showing the functional mode pattern from setup through update-state to draw*

This is the **functional mode** pattern:

1. **setup**: Initialize state (runs once).
2. **update-state**: Transform state (runs every frame).
3. **draw**: Render state (runs every frame).

State flows in one direction. No mutations, no surprises—just pure functions transforming data.

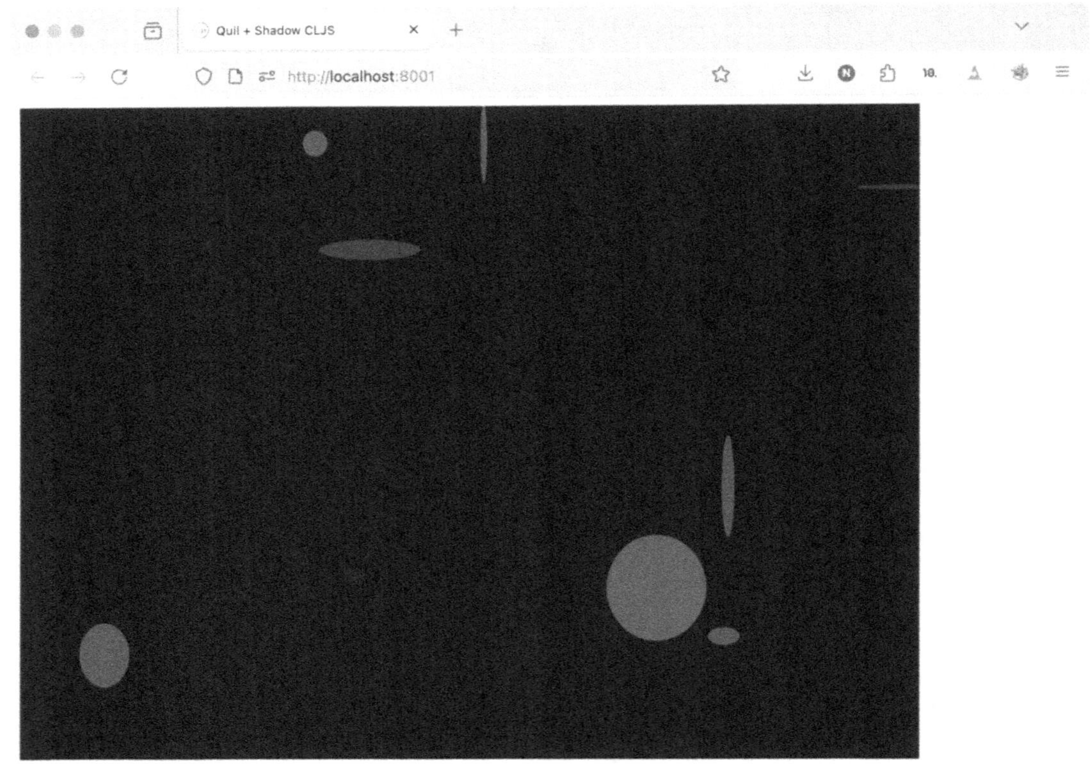

Figure 3-2. *Random pulsating shapes displaying HSB color mode with organic animation*

Iteration 1: Random Shapes

Let's start with the simplest possible generative art—random shapes that regenerate every frame.

The Complete Code

Listing 3-1. Complete Quil sketch with random pulsating shapes using HSB color mode and functional middleware

```
(ns art.e01
  (:require [quil.core :as q]
            [quil.middleware :as m]))

(defn setup []
  (q/frame-rate 10)
  (q/color-mode :hsb)
  {:shapes
   (repeatedly
     10
     #(vector (rand (q/width))
              (rand (q/height))
              (rand 255)
              (rand 100)
              (rand 100)))})

(defn draw [{:keys [shapes]}]
  (q/background 0)
  (doseq [[x y h s b] shapes]
    (q/fill h s b)
    (q/ellipse x y (rand 100) (rand 100))))

(defn init []
  (q/defsketch abstract-art
    :host "app"
    :size [800 600]
    :setup setup
    :draw draw
    :middleware [m/fun-mode]))
```

Breaking It Down

Namespace and Requires

Listing 3-2. Namespace declaration requiring Quil core drawing functions and functional mode middleware

```
(ns art.e01
  (:require [quil.core :as q]
            [quil.middleware :as m]))
```

- `quil.core`: All drawing functions (`ellipse`, `fill`, `background`, etc.)
- `quil.middleware`: The functional mode middleware

Setup: Creating Random Shapes

Listing 3-3. Setup function initializing ten random shapes with HSB color values and screen-relative positions

```
(defn setup []
  (q/frame-rate 10)
  (q/color-mode :hsb)
  {:shapes
   (repeatedly
     10
     #(vector (rand (q/width))
              (rand (q/height))
              (rand 255)
              (rand 100)
              (rand 100)))})
```

Line by line:

1. **`(q/frame-rate 10)`**: Run at 10 frames per second (slow enough to see changes).
2. **`(q/color-mode :hsb)`**: Use HSB (hue, saturation, brightness) instead of RGB.

3. **repeatedly 10**: Create ten random shapes.
4. **Each shape is a vector**: [x, y, hue, saturation, brightness].

Why HSB? It's more intuitive for generative art:

- **Hue** (0–255): The color itself (red, green, blue, etc.)
- **Saturation** (0–100): How vivid the color is
- **Brightness** (0–100): How light or dark

With RGB, getting a "random color" often looks muddy. With HSB, random hues are vibrant and distinct.

Draw: Rendering Shapes

Listing 3-4. Draw function rendering shapes with destructured HSB values and randomized ellipse dimensions for pulsation effect

```
(defn draw [{:keys [shapes]}]
  (q/background 0)
  (doseq [[x y h s b] shapes]
    (q/fill h s b)
    (q/ellipse x y (rand 100) (rand 100))))
```

The process:

1. **(q/background 0)**: Fill the canvas with black (clears previous frame).
2. **doseq**: Iterate over each shape.
3. **Destructuring**: [x y h s b] pulls out the shape's data.
4. **(q/fill h s b)**: Set the fill color.
5. **(q/ellipse x y (rand 100) (rand 100))**: Draw a circle at (x, y) with random width and height.

The magic: Notice (rand 100) for the ellipse size? This happens *every frame*, so even though the shape positions are fixed, their sizes constantly change. This creates a pulsating, organic effect.

The Sketch Definition

Listing 3-5. Sketch definition mounting canvas to DOM with functional mode for immutable state management

```
(defn init []
  (q/defsketch abstract-art
    :host "app"
    :size [800 600]
    :setup setup
    :draw draw
    :middleware [m/fun-mode]))
```

Parameters:

- **`:host "app"`**: Mount the canvas in the `<div id="app">` element.
- **`:size [800 600]`**: Canvas dimensions (width × height).
- **`:setup setup`**: Function to initialize state.
- **`:draw draw`**: Function to render each frame.
- **`:middleware [m/fun-mode]`**: Enable functional mode (state management).

What You See

Ten colorful circles, positions fixed, sizes pulsating randomly. It's hypnotic in its simplicity—like watching jellyfish drift in an aquarium.

Iteration 2: Moving Shapes with Physics

Random pulsation is fun, but what if shapes *moved*? What if they had velocity, wrapped around screen edges, and changed color over time?

Enhanced State Structure

Listing 3-6. Shape factory function creating maps with position, size, color, and velocity properties for physics-based animation

```
(defn create-shape []
  {:x (rand (q/width))
   :y (rand (q/height))
   :size (+ min-shape-size (rand (- max-shape-size min-shape-size)))
   :hue (rand 255)
   :dx (random-velocity)
   :dy (random-velocity)})
```

Now each shape is a **map** with

- **Position**: `:x`, `:y`
- **Size**: `:size` (constant per shape)
- **Color**: `:hue` (will change over time)
- **Velocity**: `:dx`, `:dy` (change in x and y per frame)

Velocity Generation

Listing 3-7. Random velocity generator producing values between negative and positive max-velocity for bidirectional movement

```
(defn random-velocity []
  (- (rand (* 2 max-velocity)) max-velocity))
```

This generates values between `-max-velocity` and `+max-velocity`. If `max-velocity` is 2.0: - Possible values: -2.0 to +2.0 - Negative values move left/up - Positive values move right/down

Toroidal Wrapping

Listing 3-8. Toroidal coordinate wrapping function using modulo for seamless edge transitions

```
(defn wrap-coordinate [value max-value]
  (mod value max-value))
```

This creates a **toroidal topology**—shapes that exit the right edge reappear on the left, and vice versa. It's like the classic game Asteroids.

The math: `(mod 850 800)` = 50. If a shape's x-coordinate is 850 on an 800-pixel-wide canvas, it wraps to x = 50.

Shape Update Logic

Listing 3-9. Shape update function applying velocity and incrementing hue with immutable assoc transformation

```
(defn update-shape [{:keys [x y hue dx dy] :as shape}]
  (let [new-x (wrap-coordinate (+ x dx) (q/width))
        new-y (wrap-coordinate (+ y dy) (q/height))
        new-hue (wrap-coordinate (+ hue 1) 255)]
    (assoc shape
           :x new-x
           :y new-y
           :hue new-hue)))
```

Every frame:

1. Add velocity to position.
2. Wrap coordinates if they exceed bounds.
3. Increment hue by 1 (color shift).
4. Return new shape (immutable update).

The Update-Draw Separation

Listing 3-10. Functional mode pattern separating pure state transformation from rendering side effects

```
(defn update-state [state]
  (update state :shapes update-shapes))

(defn draw [{:keys [shapes]}]
  (draw-shapes shapes))
```

This is the **functional mode** pattern in action:

- **update-state**: Pure function that transforms state
- **draw**: Pure function that renders state (no side effects except drawing)

Quil's middleware handles calling these functions in the right order.

Fullscreen Canvas

Listing 3-11. Fullscreen canvas configuration using browser window dimensions for immersive experience

```
:size [(.-innerWidth js/window) (.-innerHeight js/window)]
```

Instead of a fixed 800×600 canvas, we use the browser's window size. This creates an immersive, fullscreen experience.

What You See

Thirty colorful circles drifting across the screen, wrapping around edges, slowly shifting through the color spectrum. It's like watching a lava lamp designed by a mathematician.

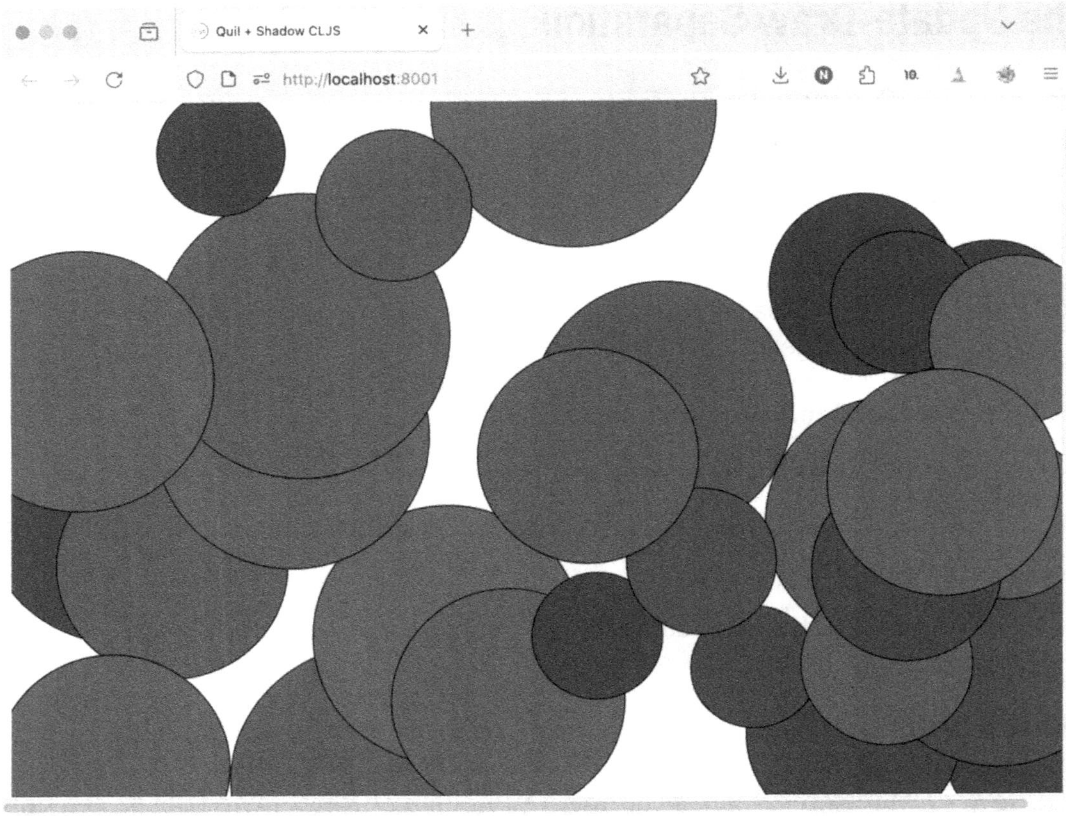

Figure 3-3. *Moving shapes with velocity-based physics drifting across the screen with color-shifting hue animation*

The Beauty of Emergence

Here's what's profound: we didn't choreograph this animation. We defined simple rules: - Shapes have velocity - Velocity is constant - Coordinates wrap - Hue increments

From these simple rules, complex patterns emerge: - Shapes cluster and separate - Colors create temporary harmonies - The overall composition is never the same

This is **emergence**—complexity arising from simplicity. It's the same principle behind flocking birds, ant colonies, and Conway's Game of Life.

Comparing Iterations

Table 3-1. *Comparison of iteration approaches showing progression from simple pulsation to complex velocity-based movement*

Aspect	Iteration 1	Iteration 2
State	Vectors	Maps
Movement	None	Velocity based
Color	Static	Shifting hue
Size	Random per frame	Fixed per shape
Complexity	~30 lines	~115 lines
Feel	Pulsating	Drifting

The lesson: More code doesn't always mean better art. Sometimes, the simplest sketch is the most mesmerizing.

Exercises: Expand Your Canvas

Exercise 1: Gravity

Difficulty: Easy **Concepts**: Physics simulation

Add gravity to make shapes fall:

1. Add a `:dy-velocity` field to each shape.
2. In `update-shape`, increment `:dy` by 0.1 each frame (gravity).
3. When a shape hits the bottom, reverse its `:dy` (bounce).

Hint Check if `new-y > (q/height)` before wrapping.

Exercise 2: Mouse Attraction

Difficulty: Medium **Concepts**: Vector math, interactivity

Make shapes attracted to the mouse:

1. Get mouse position: `(q/mouse-x)` and `(q/mouse-y)`.
2. Calculate direction vector from shape to mouse.
3. Add a fraction of that vector to the shape's velocity.
4. Limit maximum velocity to prevent runaway acceleration.

Hint Use `(q/dist x1 y1 x2 y2)` to calculate distance.

Exercise 3: Collision Detection

Difficulty: Hard **Concepts**: Spatial algorithms, physics

Make shapes bounce off each other:

1. For each shape, check distance to all other shapes.
2. If distance < sum of radii, they're colliding.
3. Calculate collision normal (direction between centers).
4. Reflect velocities based on the normal.

Hint This is $O(n^2)$. For 30 shapes, that's 900 comparisons per frame—still fast enough.

Exercise 4: Trails

Difficulty: Medium **Concepts**: Alpha blending, visual effects

Create motion trails:

1. Instead of `(q/background 0)`, use `(q/fill 0 0 0 10)` and `(q/rect 0 0 (q/width) (q/height))`.
2. This draws a semi-transparent black rectangle, fading previous frames.
3. Shapes leave trails as they move.

Hint Lower alpha values create longer trails.

Final challenge: Combine all four! Imagine shapes with gravity, mouse attraction, collision detection, and trails. That's a full physics simulation.

Wrapping Up

Before you close the tab, look at `update-state` and `draw` side by side and ask yourself honestly—could you call `update-state` in a test without touching the canvas at all? Yes. Could you call `draw` with a fixed state map and get the same picture every time? Yes. That's not a coincidence; that's the functional mode pattern working. Quil enforces the separation structurally, but you could violate it by putting side effects in `update-state`. Don't. The sketch lifecycle only helps you if you respect it.

The pulsation effect in iteration one—why does size change every frame even though the shapes don't move? Because `(rand 100)` inside `draw` runs on each render. That's a side effect inside `draw`, which is technically fine since `draw` is already impure (it paints things). But if you ever tried to move that randomness into `update-state`, you'd need to store the size in state and update it there. That distinction—what belongs in state versus what's a rendering detail—will follow you through every Quil project.

The fractals chapter is next. It uses the same lifecycle but pushes the `update-state` function into recursive territory. If the setup/update/draw loop feels natural now, you're ready.

Fractals: Infinite Patterns in Finite Code

> *"Clouds are not spheres, mountains are not cones, coastlines are not circles, and bark is not smooth, nor does lightning travel in a straight line."*
>
> —Benoit Mandelbrot

The Recursive Studio

You've moved to another room on the third floor. This one feels different—mirrors on every wall, each reflection containing infinite reflections. Welcome to the **fractal studio**, where we explore patterns that repeat at every scale.

Fractals are nature's geometry. They're in trees, rivers, coastlines, and clouds. They're how nature creates complexity from simple, recursive rules. We're building fractal trees that grow, branch, and shimmer with color.

What Are Fractals?

A **fractal** is a pattern that repeats at different scales. Zoom in, and you see the same structure. Zoom in again—still the same. Infinitely.

The term was coined by Benoit Mandelbrot in 1975, but the concept is ancient. Artists have used recursive patterns for millennia. What's new is using code to generate them.

The key property: **Self-similarity**. A fractal tree branch looks like a tiny tree. A coastline's jagged edge looks like a smaller coastline. This recursive structure makes fractals perfect for programming—they're just functions calling themselves.

Iteration 1: Simple Recursive Tree

Let's start with the classic fractal: a binary tree.

The Core Algorithm

Listing 3-12. Recursive branch function with polar coordinate endpoint calculation and binary subdivision creating fractal tree structure

```
(defn branch [x y len angle depth hue-offset]
  (when (> depth 0)
    (let [x2 (+ x (* len (q/cos angle)))
          y2 (+ y (* len (q/sin angle)))
          hue (mod (+ hue-offset (* 15 depth)) 255)]
      (q/stroke hue 255 255)
      (q/line x y x2 y2)
      (branch x2 y2 (* len 0.7) (+ angle 0.3) (dec depth) hue-offset)
      (branch x2 y2 (* len 0.7) (- angle 0.3) (dec depth) hue-offset))))
```

This is **recursion** in its purest form. Let's dissect it.

The Recursive Structure

```
branch(x, y, length, angle, depth)
  if depth > 0:
    1. Calculate endpoint
    2. Draw line from start to end
    3. Recurse left:  branch(end, length×0.7, angle+0.3, depth-1)
    4. Recurse right: branch(end, length×0.7, angle-0.3, depth-1)
```

The base case: `(when (> depth 0) ...)`. When depth reaches 0, recursion stops.

The recursive case: Call `branch` twice—once with `(+ angle 0.3)`, once with `(- angle 0.3)`. This creates the left and right sub-branches.

Calculating the Endpoint

```
(let [x2 (+ x (* len (q/cos angle)))
      y2 (+ y (* len (q/sin angle)))]
  ...)
```

This is **polar to Cartesian conversion**: - Start at `(x, y)` - Move `len` pixels in direction `angle` - End at `(x2, y2)`

The math: - `x2 = x + len × cos(angle)` - `y2 = y + len × sin(angle)`

If `angle = 0` (pointing right), `cos(0) = 1` and `sin(0) = 0`, so we move purely in the x-direction.

Color by Depth

```
(let [hue (mod (+ hue-offset (* 15 depth)) 255)]
  (q/stroke hue 255 255)
  ...)
```

Deeper branches have different hues: - Depth 10: hue = `hue-offset + 150` - Depth 5: hue = `hue-offset + 75` - Depth 1: hue = `hue-offset + 15`

This creates a rainbow gradient from trunk to tips.

The Branching Factor

```
(branch x2 y2 (* len 0.7) (+ angle 0.3) (dec depth) hue-offset)
(branch x2 y2 (* len 0.7) (- angle 0.3) (dec depth) hue-offset)
```

Key parameters: - **`(* len 0.7)`**: Each branch is 70% the length of its parent - **`(+ angle 0.3)` and `(- angle 0.3)`**: Branches diverge by 0.3 radians (~17 degrees) - **`(dec depth)`**: Reduce depth by 1

Exponential Growth

With depth 10 and binary branching: - Depth 10: 1 branch - Depth 9: 2 branches - Depth 8: 4 branches - Depth 7: 8 branches - ... - Depth 1: 512 branches

Total: **1,023 branches**. That's the power of recursion.

The Setup and Draw

Listing 3-13. Fractal tree setup with animated hue offset and translate transformation placing trunk at bottom center

```
(defn setup []
  (q/color-mode :hsb 255)
  {:angle 0
   :hue-offset 0})
```

```
(defn update-state [state]
  (-> state
      (update :angle #(mod (+ % 0.02) q/TWO-PI))
      (update :hue-offset #(mod (+ % 2) 255))))

(defn draw [state]
  (q/background 0)
  (q/translate (/ (q/width) 2) (q/height))
  (branch 0 0 120 (- q/HALF-PI) 10 (:hue-offset state)))
```

Key points:

1. **`(q/translate ...)`**: Move the origin to the bottom-center of the canvas.
2. **`(- q/HALF-PI)`**: Start pointing straight up ($\pi/2$ radians = 90 degrees, negated because y-axis is inverted).
3. **Animated hue**: `hue-offset` increments every frame, creating a color-shifting effect.

What You See

A tree growing from the bottom-center, branches splitting symmetrically, colors cycling through the rainbow. It's mesmerizing—organic yet mathematical, chaotic yet ordered.

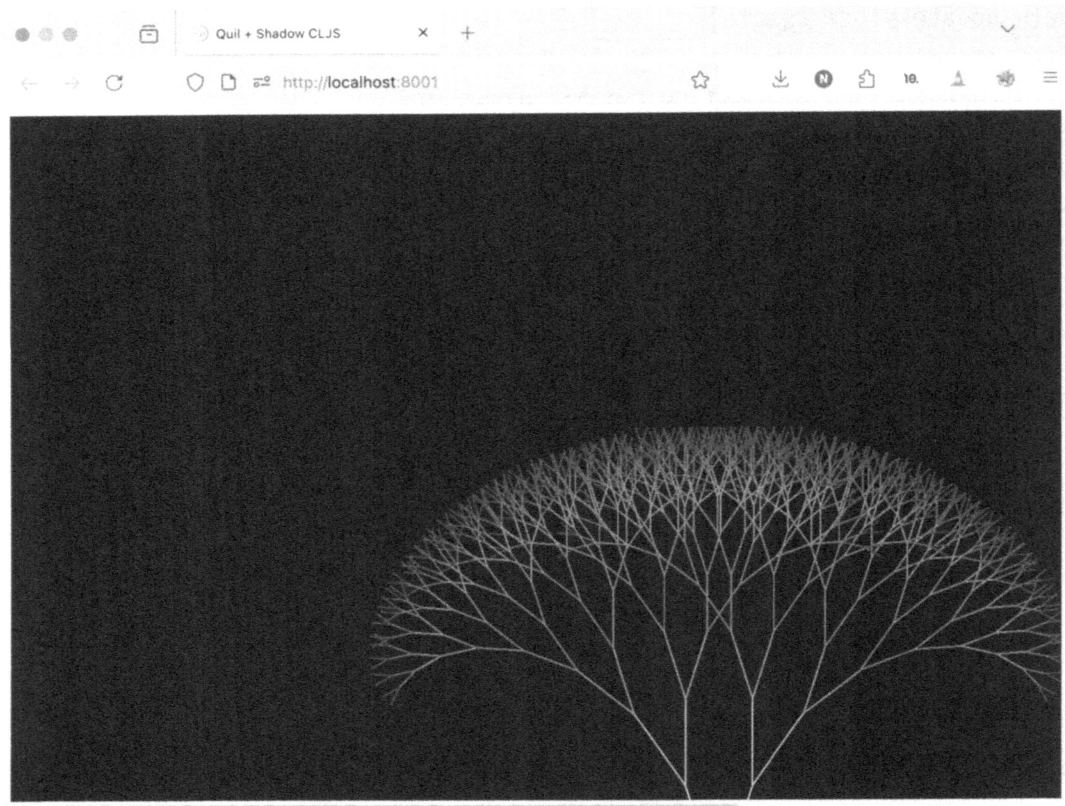

Figure 3-4. *Recursive binary tree with rainbow gradient coloring from trunk to tips*

Iteration 2: Quadruple Branching

What if each branch split into *four* sub-branches instead of two?

The Enhanced Branch Function

Listing 3-14. Quadruple branching variation with helper functions creating exponentially denser fractal patterns

```
(defn branch [x y length angle depth hue-offset]
  (when (> depth 0)
    (let [{end-x :x end-y :y} (calculate-endpoint x y length angle)
          hue (calculate-branch-hue depth hue-offset)
```

```
        new-length (* length branch-scale-factor)
        new-depth (dec depth)]

    (draw-branch-line x y end-x end-y hue)

    ;; Four sub-branches
    (branch end-x end-y new-length (+ angle branch-angle-offset)
    new-depth hue-offset)
    (branch end-x end-y new-length (- angle branch-angle-offset)
    new-depth hue-offset)
    (branch end-x end-y new-length (+ angle branch-angle-offset)
    new-depth hue-offset)
    (branch end-x end-y new-length (- angle branch-angle-offset)
    new-depth hue-offset))))
```

The change: Four recursive calls instead of two.

The impact: With depth 12: - Binary tree: 4,095 branches - Quadruple tree: **16,777,215 branches**

We can't actually render that many (the browser would freeze), so we limit depth to 12 and use a growth animation.

Gradual Growth

Listing 3-15. Growth depth calculation for gradual tree emergence animation over time

```
(defn calculate-growth-depth [frame-count]
  (min max-depth (/ frame-count 10)))
```

The tree grows over time: - Frame 0: depth 0 (no tree) - Frame 10: depth 1 (trunk only) - Frame 50: depth 5 - Frame 120+: depth 12 (full tree)

This creates a beautiful emergence effect—the tree unfolds before your eyes.

Refactored Helper Functions

Listing 3-16. Endpoint calculation helper extracting polar-to-Cartesian conversion into reusable function

```
(defn calculate-endpoint [x y length angle]
  {:x (+ x (* length (q/cos angle)))
   :y (+ y (* length (q/sin angle)))})
```

Listing 3-17. Branch hue calculation helper for color gradient

```
(defn calculate-branch-hue [depth hue-offset]
  (mod (+ hue-offset (* hue-per-depth depth)) 255))
```

Listing 3-18. Draw branch line helper encapsulating stroke color setting and line drawing

```
(defn draw-branch-line [x y end-x end-y hue]
  (q/stroke hue 255 255)
  (q/line x y end-x end-y))
```

Why refactor? Clarity. Each function does one thing. The main `branch` function reads like prose:

1. Calculate endpoint.
2. Calculate hue.
3. Draw line.
4. Recurse four times.

This is **functional decomposition**—breaking complex logic into simple, named pieces.

The Mathematics of Fractals

Dimension

Fractals have **fractional dimension**. A line is 1D, a plane is 2D, but a fractal tree is somewhere in between—maybe 1.7D.

Why? Because it's more than a line (it branches), but less than a plane (it has gaps).

Self-Similarity Ratio

Our tree has a **self-similarity ratio** of 0.7—each branch is 70% the size of its parent.

If we zoom in by $1/0.7 \approx 1.43\times$, the sub-branches look identical to the original.

Hausdorff Dimension

The **Hausdorff dimension** of our tree is approximately

```
D = log(N) / log(1/r)
  = log(2) / log(1/0.7)
  ≈ 1.94
```

where

- N = 2 (number of sub-branches)
- r = 0.7 (scale factor)

So our tree is almost two dimensional—it nearly fills the plane.

Fractals in Nature

Why do trees look like fractals? **Efficiency**.

A tree needs to

1. Maximize sunlight exposure (spread leaves wide)
2. Minimize material (wood is expensive)
3. Distribute nutrients (from roots to every leaf)

Fractal branching solves all three:

- Self-similar branching reaches everywhere.
- Exponential growth (2^n branches) with linear material (sum of decreasing lengths).
- Every leaf has a direct path to the trunk.

Nature discovered fractals billions of years before Mandelbrot named them.

Comparing Iterations

Table 3-2. *Comparison between binary and quadruple branching fractals showing exponential growth in complexity*

Aspect	Iteration 1	Iteration 2
Branches per node	2	4
Total branches (depth 10)	1,023	349,525
Growth	Instant	Gradual
Code structure	Inline	Refactored helpers
Visual density	Sparse	Dense

The lesson: Small changes to recursive rules create vastly different results.

Exercises: Grow Your Tree

Exercise 1: Asymmetric Branching

Difficulty: Easy **Concepts**: Randomness, natural variation

Make branches asymmetric:

1. Instead of `(+ angle 0.3)` and `(- angle 0.3)`, use `(+ angle (rand 0.5))` and `(- angle (rand 0.5))`.
2. Vary the length scale: `(* len (+ 0.6 (rand 0.2)))`.
3. Watch the tree become more organic.

Hint Trees in nature are never perfectly symmetric.

Exercise 2: Wind Effect

Difficulty: Medium **Concepts**: Sine waves, environmental simulation

Add swaying motion:

1. Add a `:wind` value to state that oscillates: `(* 0.2 (q/sin (* t 0.5)))`.
2. Add wind to the angle: `(+ angle wind-offset)`.
3. The tree sways in the breeze.

Hint Deeper branches should sway more (multiply by depth).

Exercise 3: Leaves

Difficulty: Medium **Concepts**: Conditional rendering, detail

Draw leaves at branch tips:

1. When `depth = 1`, instead of drawing a line, draw a small circle.
2. Use green color: `(q/fill 120 255 200)`.
3. Size based on branch length: `(q/ellipse x y (* len 0.5) (* len 0.5))`.

Hint You'll need an `if` statement to choose between line and circle.

Exercise 4: 3D Fractal

Difficulty: Expert **Concepts**: 3D graphics, advanced Quil

Render in 3D:

1. Use `(q/defsketch ... :renderer :p3d)` for 3D mode.
2. Add a z-coordinate to branches.
3. Rotate the view: `(q/rotate-y (q/mouse-x))`.
4. Branch in three dimensions.

Hint This requires understanding 3D transformations. Start with Quil's 3D examples.

Final challenge: Create a forest—multiple trees with different random seeds, swaying in synchronized wind, with leaves that change color based on season (time).

Wrapping Up

You've mastered recursion through fractals. You've learned

- **Recursive algorithms**: Functions that call themselves
- **Base cases**: When to stop recursing
- **Exponential growth**: How small changes compound
- **Polar coordinates**: Converting angles and lengths to x, y positions
- **Self-similarity**: Patterns that repeat at every scale

Fractals teach you to think recursively. Every complex problem can be broken into smaller, similar sub-problems. This is the essence of divide-and-conquer algorithms, tree data structures, and functional programming itself.

Next, we'll explore **waves**—flowing, organic patterns created with Perlin noise. But for now, watch your tree grow. Notice how branches mirror the whole. See the infinite complexity emerging from a few lines of code.

This is the power of recursion. This is the beauty of fractals.

> *"The most beautiful thing we can experience is the mysterious. It is the source of all true art and science."*
>
> —Albert Einstein

Waves: Organic Motion with Perlin Noise

> *"You can't stop the waves, but you can learn to surf."*
>
> —Jon Kabat-Zinn

The Noise Studio

Another room on the third floor. This one feels fluid—walls seem to ripple, surfaces undulate. Welcome to the **noise studio**, where we explore **Perlin noise**, the secret ingredient behind natural-looking randomness.

We're creating waves, not the mathematical sine waves you know, but organic, flowing patterns that look like water, clouds, or terrain. This is the technique used in Minecraft for terrain generation, in Photoshop for cloud filters, and in countless games for procedural content.

What Is Perlin Noise?

Perlin noise was invented by Ken Perlin in 1983 for the movie *Tron*. He needed a way to create textures that looked natural, not random.

The Problem with Random

Listing 3-19. Pure random function calls showing discontinuous value jumps creating artificial-looking patterns

```
(rand)  ; 0.234
(rand)  ; 0.891
(rand)  ; 0.102
```

Pure randomness is **discontinuous**. Values jump around. This looks artificial.

Perlin Noise

Listing 3-20. Perlin noise function calls demonstrating continuous coherent values for natural-looking randomness

```
(q/noise 0.0)    ; 0.5
(q/noise 0.1)    ; 0.52
(q/noise 0.2)    ; 0.54
```

Perlin noise is **continuous**. Adjacent values are similar. This looks natural.

The key property: **Coherent noise**. Close inputs produce close outputs. Far inputs produce unrelated outputs.

Visualizing the Difference

```
Random:    
```

```
           (jagged, harsh)
Perlin:    
```

```
           (smooth, flowing)
```

Perlin noise creates the smooth, organic randomness we see in nature.

Iteration 1: Simple Noise Grid

Let's start by visualizing Perlin noise directly.

The Core Drawing Loop

Listing 3-21. Perlin noise wave visualization using 3D noise with time parameter for animated height displacement

```
(defn draw-waves [time]
  (q/no-stroke)
  (doseq [y (range 0 height 10)]
    (doseq [x (range 0 width 10)]
      (let [offset (* 30 (q/noise (* x 0.01) (* y 0.01) time))
            wave-height (+ y offset)]
        (q/fill 200 255 (- 255 (* 0.7 wave-height)))
        (q/rect x wave-height 10 10)))))
```

Breaking It Down

Nested Loops

Listing 3-22. Nested loop structure creating grid of sample points spaced 10 pixels apart for wave rendering

```
(doseq [y (range 0 height 10)]
  (doseq [x (range 0 width 10)]
    ...))
```

This creates a grid of points, spaced 10 pixels apart. If the canvas is 1000×600: - x: 0, 10, 20, ..., 990 (100 columns) - y: 0, 10, 20, ..., 590 (60 rows) - Total: 6,000 rectangles

The Noise Call

Listing 3-23. Three-dimensional Perlin noise sampling with scaled spatial coordinates and time parameter

```
(q/noise (* x 0.01) (* y 0.01) time)
```

Three-dimensional noise:

- **First dimension**: x-position (scaled by 0.01)
- **Second dimension**: y-position (scaled by 0.01)
- **Third dimension**: Time

Why scale by 0.01? Perlin noise works best with small inputs. `(q/noise 100 200 5)` would be too "zoomed out"—the values would change too quickly. `(q/noise 1.0 2.0 0.05)` is "zoomed in"—smooth, gradual changes.

The Offset Calculation

Listing 3-24. Noise-based offset calculation displacing rectangles vertically for wave animation effect

```
(let [offset (* 30 (q/noise (* x 0.01) (* y 0.01) time))
      wave-height (+ y offset)]
  ...)
```

- `(q/noise ...)` returns a value between 0 and 1.
- Multiply by 30 to get an offset between 0 and 30 pixels.
- Add to the base y-position.

The effect: Each rectangle is displaced vertically by a noise-driven amount. As `time` changes, the displacement changes, creating animated waves.

Color by Height

Listing 3-25. HSB fill color with height-based brightness creating depth perception in wave visualization

```
(q/fill 200 255 (- 255 (* 0.7 wave-height)))
```

In HSB mode

- **Hue**: 200 (cyan/blue)
- **Saturation**: 255 (fully saturated)
- **Brightness**: Varies by height

Higher rectangles are darker, lower rectangles are brighter. This creates a depth effect—like looking down at water from above.

Time Animation

Listing 3-26. Time animation incrementing noise field offset for flowing wave motion through 3D noise space

```
(defn update-state [state]
  (update state :time #(+ % 0.02)))
```

Every frame, increment `:time` by 0.02. This shifts the noise field, making the waves flow.

The magic: We're not moving rectangles. We're changing which slice of the 3D noise field we're sampling. It's like moving through a frozen ocean—the waves don't move, but our perspective does.

What You See

A grid of blue rectangles, undulating like water. The motion is organic, never repeating exactly, yet always smooth. It's hypnotic.

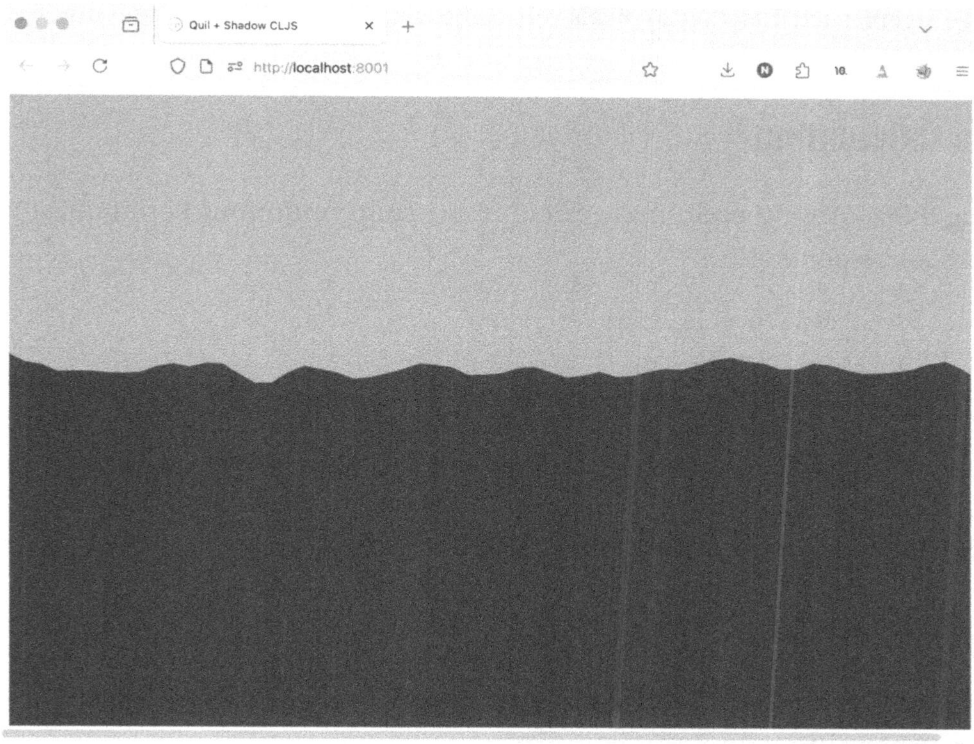

Figure 3-5. *Perlin noise visualization showing organic wave patterns with height-based coloring*

Iteration 2: Layered Waves

Simple noise is nice, but what if we added **depth**? Multiple layers, each moving at different speeds, creating parallax?

Layer Configuration

Listing 3-27. Layer configuration constants defining parallax depth with vertical offset and transparency variation

```
(def layer-count 5)
(def layer-y-offset 20)
(def layer-hue-offset 5)
(def layer-alpha-base 120)
(def layer-alpha-decrement 40)
```

Five layers, each offset by 20 pixels vertically, with slightly different hues and transparency.

Wave Calculation

Listing 3-28. Wave y-coordinate calculation using continuous Perlin noise for smooth curve generation

```
(defn calculate-wave-y [x time]
  (+ (/ canvas-height 2)
     (* wave-height (q/noise (* x noise-scale) time))))
```

Instead of a grid, we're drawing **continuous curves.** For each x-coordinate, calculate a y-coordinate using noise.

The shape: A smooth, flowing line across the canvas.

Drawing a Layer

Listing 3-29. Wave layer drawing function using begin-shape/vertex API for filled polygon with time-offset parallax

```
(defn draw-wave-layer [time layer-index]
  (let [y-offset (* layer-index layer-y-offset)
        layer-time (+ time (* layer-index 0.1))
        fill-color (calculate-layer-color layer-index)]

   (q/fill fill-color)
   (q/no-stroke)
   (q/begin-shape)

   ;; Start from bottom-left
   (q/vertex 0 canvas-height)

   ;; Draw wave points
   (doseq [x (range 0 canvas-width (/ canvas-width wave-columns))]
     (let [y (- (calculate-wave-y x layer-time) y-offset)]
       (q/vertex x y)))
```

```
  ;; End at bottom-right
  (q/vertex canvas-width canvas-height)
  (q/end-shape)))
```

The Shape API

begin-shape/end-shape: Quil's way of drawing complex polygons.

vertex: Add a point to the shape.

The sequence:

1. Start at bottom-left: `(0, canvas-height)`.
2. Add wave points across the width.
3. End at bottom-right: `(canvas-width, canvas-height)`.
4. Close the shape.

The result: A filled polygon that looks like a wave, extending to the bottom of the canvas.

Layer Parallax

Listing 3-30. Layer time offset calculation creating parallax effect by advancing each layer's animation phase

```
(let [layer-time (+ time (* layer-index 0.1))]
  ...)
```

Each layer uses a different time offset: - Layer 0: `time` - Layer 1: `time + 0.1` - Layer 2: `time + 0.2` - ...

The effect: Layers move at slightly different speeds, creating a **parallax effect**—like looking at distant mountains moving slower than nearby trees.

Alpha Transparency

Listing 3-31. Layer alpha calculation creating depth through progressive transparency based on layer index

```
(defn calculate-layer-alpha [layer-index]
  (max layer-alpha-base (- 255 (* layer-alpha-decrement layer-index))))
```

- Layer 0: alpha ≈ 255 (opaque)
- Layer 1: alpha ≈ 215
- Layer 2: alpha ≈ 175
- ...

Front layers are more opaque; back layers are more transparent. This creates **depth**.

What You See

Five undulating waves, layered on top of each other, each moving at a different speed. The effect is mesmerizing—like watching ocean waves from a cliff or clouds drifting across the sky.

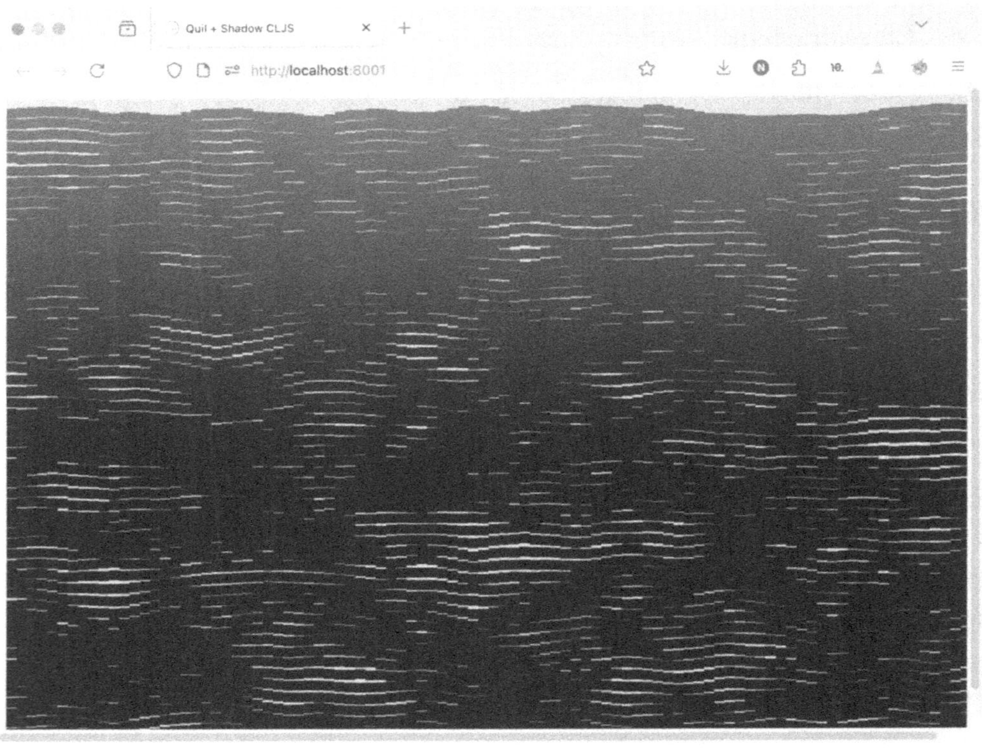

Figure 3-6. *Layered waves with parallax effect creating depth through multiple overlapping animated layers*

The Mathematics of Noise

Octaves

Perlin noise can be **layered** (like our waves, but in the noise itself). Each layer is called an **octave**:

Listing 3-32. Multi-octave noise function combining multiple frequency layers for terrain-like detail variation

```
(defn multi-octave-noise [x y]
  (+ (* 0.5 (q/noise x y))
     (* 0.25 (q/noise (* x 2) (* y 2)))
     (* 0.125 (q/noise (* x 4) (* y 4)))))
```

Each octave

- Has half the amplitude
- Has double the frequency

The result: Noise with both large, smooth features and small, detailed features. This is how Minecraft generates terrain—large mountains with small pebbles.

Frequency and Amplitude

Listing 3-33. Frequency and amplitude parameters controlling noise detail level and displacement magnitude

```
(* amplitude (q/noise (* x frequency) time))
```

- **Frequency**: How quickly the noise changes (higher = more detail)
- **Amplitude**: How much the noise affects the result (higher = bigger waves)

Our waves use

- Frequency: 0.02 (very smooth)
- Amplitude: 50 (moderate displacement)

Persistence and Lacunarity

For multi-octave noise

- **Persistence**: How much each octave contributes (usually 0.5)
- **Lacunarity**: How much frequency increases per octave (usually 2.0)

These parameters control the "character" of the noise—smooth vs. rough, simple vs. complex.

Comparing Iterations

Table 3-3. *Comparison of wave rendering techniques from discrete rectangles to continuous polygons*

Aspect	Iteration 1	Iteration 2
Rendering	Grid of rectangles	Filled polygons
Layers	Single	Multiple (5)
Depth	None	Parallax + alpha
Smoothness	Discrete	Continuous
Performance	6,000 rects/frame	300 vertices/frame

The lesson: Fewer primitives, rendered smartly, can create richer visuals.

Waves in Nature

Why does Perlin noise look like water? Because **water is a continuous medium**.

- **Ocean waves**: Created by wind transferring energy to water
- **Wave interference**: Multiple waves combine (like our layers)
- **Shallow water**: Waves slow down and steepen (like our height-based color)

Our simulation isn't physically accurate, but it captures the **essence** of waves—smooth, flowing, layered motion.

Exercises: Ride the Wave

Exercise 1: Wave Speed Control

Difficulty: Easy **Concepts**: User input, parameter tuning

Add keyboard control for wave speed:

1. Add a `:speed` field to state (default 0.02).
2. On up arrow: increase speed by 0.01.
3. On down arrow: decrease speed by 0.01.
4. Use `:speed` instead of hardcoded 0.02.

Hint Use `:key-pressed` event in `defsketch`.

Exercise 2: Mouse-Driven Waves

Difficulty: Medium **Concepts**: Interactivity, spatial effects

Make waves react to mouse position:

1. Get mouse x-position: `(q/mouse-x)`.
2. Add a "ripple" centered at mouse-x.
3. Use distance from mouse to modulate wave height.
4. Waves are taller near the cursor.

Hint `(q/dist x 0 mouse-x 0)` gives horizontal distance.

Exercise 3: Color Gradient

Difficulty: Medium **Concepts**: Color interpolation, visual polish

Create a sunset gradient:

1. Instead of fixed hue 180, interpolate from 0 (red) at top to 240 (blue) at bottom.

2. Use `(q/lerp start end amount)` for smooth transitions.
3. Each layer gets a different hue based on its y-position.

Hint `amount = (/ y canvas-height)` gives a 0-1 value from top to bottom.

Exercise 4: Foam and Crests

Difficulty: Hard **Concepts**: Derivative estimation, detail rendering

Add white foam to wave crests:

1. For each wave point, compare its height to neighbors.
2. If it's a local maximum (crest), draw a white circle.
3. Size of circle based on wave steepness.
4. Creates realistic foam effect.

Hint Steepness ≈ `(abs (- y-current y-previous))`.

Final challenge: Create a full ocean scene—multiple wave layers, sunset gradient, foam on crests, and a boat that bobs with the waves (sample noise at boat's x-position for y-position).

Wrapping Up

You've mastered Perlin noise. You've learned

- **Coherent noise**: Smooth, natural-looking randomness
- **Multi-dimensional noise**: Using x, y, and time for animation
- **Layering**: Creating depth with parallax and transparency
- **Shape API**: Drawing complex polygons with `begin-shape`/`end-shape`
- **Organic motion**: Making things move naturally

Perlin noise is one of the most powerful tools in generative art. It's used for: - Terrain generation (Minecraft, No Man's Sky) - Cloud and fire effects (movies, games) - Procedural textures (Photoshop, Blender) - Natural motion (character animation, camera shake)

Next, we'll explore **bubbles**—interactive particles with physics and gradients. But for now, watch your waves flow. Notice how they never repeat. See the depth created by simple layering.

This is the power of noise. This is the beauty of continuous randomness.

> *"Nature uses only the longest threads to weave her patterns, so that each small piece of her fabric reveals the organization of the entire tapestry."*
>
> —Richard Feynman

Bubbles: Interactive Physics and Gradients

> *"Life is mostly froth and bubble, two things stand like stone: kindness in another's trouble, courage in your own."*
>
> —Adam Lindsay Gordon

The Interactive Studio

The final room on the third floor. This one responds to you—move your hand, and colors shift. Click, and forms multiply. Welcome to the **interactive studio**, where art becomes a conversation.

We're creating bubbles, floating, colorful spheres that respond to your mouse, split when clicked, and shimmer with radial gradients. This combines everything we've learned: animation, physics, interactivity, and visual polish.

What Makes Bubbles Special?

Bubbles are **interactive particles**. Unlike our previous projects

- **Abstract art**: Shapes moved on their own.
- **Fractals**: Patterns were deterministic.
- **Waves**: Motion was continuous but non-interactive.

Bubbles **respond to you**. They're a dialogue between code and user, between algorithm and intention.

The Architecture: Atoms and State

For the first time in Quil, we're using **atoms** outside the functional mode.

Listing 3-34. Atom-based state management for interactive event handling outside functional mode constraints

```
(defonce bubbles (atom []))
(defonce mouse-position (atom {:x 0 :y 0}))
```

Why? We need to modify bubbles from event handlers (`mouse-clicked`, `mouse-moved`). Functional mode's immutable state doesn't work well with events that happen outside the update/draw cycle.

This is a pragmatic choice—sometimes, mutable state is the right tool.

Bubble Structure

Each bubble is a map.

Listing 3-35. Bubble data structure map with position, size, motion, and radial gradient color specification

```
{:x 400
 :y 300
 :size 100
 :base-speed -0.3
 :speed 0
 :gradient {:color1 [120 80 200 255]
            :color2 [200 160 255 50]}}
```

- **Position**: `:x`, `:y`
- **Size**: `:size` (diameter)

- **Motion**: `:base-speed` (constant upward drift), `:speed` (current speed including mouse influence)
- **Appearance**: `:gradient` (two colors for radial gradient)

Creating Bubbles

Random Color Gradients

Listing 3-36. Random gradient generator creating two-color specifications with opaque center and transparent edge

```
(defn random-color-component []
  (rand-int 150))

(defn random-gradient []
  (let [r (random-color-component)
        g (random-color-component)
        b (random-color-component)]
    {:color1 [r g b 255]
     :color2 [(+ r (rand-int 80))
              (+ g (rand-int 80))
              (+ b (rand-int 80))
              50]}))
```

The strategy:

1. Pick a random base color (r, g, b).
2. **color1** (center): Base color, fully opaque.
3. **color2** (edge): Slightly lighter, mostly transparent.

Why add random amounts? Creates subtle variation—some bubbles are more vibrant, others more muted.

Why limit to 150? Prevents overly bright colors. We want soft, pastel tones.

Bubble Factory

Listing 3-37. Bubble factory functions creating randomized bubbles with position, size, and bidirectional drift speeds

```
(defn create-bubble [x y size]
  {:x x
   :y y
   :size size
   :base-speed (- 0.5 (rand 1.0))
   :speed 0
   :gradient (random-gradient)})

(defn random-bubble []
  (create-bubble
   (rand (q/width))
   (rand (q/height))
   (+ min-bubble-size (rand (- max-bubble-size min-bubble-size)))))
```

base-speed: Random value between -0.5 and +0.5. Some bubbles drift up, some down, some barely move.

Size: Between 60 and 140 pixels (configurable constants).

Physics: Mouse Influence

Calculating Speed Boost

Listing 3-38. Mouse influence physics calculating speed boost inversely proportional to distance from cursor

```
(defn calculate-mouse-boost [bubble-x bubble-y]
  (let [{:keys [x y]} @mouse-position
        distance (q/dist bubble-x bubble-y x y)]
    (if (< distance mouse-influence-radius)
      (* (- 1 (/ distance mouse-influence-radius)) max-speed-boost)
      0)))
```

The formula:

```
if distance < radius:
  boost = (1 - distance/radius) × max_boost
else:
  boost = 0
```

Example: - Mouse at (500, 300) - Bubble at (500, 200) - Distance = 100 - Radius = 150 - Boost = (1 - 100/150) × 4.0 = 0.333 × 4.0 = 1.33

The effect: Bubbles near the mouse move faster. The closer they are, the stronger the boost.

Updating Bubble Position

```
(defn update-bubble [{:keys [x y base-speed] :as bubble}]
  (let [boost (calculate-mouse-boost x y)
        new-speed (+ base-speed boost)
        new-y (+ y new-speed)]
    (assoc bubble
           :y new-y
           :speed new-speed)))
```

Every frame:

1. Calculate mouse boost based on distance.
2. Add boost to base speed.
3. Update y-position.
4. Store new speed (for potential visual feedback).

The result: Bubbles drift naturally, but accelerate when you move the mouse near them. It's like they're attracted to your cursor.

Drawing: Radial Gradients

The Gradient Algorithm

Listing 3-39. Radial gradient rendering using concentric circles with linear color interpolation from center to edge

```
(defn draw-gradient-circle [x y size gradient]
  (let [{[r1 g1 b1 a1] :color1
         [r2 g2 b2 a2] :color2} gradient]
    (q/no-stroke)
    (doseq [i (range 0 size 1)]
      (let [t (/ i size)]
        (q/fill (q/lerp r1 r2 t)
                (q/lerp g1 g2 t)
                (q/lerp b1 b2 t)
                (q/lerp a1 a2 t))
        (q/ellipse x y (- size i) (- size i))))))
```

The technique: Draw concentric circles, each slightly smaller and with interpolated color.

Step by step:

1. Outer circle (i=0): Full size, color1
2. Next circle (i=1): Size-1, slightly toward color2
3. ...
4. Inner circle (i=size): Size 0 (point), color2

Linear interpolation:

```
(q/lerp r1 r2 t)
```

When `t = 0`: returns `r1`. When `t = 1`: returns `r2`. When `t = 0.5`: returns `(r1 + r2) / 2`.

The math: `lerp(a, b, t) = a + (b - a) × t`.

The result: A smooth color transition from center to edge.

Why Not Use Built-In Gradients?

Quil (and Processing) don't have built-in radial gradients. This technique—drawing concentric circles—is a classic workaround.

The trade-off: Performance. Drawing 100+ circles per bubble is expensive. For eight bubbles, that's 800+ circles per frame. But it looks beautiful, and modern browsers can handle it.

Interaction: Splitting Bubbles

Click Detection

Listing 3-40. Point-in-circle collision detection comparing distance to bubble radius for click targeting

```
(defn point-in-bubble? [bubble point-x point-y]
  (< (q/dist (:x bubble) (:y bubble) point-x point-y)
     (:size bubble)))
```

Circle collision: If distance from point to center < radius, the point is inside.

Splitting Logic

Listing 3-41. Bubble splitting function using golden ratio scaling and gradient preservation for visual continuity

```
(defn split-bubble [{:keys [x y size gradient]}]
  (let [new-size (/ size 1.6)
        offset (/ size 3)]
    [(assoc (create-bubble (- x offset) y new-size) :gradient gradient)
     (assoc (create-bubble (+ x offset) y new-size) :gradient gradient)]))
```

The algorithm:

1. New size = old size / 1.6 (≈ 62% of original).
2. Offset = size / 3 (bubbles appear left and right of original).
3. Create two new bubbles with same gradient.

Why 1.6? It's the golden ratio ($\varphi \approx 1.618$). Aesthetically pleasing proportions.

Preserving gradient: Both child bubbles inherit the parent's colors, maintaining visual continuity.

Event Handler

Listing 3-42. Click event handler using reduce pattern to transform bubble collection replacing clicked bubble with split pair

```
(defn handle-bubble-click! []
  (let [click-x (q/mouse-x)
        click-y (q/mouse-y)]
    (swap! bubbles
           (fn [bubbles]
             (reduce
              (fn [result bubble]
                (if (point-in-bubble? bubble click-x click-y)
                  (into result (split-bubble bubble))
                  (conj result bubble)))
              []
              bubbles)))))
```

The process:

1. Get click coordinates.
2. For each bubble
   - **If clicked**: Replace with two smaller bubbles
   - **If not clicked**: Keep as is
3. Update the bubbles atom.

reduce pattern: Transform a collection by accumulating results. This is functional programming's answer to loops.

Mouse Tracking

Listing 3-43. Mouse movement tracking updating position atom for decoupled physics influence calculations

```
(defn handle-mouse-moved! []
  (reset! mouse-position {:x (q/mouse-x) :y (q/mouse-y)}))
```

Every time the mouse moves, update the atom. The physics system reads this atom to calculate influence.

Decoupling: Mouse events and physics updates are separate. The event just records position; the update loop uses it. This is **separation of concerns**.
The Sketch Definition

Listing 3-44. Sketch definition with mouse event handlers integrating interactive callbacks into Quil lifecycle

```
(defn init []
  (q/defsketch floating-bubbles
    :size [(.-innerWidth js/window) (.-innerHeight js/window)]
    :host "app"
    :setup setup
    :draw draw
    :mouse-moved handle-mouse-moved!
    :mouse-pressed handle-bubble-click!
    :middleware [m/fun-mode]))
```

New event handlers:

- **`:mouse-moved`**: Called whenever the mouse moves
- **`:mouse-pressed`**: Called when any mouse button is clicked

These are Quil's hooks into browser events.

What You See

Eight bubbles floating across a dark canvas. Move your mouse—bubbles near it accelerate. Click one—it splits into two smaller bubbles. The colors shimmer, the motion is organic, and the interaction is immediate.

It's playful, meditative, and endlessly satisfying.

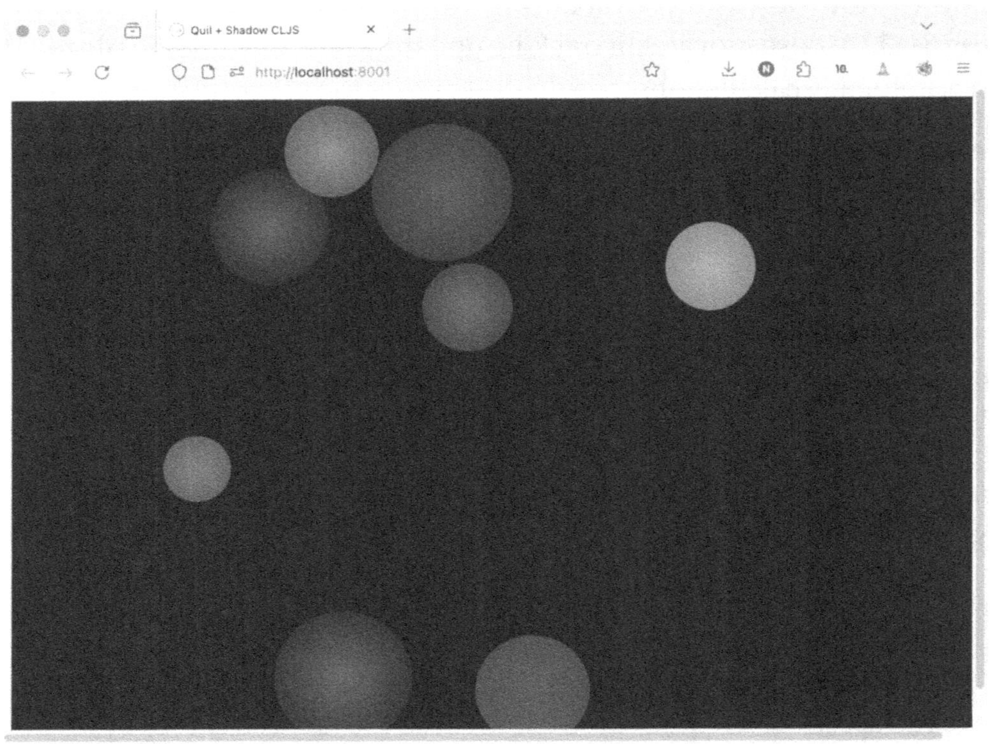

Figure 3-7. *Interactive bubbles with radial gradients responding to mouse position and splitting on click*

The Physics of Bubbles

Real bubbles have fascinating physics.

Surface Tension

Bubbles are spherical because surface tension minimizes surface area. A sphere has the smallest surface area for a given volume.

Our bubbles are always circular—we're simulating this property implicitly.

Buoyancy

Real bubbles rise because they're filled with gas lighter than air. Our :base-speed simulates this—most bubbles drift upward.

Coalescence

When real bubbles collide, they merge. We could add this:

```
(defn merge-bubbles [b1 b2]
  (let [new-size (Math/sqrt (+ (* (:size b1) (:size b1))
                               (* (:size b2) (:size b2))))]
    (create-bubble
     (/ (+ (:x b1) (:x b2)) 2)
     (/ (+ (:y b1) (:y b2)) 2)
     new-size)))
```

The math: Volume is proportional to radius^3. To conserve volume, we use the Pythagorean theorem on radii.

Exercises: Bubble Lab

Exercise 1: Gravity

Difficulty: Easy **Concepts**: Acceleration, physics

Add gravity to make bubbles fall:

1. Add a :vy (vertical velocity) field to each bubble.
2. Each frame, add 0.1 to :vy (gravity).
3. Add :vy to :y (apply velocity).
4. When bubble hits bottom, reverse :vy (bounce).

Hint This creates a bouncing effect.

Exercise 2: Bubble Trails

Difficulty: Medium **Concepts**: Particle systems, visual effects

Leave trails as bubbles move:

1. Store last N positions for each bubble.
2. Draw semi-transparent circles at each position.
3. Older positions are smaller and more transparent.
4. Creates a motion trail effect.

Hint Use a queue (vector with `conj` and `drop`).

Exercise 3: Bubble Sounds

Difficulty: Medium **Concepts**: Web Audio API, interactivity

Play a sound when bubbles split:

1. Load a "pop" sound file.
2. In `handle-bubble-click!`, play the sound.
3. Pitch varies by bubble size (smaller = higher pitch).
4. Creates satisfying audio feedback.

Hint Use `js/Audio` or Web Audio API.

Exercise 4: Bubble Merging

Difficulty: Hard **Concepts**: Collision detection, physics

Make bubbles merge when they touch:

1. For each pair of bubbles, check if they overlap.
2. If distance < sum of radii, they're colliding.
3. Remove both bubbles, create one merged bubble.
4. Merged bubble has combined volume.

Hint This is $O(n^2)$. Optimize with spatial partitioning for many bubbles.

Final challenge: Create a full bubble simulation—gravity, mouse influence, splitting, merging, trails, and sounds. Make it feel like a real bubble bath.

Wrapping Up

You've mastered interactive generative art. You've learned

- **Atoms for mutable state**: When functional purity isn't practical
- **Event handlers**: Responding to mouse and keyboard
- **Physics simulation**: Speed, acceleration, influence fields
- **Radial gradients**: Drawing smooth color transitions
- **Collision detection**: Point-in-circle tests
- **Particle splitting**: Creating emergent complexity from interaction

Bubbles teach you that art can be a conversation. The user isn't just a viewer—they're a collaborator. Every click, every mouse movement, shapes the experience.

This is the power of interactive art. This is the beauty of generative systems that respond.

> *"Art is not a thing; it is a way."*
>
> —Elbert Hubbard

Epilogue: The Third Floor Complete

You've explored four studios on the third floor, each teaching a different aspect of generative art.

Abstract art taught you **emergence**—complex patterns from simple rules. **Fractals** taught you **recursion**—infinite detail from self-similar structures. **Waves** taught you **noise**—organic motion from coherent randomness. **Bubbles** taught you **interaction**—art as dialogue between code and user.

All powered by **Quil**, the creative coding framework that makes visual programming accessible and expressive.

What You've Learned on the Third Floor

1. **Quil fundamentals**: Setup, update, draw lifecycle
2. **Color modes**: HSB for intuitive color manipulation
3. **Functional mode**: Immutable state management
4. **Recursion**: Functions that call themselves
5. **Perlin noise**: Smooth, natural-looking randomness
6. **Event handling**: Mouse and keyboard interaction
7. **Visual techniques**: Gradients, shapes, transformations
8. **Physics simulation**: Velocity, acceleration, influence fields

These aren't just art skills—they're **computational thinking** skills. The patterns you've learned apply to: - Game development (particle systems, procedural generation) - Data visualization (smooth animations, interactive charts) - Simulations (physics, biology, economics) - UI/UX design (micro-interactions, transitions)

Comparing Floors

Let's see how the third floor builds on the previous two.

Table 3-4. *Progression across three floors from fundamentals through animations to generative art*

Aspect	First Floor	Second Floor	Third Floor
Focus	Fundamentals	Visual Effects	Generative Art
Libraries	None, Reagent	Motion.js	Quil
Paradigm	Reactive, Game Loop	Declarative	Creative Coding
Interactivity	Keyboard, Mouse	Hover, Click	Physics, Events
Output	Utilities, Games	Animations	Art
Randomness	None	Parametric	Perlin Noise

The progression: The first floor taught fundamentals. The second floor taught animation. The third floor taught creation.

The Road Ahead

This was the third floor: generative art with Quil. You've learned to think like an artist-programmer, to see code as a creative medium, to embrace randomness and emergence.

But this hotel has seven more floors above you. Each one builds on what you've learned here.

On the fourth floor, you'll discover **state management at scale**—how to build complex applications with many moving parts. The fifth floor teaches **asynchronous programming**—dealing with time, promises, and side effects. Higher up, there are floors dedicated to **back-end development**, **databases**, **deployment**, and **production systems**.

But you can't skip floors. The elevator only goes up when you're ready.

For now, take a moment. Look at what you've created: - Shapes that drift and morph - Trees that grow recursively - Waves that flow organically - Bubbles that respond to your touch

This is the power of ClojureScript. This is the beauty of generative art. This is what happens when you combine functional programming with creative coding.

The third floor is complete. The studios are yours to revisit anytime. The code is yours to modify, extend, and make your own.

When you're ready—when you've experimented with the exercises, created your own variations, and truly internalized these patterns—the fourth floor will be waiting.

Until then, create. Experiment. Play. Let the code surprise you. Let the randomness guide you. Let the art emerge.

You're not just a programmer anymore. You're an artist who codes.

Welcome to the third floor. You've earned your place here.

> *"Every child is an artist. The problem is how to remain an artist once we grow up."*
>
> —Pablo Picasso

CHAPTER 4

Reactive UI with Reagent: The Reception Desk

> "The best interface is no interface, but the second best is one that responds immediately to your every input."

Welcome to the Fourth Floor

You've arrived at the fourth floor, the UI toolkit floor. We're leaving the realm of pure visual art and entering the practical world of user interfaces. This floor has three distinct rooms, each showcasing a different approach to building interactive applications. We're starting with **Reagent**, a ClojureScript wrapper around React for building reactive user interfaces.

We're building with Reagent, where everything revolves around immediate response and reactive state. You type, the UI responds. You submit, validation happens instantly. It's all about creating interfaces that feel alive.

The Concept

Forms are everywhere. Contact forms, login screens, checkout pages—they're the handshake between user and application. But how many times have you filled out a form, clicked submit, and then discovered you'd made a mistake three fields ago? That's frustrating. That's bad UX.

Reactive interfaces solve this. As you type, the interface validates. As you interact, state updates. There's no disconnect between input and feedback—it's all one continuous flow.

N. Modrzyk, *The ClojureScript Playbook*, https://doi.org/10.1007/979-8-8688-2879-9_4

Reagent makes this natural in ClojureScript by treating your UI as a **pure function of state**. When state changes, the UI automatically re-renders. No manual DOM manipulation, no forgetting to update a display—just data flowing through functions.

This is the philosophy pioneered by React in 2013 and embraced by the functional programming community ever since. Reagent brings it to ClojureScript with a beautifully minimal API that feels native to the language.

At the Reception Desk: A Contact Form

We're building a simple contact form with three fields:

- **Name** (required)
- **Email** (required, must be valid format)
- **Message** (required)

As the user types, we validate in real time. When they submit, we check everything one final time. It's straightforward, but it demonstrates the core principles of reactive UI.

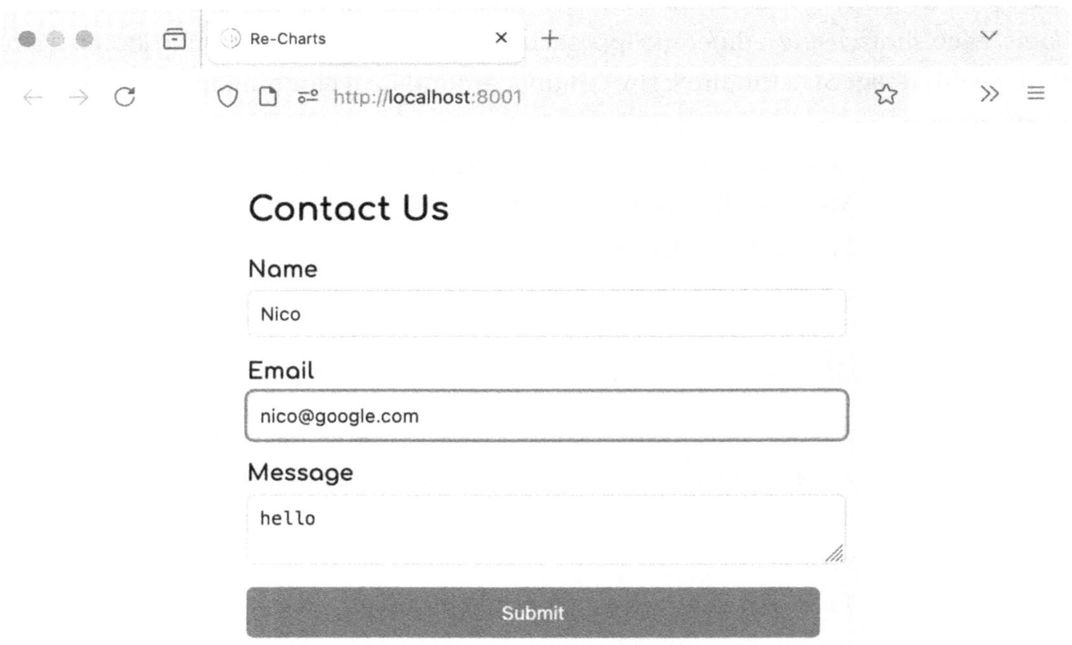

Figure 4-1. *The reactive contact form interface with real-time validation feedback*

The Architecture: Reactive Data Flow

Before diving into code, let's visualize how Reagent applications work.

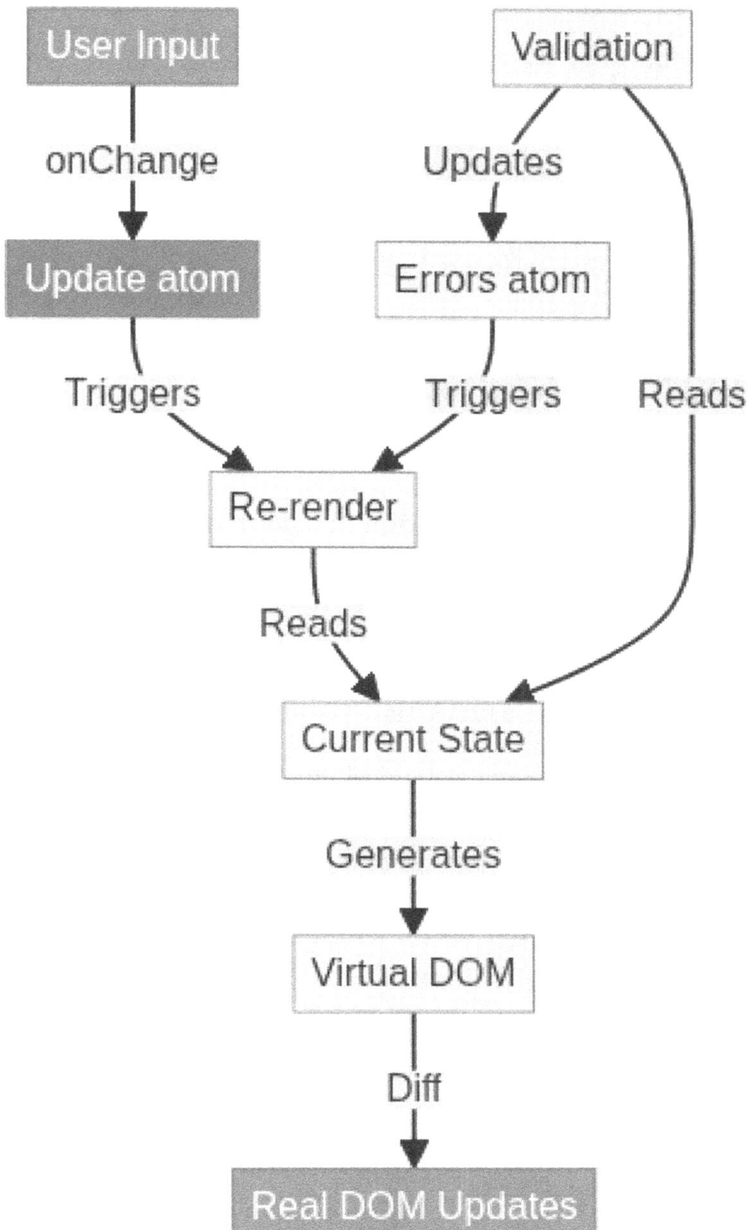

Figure 4-2. *Reactive data flow diagram showing how user input triggers atom updates and component re-renders*

The flow:

1. User types in an input field.
2. Event handler updates a Reagent atom.
3. Atom change triggers re-render.
4. Components read new state and re-generate UI.
5. React efficiently updates only what changed.

This is **unidirectional data flow**. Data has one path: from state to UI. Changes go through state, never directly modifying the DOM.

The Foundation: Project Setup

Our deps.edn introduces a new dependency—Reagent.

Listing 4-1. Project dependencies adding Reagent for reactive UI component library wrapping React

```
{:paths ["src" "resources"]
 :deps {org.clojure/clojurescript {:mvn/version "1.12.42"}
        reagent/reagent {:mvn/version "2.0.1"}}}
```

Reagent is our only dependency beyond ClojureScript itself. It bundles React internally, so we don't need to manage React separately.

The shadow-cljs.edn is familiar.

Listing 4-2. Shadow-cljs configuration with development server and browser build targeting reactive UI application

```
{:source-paths ["src"]
 :dependencies []
 :dev-http {8001 "public"}
 :builds
 {:app
  {:target :browser
   :output-dir "public/js"
```

```
:asset-path "/js"
:modules {:main {:entries [contact-form.core]
                 :init-fn contact-form.core/init}}}}}
```

Our HTML is minimal—we just need a mounting point.

Listing 4-3. HTML template with inline CSS styling for modern contact form interface with Material Design aesthetics

```
<!DOCTYPE html>
<html lang="en">
<head>
    <meta charset="UTF-8">
    <title>Contact Form - Reagent</title>
    <style>
        body {
            font-family: -apple-system, BlinkMacSystemFont, "Segoe UI",
            Roboto, sans-serif;
            max-width: 500px;
            margin: 50px auto;
            padding: 20px;
            background: #f5f5f5;
        }
        .container {
            background: white;
            padding: 30px;
            border-radius: 8px;
            box-shadow: 0 2px 4px rgba(0,0,0,0.1);
        }
        h2 { color: #333; margin-top: 0; }
        .field { margin-bottom: 20px; }
        label { display: block; margin-bottom: 5px; color: #555; font-
        weight: 500; }
        input, textarea {
            width: 100%;
            padding: 10px;
            border: 1px solid #ddd;
```

```
            border-radius: 4px;
            font-size: 14px;
            box-sizing: border-box;
        }
        textarea { min-height: 100px; resize: vertical; }
        .error { color: #d32f2f; font-size: 12px; margin-top: 5px; }
        button {
            background: #1976d2;
            color: white;
            padding: 12px 24px;
            border: none;
            border-radius: 4px;
            cursor: pointer;
            font-size: 16px;
            font-weight: 500;
        }
        button:hover { background: #1565c0; }
    </style>
</head>
<body>
    <div id="app"></div>
    <script src="js/main.js"></script>
</body>
</html>
```

We've included inline CSS for a clean, modern form design. This keeps the project self-contained and easy to understand.

The State: Atoms for Data

Let's look at our namespace and state definitions.

Listing 4-4. Namespace declaration with Reagent atoms for reactive form state and validation error tracking

```
(ns contact-form.core
 (:require [reagent.core :as r]
           [reagent.dom.client :as rdc]))

;; State for form data and errors
(defonce form-data (r/atom {:name "" :email "" :message ""}))
(defonce errors (r/atom {}))
```

Key concepts:

- **`(r/atom {...})`**: Creates a Reagent atom (reactive state container)
- **`form-data`**: Holds the current values of all form fields
- **`errors`**: Holds validation error messages for each field
- **`defonce`**: Ensures hot-reloading doesn't reset our state during development

Reagent atoms are special. When you `deref` them (with `@`) inside a Reagent component, that component automatically re-renders when the atom changes. This is the "magic" of reactive programming—but it's not magic, it's just careful bookkeeping.

Validation: Pure Logic

Before we build UI, we need validation logic. This is a pure function—no side effects, no dependencies on atoms.

Listing 4-5. Form validation function with email regex pattern checking and error atom accumulation returning boolean validity

```
;; Validation function
(defn validate-form []
 (reset! errors {})
 (let [{:keys [name email message]} @form-data]
  (when (empty? name) (swap! errors assoc :name "Name is required"))
  (when (empty? email) (swap! errors assoc :email "Email is required"))
```

```
(when (and (not (empty? email)) (not (re-matches #"^[\w._%+-]+@[\w.-]+\.
[a-zA-Z]{2,}$" email)))
 (swap! errors assoc :email "Invalid email format"))
(when (empty? message) (swap! errors assoc :message "Message cannot be
empty"))
(empty? @errors)))
```

Breaking it down:

1. **(reset! errors {})**: Clear all previous errors.
2. **{:keys [name email message]} @form-data**: Destructure form values.
3. **(when (empty? name) ...)**: If name is empty, add error.
4. **Email regex**: `^[\w._%+-]+@[\w.-]+\.[a-zA-Z]{2,}$` matches standard email format.
5. **Return value**: `true` if no errors, `false` otherwise.

The function modifies the `errors` atom as a side effect, but the validation logic itself is pure—same input always produces same output.

Form Submission: Handling Events

When the user clicks Submit, we validate and either show errors or confirm success.

Listing 4-6. Submit event handler preventing default browser behavior and conditionally showing success on validation pass

```
;; Submit handler
(defn handle-submit [event]
 (.preventDefault event)
 (when (validate-form)
  (js/alert "Form submitted successfully!")))
```

Key points:

- **`(.preventDefault event)`**: Stops the browser's default form submission (which would reload the page)
- **`(when (validate-form) ...)`**: Only proceed if validation passes
- **`js/alert`**: Shows a simple success message (in a real app, you'd call an API)

This is event handling in ClojureScript—direct JavaScript interop for browser APIs, wrapped in ClojureScript's cleaner syntax.

Building Components: Hiccup Syntax

Reagent uses **Hiccup**, a ClojureScript DSL for representing HTML. Instead of writing `<div class="field">`, you write `[:div.field]`. It's more concise and composable.

Input Field Component

Listing 4-7. Reusable input field component using Hiccup syntax with controlled component pattern and conditional error display

```
;; Input component
(defn input-field [label key type]
 [:div.field
  [:label label]
  [:input {:type      type
           :value     (@form-data key)
           :on-change #(swap! form-data assoc key (-> % .-target
           .-value))}]
  (when-let [err (@errors key)] [:p.error err])])
```

Hiccup explained:

- **`[:div.field]`**: A `<div>` with class `field`
- **`[:label label]`**: A `<label>` with text content from the `label` parameter
- **`[:input {...}]`**: An `<input>` with a map of attributes

The input attributes:

- **`:type type`**: Text, email, etc. (passed as parameter)
- **`:value (@form-data key)`**: Controlled component—value comes from state
- **`:on-change #(...)`**: Event handler that updates state

The event handler:

```
#(swap! form-data assoc key (-> % .-target .-value))
```

This is a concise anonymous function: - **`%`**: The event object - **`(-> % .-target .-value)`**: Thread-first macro to get `event.target.value` - **`swap! form-data assoc key ...`**: Update the atom by associating the new value with the key

The error display:

```
(when-let [err (@errors key)] [:p.error err])
```

- **`when-let`**: Only executes body if binding is truthy
- **`(@errors key)`**: Get error message for this field (nil if no error)
- **`[:p.error err]`**: Render error message in red text

This component is **reusable**. We can create any input field by passing different parameters.

Textarea Component

The textarea is nearly identical, just a different HTML element.

Listing 4-8. Textarea component following the same controlled pattern as input field with reactive state binding

```
;; Textarea component
(defn textarea-field [label key]
 [:div.field
  [:label label]
  [:textarea {:value     (@form-data key)
              :on-change #(swap! form-data assoc key (-> % .-target
              .-value))}]
  (when-let [err (@errors key)] [:p.error err])])
```

Same patterns: Controlled component, state updates on change, error display when needed.

The Complete Form: Composing Components

Now we assemble everything.

Listing 4-9. Form component composing reusable field components with Hiccup syntax and submit event handler integration

```
;; Form component
(defn form-component []
 [:div.container
  [:h2 "Contact Us"]
  [:form {:on-submit handle-submit}
   [input-field "Name" :name "text"]
   [input-field "Email" :email "email"]
   [textarea-field "Message" :message]
   [:button "Submit"]]])
```

Hiccup composition:

- **`[:div.container ...]`**: Container with styling
- **`[:form {:on-submit handle-submit}]`**: Form with submit handler

- **`[input-field ...]`**: Invoke our component functions (note the square brackets—this is how Reagent renders components)
- **`[:button "Submit"]`**: Simple submit button

This is **functional composition** in UI form. Each component is a function that returns Hiccup. We nest them naturally, like any other data structure.

Mounting to the DOM: The Entry Point

Finally, we need to render our app.

Listing 4-10. Application initialization creating a persistent React root with `defonce`, then rendering the form component into it

```
(defonce root (rdc/create-root (js/document.getElementById "app")))

(defn init []
 (rdc/render root [form-component]))
```

What happens here:

1. **`[form-component]`**: Our root component (in a vector for Reagent)
2. **`(js/document.getElementById "app")`**: The DOM element to mount into
3. **`rdc/render root`**: Reagent's render function that kicks off the reactive system

When this runs, Reagent

1. Renders `form-component` to virtual DOM
2. Compares virtual DOM to real DOM
3. Updates real DOM efficiently
4. Sets up listeners for atom changes

From this point on, **any change to `form-data` or `errors` automatically triggers re-renders**. You never manually update the DOM again.

The User Experience

Let's walk through what the user experiences:

1. **Page loads**: Empty form, no errors
2. **User types in Name field**: `form-data` updates, no validation yet
3. **User leaves Email field empty and clicks Submit**:
    - `validate-form` runs.
    - `errors` atom gets `{:email "Email is required"}`.
    - Component re-renders.
    - Error message appears in red.
4. **User types invalid email:**
    - Field updates as they type.
    - On submit, "Invalid email format" appears.
5. **User types valid email and fills all fields:**
    - Validation passes.
    - Alert shows success.

This is **immediate feedback**. The user never wonders what went wrong—the interface tells them instantly.

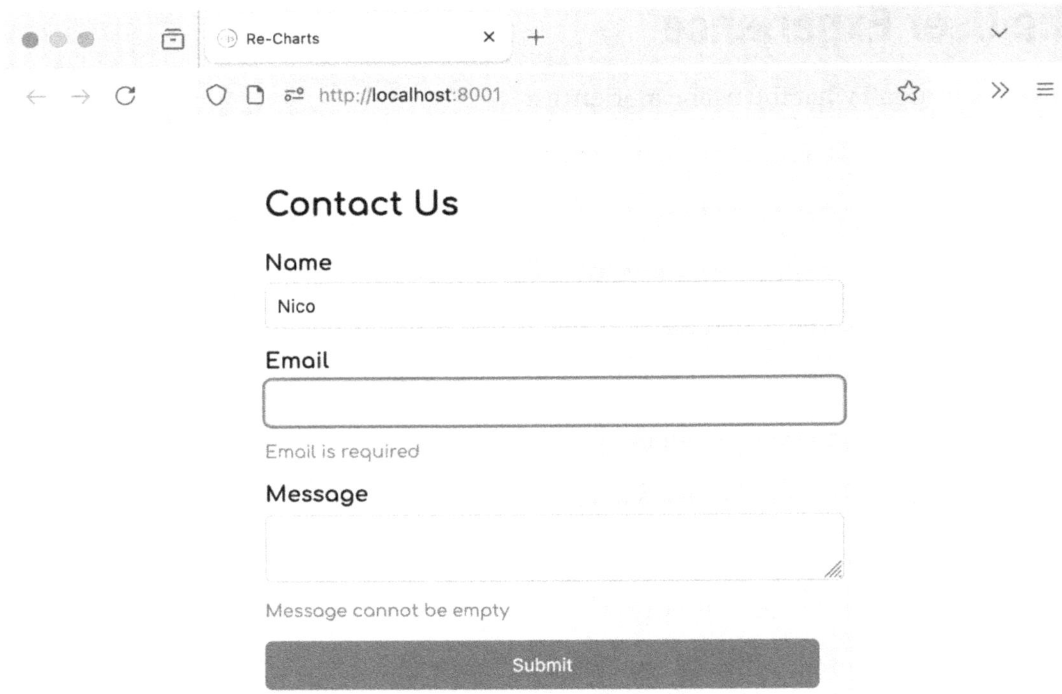

Figure 4-3. *Form validation in action showing error messages and immediate user feedback*

The Reagent Philosophy

Let's step back and appreciate what we've built.

Separation of concerns: - **Data**: Atoms hold state - **Logic**: Pure functions validate and transform - **View**: Components render state

Declarative UI: - We describe *what* the UI should look like given state - We never say *how* to update the DOM - Reagent handles the imperative details

Reactive updates: - When atoms change, UI updates automatically - No callbacks, no observers, no pub/sub - Just atoms and deref (@)

This is the React model, but expressed in ClojureScript's functional style. It's elegant, testable, and scales from simple forms to complex applications.

Comparing Floors

Let's see how the fourth floor builds on the third.

Table 4-1. *Comparison of state management and rendering approaches between Quil and Reagent*

Aspect	Third Floor (Quil)	Fourth Floor (Reagent)
Purpose	Generative art	User interfaces
Rendering	Canvas API	React/DOM
State	Atoms (explicit updates)	Atoms (reactive)
Animation	requestAnimationFrame	Event driven
User Input	Mouse position	Forms, clicks, typing
Data Flow	Update → Draw	Event → Update → Render

The pattern: Both use atoms for state, but Reagent adds reactivity—the UI automatically re-renders when state changes.

Exercises: Enhance Your Form

Exercise 1: Real-Time Validation

Difficulty: Easy **Concepts**: Side effects, reactive updates

Currently, validation only runs on submit. Make it run on every keystroke:

1. Create a new function `validate-field` that validates a single field.
2. Modify the `:on-change` handlers to call `validate-field` after updating state.
3. Use `(go-loop [...] (<! (timeout 300)) ...)` from `core.async` to debounce validation (wait 300 ms after user stops typing).

Hint You'll need to add `[cljs.core.async :refer [go-loop timeout <!]]` to your requires.

Exercise 2: Password Strength Meter

Difficulty: Medium **Concepts**: Derived state, visual feedback

Add a password field with a strength indicator:

1. Add `:password` field to `form-data`.
2. Create a `password-strength` function that returns `:weak`, `:medium`, or `:strong`.
3. Create a `password-indicator` component that shows colored bars based on strength.
4. Use green for strong, yellow for medium, and red for weak.

Hint Check for length, numbers, uppercase, and special characters.

Exercise 3: Multi-step Form

Difficulty: Hard **Concepts**: State machines, conditional rendering

Convert the form into a three-step wizard:

1. **Step 1**: Name and Email
2. **Step 2**: Message
3. **Step 3**: Review and Submit

Add **Next** and **Previous** buttons. Show progress indicator (1/3, 2/3, 3/3). Validate each step before allowing "Next".

Hint Add a `:current-step` field to your state atom.

Exercise 4: Async Submission

Difficulty: Medium **Concepts**: AJAX, loading states

Simulate sending data to a server:

1. Replace `js/alert` with a timeout: `(js/setTimeout #(show-success) 2000)`.
2. Add a `:loading?` field to state.
3. Show a spinner or "Submitting..." message while loading.
4. Disable the submit button during load.

Hint Use `(set! (.-disabled button-el) true)` or add a `:disabled` attribute conditionally.

Final challenge: Combine all four! A multi-step wizard with real-time validation, password strength feedback, and async submission with loading states. That's a production-ready form.

Wrapping Up

A quick check before you move to the next room: do you understand why the inputs are *controlled*?

It comes down to `:value (@form-data key)`. That attribute means the input's displayed value always comes from the atom—not from the browser's own internal state. If you remove that line, the input still accepts text, but the atom stops being the source of truth. The form "works," but validation breaks silently, because `@form-data` never reflects what the user typed. This is one of those bugs that takes 40 minutes to find the first time.

The other thing worth internalizing: `validate-form` modifies `errors` as a side effect, but it's still worth calling "validation logic" rather than "UI logic." It knows nothing about the DOM. You could call it in a test with mock atom values and it would work fine. The side effect is real, but the validation thinking is separate from the rendering thinking. That's the pattern.

Two more rooms on this floor. The next one uses re-frame, which will feel like Reagent plus a lot of structure. Go in wondering: "what problem does this extra structure solve?" The answer will be clearer once you've felt the limits of plain atoms.

UIkit: The Conference Room

"Great design is invisible. Great frameworks make great design inevitable."

Welcome to the Conference Room

Welcome to the second room on the fourth floor, where we explore **UIkit**, a comprehensive CSS framework that brings professional design and responsive layouts to your applications without writing custom CSS.

While Reagent taught us about reactive state, UIkit teaches us about responsive design. This is where data presentation meets visual polish, where CSV files become beautiful card grids, and where professional design is just a class name away.

The Concept: From Data to Design

We're building a player showcase—a common pattern in sports sites, gaming platforms, and team directories. You have data (names, countries, bios) in a CSV file, and you want to display it beautifully, responsively, and with zero design effort.

This is where **component frameworks** shine. UIkit provides pre-built, battle-tested components: - **Cards** for content containers - **Grid systems** for responsive layouts - **Typography** for readable text - **Utilities** for spacing and shadows

You focus on the data and structure; UIkit handles the aesthetics. It's separation of concerns applied to design.

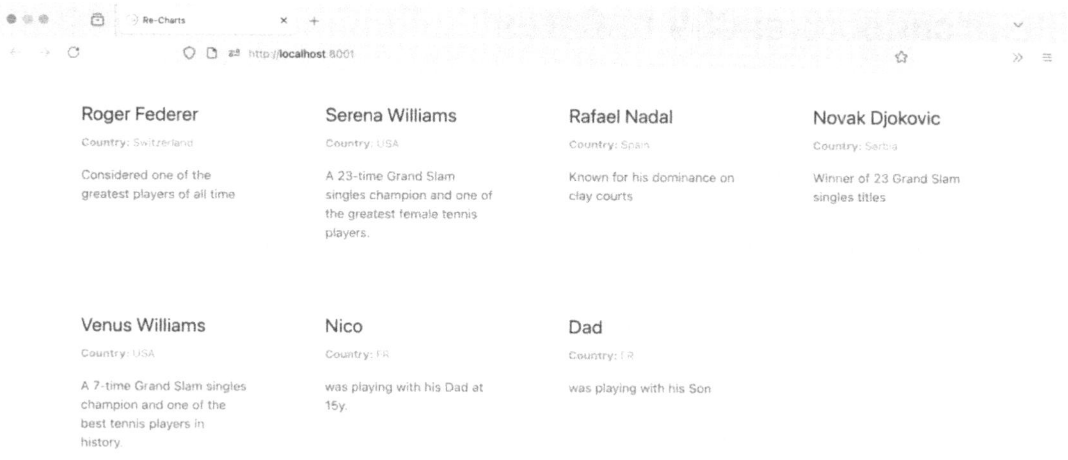

Figure 4-4. *Player showcase application displaying soccer player cards in a responsive grid layout using UIkit components*

The UIkit Philosophy

UIkit, created by YOOtheme in 2013, takes a different approach than libraries like Tailwind CSS or Bootstrap:

> **Class-based design**: You apply semantic class names like `uk-card`, `uk-grid`, and `uk-padding` to your HTML. No inline styles, no utility explosion—just clear, descriptive classes.
>
> **Modular components**: Each component (cards, navigation, modals) is self-contained with its own styles and sometimes JavaScript.
>
> **Responsive by default**: Everything adapts to screen size automatically. The grid system uses suffixes like `@s` (small), `@m` (medium), and `@l` (large).
>
> **Customizable but opinionated**: It looks good out of the box, but you can theme it if needed.

The philosophy: **Professional design should be accessible to everyone, not just designers.**

The Architecture: CSV to Cards

Before we write code, let's understand the data flow.

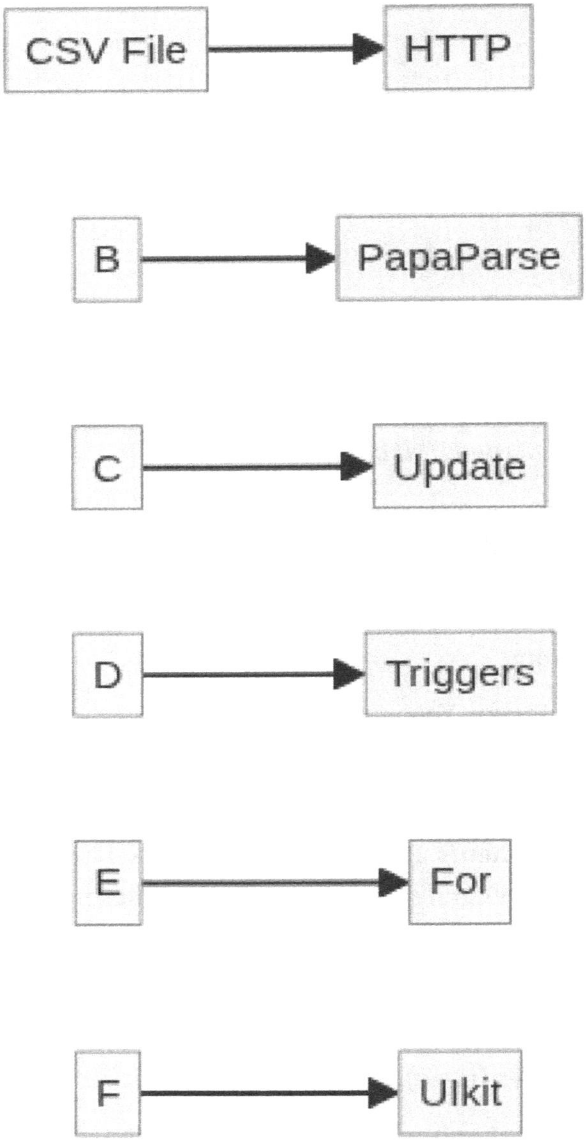

Figure 4-5. *Integration pattern for UIkit components showing JavaScript interop and ClojureScript lifecycle management*

The flow:

1. Load CSV file via HTTP.
2. Parse it with PapaParse (JavaScript CSV library).
3. Convert to ClojureScript data structures.
4. Store in a Reagent atom.
5. Render cards with UIkit styling.
6. Grid automatically adjusts to screen size.

This combines **external data**, **third-party libraries**, and **framework CSS**—a realistic web development workflow.

The Foundation: Project Setup

Our `deps.edn` adds new dependencies for HTTP requests:

```
{:paths ["src" "resources"]
 :deps {org.clojure/clojurescript {:mvn/version "1.12.42"}
        reagent/reagent {:mvn/version "2.0.1"}
        cljs-ajax/cljs-ajax {:mvn/version "0.8.4"}}}
```

`cljs-ajax`: A ClojureScript library for making AJAX requests. It wraps JavaScript's fetch API with a more functional interface.

The `shadow-cljs.edn` is standard, but note the namespace:

```
{:source-paths ["src"]
 :dependencies [["papaparse" "5.4.1"]]  ;; NPM dependency for CSV parsing
 :dev-http {8001 "public"}
 :builds
 {:app
  {:target :browser
   :output-dir "public/js"
   :asset-path "/js"
   :modules {:main {:entries [abstract-art.core]
                    :init-fn abstract-art.core/init}}}}}
```

Notice **["papaparse" "5.4.1"]**—shadow-cljs lets you use NPM packages directly. PapaParse is a robust JavaScript CSV parser; we'll use it via JavaScript interop.

The HTML with UIkit

Our HTML includes UIkit's CSS and JavaScript:

```
<!DOCTYPE html>
<html lang="en">
<head>
    <meta charset="UTF-8">
    <meta name="viewport" content="width=device-width, initial-scale=1.0">
    <title>Player Showcase - UIkit</title>
    <!-- UIkit CSS -->
    <link rel="stylesheet" href="https://cdn.jsdelivr.net/npm/
    uikit@3.16.14/dist/css/uikit.min.css" />
    <style>
        body {
            background: #f8f8f8;
            padding: 20px;
        }
    </style>
</head>
<body>
    <div id="app"></div>
    <!-- UIkit JS and Icons -->
    <script src="https://cdn.jsdelivr.net/npm/uikit@3.16.14/dist/js/uikit.
    min.js"></script>
    <script src="https://cdn.jsdelivr.net/npm/uikit@3.16.14/dist/js/uikit-
    icons.min.js"></script>
    <script src="js/main.js"></script>
</body>
</html>
```

Why three script tags?

1. **`uikit.min.js`**: Core JavaScript for interactive components (modals, dropdowns, etc.)
2. **`uikit-icons.min.js`**: Icon set (we're not using icons here, but it's common to include them)
3. **`main.js`**: Our compiled ClojureScript

UIkit uses a CDN (content delivery network), so we don't need to bundle it locally. Fast, cached, and always up to date.

The CSV Data

Create `public/players.csv`:

```
name,country,bio Lionel Messi,Argentina,Widely regarded as one of the
greatest players of all time. Eight-time Ballon d'Or winner.
Cristiano Ronaldo,Portugal,Five-time Ballon d'Or winner known for his
incredible athleticism and goal-scoring ability.
Neymar Jr,Brazil,Creative forward known for his dribbling skills and flair
on the pitch.
Kylian Mbappé,France,explosive pace and clinical finishing have made him
one of the most exciting players in the world.
Robert Lewandowski,Poland,Prolific striker with exceptional positioning and
finishing skills.
Kevin De Bruyne,Belgium,Masterful playmaker with vision and passing ability
that set him apart.
Luka Modrić,Croatia,Elegant midfielder who controls the tempo of the game
with his technical skills.
Mohamed Salah,Egypt,Lightning-fast winger with a deadly left foot and
incredible work rate.
```

Real data, real structure. This could be thousands of rows; the technique scales.

The Code: Namespace and Dependencies

```
(ns abstract-art.core
 (:require
  [reagent.core :as reagent]
  [reagent.dom.client :as rdc]
  [ajax.core :refer [GET POST]]))
```

New require: `ajax.core` provides `GET` and `POST` for HTTP requests. These are macros that make AJAX calls functional and concise.

State: The Players Atom

```
;; Atom to hold the players' data
(defonce players (reagent/atom []))
```

Simple and clean. We start with an empty vector. When data loads, we populate it. Reagent will re-render automatically.

Loading and Parsing CSV

Here's where JavaScript interop gets interesting:

```
;; Function to parse CSV text using PapaParse
(defn parse-csv [csv-text]
 (.parse js/Papa csv-text
        (clj->js {:header         true
                  :skipEmptyLines true
                  :complete       (fn [result]
                                   (reset! players (js->clj (.-data
                                   result) :keywordize-keys true)))})))
```

Breaking it down:

JavaScript Interop for PapaParse

js/Papa: Access the global Papa object (from PapaParse library).

.parse js/Papa csv-text ...: Call the `parse` method on Papa.

(clj->js {...}): Convert ClojureScript map to JavaScript object.

Parse Options

:header true: Treat the first row as headers (becomes object keys).

:skipEmptyLines true: Ignore blank lines.

:complete (fn [result] ...): Call back when parsing finishes.

The Callback

```
(fn [result]
 (reset! players (js->clj (.-data result) :keywordize-keys true)))
```

(.-data result): Access the `data` property (JavaScript interop).

js->clj ... :keywordize-keys true: Convert JavaScript array to ClojureScript vector, turning JSON keys into keywords.

Result: A vector of maps like

```
[{:name "Lionel Messi" :country "Argentina" :bio "..."}
 {:name "Cristiano Ronaldo" :country "Portugal" :bio "..."}
 ...]
```

Fetching the CSV File

```
;; Fetch CSV file and parse it
(defn fetch-players [url]
 (GET url
      {:handler       parse-csv
       :error-handler #(js/console.error "Failed to load CSV" %)}))
```

AJAX with `cljs-ajax`:

- **`GET url`**: Make a GET request to the URL.
- **`:handler parse-csv`**: On success, call `parse-csv` with response body.
- **`:error-handler #(...)`**: On failure, log error to console.

This is **functional error handling**. No try/catch, no promises—just success and error handlers.

The Player Card Component

Now we build the visual component:

```
;; UI for displaying a player card
(defn player-card [player]
 [:div {:class "uk-card uk-card-default uk-card-body uk-padding uk-box-
 shadow-medium"}
  [:h3 {:class "uk-card-title uk-margin-small-bottom"} (:name player)]
  [:p {:class "uk-text-meta uk-margin-remove-top uk-margin-small-bottom"}
   [:strong "Country: "] (:country player)]
  [:p {:class "uk-margin-small-bottom"} (:bio player)]])
```

UIkit classes explained:

Card Structure

- **`uk-card`**: Base card component
- **`uk-card-default`**: Default card styling (white background, subtle border)
- **`uk-card-body`**: Adds padding inside the card
- **`uk-padding`**: Extra padding
- **`uk-box-shadow-medium`**: Subtle shadow for depth

Typography

uk-card-title: Larger font size for titles

uk-text-meta: Smaller, muted text for metadata

uk-margin-small-bottom: Small bottom margin (spacing utility)

uk-margin-remove-top: Remove top margin (fine-tuning)

This is **declarative styling**. You describe *what* you want (a card, a title), and UIkit provides *how* it looks.

The Grid Layout

```
;; UI to display all players' cards
(defn player-cards []
 [:div {:class "uk-container"}
  [:div {:class "uk-grid uk-grid-small uk-child-width-1-1 uk-child-
  width-1-2@s uk-child-width-1-3@m uk-child-width-1-4@l"
         :uk-grid true}
   (for [player @players]
    ^{:key (:name player)}
    [:div [player-card player]])]])
```

UIkit grid classes:

The Container

uk-container: Centers content and adds max-width (responsive container)

The Grid

uk-grid: Enables grid layout

uk-grid-small: Smaller gutter (gap) between items

Grid Width Classes (the magic of responsive design):

`uk-child-width-1-1`: On tiny screens, 1 column (100% width)

`uk-child-width-1-2@s`: On small screens (`@s`), 2 columns (50% each)

`uk-child-width-1-3@m`: On medium screens (`@m`), 3 columns (33.3% each)

`uk-child-width-1-4@l`: On large screens (`@l`), 4 columns (25% each)

`:uk-grid true`: Activates UIkit's JavaScript for grid calculations

The Loop

```
(for [player @players]
 ^{:key (:name player)}
 [:div [player-card player]])
```

`for`: List comprehension over players

`^{:key (:name player)}`: React key (for efficient re-rendering)

`[:div [player-card player]]`: Each card wrapped in a grid item

The result? **Responsive magic**. Resize your browser, and the grid adapts

- Phone: 1 column
- Tablet: 2 columns
- Laptop: 3 columns
- Desktop: 4 columns

You wrote zero CSS. UIkit handles breakpoints, flexbox, and layout.

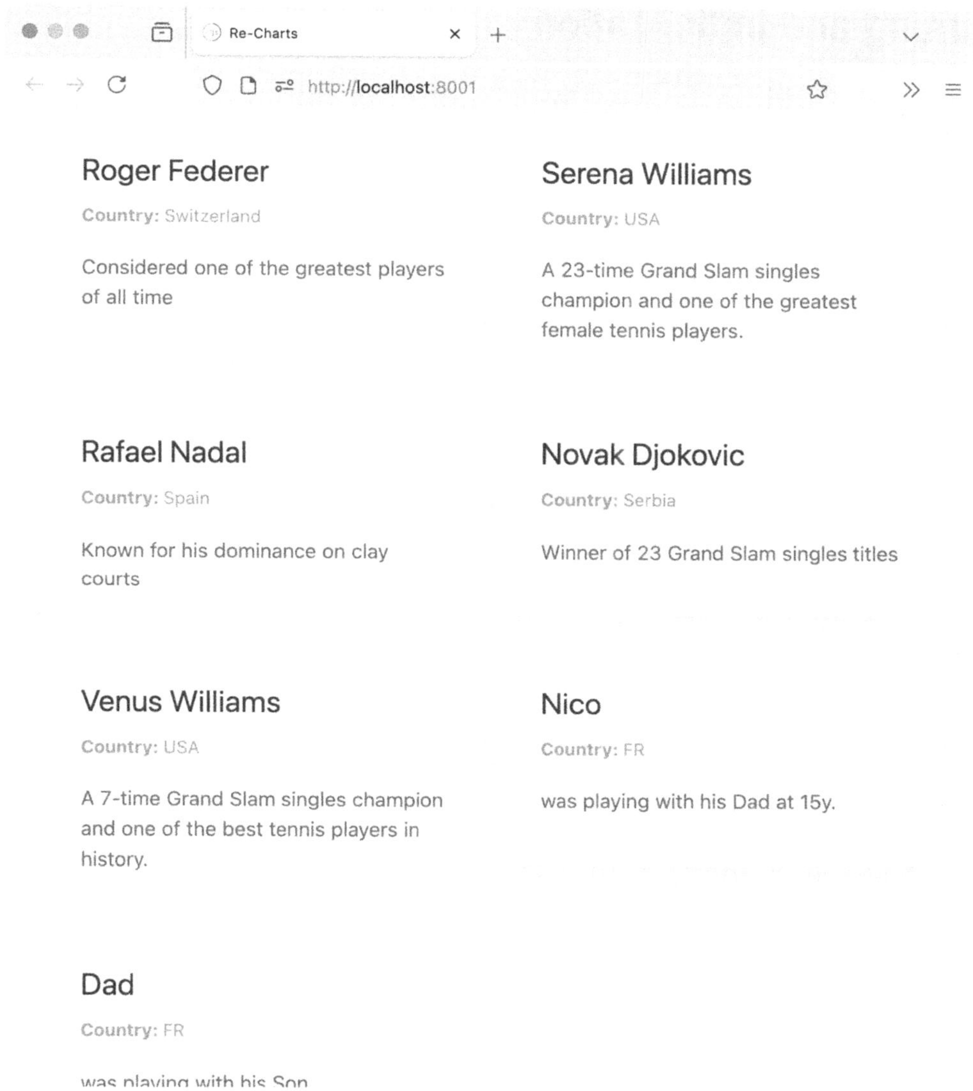

***Figure 4-6.** Responsive grid layout adapting from four columns (desktop) to two columns (tablet) demonstrating UIkit's breakpoint system*

Mounting and Initialization

```
(defn mount-root []
 (rdc/render root [player-cards] (.getElementById js/document "app")))

(defn ^:export init []
 (fetch-players "players.csv")
 (mount-root))
```

The sequence:

1. **`fetch-players "players.csv"`**: Start loading CSV.
2. **`mount-root`**: Render empty grid immediately.
3. When CSV loads → `parse-csv` runs → `players` atom updates → grid re-renders with data.

This creates a **loading pattern**. The UI appears instantly (even if empty), then populates when data arrives. In a production app, you'd show a loading spinner.

The User Experience

Let's walk through what happens:

1. **Page loads**: Empty grid appears.
2. **HTTP request fires**: CSV file fetched from server.
3. **PapaParse processes**: CSV text becomes ClojureScript data.
4. **Atom updates**: `players` goes from `[]` to `[{...} {...} ...]`.
5. **Reagent re-renders**: Grid populates with cards.
6. **UIkit applies styles**: Cards appear with shadows, spacing, and typography.

Resize the browser:

- **Wide**: Four columns side-by-side
- **Medium**: Three columns

- **Narrow**: Two columns
- **Phone**: 1 column stacked

No JavaScript, no media queries written by you. UIkit's grid system handles all breakpoints.

The UIkit Advantage

Let's compare approaches.

Table 4-2. *Comparison of CSS framework approaches from custom styling to utility-first and component libraries*

Aspect	Custom CSS	Bootstrap	Tailwind CSS	UIkit
Setup	Manual	CDN/NPM	Build process	CDN/NPM
Class Names	You decide	`.card`, `.col-md-3`	`.flex`, `.p-4`	`.uk-card`, `.uk-grid`
Responsive	Media queries	Column classes	Responsive utilities	`@s`, `@m`, `@l` suffixes
Customization	Full control	Variables	Config file	LESS variables
Learning Curve	High	Medium	Low (verbose)	Low (semantic)

UIkit balances simplicity and power. It's semantic (`.uk-card` means something), responsive (breakpoint suffixes), and comprehensive (50+ components).

Comparing Floors

Let's see how this room differs from the reception desk.

Table 4-3. *Architectural differences between Reagent's functional approach and UIkit's imperative component system*

Aspect	Reception (Reagent)	Conference Room (UIkit)
Focus	Interactive logic	Visual presentation
Styling	Custom CSS	Framework classes
Data Source	User input	External file (CSV)
Challenge	State management	Responsive layout
JavaScript Interop	Browser APIs	Third-party libraries

The lesson: Reagent handles *behavior*; UIkit handles *appearance*. Together, they create polished, interactive UIs with minimal code.

Exercises: Expand Your Showcase

Exercise 1: Search Filter

Difficulty: Easy **Concepts**: Derived state, string matching

Add a search box that filters players by name:

1. Add a `search-query` atom.
2. Create an input field bound to this atom.
3. In `player-cards`, filter `@players` based on query.
4. Use `(filter #(includes? (:name %) @search-query) @players)`.

Hint `includes?` checks if a string contains a substring (case sensitive).

Exercise 2: Sorting

Difficulty: Medium **Concepts**: Comparators, UI controls

Add buttons to sort players alphabetically or by country:

1. Add a `sort-by` atom with values `:name`, `:country`, and `:default`.
2. Create three buttons that set this atom.
3. In `player-cards`, apply `(sort-by sort-key @players)`.
4. Style active button with `uk-button-primary`.

Hint Use `case` to switch between sort keys.

Exercise 3: Modal Detail View

Difficulty: Hard **Concepts**: UIkit JavaScript, event handling

Make cards clickable to show full details in a modal:

1. Add a `:on-click` handler to each card.
2. Store selected player in a `selected-player` atom.
3. Create a modal component using UIkit's modal classes.
4. Call `(.modal js/UIkit "#player-modal")` with `.show()` to open it.
5. Display full bio, country flag (emoji?), and stats.

Hint UIkit modals need JavaScript: `(.show (.modal js/UIkit "#my-modal"))`.

Exercise 4: Load from API

Difficulty: Medium **Concepts**: JSON parsing, real APIs

Instead of CSV, load from a REST API:

1. Replace `GET "players.csv"` with `GET "https://api.example.com/players"`.
2. Set `:response-format (ajax/json-response-format {:keywords? true})`.
3. Remove PapaParse parsing (JSON is native).
4. Handle loading state with a `loading?` Atom.
5. Show UIkit spinner while loading: `[:div {:uk-spinner true}]`.

Hint Many free APIs exist (JSONPlaceholder, PokéAPI, etc.).

Final challenge: Combine all four! Searchable, sortable player cards that open modals and load from an API with loading states. That's a production-quality data showcase.

Wrapping Up

You've built a responsive player showcase. You've learned

- **UIkit basics**: Cards, grids, and responsive classes
- **CSV parsing**: Using PapaParse via JavaScript interop
- **AJAX with cljs-ajax**: Functional HTTP requests
- **Responsive design**: Breakpoint-based layouts
- **Component frameworks**: Balancing abstraction and control

UIkit represents a philosophy: great design shouldn't require great designers. By providing thoughtfully designed components and a flexible grid system, it lets developers create professional interfaces without deep CSS knowledge.

Presentation matters. Your data might be perfect, your logic flawless, but if the UI looks amateurish, users won't trust it. Frameworks like UIkit democratize design, making polish accessible.

But UIkit is just one approach. There are dozens of CSS frameworks, each with trade-offs. The patterns you learned here—external data, responsive grids, component composition—transfer to any framework.

Summary: What We Learned

In the conference room, we discovered

1. **Component CSS frameworks**: UIkit provides pre-built components with semantic class names, making professional design accessible without custom CSS.
2. **Responsive grid systems**: Breakpoint suffixes (`@s`, `@m`, `@l`) create adaptive layouts that work on any screen size without media queries.
3. **JavaScript interop for libraries**: Using PapaParse via `js/Papa` shows how to leverage the vast JavaScript ecosystem from ClojureScript.
4. **Functional AJAX**: The `cljs-ajax` library makes HTTP requests functional with `:handler` and `:error-handler` instead of promises or callbacks.
5. **Data transformation pipeline**: CSV → JavaScript object → ClojureScript map → Reagent component demonstrates the full data flow in a modern web app.
6. **Declarative styling**: Instead of "how to make it pretty," we declare "this is a card, this is a grid," and the framework handles implementation.

The conference room shows that beautiful UIs don't require beautiful code—they require **thoughtful abstractions**. UIkit is one such abstraction, trading customization for speed and consistency.

"Good design is obvious. Great design is transparent."

Webix: The Executive Dashboard

> "Data without structure is noise. Structure without beauty is bureaucracy. Beautiful structure that responds? That's a dashboard."

Welcome to the Executive Suite

You've walked through the reception desk, past the conference room, and now you stand before double doors of polished wood. Inside, floor-to-ceiling windows bathe the room in natural light. On the wall hangs a row of monitors displaying real-time data grids—sortable columns, filterable rows, clean typography, and not a single error message in sight.

Welcome to the third and final room on the fourth floor, where we explore **Webix**—a professional JavaScript UI library that transforms raw data into interactive dashboards without the complexity of modern frameworks. This is the suite where spreadsheets become applications, where business logic meets visual precision.

While Reagent taught us about *reactive state* and UIkit showed us *responsive design*, Webix teaches us about *data presentation*. This is the room where data structures become interactive tables, where configuration replaces construction, and where enterprise-grade interfaces require surprisingly little code.

The Concept: From Data to Dashboard

Imagine you're building an internal tool for a film database. You have movie data—titles, years, votes, ratings—and you need to display it in a way that is professional, sortable, and filterable and requires zero custom CSS. You don't need a complex state management system. You don't need routing. You just need a **really good table**.

This is where **enterprise UI libraries** shine. Webix provides: - **DataTable** components with built-in sorting and filtering - **Layouts** that organize content with minimal configuration - **Professional styling** out of the box - **JavaScript interop** that plays nicely with ClojureScript

You focus on the data and configuration; Webix handles rendering, interaction, and visual polish. It's the difference between building a spreadsheet from scratch and using Excel.

ClojureScript and Webix

Title	Year	Votes	Rating ^	Rank
The Good, the Bad and the Ugly	1966	213030	8.9	4
My Fair Lady	1964	533848	8.9	5
12 Angry Men	1957	164558	8.9	6
The Godfather: Part II	1974	319352	9	3
The Shawshank Redemption	1994	678790	9.2	1
The Godfather	1972	511495	9.2	2

Figure 4-7. *Movie database application with Webix datatable displaying top-rated films with sortable columns*

The Webix Philosophy

Webix, created by XB Software in 2013, takes a radically different approach than frameworks like React or Vue:

> **Configuration over code**: You describe what you want using JavaScript objects. No JSX, no virtual DOM, no template language—just nested configuration.
>
> **Component library**: Webix ships with 100+ UI components—datatables, charts, forms, calendars, file managers—all styled consistently.
>
> **No build step required**: Include one CSS file and one JS file via CDN. No webpack, no babel, no npm sprawl. It's refreshingly old school.
>
> **Enterprise focus**: Designed for business applications where data density, performance, and professional appearance matter more than animations or mobile-first design.

The philosophy: **Complex UIs should not require complex code.** If 90% of dashboards look similar, why reinvent the wheel?

The Architecture: Data to Table

Before we write code, let's understand the data flow.

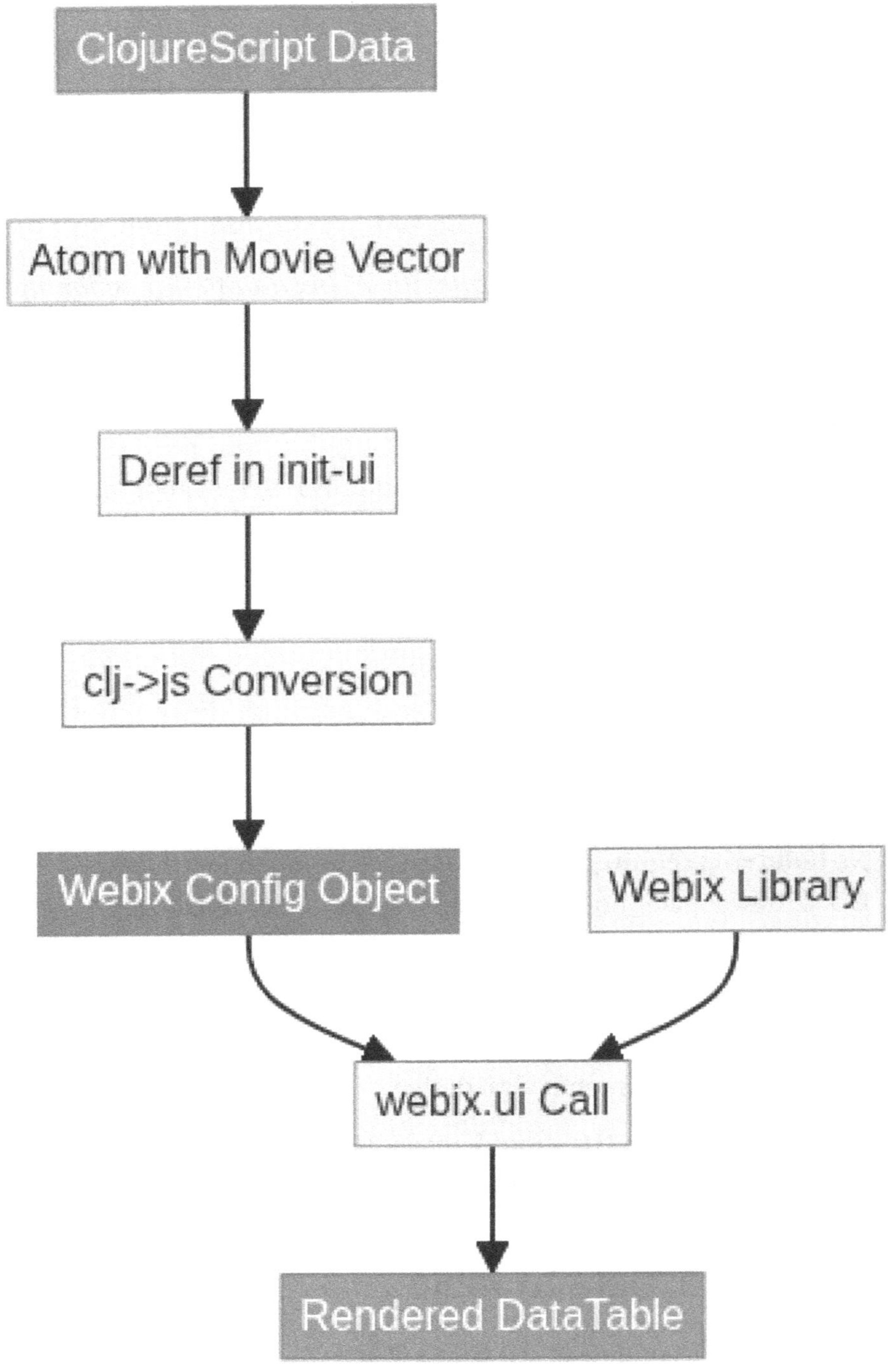

Figure 4-8. *Webix configuration-based architecture showing declarative UI definition through JavaScript objects*

The flow:

1. Define movie data as ClojureScript maps in an atom.
2. Dereference the atom to get current state.
3. Convert ClojureScript data to JavaScript objects.
4. Pass to Webix as configuration.
5. Webix renders interactive table with sorting built in.
6. No manual DOM manipulation needed.

This is **declarative UI through configuration**—a different paradigm than Reagent's components or UIkit's class-based styling.

The Foundation: Project Setup

Our `deps.edn` is minimal—no special Clojure dependencies needed:

```
{:paths ["src" "resources"]
 :deps {org.clojure/clojurescript {:mvn/version "1.12.42"}}}
```

Just ClojureScript. Webix is a JavaScript library we'll load via CDN and use through interop.

The `shadow-cljs.edn` adds Webix as an NPM dependency:

```
{:source-paths ["src"]
 :dependencies [["webix" "10.0.4"]]  ;; NPM package
 :dev-http {8001 "public"}
 :builds
 {:app
  {:target :browser
   :output-dir "public/js"
   :asset-path "/js"
   :modules {:main {:entries [abstract-art.core]
                    :init-fn abstract-art.core/init}}}}}
```

Notice **`["webix" "10.0.4"]`**—shadow-cljs lets us require NPM packages directly in our ClojureScript code. This is cleaner than global CDN references, though both work.

The HTML with Webix CSS

Our HTML is remarkably simple:

```
<!DOCTYPE html>
<html lang="en">
<head>
    <meta charset="UTF-8">
    <title>Webix</title>
    <link rel="stylesheet" href="//cdn.webix.com/edge/webix.css"
type="text/css">
</head>
<body>
<div height="100%" id="app"></div>
<script src="js/main.js"></script>
</body>
</html>
```

Why so minimal?

1. **One CSS file**: `webix.css` contains all styles for all components.
2. **No container styling**: Webix manages layout internally.
3. **`height="100%"`**: Ensures Webix can calculate dimensions properly.

The entire Webix ecosystem—typography, colors, spacing, grids—comes from that single stylesheet. No Bootstrap, no Tailwind CSS, no custom CSS at all.

The Data: Movies As Maps

Our data lives in a ClojureScript atom:

```
(def grid-data
  (atom
    [{:id 1 :title "The Shawshank Redemption" :year 1994 :votes 678790
    :rating 9.2 :rank 1}
     {:id 2 :title "The Godfather" :year 1972 :votes 511495 :rating 9.2
     :rank 2}
```

```
{:id 3 :title "The Godfather: Part II" :year 1974 :votes 319352
:rating 9.0 :rank 3}
{:id 4 :title "The Good, the Bad and the Ugly" :year 1966 :votes
213030 :rating 8.9 :rank 4}
{:id 5 :title "My Fair Lady" :year 1964 :votes 533848 :rating 8.9
:rank 5}
{:id 6 :title "12 Angry Men" :year 1957 :votes 164558 :rating 8.9
:rank 6}]))
```

Structure:

- **Vector of maps**: Each map represents one movie.
- **Consistent keys**: `:id`, `:title`, `:year`, `:votes`, `:rating`, `:rank.`
- **Realistic data**: Based on actual IMDB top-rated films.

This could come from a database, CSV file, or API. The pattern stays the same: data as ClojureScript collections, converted to JavaScript for Webix.

The Code: Namespace and Requires

```
(ns abstract-art.core
  (:require ["webix" :as webix]))
```

Breaking it down:

`["webix" :as webix]`: Require the Webix NPM package - **Square brackets**: Signal an NPM/JavaScript module - **`:as webix`**: Bind it to the name `webix` in our namespace - **Access via `webix`**: We'll call `webix.ui(...)` later

This is **JavaScript module interop** in ClojureScript—clean, typed, and modern.

Building the UI: Configuration As Code

Here's where Webix shines. We don't build components—we configure them:

```
(defn init-ui []
  (.ui webix
       (clj->js
         {:rows [
```

```
{:view "template" :type "header" :template "ClojureScript
and Webix"}
{:view "datatable" :autoConfig true :data @grid-data}]})))
```

Breaking it down:

The Webix API

`.ui webix`: Call the `ui` method on the Webix object - This is the main entry point for Webix - It takes a configuration object and renders UI - Returns a reference to the created component

ClojureScript to JavaScript Conversion

`(clj->js {...})`: Convert ClojureScript map to JavaScript object - **Necessary**: Webix expects JavaScript objects, not ClojureScript data - **Recursive**: Converts nested structures too - **Keys become strings**: `:rows` becomes `"rows"`

The Configuration Object

`:rows [...]`: Webix layout with multiple components stacked vertically - **Alternative**: `:cols` for horizontal layout - **Nested layouts**: You can nest `:rows` within `:cols` for complex grids

The Header Component

```
{:view "template" :type "header" :template "ClojureScript and Webix"}
```

`:view "template"`: A simple HTML container component. **`:type "header"`**: Pre-styled as a header (bold, larger text, background color). **`:template "..."`**: The text content to display

This creates a blue header bar with white text—standard Webix styling, zero CSS written by us.

The DataTable Component

```
{:view "datatable" :autoConfig true :data @grid-data}
```

`:view "datatable"`: Webix's powerful table component. **`:autoConfig true`**: Automatically detect columns from data. **`:data @grid-data`**: The actual data to display.

What happens:

1. Webix looks at `@grid-data`
2. Sees keys like `:id`, `:title`, `:year`
3. Creates columns automatically
4. Renders sortable, interactive table
5. Adds hover effects, alternating row colors, scrolling

All from three configuration keys. No column definitions, no cell renderers, no styling.

The Init Function: Entry Point

```
(defn init []
  (init-ui))
```

Simple and clean. When shadow-cljs loads our app, it calls `init`, which calls `init-ui`, which renders the Webix table into the #app div.

Why separate `init` and `init-ui`?

- **Hot reloading**: During development, you might want to reinitialize UI without full page refresh
- **Testing**: Easier to test `init-ui` in isolation
- **Extensibility**: `init` might do other setups (load data, set up routing, etc.)

The User Experience

Let's walk through what the user sees:

1. **Page loads**: Webix CSS loads first, setting up fonts and colors.
2. **JavaScript initializes**: Our ClojureScript calls `webix.ui(...)`.
3. **Header appears**: Blue bar with "ClojureScript and Webix."
4. **Table renders**: Columns auto-detected, data populates, sorting enabled.

User interactions:

- **Click column header**: Table sorts by that column (ascending/descending toggle).
- **Hover rows**: Background color changes slightly.
- **Scroll**: Smooth scrolling with sticky headers.
- **Resize columns**: Drag column borders to adjust width.

All of this comes **for free**. We wrote zero event handlers, zero CSS, and zero DOM manipulation. Just data + configuration = interactive table.

Title	Year	Votes	Rating	Rank
The Shawshank Redemption	1994	678790	9.2	1
The Godfather	1972	511495	9.2	2
The Godfather: Part II	1974	319352	9	3
The Good, the Bad and the Ugly	1966	213030	8.9	4
My Fair Lady	1964	533848	8.9	5
12 Angry Men	1957	164558	8.9	6

Figure 4-9. *Advanced datatable configuration showing custom column widths, formatting, and sorting for movie data*

Comparing Paradigms

Let's see how Webix differs from previous rooms.

Table 4-4. *Feature comparison between Reagent, UIkit, and Webix highlighting their different philosophies and use cases*

Aspect	Reagent (Reception)	UIkit (Conference)	Webix (Executive)
Philosophy	Reactive components	Responsive classes	Configuration objects
Code Style	Hiccup vectors	HTML with CSS classes	JavaScript objects
State	Reagent atoms	Static data	JavaScript data
Interactivity	Event handlers	CSS/JS utilities	Built-in component behavior
Best For	Forms, SPAs	Responsive layouts	Data-heavy dashboards
Learning Curve	Medium	Low	Low (if you know the API)

The lesson: There's no single "right" approach. Reagent excels at interactive state, UIkit at responsive design, and Webix at data presentation. Choose based on your problem.

The Webix Advantage

Why would you use Webix instead of building a table with React or Vue?

Pros:

- **Speed of development**: DataTable in 3 lines vs. 100+ with custom React component
- **Consistency**: All components styled uniformly
- **Performance**: Optimized for thousands of rows (virtual scrolling, efficient rendering)
- **Rich features**: Filtering, grouping, editing, exporting—all built-in
- **No bloat**: One CSS file, one JS file, done

Cons:

- **Less flexible**: Styling customization requires digging into Webix's theming API
- **Proprietary**: Not open source (free version has limitations, commercial license for full features)

- **JavaScript centric**: Designed for imperative code, feels less natural in functional languages
- **Niche ecosystem**: Smaller community than React/Vue

Verdict: Webix is perfect for **internal tools, admin panels, and B2B dashboards** where time-to-market matters more than pixel-perfect design. It's less suited for **consumer-facing apps** where brand identity and custom UX are critical.

JavaScript Interop Deep Dive

Let's examine how ClojureScript and JavaScript work together here.

Requiring JavaScript Modules

```
(:require ["webix" :as webix])
```

This is enabled by **shadow-cljs**, which understands NPM packages. Behind the scenes, shadow-cljs

1. Finds `node_modules/webix/webix.js`
2. Bundles it with our compiled ClojureScript
3. Makes it available as `webix` in our namespace

Calling JavaScript Methods

```
(.ui webix ...)
```

Dot syntax: `.methodName` calls a method on an object **Equivalent JavaScript**: `webix.ui(...)`.

This is **method invocation syntax** in ClojureScript—clean and unambiguous.

Converting Data Structures

```
(clj->js {:rows [...]})
```

`clj->js`: Recursively converts ClojureScript to JavaScript - **Maps** → Objects: `{:key "value"}` → `{key: "value"}` - **Vectors** → Arrays: `[1 2 3]` → `[1, 2, 3]` - **Keywords** → Strings: `:view` → `"view"`

Alternative: `js-obj` for non-recursive, flat objects

Dereferencing Atoms

```
:data @grid-data
```

`@grid-data`: Deref the atom to get its value. **Returns**: The vector of movie maps. **Then**: Converted to JavaScript array by `clj->js`

This is a **snapshot**—Webix doesn't react to atom changes. If you update `grid-data` later, you'd need to manually refresh the table. This is unlike Reagent, where atoms trigger automatic re-renders.

Enhancing the Table: Manual Configuration

`autoConfig` is convenient but limited. For more control, define columns explicitly:

```
(defn init-ui-advanced []
  (.ui webix
       (clj->js
         {:rows [
                 {:view "template" :type "header" :template "Top
                 Rated Films"}
                 {:view "datatable"
                  :columns [{:id "rank" :header "Rank" :width 60}
                            {:id "title" :header "Title" :width 250
                            :fillspace true}
                            {:id "year" :header "Year" :width 80}
                            {:id "rating" :header "Rating" :width 80
                            :sort "int"}
                            {:id "votes" :header "Votes" :width 100 :format
                            "#,###"}]
                  :data @grid-data}]})))
```

New features:

Column Definitions

`:columns [...]`: Array of column configuration objects. **`:id "rank"`**: Maps to the data key (`:rank` in our maps). **`:header "Rank"`**: Display name in the table header. **`:width 60`**: Column width in pixels. **`:fillspace true`**: Column expands to fill available space. **`:sort "int"`**: Enable sorting as integers (default is string sort). **`:format "#,###"`**: Format numbers with thousands separator (678790 → 678,790)

This gives you **pixel-perfect control** over presentation while keeping the code declarative.

Exercises: Build Your Dashboard

Exercise 1: Add Search Filter

Difficulty: Easy **Concepts**: Webix toolbar, event handlers

Add a search input above the table:

1. Change `:rows` to include a new component before the datatable.
2. Add `{:view "text" :id "searchField" :placeholder "Search movies..."}`.
3. Add `:on {:onTimedKeyPress (fn [] (.filter datatable ...))}` to the search input.
4. Use Webix's `.filter()` method to filter rows by title.

Hint You'll need to get a reference to the datatable with `(.getDom webix "myTableId")`.

Exercise 2: Add New Movie

Difficulty: Medium **Concepts**: Forms, data manipulation

Create a form to add new movies:

1. Add a toolbar with an "Add Movie" button.
2. Create a Webix window (modal) with a form.

3. On submit, use `swap!` to add the new movie to `grid-data`.
4. Call `.clearAll()` and `.parse()` on the datatable to refresh.

Hint Webix windows are configured like `{:view "window" :body {...}}`.

Exercise 3: Export to CSV

Difficulty: Easy **Concepts**: Webix plugins

Enable CSV export:

1. Add `{:view "button" :value "Export CSV" :click #(...)}` to the toolbar.
2. Inside the click handler, call `(.exportToCSV ($ "myTableId"))`.
3. Require Webix's export plugin: `{:dependencies [["@webix/csv" "latest"]]}`.

Hint Webix's export functionality requires PRO license or external plugins.

Exercise 4: Load from API

Difficulty: Hard **Concepts**: AJAX, async data

Replace hardcoded data with API call:

1. Use `(js/fetch "https://api.example.com/movies")`.
2. Parse JSON response with `(.then response #(.json %))`.
3. Convert to ClojureScript with `js->clj`.
4. Update `grid-data` atom.
5. Refresh table with `.clearAll()` and `.parse()`.

Hint Use `core.async` or promises to handle async flow.

Final challenge: Combine all four! Build a movie dashboard with search, filtering, add/edit functionality, CSV export, and real API integration. That's a production-ready admin panel.

Wrapping Up

You've built a professional data table. You've learned

- **Webix basics**: Configuration-driven UI development
- **DataTable component**: Sortable, interactive tables with minimal code
- **JavaScript interop**: Requiring NPM modules and calling JS methods from ClojureScript
- **Data conversion**: Moving between ClojureScript and JavaScript with `clj->js`
- **Enterprise UI libraries**: When and why to use them

Webix represents a philosophy: **sophisticated UIs don't require sophisticated code**. By providing powerful, opinionated components, it lets developers build complex interfaces in hours, not weeks.

This is the executive suite lesson: **speed matters**. In business, the ability to spin up a functional dashboard quickly can be the difference between insight and missed opportunity. Webix optimizes for that speed.

But Webix is just one option in a vast ecosystem. Dozens of enterprise UI libraries—Ag-Grid, DevExtreme, Kendo UI—exist, each with trade-offs. The patterns you learned here—data-driven configuration, interop, component composition—transfer to all of them.

The double doors close quietly behind you. You've completed the fourth floor—three rooms, three approaches to UI, three philosophies. Reactive state, responsive design, data presentation. Together, they form a complete toolkit for modern web development.

Summary: What We Learned

In the executive suite, we discovered

1. **Configuration-driven UI**: Webix uses nested JavaScript objects to define components, layouts, and behavior—code becomes data.
2. **Enterprise component library**: Webix provides 100+ components (tables, charts, forms) styled consistently and optimized for business applications.
3. **JavaScript interop in shadow-cljs**: Requiring NPM packages with `["webix" :as webix]` and calling methods with `.ui` demonstrate seamless JS/ClojureScript integration.
4. **Data conversion patterns**: `clj->js` converts ClojureScript data to JavaScript, enabling libraries like Webix to consume our native data structures.
5. **Declarative datatables**: With `autoConfig` and manual column definitions, Webix creates sortable, filterable tables with features that would take hundreds of lines in custom code.
6. **Trade-offs in UI libraries**: Webix trades flexibility for speed—perfect for internal tools, less ideal for consumer-facing apps with custom designs.

The executive suite shows that **sometimes the best code is the code you don't write**. Webix abstracts away complexity, handling sorting, styling, and interaction so you can focus on data and business logic.

When your users are colleagues, not customers—when data density matters more than brand identity—libraries like Webix shine. They're not glamorous, but they ship fast.

"In the executive suite, time is money. Webix is the exchange rate."

CHAPTER 5

Mind Map: Thinking in Trees

> "The mind is not a vessel to be filled, but a fire to be kindled. And sometimes, that fire needs a map."

Welcome to the Fifth Floor

The fifth floor is different. This is the **innovation lab**, where ideas take shape and structure emerges from chaos. You see whiteboards full of mind maps: circles connected by lines, ideas branching like trees, central concepts exploding into satellites of related thoughts.

Welcome to Chapter 5, Mind Map: Thinking in Trees. This floor isn't about learning frameworks or mastering techniques; it's about building things that feel good to use. Small applications with personality, tools that make you smile, interfaces that respect the way humans think.

We're starting with a mind map, a tool as old as thought itself, now rendered in SVG, powered by ClojureScript, and responsive to every click.

The Concept: Ideas As Interactive Trees

Mind mapping is a visual thinking tool invented by Tony Buzan in the 1970s. The idea is simple: start with a central concept, then branch outward with related ideas. Each branch can have sub-branches, creating a tree structure that mirrors how our brains actually work—not linear, not hierarchical, but **radial and associative**.

N. Modrzyk, *The ClojureScript Playbook*, https://doi.org/10.1007/979-8-8688-2879-9_5

We're building an interactive mind map where

- You **click a node** to add a child idea
- You **shift+click a node** to delete it and all descendants
- **Nodes fan out** automatically to avoid overlap
- **Everything renders in SVG** for crisp, scalable graphics

This isn't about building a to-do list or a data dashboard. This is about **thinking spatially**, about letting structure emerge naturally, about making the computer work the way your brain works.

Figure 5-1. *Interactive mind map application interface with hierarchical node structure and drag-and-drop functionality*

The Mind Map Philosophy

Why mind maps? Why this pattern?

> **Hierarchical but not rigid**: Unlike bullet points or outlines, mind maps grow organically. You can add branches anywhere, nest ideas deeply, and see the whole structure at once.

Visual and spatial: Our brains excel at spatial memory. Seeing ideas positioned in space—not just listed—creates stronger mental models.

Interactive discovery: Building a mind map is a thinking process. Each node you add sparks new connections. It's not documentation—it's **exploration**.

SVG as canvas: We're using SVG (scalable vector graphics) instead of HTML. SVG gives us: - Infinite canvas (no fixed width/height constraints) - Geometric primitives (circles, lines, text) - Coordinate-based positioning (x, y instead of CSS layouts) - Crisp rendering at any zoom level

This is ClojureScript doing what it does best: managing **nested, recursive data structures** and rendering them elegantly.

The Architecture: From Data to Diagram

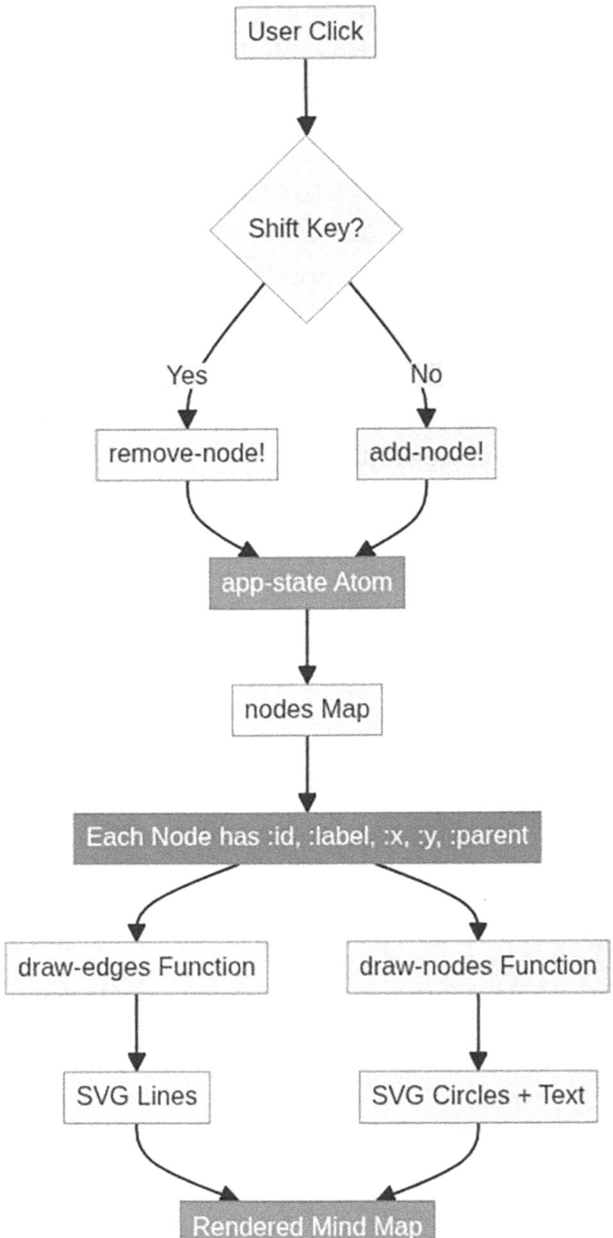

Figure 5-2. *Mind map data structure showing nested tree architecture with parent-child relationships*

The flow:

1. **State is a map of nodes**, each with position and parent reference.
2. **Rendering loops over nodes** to draw circles (nodes) and lines (connections).
3. **Click handlers** modify state (add/remove nodes).
4. **Reagent auto-re-renders** the SVG when state changes.
5. **New nodes position automatically** using a fan-out algorithm.

The beauty: State is just **a map of maps**. All visual complexity comes from interpretation, not storage.

The Foundation: Project Setup

Our `deps.edn` is minimal—just Reagent.

Listing 5-1. Minimal project dependencies with Reagent for interactive SVG-based mind mapping application

```
{:paths ["src" "resources"]
 :deps {org.clojure/clojurescript {:mvn/version "1.12.42"}
        reagent/reagent {:mvn/version "2.0.1"}}}
```

No charting libraries, no mind map frameworks. Just state, functions, and SVG.

The `shadow-cljs.edn` is as follows.

Listing 5-2. Shadow-cljs build configuration for mind map application with development server setup

```
{:source-paths ["src"]
 :dependencies []
 :dev-http {8001 "public"}
 :builds
 {:app
  {:target :browser
   :output-dir "public/js"
```

```
:asset-path "/js"
:modules {:main {:entries [mindmap.core]
                 :init-fn mindmap.core/init}}}}}
```

Standard setup. The magic is in the algorithms, not the tooling.

The State: Nodes As a Map

Listing 5-3. Application state atom with node map structure using parent references for tree hierarchy

```
(defonce app-state
  (r/atom
    {:next-id 2
     :nodes   {1 {:id     1
                  :label  "Root"
                  :x      300
                  :y      50
                  :parent nil}}}))
```

Structure:

- **`:next-id`**: Counter for generating unique IDs.
- **`:nodes`**: Map from ID to node data.
- **Each node** has `:id`, `:label`, `:x`, `:y`, and `:parent`.

Why a map, not a vector?

- **O(1) lookup**: Finding a node by ID is instant.
- **Easy deletion**: `(dissoc nodes id)` removes a node.
- **No order assumptions**: Nodes aren't inherently ordered (unlike a list).

The root node:

- **`:parent nil`**: It has no parent (it's the starting point).
- **Position (300, 50)**: Centered near the top of our 800x600 SVG.
- **Label "Root"**: Starting point for all ideas.

This is **data-oriented design**. The tree structure isn't encoded in special classes or pointers—it's just maps with `:parent` references.

The Algorithm: Finding Descendants

When we delete a node, we need to delete **all its children and grandchildren**. This requires recursion.

Listing 5-4. Recursive descendants function finding all children and grandchildren using functional tree traversal

```
(defn descendants
  "Return a set of all descendant IDs of the node with `id` in the
  `nodes` map."
  [nodes id]
  (let [direct-children (->>
nodes
                               vals
                               (filter #(= id (:parent %)))
                               (map :id)
                               set)]
    (reduce
      (fn [acc child-id]
        (set/union acc (descendants nodes child-id)))
      direct-children
      direct-children)))
```

Breaking it down:

Finding Direct Children

```
(let [direct-children (->> nodes
                           vals
                           (filter #(= id (:parent %)))
                           (map :id)
                           set)]
  ...)
```

vals: Get all node objects (we don't care about keys here).

(filter #(= id (:parent %))): Keep only nodes whose `:parent` is our ID.

(map :id): Extract just the IDs.

set: Convert to a set (for efficient union later).

Recursive Descent

```
(reduce
  (fn [acc child-id]
    (set/union acc (descendants nodes child-id)))
  direct-children
  direct-children)
```

Base case: Start with `direct-children` (the accumulator).

Recursive case: For each child, get *its* descendants and union them into the accumulator.

Return: A set containing the node's children, grandchildren, great-grandchildren, etc.

This is **functional recursion**—no loops, no mutation, just function calls building up a result.

Deleting Nodes: Confirmation and Cleanup

Listing 5-5. Node removal function with descendant cleanup using apply dissoc for batch deletion with confirmation

```
(defn remove-node!
  "Given a node-id, confirm with the user and remove that node plus all its
  descendants."
  [node-id]
  (let [{:keys [nodes]} @app-state
        node (get nodes node-id)
        label (:label node)
        child-ids (descendants nodes node-id)
        to-remove (set/union child-ids #{node-id})]
```

```
  (when (js/confirm (str "Delete node \"" label "\" and all its
  children?"))
    (swap! app-state update :nodes
           (fn [old-nodes]
             (apply dissoc old-nodes to-remove))))))
```

The flow:

1. **Get current state**: `{:keys [nodes]} @app-state`
2. **Find the node**: `(get nodes node-id)`
3. **Get all descendants**: `(descendants nodes node-id)`
4. **Build removal set**: Union of descendants + the node itself
5. **Confirm with user**: Native browser `confirm()` dialog
6. **Remove atomically**: `(apply dissoc old-nodes to-remove)`

Why `apply dissoc`?
`dissoc` removes keys from a map: `(dissoc {:a 1 :b 2} :a)` → `{:b 2}`.
But we have a *set* of keys to remove. `apply` spreads the set into arguments:

```
(apply dissoc {:a 1 :b 2 :c 3} [:a :c])
;; becomes: (dissoc {:a 1 :b 2 :c 3} :a :c)
;; returns: {:b 2}
```

This is **batch deletion** in one atomic operation.

Adding Nodes: The Fan-Out Algorithm

When you click a node, a new child is added. But where should it appear? We use a **staggered fan-out**.

Listing 5-6. Add node function with symmetric fan-out positioning algorithm creating balanced tree layout automatically

```
(defn add-node!
  "Given a parent-id, prompt the user for a label and add a new node under
  that parent.
```

```
   Each new child is offset so that they fan out evenly (0, +120, -120,
   +240, -240, ...)."
  [parent-id]
  (let [label (js/prompt "New node label:" "")
        {:keys [nodes next-id]} @app-state]
    (when (and label (not (str/blank? label)))
      (let [parent (get nodes parent-id)
            sibling-ids (->>
nodes
                              vals
                              (filter #(= parent-id (:parent %)))
                              count)
            k sibling-ids
            multiplier (quot (inc k) 2)
            sign (if (odd? k) 1 -1)
            dx (* 120 multiplier sign)
            dy 100
            new-x (+ (:x parent) dx)
            new-y (+ (:y parent) dy)
            new-node {:id     next-id
                      :label  label
                      :x      new-x
                      :y      new-y
                      :parent parent-id}]
        (swap! app-state update :nodes assoc next-id new-node)
        (swap! app-state assoc :next-id (inc next-id))))))
```

The fan-out math:

Children are positioned in this sequence:

- **First child (k=0)**: dx = 0 (directly below parent)
- **Second child (k=1)**: dx = +120 (right)
- **Third child (k=2)**: dx = -120 (left)
- **Fourth child (k=3)**: dx = +240 (further right)
- **Fifth child (k=4)**: dx = -240 (further left)

The formula:

```
multiplier (quot (inc k) 2)    ; 0, 1, 1, 2, 2, 3, 3, ...
Sign (if (odd? k) 1 -1)        ; +, -, +, -, +, -, ...
Dx (* 120 multiplier sign)     ; 0, +120, -120, +240, -240, ...
```

This creates a **balanced, symmetric tree** without manual positioning. The nodes naturally spread out as you add more.

Rendering Edges: Connecting the Dots

Listing 5-7. SVG edge rendering function drawing lines from parent to child nodes using coordinate lookups

```
(defn draw-edges []
  "Return a sequence of [:line ...] hiccup for each parent→child link."
  (let [{:keys [nodes]} @app-state]
    (for [{:keys [id x y parent]} (vals nodes)
          :when parent]
      (let [{px :x py :y} (get nodes parent)]
        [:line {:key          (str "edge-" parent "-" id)
                :x1           px
                :y1           py
                :x2           x
                :y2           y
                :stroke       "#555"
                :stroke-width 2}]))))
```

The logic:

1. **Loop over all nodes**: `(for [{:keys [id x y parent]} (vals nodes) ...]`.
2. **Skip the root**: `:when parent` (root has `nil` parent).
3. **Get parent's position**: `(get nodes parent)` returns `{:x ... :y ...}`.
4. **Draw line**: From `(px, py)` to `(x, y)`.

SVG line syntax:

- **:x1, :y1**: Start point
- **:x2, :y2**: End point
- **:stroke**: Line color
- **:stroke-width**: Line thickness

Each line gets a unique :key for React's reconciliation. This ensures smooth updates when nodes are added/removed.

Rendering Nodes: Circles and Labels

Listing 5-8. SVG node rendering with coordinate transforms and shift-key-aware click handlers for add/delete operations

```
(defn draw-nodes []
  "Return a sequence of [:g ...] hiccup for each node (circle + text),
   with an on-click that either removes (if shift-click) or adds a child."
  (let [{:keys [nodes]} @app-state]
    (for [{:keys [id x y label]} (vals nodes)]
      [:g {:key       (str "node-" id)
           :transform (str "translate(" x "," y ")")
           :on-click  (fn [e]
                        (.stopPropagation e)
                        (if (.-shiftKey e)
                          (remove-node! id)
                          (add-node! id)))}
       ;; Draw circle
       [:circle {:r            30
                 :fill         "#FFD"
                 :stroke       "#333"
                 :stroke-width 2}]
       ;; Draw label centered
       [:text {:text-anchor "middle"
               :y           5
```

```
           :font-size   "12px"
           :fill        "#000"}
      label]])))
```

SVG Groups (<g>):

Each node is a **group** containing a circle and text. The `:transform` attribute moves the entire group to `(x, y)`.

Why `translate`?

Instead of setting `:cx` and `:cy` on the circle, we translate the *group*. This means: - Circle at `(0, 0)` within the group → appears at `(x, y)` on screen - Text at `(0, 5)` within the group → centered on the circle

This is **coordinate space transformation**—a powerful SVG pattern.

Click handling:

```
:on-click (fn [e]
            (.stopPropagation e)
            (if (.-shiftKey e)
              (remove-node! id)
              (add-node! id)))
```

`(.stopPropagation e)`: Prevent click from bubbling to SVG canvas (which might have a background click handler).

`(.-shiftKey e)`: Check if Shift was held during click.

Result: Normal click adds a child; Shift+click deletes the node.

The Complete Component: Putting It Together

Listing 5-9. Complete mind map component composing edges and nodes with painter's model rendering order for visual layering

```
(defn mindmap-component []
  [:div {:style {:text-align "center"}}
   [:h2 "Simple ClojureScript Mind-Map"]
   [:p "Click on a node to add a child. Shift+Click on a node to delete it
   and its descendants."]
   [:svg {:width  800
          :height 600
```

```
        :style  {:border "1px solid #CCC"}}
   ;; Draw edges first
   (draw-edges)
   ;; Then draw nodes on top
   (draw-nodes)]])
```

Rendering order matters:

SVG is a **painter's model**—elements drawn first appear behind elements drawn later.

1. **Draw edges first**: Lines appear in the background.
2. **Draw nodes on top**: Circles and text overlay the lines.

This creates visual depth without z-index hacks.

Figure 5-3. *Completed mind map with multiple levels showing visual hierarchy and connection lines*

The User Experience

Let's walk through a session:

1. **Page loads**: Single "Root" node visible.
2. **Click "Root"**: Prompt asks for label → type "Ideas" → new node appears below.
3. **Click "Ideas"**: Add "Feature A" → appears to the right of center.
4. **Click "Ideas" again**: Add "Feature B" → appears to the left (balanced layout).
5. **Click "Feature A"**: Add "Detail 1" → nested deeper, offset right.
6. **Shift+click "Feature A"**: Confirmation dialog → "Feature A" and "Detail 1" both disappear.

The map grows organically, reflects your thought process, and cleans up when you change your mind.

Why This Pattern Works

Mind maps succeed because they match **how we think**:

Non-linear: You don't think in bullet points. You jump between ideas, make connections, and explore tangents. Mind maps accommodate that chaos.

Visual memory: We remember spatial layouts better than lists. "That idea was upper-right" is easier to recall than "item #7."

Low friction: Adding a node is one click. Deleting is one Shift+click. No forms, no menus, no modals. The interface disappears.

Immediate feedback: Every click changes the diagram instantly. There's no save button, no loading state—just you and your thoughts.

This is **humane software design**: tools that adapt to humans, not the other way around.

Exercises: Expand Your Mind Map

Exercise 1: Edit Node Labels

Difficulty: Easy **Concepts**: Inline editing, controlled inputs

Allow editing node labels:

1. Add an `:editing?` field to each node.
2. On double-click, set `:editing? true` for that node.
3. Replace `[:text ...]` with `[:foreignObject ...]` containing an `[:input]`.
4. On blur or Enter, save the new label and set `:editing? false`.

Hint SVG's `<foreignObject>` lets you embed HTML inside SVG.

Exercise 2: Drag to Reposition

Difficulty: Hard **Concepts**: Mouse events, drag state

Make nodes draggable:

1. Add `:on-mouse-down` to start tracking mouse position.
2. Store dragging state: `{:dragging-id node-id :offset-x dx :offset-y dy}`.
3. On `:on-mouse-move` (on the SVG), update node position.
4. On `:on-mouse-up`, clear dragging state.

Hint Calculate offset as `mouse-x - node-x` to prevent jumping.

Exercise 3: Export to JSON

Difficulty: Easy **Concepts**: Serialization, download

Add an "Export" button:

1. Convert `@app-state` to JSON with `(js/JSON.stringify (clj->js @app-state))`.

2. Create a blob: `(js/Blob. [json] #js {:type "application/json"})`.
3. Create download link: `(js/URL.createObjectURL blob)`.
4. Trigger download with a hidden `<a>` element.

Hint Use `:download "mindmap.json"` attribute on the link.

Exercise 4: Color-Coded Branches

Difficulty: Medium **Concepts**: Derived properties, HSL colors

Color nodes by depth:

1. Write a function `node-depth` that counts levels from root.
2. Map depth to HSL hue: `(str "hsl(" (* depth 30) ", 70%, 80%)")`.
3. Use this as `:fill` color for circles.

Hint Root is depth 0; its children are depth 1, etc. Use recursion.

Final challenge: Combine all four! A fully interactive mind map with editing, dragging, exporting, and color-coded depth visualization. That's a production tool.

Wrapping Up

There's one design decision in this chapter I want you to own before moving on: why is the node store a flat map (`{1 {:id 1 :parent nil ...} 2 {...}}`) rather than a nested tree (`{:id 1 :children [{:id 2 :children [...]}]}`)?

Both would render the same mind map. But try deleting a node in the nested version. You'd have to walk the tree, find the node, remove it from its parent's children array, do the same recursively for its descendants, and rebuild the structure up the chain. With the flat map, deletion is `(apply dissoc nodes to-remove)`—one line. Looking up a node's parent is `(get nodes parent-id)`—one line. The flat structure makes operations cheap at the cost of slightly more explicit traversal in `descendants`. That trade-off is worth it here and will be worth it in most cases involving hierarchical data.

Take a moment to also notice `defonce` in the state definition. Hot-reload is running while you develop—every time you save a file, your code re-evaluates. Without `defonce`, the atom resets to its initial value on every save, wiping your map. With it, the state survives. It's a development detail, not production code, but it's the difference between a pleasant and a frustrating dev loop.

The fifth floor has two more apps. If this one felt comfortable, the next will push harder. If anything here felt shaky—especially the `descendants` recursion—trace through it one more time with a three-level tree on paper before continuing.

Re-frame Pomodoro: Time, State, and Effects

> "Good architecture is not about building cathedrals. It's about building cities—places where complexity can grow without becoming chaos."

The Second Room

You step away from the mind map whiteboard and into a quieter space. The walls here are covered with diagrams—not sprawling creative sketches, but precise architectural drawings. Event flows, data flows, subscription graphs. Everything labeled, everything connected.

In the center of the room sits a clean workspace with a timer ticking down on screen. But this isn't just any timer. Behind the simple interface lies a **sophisticated architecture**—a pattern that has powered some of the largest ClojureScript applications in production.

Welcome to **re-frame**: a framework for building maintainable single-page applications. If Reagent taught us reactive UI, re-frame teaches us **reactive architecture**. This is where your app grows from a toy project to a real system.

The Concept: Events, Not Callbacks

Every web application faces the same problem: **how do you manage complexity as your app grows?**

With vanilla Reagent, you might start with atoms and event handlers. That works for a contact form. But what about

- **Undo/redo?** You need to track every state change.
- **Dev tools?** You need to inspect and replay events.
- **Testing?** You need to separate logic from UI.
- **Team collaboration?** You need clear boundaries between features.

This is where **re-frame** enters. It's an architecture, a pattern, and a library—all in one. The core idea:

Everything that happens is an event. Events trigger pure functions. Pure functions update state. State flows to UI through subscriptions.

It's **unidirectional data flow** taken to its logical conclusion. No callbacks, no `this`, no side effects hidden in components. Just events flowing through a system.

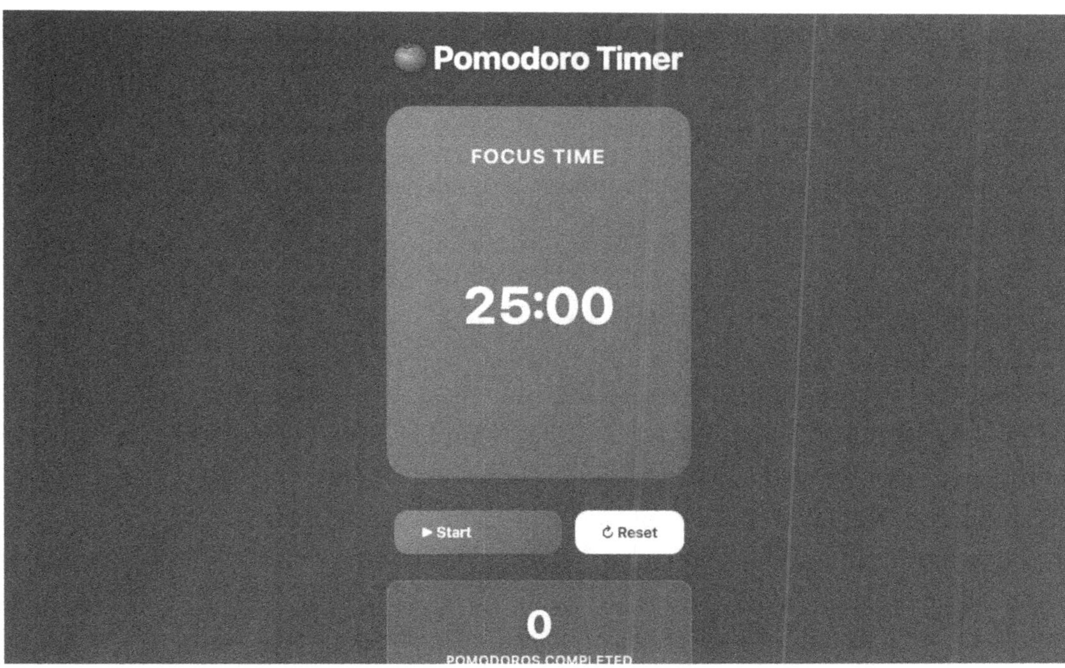

Figure 5-4. *Re-frame Pomodoro Timer demonstrating unidirectional data flow and effect-driven architecture*

The Re-frame Philosophy

Re-frame is built on a pattern called **six dominoes**:

`Event → Handler → Effect → State → Subscription → View`

Let's break it down:

1. **Event dispatch**: Something happens (user clicks, timer ticks, session completes).
2. **Event handler**: A pure function receives the event and returns **effects** (things to do).
3. **Effects**: Side effects like "update state," "start timer," and "show notification."
4. **State update**: The `app-db` (global state atom) is modified.
5. **Subscriptions**: Components subscribe to derived data from `app-db`.
6. **View re-render**: React efficiently updates only what changed.

The genius: **Every step is a pure function** (except the final render). This makes the entire system testable, inspectable, and predictable.

A Pomodoro Timer, Architecturally

We're building a Pomodoro Timer with: - 25-minute work sessions - 5-minute short breaks - 15-minute long breaks (after four Pomodoros) - Start/Pause/Reset controls - Visual progress indicator - Session counter - Browser notifications

Simple features, but implemented using re-frame's full architecture. This is a **reference implementation**—a template you can scale to apps with hundreds of features.

The Architecture: Data Flow Diagram

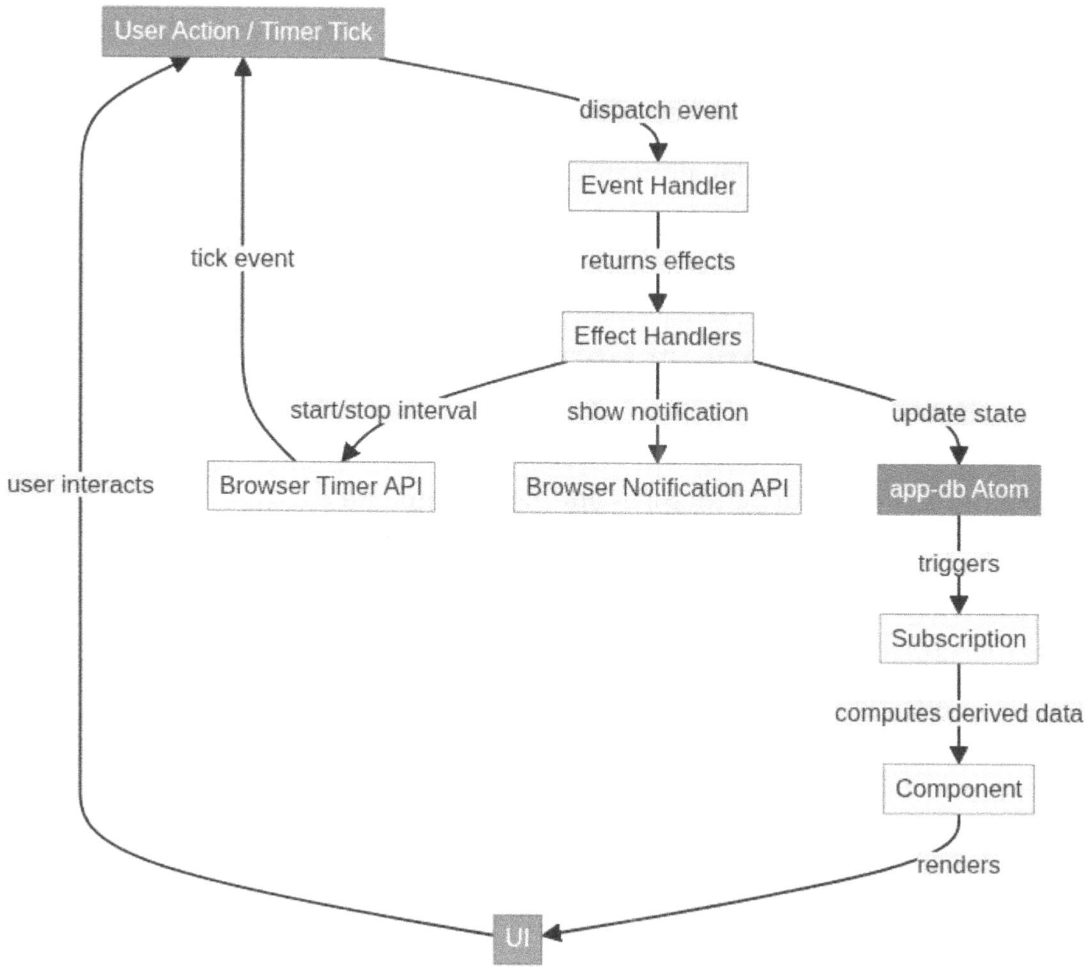

Figure 5-5. *Re-frame architecture diagram showing the cycle of events, effects, subscriptions, and reactive updates*

The circle:

1. User clicks "Start."
2. Component dispatches `:start-timer` event.
3. Handler returns `:start-interval` effect.
4. Effect starts JavaScript interval.
5. Every second, interval dispatches `:tick` event.

6. `:tick` handler decrements time and updates `app-db`.
7. Subscription recomputes progress percentage.
8. Component re-renders with new time.
9. When time reaches 0, `:complete-session` event fires.
10. Cycle continues with the next session.

This cycle repeats for every interaction. The beauty: **Each step is isolated.** You can test handlers, subscriptions, and components independently.

The Foundation: Project Setup

Our `deps.edn` adds re-frame.

Listing 5-10. Project dependencies adding re-frame for event-driven architecture on top of Reagent

```
{:paths ["src" "resources"]
 :deps {org.clojure/clojurescript {:mvn/version "1.12.42"}
        reagent/reagent {:mvn/version "2.0.1"}
        re-frame/re-frame {:mvn/version "1.3.0"}}}
```

re-frame sits on top of Reagent. It doesn't replace it—it **organizes** it.

The shadow-cljs setup is standard.

Listing 5-11. Shadow-cljs configuration for re-frame Pomodoro application

```
{:source-paths ["src"]
 :dependencies []
 :dev-http {8001 "public"}
 :builds
 {:app
  {:target :browser
   :output-dir "public/js"
   :asset-path "/js"
   :modules {:main {:entries [pomodoro.core]
                    :init-fn pomodoro.core/init}}}}}
```

The State: Initial Database

Listing 5-12. Default application database structure with timer state and Pomodoro tracking

```
(def work-duration (* 25 60))        ;; 25 minutes in seconds
(def short-break (* 5 60))           ;; 5 minutes
(def long-break (* 15 60))           ;; 15 minutes

(def default-db
  {:time-remaining work-duration     ;; seconds left in current session
   :mode :work                       ;; :work, :short-break, :long-break
   :running? false                   ;; is timer active?
   :pomodoros-completed 0            ;; count of work sessions finished
   :interval-id nil})                ;; JavaScript interval ID for cleanup
```

Structure:

- **`:time-remaining`**: Current countdown (in seconds)
- **`:mode`**: Current session type (work vs. breaks)
- **`:running?`**: Whether timer is actively counting down
- **`:pomodoros-completed`**: How many work sessions finished (determines break type)
- **`:interval-id`**: Reference to JavaScript interval (for cleanup)

Why track `:interval-id`?

When stopping the timer, we need to call `js/clearInterval`. By storing the ID in state, we ensure proper cleanup—no leaked timers running in the background.

Event Handlers: The Core Logic

Initialization

Listing 5-13. Database initialization event handler resetting app state to defaults on startup

```
(re-frame/reg-event-db
  :initialize-db
  (fn [_ _]
   default-db))
```

reg-event-db: Register an event handler that returns a new app-db.
Arguments:

- **First _**: The current database (we ignore it, returning fresh state)
- **Second _**: The event vector (we don't need parameters here)

Return: The default-db map
This runs once on app load, setting up initial state.

The Tick: Heart of the Timer

Listing 5-14. Tick event handler decrementing time and triggering session completion when timer reaches zero

```
(re-frame/reg-event-fx
  :tick
  (fn [{:keys [db]} _]
    (let [new-time (dec (:time-remaining db))]
      (if (<= new-time 0)
        ;; Time's up! Complete session
        {:dispatch [:complete-session]}
        ;; Keep counting down
        {:db (assoc db :time-remaining new-time)}))))
```

Event vector: [:tick] (dispatched every second by interval)

The logic:

1. **Decrement time**: `(dec (:time-remaining db))`.
2. **Check completion**: If time reaches 0, dispatch `:complete-session`.
3. **Otherwise**: Update `:time-remaining` in state.

Why return effects?

We use `reg-event-fx` (not `reg-event-db`) because we might dispatch another event (`:complete-session`). Effects let us coordinate multiple actions.

Starting the Timer

Listing 5-15. Start timer event handler setting running state and triggering interval effect

```
(re-frame/reg-event-fx
  :start-timer
  (fn [{:keys [db]} _]
    {:db (assoc db :running? true)
     :start-interval nil}))
```

Effects returned:

- **`:db`**: Set `:running? true`
- **`:start-interval`**: Custom effect to start JavaScript interval

Wait, what's `:start-interval`?

This is a **custom effect** we'll register. By separating the side effect (starting a timer) from the handler, we keep the handler pure—it just returns "what should happen," not "how to do it."

Pausing and Resetting

Listing 5-16. Pause and reset event handlers with interval cleanup via custom effect

```
(re-frame/reg-event-fx
  :pause-timer
  (fn [{:keys [db]} _]
```

```
    {:db (assoc db :running? false)
     :stop-interval (:interval-id db)}))

(re-frame/reg-event-fx
  :reset-timer
  (fn [{:keys [db]} _]
    (let [duration (case (:mode db)
                     :work work-duration
                     :short-break short-break
                     :long-break long-break)]
      {:db (assoc db
                  :time-remaining duration
                  :running? false)
       :stop-interval (:interval-id db)})))
```

Pause: Set `:running? false` and stop the interval.

Reset: Restore time to current mode's duration and stop the timer.

Both use the `:stop-interval` effect for cleanup.

Session Completion and Mode Transitions

Listing 5-17. Session completion handler with mode transition logic and browser notification effect

```
(re-frame/reg-event-fx
  :complete-session
  (fn [{:keys [db]} _]
    (let [current-mode (:mode db)
          completed-count (:pomodoros-completed db)

          ;; Determine next mode
          [next-mode new-count]
          (case current-mode
            :work (if (= (mod (inc completed-count) 4) 0)
                    [:long-break (inc completed-count)]  ;; Every 4th work
                    session → long break
                    [:short-break (inc completed-count)]) ;; Otherwise →
                    short break
```

```
      ;; Breaks always return to work (don't increment counter)
      :short-break [:work completed-count]
      :long-break [:work completed-count])

    ;; Get duration for next mode
    next-duration (case next-mode
                    :work work-duration
                    :short-break short-break
                    :long-break long-break)]

{:db (assoc db
           :mode next-mode
           :time-remaining next-duration
           :pomodoros-completed new-count
           :running? false)
 :stop-interval (:interval-id db)
 :notify {:title "Session Complete!"
          :body (case current-mode
                  :work "Time for a break!"
                  :short-break "Back to work!"
                  :long-break "Back to work!")}})))
```

The flow:

1. **Determine next mode**: - After work session: Check if fourth Pomodoro → long break, else → short break - After any break → back to work.

2. **Update counters**: Increment `:pomodoros-completed` only after work sessions.

3. **Set duration**: Look up next mode's time requirement.

4. **Stop timer**: User must manually start next session.

5. **Notify user**: Browser notification with appropriate message.

Why stop automatically?

The Pomodoro technique encourages intentional breaks. Auto-starting would defeat the purpose—you need to consciously choose to start the next session.

Custom Effects: Timer and Notifications

Here's where re-frame's effect system shines.

Start Interval Effect

Listing 5-18. Custom effect handler for starting JavaScript interval and storing its ID for cleanup

```
(re-frame/reg-fx
  :start-interval
  (fn [_]
    (let [interval-id (js/setInterval
                        #(re-frame/dispatch [:tick])
                        1000)]
      (re-frame/dispatch [:store-interval-id interval-id]))))
```

What it does:

1. **Start interval**: Call `:tick` event every 1000 ms (1 second).
2. **Store ID**: Dispatch event to save `interval-id` in state.

Why dispatch to store ID?

Effects can't directly modify state—only event handlers can. So we dispatch an event to update `app-db` with the interval ID.

Store Interval ID Handler

Listing 5-19. Event handler for storing interval ID enabling cleanup when timer stops

```
(re-frame/reg-event-db
  :store-interval-id
  (fn [db [_ id]]
    (assoc db :interval-id id)))
```

Simple: save the ID so we can clean it up later.

Stop Interval Effect

Listing 5-20. Custom effect handler for cleaning up JavaScript interval to prevent memory leaks

```
(re-frame/reg-fx
  :stop-interval
  (fn [interval-id]
    (when interval-id
      (js/clearInterval interval-id))))
```

Cleanup: If we have an interval ID, clear it. This prevents memory leaks from abandoned timers.

Browser Notification Effect

Listing 5-21. Custom effect handler for browser notifications with permission handling

```
(re-frame/reg-fx
  :notify
  (fn [{:keys [title body]}]
    (when (.-Notification js/window)
      (if (= (.-permission js/Notification) "granted")
        (js/Notification. title #js {:body body})
        (when (not= (.-permission js/Notification) "denied")
          (.then (.requestPermission js/Notification)
                 (fn [permission]
                   (when (= permission "granted")
                     (js/Notification. title #js {:body body})))))))))
```

Permission flow:

1. **Check support**: Does browser support notifications?
2. **Check permission**: Already granted? → Show notification.
3. **Request permission**: If not denied, ask user.
4. **On grant**: Show notification.

This handles all the browser notification API complexity in one effect. Event handlers stay pure—they just say `:notify {...}` and this effect does the rest.

Subscriptions: Querying State

Components don't read `app-db` directly. They **subscribe** to derived data.

Basic Subscriptions

Listing 5-22. Basic state subscriptions for timer properties providing reactive updates to components

```
(re-frame/reg-sub
  :time-remaining
  (fn [db _]
    (:time-remaining db)))

(re-frame/reg-sub
  :mode
  (fn [db _]
    (:mode db)))

(re-frame/reg-sub
  :running?
  (fn [db _]
    (:running? db)))

(re-frame/reg-sub
  :pomodoros-completed
  (fn [db _]
    (:pomodoros-completed db)))
```

Direct accessors—no computation needed.

Derived Data: Progress Percentage

Listing 5-23. Derived subscription computing progress percentage from time and mode using signal graph

```
(re-frame/reg-sub
  :progress-percent
  :<- [:time-remaining]
  :<- [:mode]
  (fn [[time-remaining mode] _]
    (let [total (case mode
                  :work work-duration
                  :short-break short-break
                  :long-break long-break)
          elapsed (- total time-remaining)]
      (* 100 (/ elapsed total)))))
```

Signal graph: `:<- [:time-remaining]` means "subscribe to `:time-remaining`."

Composition: This subscription depends on two others. When either changes, this recomputes.

Calculation:

1. Get total duration for current mode.
2. Calculate elapsed time.
3. Return percentage (0–100).

Why derived?

Components shouldn't do math. Subscriptions centralize logic, making it testable and reusable.

Formatted Time Display

Listing 5-24. Derived subscription formatting seconds as MM:SS time string for display

```
(re-frame/reg-sub
  :time-display
  :<- [:time-remaining]
```

```
(fn [seconds _]
  (let [mins (quot seconds 60)
        secs (mod seconds 60)]
    (str (when (< mins 10) "0") mins
         ":"
         (when (< secs 10) "0") secs))))
```

Formatting:

- quot: Integer division (get minutes)
- mod: Remainder (get seconds)
- **Zero-padding**: "5:3" → "05:03"

Again, presentation logic belongs in subscriptions, not components.

Views: Connecting to Architecture

Timer Display Component

Listing 5-25. Timer display component with mode-based styling and SVG circular progress indicator

```
(defn timer-display []
  (let [time-display (re-frame/subscribe [:time-display])
        mode (re-frame/subscribe [:mode])
        progress (re-frame/subscribe [:progress-percent])]
    (fn []
      [:div {:class (str "timer-container mode-" (name @mode))}
       [:div {:class "mode-label"}
        (case @mode
          :work "Focus Time"
          :short-break "Short Break"
          :long-break "Long Break")]

       ;; Circular progress indicator
       [:svg {:class "progress-ring" :width 300 :height 300}
        (let [radius 140
```

```
         circumference (* 2 Math/PI radius)
         offset (* circumference (- 1 (/ @progress 100)))]
     [:circle {:class "progress-ring-circle"
               :cx 150 :cy 150 :r radius
               :style {:stroke-dasharray circumference
                       :stroke-dashoffset offset}}])]

   [:div {:class "time-text"} @time-display]])))
```

Three subscriptions:

1. **Time display**: Formatted string
2. **Mode**: Current session type
3. **Progress**: Percentage for visual indicator

Dynamic class: mode-work, mode-short-break, etc., for CSS styling
SVG progress ring:

- **Circle**: 140 px radius
- **Circumference**: 2πr
- **Offset**: Adjusted based on progress percentage
- **Result**: Animated circular progress bar

Control Button Component

Listing 5-26. Control button component with conditional start/pause rendering based on timer state

```
(defn controls []
  (let [running? (re-frame/subscribe [:running?])]
    (fn []
      [:div {:class "controls"}
       (if @running?
         [:button {:class "btn-pause"
                   :on-click #(re-frame/dispatch [:pause-timer])}
          "Pause"]
         [:button {:class "btn-start"
```

```
                :on-click #(re-frame/dispatch [:start-timer])}
      "Start"])

    [:button {:class "btn-reset"
              :on-click #(re-frame/dispatch [:reset-timer])}
     "Reset"]])))
```

Conditional rendering: Show "Pause" when running and "Start" when paused.

Event dispatching: Every button click dispatches an event. No direct state manipulation.

Stats Display Component

Listing 5-27. Statistics component displaying completed Pomodoro count with subscribe pattern

```
(defn stats []
  (let [completed (re-frame/subscribe [:pomodoros-completed])]
    (fn []
      [:div {:class "stats"}
       [:div {:class "stat-item"}
        [:div {:class "stat-value"} @completed]
        [:div {:class "stat-label"} "Pomodoros Today"]]])))
```

Simple display of session count. In a production app, you'd add: - Daily totals - Weekly averages - Streak tracking - Goal progress

All using the same subscription pattern.

Main App Component

Listing 5-28. Main application component composing timer display, controls, and statistics

```
(defn app []
  [:div {:class "app"}
   [:h1 {:class "title"} "Pomodoro Timer"]
```

```
  [timer-display]
  [controls]
  [stats]])
```

Clean composition. Each component is self-contained, subscribing to its own data.

Mounting and Initialization

Listing 5-29. Application initialization with notification permission request and synchronous database setup

```
(defonce root (rdc/create-root (.getElementById js/document "app")))

(defn ^:export init []
  ;; Request notification permission on load
  (when (.-Notification js/window)
    (when (= (.-permission js/Notification) "default")
      (.requestPermission js/Notification)))

  ;; Initialize app state
  (re-frame/dispatch-sync [:initialize-db])

  ;; Render into <div id="app">
  (rdc/render root [app]))
```

Startup sequence:

1. **Request notification permission**: Proactive UX—ask before session completes
2. **Initialize state**: `dispatch-sync` ensures state ready before render
3. **Mount app**: Render into DOM

Why sync?

We need `app-db` initialized before rendering. `dispatch` is asynchronous, but `dispatch-sync` blocks until the handler finishes.

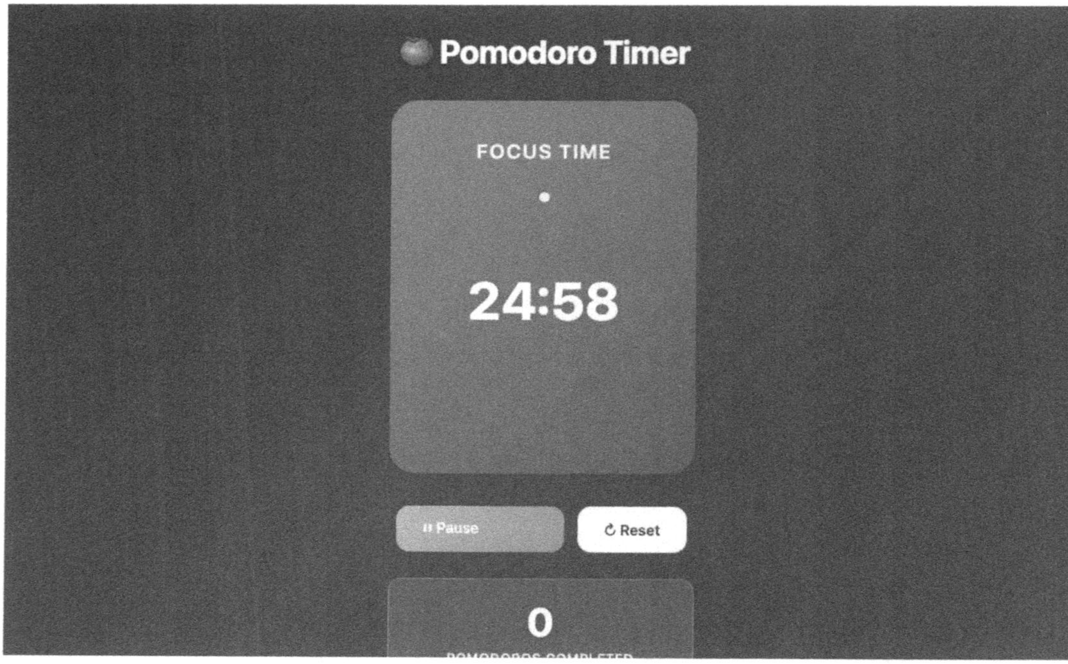

Figure 5-6. *Pomodoro Timer in break mode showing circular progress and session statistics*

The Re-frame Advantage

Let's compare to vanilla Reagent.

Table 5-1. *Comparison between plain Reagent and re-frame approaches to state management and application architecture*

Aspect	Reagent Only	Re-frame
State	Scattered atoms	Single `app-db`
Updates	Direct `swap!`	Event dispatch
Logic	In components	In handlers
Side effects	Anywhere	Registered effects
Time travel	Manual undo stack	Built into architecture
Testing	Hard (mocks, stubs)	Easy (pure functions)

Re-frame scales. What starts as "overkill for a timer" becomes **essential** at 50 features.

Why Events Change Everything

Events are **data**. The event `[:tick]` is just a vector. This means as follows:

Logging: Record every event. Replay user sessions.

Debugging: See exactly what happened and when. "User clicked start at 14:32, tick fired 47 times, session completed at 14:57."

Testing: Call handlers with test events, assert on resulting state.

```
(deftest tick-handler-test
  (let [initial-db {:time-remaining 10 :mode :work}
        result (tick-handler {:db initial-db} [:tick])]
   (is (= 9 (get-in result [:db :time-remaining])))))
```

Time travel: Store events, replay them, undo by rewinding event history.

Reproducibility: User reports a bug? Ask for event log. Replay exact sequence in your environment.

This is **event sourcing** applied to front-end architecture. Your app's history is just a sequence of events.

Styling: Mode-Based Themes

The timer changes color based on mode—here's how.

Listing 5-30. CSS styling with mode-based gradient themes and animated SVG progress ring

```
.timer-container {
  transition: all 0.5s ease;
  padding: 2rem;
  border-radius: 1rem;
}

.mode-work {
  background: linear-gradient(135deg, #667eea 0%, #764ba2 100%);
  color: white;
}

.mode-short-break {
```

```
  background: linear-gradient(135deg, #f093fb 0%, #f5576c 100%);
  color: white;
}

.mode-long-break {
  background: linear-gradient(135deg, #4facfe 0%, #00f2fe 100%);
  color: white;
}

.progress-ring-circle {
  fill: transparent;
  stroke: white;
  stroke-width: 12;
  transition: stroke-dashoffset 0.3s ease;
  transform: rotate(-90deg);
  transform-origin: 50% 50%;
}
```

Dynamic classes: `mode-work`, `mode-short-break`, and `mode-long-break` applied via subscription

Smooth transitions: Color changes animate over 0.5 s

SVG styling: White stroke on circle, rotated -90° so progress starts at top

Exercises: Extend the Architecture

Exercise 1: Custom Durations

Difficulty: Easy **Concepts**: State management, forms

Add settings to customize work/break durations:

1. Add `:settings` to `default-db` with `:work-mins`, `:short-break-mins`, and `:long-break-mins`.
2. Create `:update-setting` event handler.
3. Add settings panel with number inputs.
4. Use settings values instead of hardcoded constants.

Hint Multiply minutes by 60 to convert to seconds.

Exercise 2: Sound Alerts

Difficulty: Medium **Concepts**: Effects, audio API

Play a sound when session completes:

1. Add `<audio id="alert-sound" src="alert.mp3">` to HTML.
2. Register `:play-sound` effect that calls `.play()` on audio element.
3. Add `:play-sound` to `:complete-session` effects.
4. Add `:sound-enabled?` to state with toggle button.

Hint Use `(.getElementById js/document "alert-sound")` to get element.

Exercise 3: Session History

Difficulty: Medium **Concepts**: State accumulation, derived data

Track completed sessions with timestamps:

1. Add `:session-history` to state (vector of maps with `:mode`, `:timestamp`, and `:completed-at`).
2. On `:complete-session`, append to history.
3. Add subscription `:todays-sessions` that filters by today's date.
4. Display history in UI (e.g., "10:30 AM - Work - 25:00").

Hint Use `(js/Date.)` for timestamps and `.toLocaleDateString()` for comparison.

Exercise 4: LocalStorage Persistence

Difficulty: Medium **Concepts**: Effects, interceptors

Persist state across browser refreshes:

1. Register `:save-to-storage` effect using `js/localStorage.setItem`.
2. Create `after-save` interceptor that triggers this effect after updates.
3. On `:initialize-db`, check for saved state in localStorage.
4. Merge with `default-db` (keep defaults for new fields).

Hint Serialize with `(.stringify js/JSON (clj->js db))`; parse with `(js->clj (.parse js/JSON stored) :keywordize-keys true)`.

Exercise 5: Auto-start Next Session (Optional)

Difficulty: Easy **Concepts**: Event chaining

Automatically start the next session after completion:

1. Add `:auto-start?` to state (default `false`).
2. Add toggle button to enable/disable.
3. In `:complete-session`, conditionally dispatch `:start-timer` if `:auto-start?` is `true`.
4. Add 3-second countdown before auto-start with visual indicator.

Hint Use `:delayed-dispatch` effect similar to the to-do tutorial's `:delayed-delete`.

Final challenge: Build a full-featured Pomodoro app with custom durations, sound alerts, session history, persistence, and daily statistics dashboard. That's production-grade architecture.

Wrapping Up

You've built a Pomodoro Timer with re-frame. You've learned

- **The six-domino pattern**: Event → handler → effect → state → subscription → view
- **Event handlers**: Pure functions that transform state
- **Custom effects**: Managed side effects (timers, notifications, audio)
- **Subscriptions**: Derived data queries with memoization and signal graphs
- **State transitions**: Clean mode switching (work → break → long break)
- **Effect coordination**: Starting/stopping intervals, browser notifications

Re-frame is more than a library—it's a **discipline**. It forces you to think about: - Where does this logic belong? - Is this function pure? - Can I test this in isolation? - What happens when this scales to 100 features?

The answers to these questions produce better software. Not just working software—**maintainable** software.

This Pomodoro Timer is simple. But it's built like a complex app. Every pattern you learned here scales: event sourcing, effect management, derived data, pure handlers, custom effects for browser APIs. Companies use re-frame to build dashboards with thousands of components and years of development.

The architectural diagrams on the walls make sense now. Every arrow, every box, every label—they all map to code you've written.

One more room remains on this floor. One more mini-app, one more philosophy.

Summary: What We Learned

In the re-frame room, we discovered

1. **Unidirectional data flow**: Events flow to handlers, handlers update state, state flows to subscriptions, and subscriptions update views—a clean cycle with timer ticks as the heartbeat.

2. **Event-driven architecture**: Every action is an event (a vector like `[:tick]`, `[:complete-session]`), making the entire app history auditable and replayable.

3. **Pure event handlers**: Handlers are pure functions `(fn [db event] new-db)` or `(fn [db event] {:db new-db :effect data})`—no side effects, fully testable.

4. **Custom effect system**: Side effects (timers, notifications, audio) are registered separately with `reg-fx`, keeping handlers pure while enabling rich interactions with browser APIs.

5. **Subscriptions with signal graphs**: Components subscribe to computed state via `reg-sub` with `:<-` dependencies, which memoizes results and enables composable derived data.

6. **State transitions**: Mode switching (work → short break → long break) handled purely in event handlers based on session count.

7. **Effect coordination**: Multiple effects per event (stop interval, update state, send notification) orchestrated through effect maps.

Re-frame shows that **architecture is a design pattern applied consistently**. Not a framework imposed from outside, but a discipline chosen deliberately. When every event is data, when every handler is pure, when every side effect is managed—complexity becomes manageable, even when your app talks to timers, notifications, and audio APIs.

> *"Good architecture isn't about preventing bad code. It's about making good code inevitable."*

CHAPTER 6

Recharts: Data Visualization Made Simple

> "A chart is a conversation between data and understanding. Make it speak clearly."

Welcome to the Sixth Floor

The elevator doors slide open to reveal a different world entirely. The sixth floor is all glass walls—literally. Floor-to-ceiling windows overlook the city, but they're not just windows. They're screens, dashboards, and visualizations. Data flowing like rivers of light, patterns emerging from numbers, stories told in bars and lines and arcs.

You step out onto polished floors that reflect the glow of a hundred charts. To your left, a wall displays stock prices dancing in real-time waves. To your right, sales figures march upward in steady bars. Ahead, a radar chart spins slowly, its polygonal shape shifting as metrics update. This is the **data visualization floor**, where information becomes insight, where numbers tell stories.

Welcome to Chapter 6, where ClojureScript meets the art and science of making information visible, comprehensible, and beautiful. You've climbed through games, animations, UI components, and mini-apps. Now you're ready for something more analytical: **charts**. Not just any charts, though. We are building interactive, declarative, React-powered visualizations that transform raw tables of data into immediate understanding.

N. Modrzyk, *The ClojureScript Playbook*, https://doi.org/10.1007/979-8-8688-2879-9_6

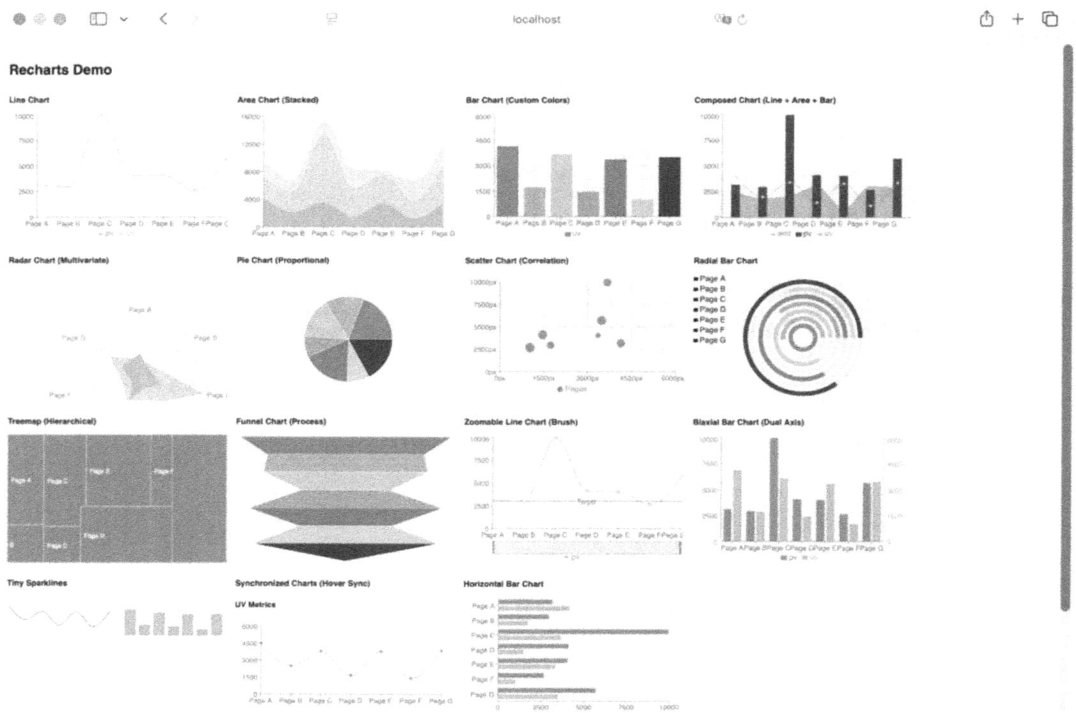

***Figure 6-1.** The data visualization floor displaying interactive charts and real-time analytics dashboards*

We begin our tour in the **Recharts wing**, a bright, efficient space where charts are built like LEGO blocks—simple pieces that snap together elegantly. Recharts is a composable charting library built on React and D3, and it's perfect for ClojureScript because it embraces the same philosophy we've been practicing all along: components as data, declarative composition, and pure functions.

The Philosophy of Composition

Data visualization isn't just about making pretty graphics. It's about answering specific questions. When you look at your data, you're asking something specific. Which metric is winning? What's the trend? How do these variables correlate? Where's the bottleneck in our process?

Recharts treats these questions as composable problems. Instead of a monolithic "Chart" object that takes a thousand configuration options, Recharts gives you small, focused components. You want a line? You add a `<Line />`. You want a grid? You add a `<CartesianGrid />`. You want a second axis? You add another `<YAxis />`.

It looks something like this.

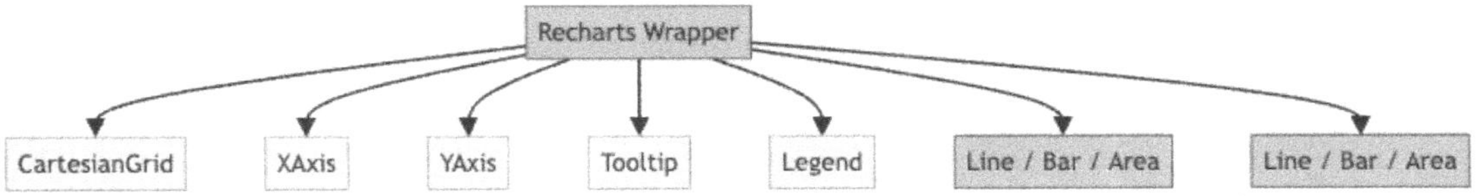

Figure 6-2. *Recharts component composition showing how small, focused components combine to create complete visualizations*

This composability allows us to layer information naturally, building complex visualizations from simple primitives.

The Foundation

Before we start painting with data, we need our canvas. Our setup remains delightfully minimal, relying on Reagent to bridge the gap between ClojureScript's immutable data structures and React's component model.

The `deps.edn` is straightforward.

Listing 6-1. Project dependencies with Reagent for React-based charting library integration

```
{:paths ["src" "resources"]
 :deps {org.clojure/clojurescript {:mvn/version "1.12.42"}
        reagent/reagent {:mvn/version "2.0.1"}}}
```

And our build configuration in `shadow-cljs.edn` targets the browser, pointing to our main namespace. The real heavy lifting is done by the npm libraries `recharts`, `react`, and `react-dom`, which provide the engine for our visualizations.

The Heartbeat: Dynamic Data

Static charts are useful, but living data is compelling. To truly understand how Recharts reacts to change, we'll build a "heartbeat" into our application—a dataset that breathes.

We define a Reagent atom to hold our state, representing a typical analytics scenario: page views, unique visitors, and engagement metrics across different pages. But we don't let it sit still. Utilizing a simple interval timer, we gently mutate the data every few seconds, fluctuating the values.

Listing 6-2. Reactive dataset with interval-based random mutations simulating real-time analytics data updates

```
(defonce data
  (r/atom [{:name "Page A" :uv 4000 :pv 2400 :amt 2400}
           {:name "Page B" :uv 3000 :pv 1398 :amt 2210}
           {:name "Page C" :uv 2000 :pv 9800 :amt 2290}
           {:name "Page D" :uv 2780 :pv 3908 :amt 2000}
           {:name "Page E" :uv 1890 :pv 4800 :amt 2181}
           {:name "Page F" :uv 2390 :pv 3800 :amt 2500}
           {:name "Page G" :uv 3490 :pv 4300 :amt 2100}]))

(defn update-data []
  (js/setInterval
   (fn []
     (swap! data
            (fn [items]
              (mapv #(assoc %
                             :uv (+ (:uv %) (- (rand-int 200) 100))
                             :pv (+ (:pv %) (- (rand-int 200) 100)))
                    items))))
   3000))
```

This creates a dashboard that feels alive. When we render our charts, they won't just appear; they will evolve, demonstrating the seamless reactivity of the Reagent-Recharts binding.

The Fundamentals: Lines, Areas, and Bars

We begin our exploration with the "Big Three" of charting. These are the workhorses of data visualization, the charts you will reach for 90% of the time.

The Narrative of Trends: The Line Chart

Invented by William Playfair in 1786, the line chart was a radical departure from the tabular data of the time. It shifted the mental model from "reading values" to "perceiving slopes." It conveys momentum—acceleration, deceleration, and volatility—drawing the eye to the **rate of change** rather than individual magnitudes.

The line chart is the storyteller of the group. It speaks of time, of momentum, of direction. When you want to answer "Where are we going?", you use a line chart.

In Recharts, building one is an exercise in declarative simplicity. You create a `<LineChart>` distinct container, giving it dimensions and data. Inside, you place your axes—an X-axis for category names, a Y-axis for values. You drop in a grid for readability, a tooltip for interaction, and, then, the star of the show: the `<Line>` component itself.

How it works: The `<LineChart>` is the container. Inside, we define `<Line>` components that link to keys in our data map (e.g., `:dataKey "pv"`). The `type="monotone"` prop smooths the line into a gentle curve. We use `activeDot={{:r 8}}` to emphasize the hovered point, giving immediate feedback to the user.

Listing 6-3. Line chart component with dual data series, monotone curves, and active dot hover effects

```
(defn line-chart []
  [:div
   [:h3 "Line Chart"]
   [:> LineChart {:width 500 :height 300 :data @data}
    [:> CartesianGrid {:strokeDasharray "3 3"}]
    [:> XAxis {:dataKey "name"}]
    [:> YAxis]
    [:> Tooltip]
    [:> Legend]
    [:> Line {:type "monotone" :dataKey "pv" :stroke "#8884d8" :activeDot
    {:r 8}}]
    [:> Line {:type "monotone" :dataKey "uv" :stroke "#82ca9d"}]]])
```

Notice the syntax `[:> Component ...]`. This is Reagent's way of creating React components directly. We define two lines here, monitoring "pv" (page views) and "uv" (unique visitors). They coexist on the same grid, telling a parallel story of traffic quality versus quantity.

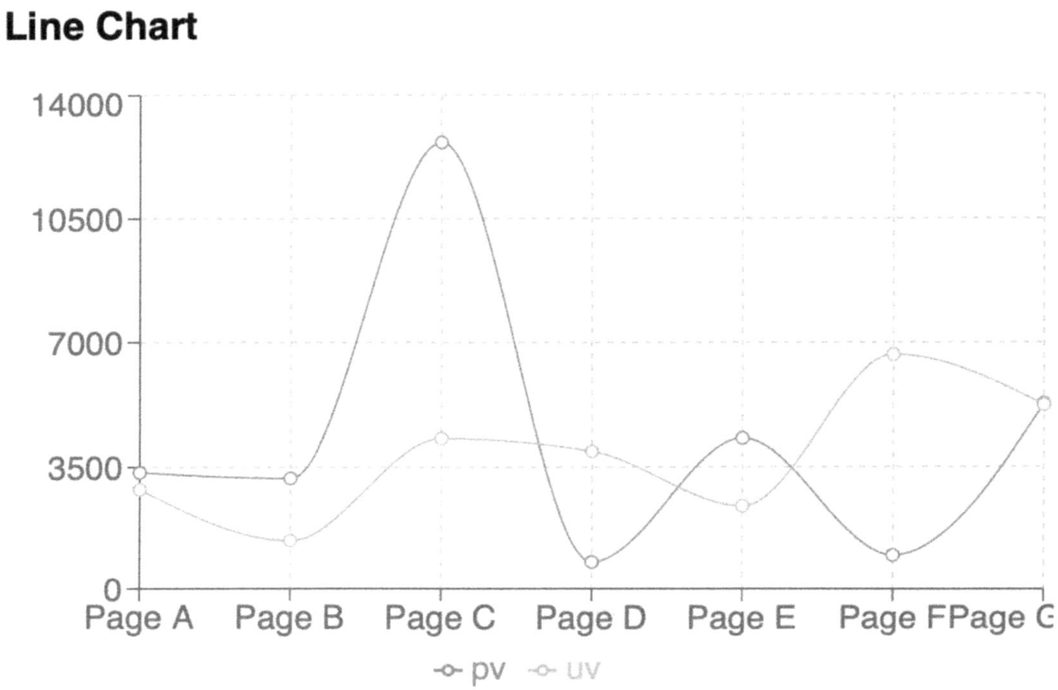

Figure 6-3. *A line chart displaying page views and unique visitors over time with interactive tooltips*

The Weight of Volume: The Area Chart

This is the line chart with mass. Also popularized by Playfair, the area chart fills the void below the curve, shifting the psychological focus from the "trend" to the "accrued value." It is particularly effective for showing part-to-whole relationships over time (stacked area), allowing the viewer to assess not just the total volume, but the changing composition of that volume.

Sometimes, a line feels too thin, too ephemeral. You want to convey volume, accumulation, and the sheer mass of the data. This is where the area chart steps in. It fills the void beneath the line, giving visual weight to the numbers.

We can stack these areas, showing how different segments contribute to a total. By adding a `stackId` prop to our components, Recharts knows to pile them atop one another. The top edge of the stack represents the total volume, while the colored bands reveal the composition. It's a powerful way to visualize resources, budgets, or server load—anything where the sum of the parts matters as much as the parts themselves.

How it works: The magic prop here is `stackId`. By assigning the same string value (e.g., `"1"`) to multiple `<Area>` components, we tell Recharts to accumulate their values. If we removed `stackId`, the areas would overlap transparently. We also remove the left and bottom margins to let the color fill the frame completely.

Listing 6-4. Stacked area chart showing accumulated volumes with stackId pattern for part-to-whole visualization

```
(defn area-chart []
  [:div
   [:h3 "Area Chart (Stacked)"]
   [:> AreaChart {:width 500 :height 300 :data @data
                  :margin {:top 10 :right 30 :left 0 :bottom 0}}
    [:> CartesianGrid {:strokeDasharray "3 3"}]
    [:> XAxis {:dataKey "name"}]
    [:> YAxis]
    [:> Tooltip]
    [:> Area {:type "monotone" :dataKey "uv" :stackId "1" :stroke "#8884d8"
    :fill "#8884d8"}]
    [:> Area {:type "monotone" :dataKey "pv" :stackId "1" :stroke "#82ca9d"
    :fill "#82ca9d"}]
    [:> Area {:type "monotone" :dataKey "amt" :stackId "1" :stroke
    "#ffc658" :fill "#ffc658"}]]]])
```

The Clarity of Comparison: The Bar Chart

While Playfair also popularized the bar chart, its utility is timeless. Unlike the line, which implies continuity, the bar asserts **distinctness**. It is the visual equivalent of a leaderboard. Use this when the "identity" of the data point (e.g., "Page A" vs. "Page B") is more important than the chronological sequence.

If the line chart is a storyteller, the bar chart is a judge. It's not interested in continuity or trends; it cares about ranking. Who is the tallest? Who sold the most? Which category is winning?

Bars separate data into discrete chunks, making comparison instantaneous for the human eye. In our implementation, we add a twist: we color individual bars differently using the `<Cell>` component. This requires mapping over our data and generating a cell for each entry, a pattern that demonstrates mixing Clojure's functional loops with React's component tree.

How it works: To achieve the distinct coloring, we can't just set a `fill` on the `<Bar>`. Instead, we manually iterate over our data using `map-indexed` and generate a `<Cell>` component for each bar. This overrides the default color. This pattern shows how seamless the interop is—we are using standard Clojure functions (`map`, `nth`, `mod`) inside the React render tree.

Listing 6-5. Bar chart with per-bar custom colors using map-indexed and Cell components for distinct visual identity

```
(def colors ["#0088FE" "#00C49F" "#FFBB28" "#FF8042" "red" "pink" "blue"])

(defn bar-chart []
  [:div
   [:h3 "Bar Chart (Custom Colors)"]
   [:> BarChart {:width 500 :height 300 :data @data}
    [:> CartesianGrid {:strokeDasharray "3 3"}]
    [:> XAxis {:dataKey "name"}]
    [:> YAxis]
    [:> Tooltip]
    [:> Legend]
    [:> Bar {:dataKey "uv" :fill "#8884d8"}
     (doall
      (map-indexed (fn [index _entry]
                     [:> Cell {:key index :fill (nth colors (mod index
                     (count colors)))}])
                   @data))]]])
```

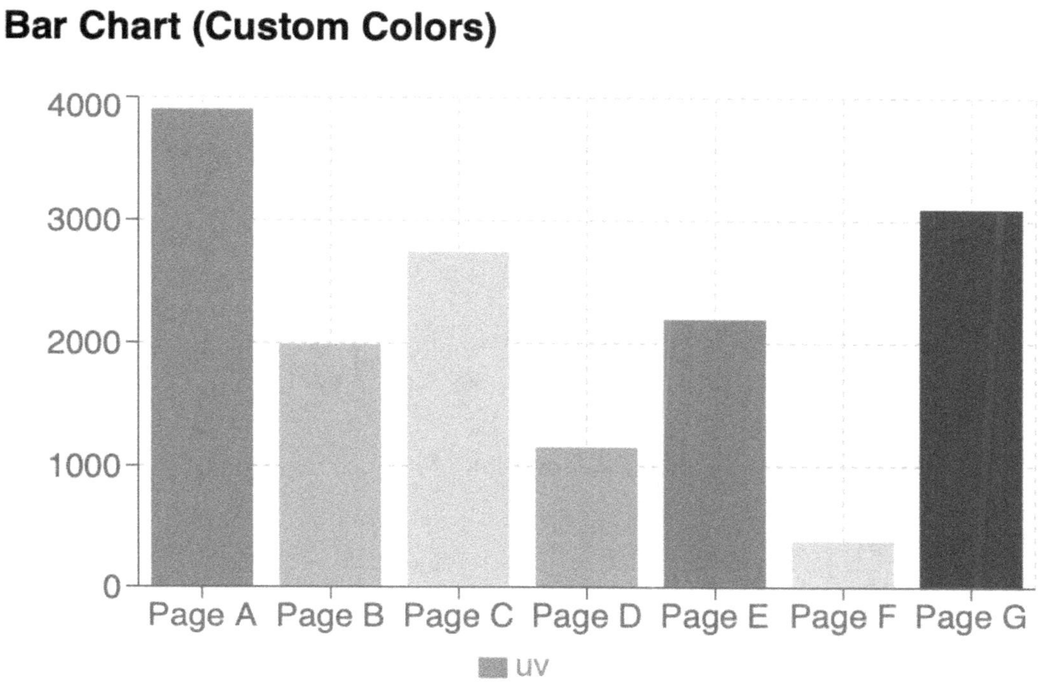

Figure 6-4. *A bar chart with custom colors showing comparative metrics across categories*

Beyond the Basics: Composition and Complexity

Having mastered the fundamentals, we move deeper into the wing, where the charts become more sophisticated, combining multiple data types and dimensions.

The Swiss Army Knife: The Composed Chart

Life is rarely just lines or just bars. Sometimes you need to compare a volume (bars) against a trend (line) and a background context (area). The composed chart behaves like a container that accepts all types of children.

We lay down an `<Area>` for context, maybe showing the target budget. On top of that, we place `<Bar>`s for actual sales. Finally, a `<Line>` cuts across, showing the profit margin. This layering allows highly dense information to remain readable because the different visual shapes (blocky bars vs. smooth lines) are distinct to the cognitive brain.

How it works: We use the `<ComposedChart>` container. We then explicitly set the `barSize` on the `<Bar>` to make it narrower than the column width, allowing the other lines to be seen clearly. The `<XAxis> scale="band"` prop ensures the categories are spaced evenly.

Listing 6-6. Composed chart layering area, bar, and line components for multi-dimensional data comparison

```
(defn composed-chart []
  [:div
   [:h3 "Composed Chart (Line + Area + Bar)"]
   [:> ComposedChart {:width 500 :height 300 :data @data}
    [:> CartesianGrid {:stroke "#f5f5f5"}]
    [:> XAxis {:dataKey "name" :scale "band"}]
    [:> YAxis]
    [:> Tooltip]
    [:> Legend]
    [:> Area {:type "monotone" :dataKey "amt" :fill "#8884d8" :stroke
    "#8884d8"}]
    [:> Bar {:dataKey "pv" :barSize 20 :fill "#413ea0"}]
    [:> Line {:type "monotone" :dataKey "uv" :stroke "#ff7300"}]]])
```

The Shape of Balance: The Radar Chart

Walking further, we encounter the radar chart, often called the spider chart. Ideally suited for multivariate data with an arbitrary number of variables, this format is historically linked to Florence Nightingale's "coxcomb" diagrams, which she used to visualize mortality causes in the Crimean War.

It excels at creating a unique "fingerprint" for an entity. It reveals skewness and symmetry instantly—a balanced team, a well-rounded coffee blend, or a lopsided skill set. Imagine you are evaluating a specialized RPG character—strength, agility, magic, defense. Or perhaps a coffee blend—acidity, body, sweetness, aroma.

The radar chart wraps the axes into a circle. A perfect score is a large, regular polygon filling the outer edge. A skewed profile looks jagged and lopsided. It allows you to see "balance" at a glance. We use `<PolarGrid>` and `<PolarAngleAxis>` here, shifting from Cartesian (x,y) to polar (angle, radius) thinking, yet the Recharts API remains consistent.

How it works: The coordinate system changes here. We use `<PolarGrid>` for the spiderweb background and `<PolarAngleAxis>` for the points on the perimeter. The `outerRadius` prop controls the overall size of the chart. Note that we define two `<Radar>` shapes with different colors and `fillOpacity`, allowing them to overlap visibly.

Listing 6-7. Radar chart with polar coordinates creating multivariate fingerprint visualization for profile comparison

```
(defn radar-chart []
  [:div
   [:h3 "Radar Chart (Multivariate)"]
   [:> RadarChart {:cx 300 :cy 250 :outerRadius 150 :width 500 :height 300
   :data @data}
    [:> PolarGrid]
    [:> PolarAngleAxis {:dataKey "name"}]
    [:> PolarRadiusAxis]
    [:> Radar {:name "UV" :dataKey "uv" :stroke "#8884d8" :fill "#8884d8"
    :fillOpacity 0.6}]
    [:> Radar {:name "PV" :dataKey "pv" :stroke "#82ca9d" :fill "#82ca9d"
    :fillOpacity 0.6}]]])
```

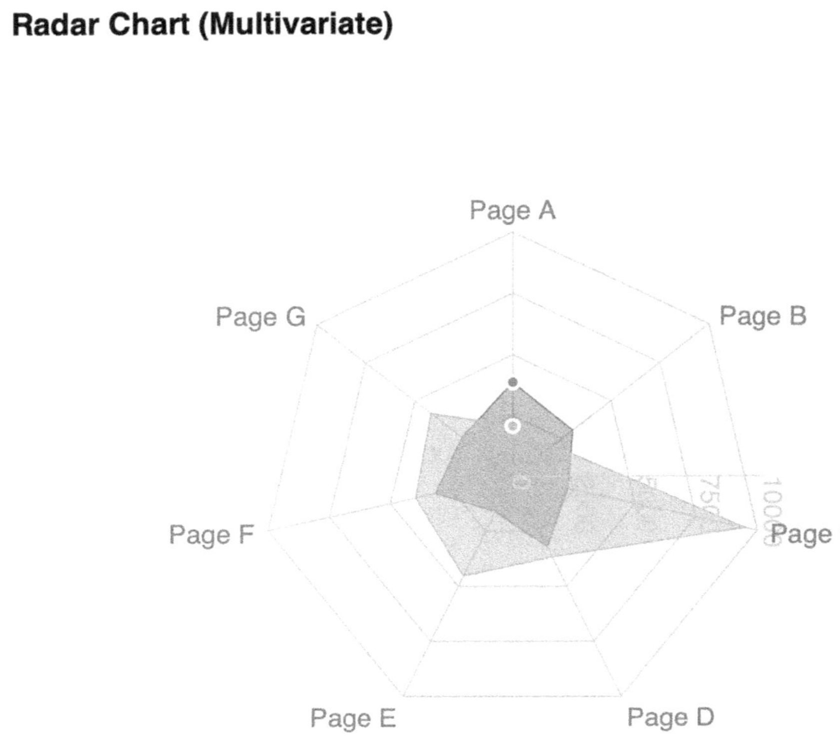

Figure 6-5. *A radar chart displaying multivariate data for profile comparison across multiple dimensions*

The Search for Correlation: The Scatter Chart

Most charts plot a variable against an independent index (usually time or category). The scatter plot, popularized by Francis Galton for statistical correlation, plots two dependent variables against each other. It is the only chart in our arsenal that purely visualizes **relationships**—clustering, outliers, and correlation trends—without the crutch of an ordered axis.

Correlation is the holy grail of analytics. Does spending more on ads actually increase sales? The scatter chart answers this. It doesn't plot categories; it maps two numerical variables against each other.

If the dots form a line moving up and to the right, you have correlation. If they look like a swarm of bees, you have chaos. We even add a third dimension—the Z-axis—by varying the size of the dots based on a third metric (`amt`). This creates a "bubble chart," packing three dimensions of data onto a two-dimensional screen.

How it works: We map three variables: `uv` to the X-axis, `pv` to the Y-axis. The interaction happens in `<ZAxis dataKey="amt" ... />`. By setting a `range` (e.g., `[60 400]`), we tell Recharts to map the min/max values of "amt" to circle pixel sizes between 60 px and 400 px squared area.

Listing 6-8. Scatter chart with three-dimensional bubble sizing via ZAxis for correlation and clustering analysis

```
(defn scatter-chart []
  [:div
   [:h3 "Scatter Chart (Correlation)"]
   [:> ScatterChart {:width 500 :height 300 :margin {:top 20 :right 20
   :bottom 20 :left 20}}
    [:> CartesianGrid]
    [:> XAxis {:type "number" :dataKey "uv" :name "UV" :unit "px"}]
    [:> YAxis {:type "number" :dataKey "pv" :name "PV" :unit "px"}]
    [:> ZAxis {:dataKey "amt" :range [60 400] :name "score" :unit "px"}]
    [:> Tooltip {:cursor {:strokeDasharray "3 3"}}]
    [:> Legend]
    [:> Scatter {:name "Pages" :data @data :fill "#8884d8"}]]])
```

Specialized Visualizations

Not all data fits on a standard grid. Some stories are circular, some are hierarchical, and some are process oriented.

The Architecture of Hierarchy: The Treemap

Invented by Ben Shneiderman in the early 1990s to solve the problem of visualizing full hard drives, the treemap is a recursive algorithm that slices 100% of the available screen estate into rectangles proportional to data size. It conveys relative weight in a hierarchy: big folders get big rectangles. It is efficient, dense, and one of the few charts that can handle thousands of nodes in a single view.

Hierarchical data—file systems, organizational charts, market sectors—is notoriously hard to visualize. The treemap solves this by turning the hierarchy into nested rectangles. The size of each rectangle corresponds to a value.

It's a "space-filling" visualization. Unlike a tree diagram which gets sprawling and messy, a treemap stays contained within its box, slicing the available pixels into smaller and smaller partitions. It allows you to spot the "heavy hitters" in a complex hierarchy instantly—they are simply the biggest boxes.

How it works: The `<Treemap>` is self-contained. It calculates the layout automatically. The `ratio` prop helps it decide how to squash the rectangles (4/3 looks standard). Note that styling is simple: just `stroke` (for borders) and `fill`.

Listing 6-9. Treemap chart for space-filling hierarchical visualization with automatic proportional layout

```
(defn treemap-chart []
  [:div
   [:h3 "Treemap (Hierarchical)"]
   [:> Treemap {:width 500 :height 300 :data @data :dataKey "uv" :ratio
   (/ 4 3) :stroke "#fff" :fill "#8884d8"}]])
```

The Flow of Attrition: The Funnel Chart

Sales pipelines and user conversion flows are processes of attrition. You start with many potential leads, and at each step, some drop off. The funnel chart visualizes this narrowing path.

Visually, it looks like an inverted pyramid. The wide top represents the starting pool, and the narrow tip represents the final success state. It's a diagnostic tool: if one segment narrows drastically compared to the others, you've found your bottleneck.

How it works: The `<Funnel>` component does the heavy lifting. We use `<LabelList>` to overlay the stage names ("Page A", etc.) directly on the funnel segments. The `isAnimationActive` prop ensures that as data changes, the funnel segments slide smoothly to their new widths.

Listing 6-10. Funnel chart with label lists and cell-based coloring showing conversion process attrition

```
(defn funnel-chart []
  [:div
   [:h3 "Funnel Chart (Process)"]
   [:> FunnelChart {:width 500 :height 300}
```

```
[:> Tooltip]
[:> Funnel {:dataKey "uv" :data @data :isAnimationActive true}
 [:> LabelList {:position "right" :fill "#000" :stroke "none" :dataKey
 "name"}]
 (doall
  (map-indexed (fn [index _entry]
                 [:> Cell {:key index :fill (nth colors (mod index
                 (count colors)))}])
               @data))]]])
```

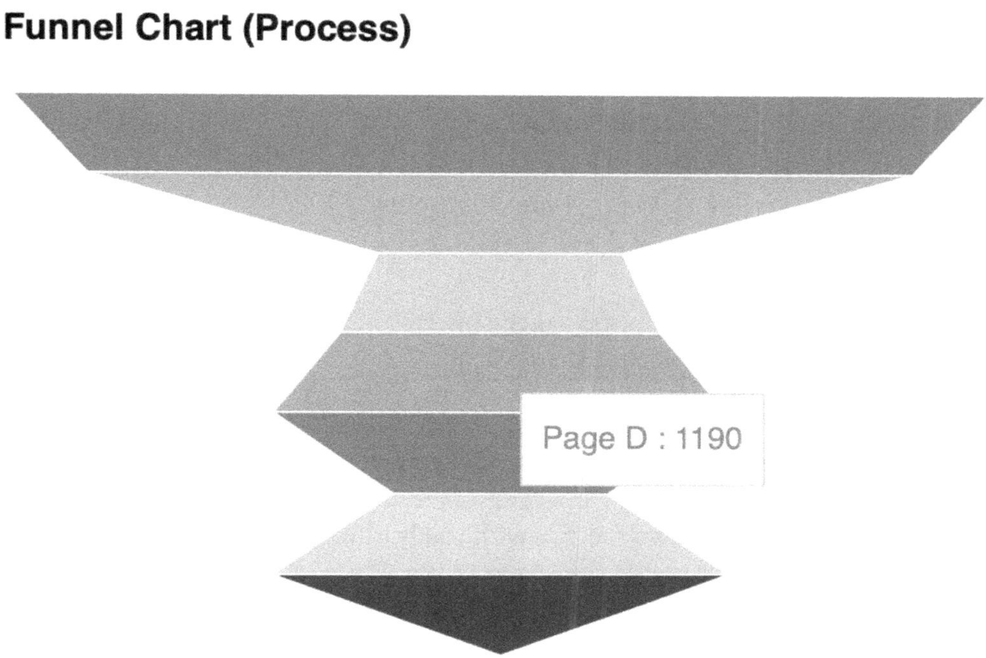

Figure 6-6. *A funnel chart visualizing conversion process stages with progressive narrowing*

The Horizontal Bar Chart

Sometimes labels are long, or the vertical screen space is limited. A horizontal bar chart solves this by flipping the axes.

How it works: We simply set the layout property of the <BarChart> to "vertical". Crucially, we must also swap the axis types: the X-axis becomes a numerical type (type="number"), and the Y-axis becomes the category type (dataKey="name" type="category").

Listing 6-11. Horizontal bar chart with vertical layout and swapped axis types for long category labels

```
(defn horizontal-bar-chart []
  [:div
   [:h3 "Horizontal Bar Chart"]
   [:> BarChart {:width 500 :height 300 :data @data :layout "vertical"
   :margin {:top 5 :right 30 :left 20 :bottom 5}}
    [:> CartesianGrid {:strokeDasharray "3 3"}]
    [:> XAxis {:type "number"}]
    [:> YAxis {:dataKey "name" :type "category"}]
    [:> Tooltip]
    [:> Legend]
    [:> Bar {:dataKey "pv" :fill "#8884d8"}]
    [:> Bar {:dataKey "uv" :fill "#82ca9d"}]]])
```

The Biaxial Chart: Apples and Oranges

What if you need to compare two metrics with vastly different scales? Say, "Revenue" (in millions) vs. "Profit Margin" (in percentage).

How it works: We use the yAxisId prop to decouple the data series. We define two <YAxis> components, giving them unique IDs ("left" and "right"). Then, we assign each <Bar> (or line) to one of these IDs. Recharts handles the scaling independently for each axis.

Listing 6-12. Biaxial bar chart with dual Y-axes for comparing metrics with different scales using yAxisId pattern

```
(defn biaxial-bar-chart []
  [:div
   [:h3 "Biaxial Bar Chart (Dual Axis)"]
   [:> BarChart {:width 500 :height 300 :data @data}
```

```
   [:> CartesianGrid {:stroke Dasharray "3 3"}]
   [:> XAxis {:dataKey "name"}]
   [:> YAxis {:yAxisId "left" :orientation "left" :stroke "#8884d8"}]
   [:> YAxis {:yAxisId "right" :orientation "right" :stroke "#82ca9d"}]
   [:> Tooltip]
   [:> Legend]
   [:> Bar {:yAxisId "left" :dataKey "pv" :fill "#8884d8"}]
   [:> Bar {:yAxisId "right" :dataKey "uv" :fill "#82ca9d"}]]]])
```

Interaction and Density

As we reach the end of the wing, we find tools designed for density—handling large datasets or limited screen real estate.

The Microscope: The Brush Chart

When you have thousands of data points—say, stock data over five years—showing it all at once creates noise. But showing only a week loses context. The brush chart offers the solution: "focus plus context."

We render the full dataset in a small strip at the bottom (the context) and a zoomed-in view above (the focus). The user can drag handles on the small strip to "brush" a specific time window, instantly updating the main chart. It empowers the user to explore the data, diving from the macro view of years down to the micro view of days.

How it works: We add a `<Brush>` component inside the chart. By default, it controls the X-axis. We also use a `<ReferenceLine>` to draw a static red threshold at Y=3000. This combination of interactive exploration (brushing) and static benchmarking (reference line) is powerful for analysis.

Listing 6-13. Brush chart with zoomable focus-plus-context interaction and reference line benchmark

```
(defn brush-chart []
  [:div
   [:h3 "Zoomable Line Chart (Brush)"]
   [:> LineChart {:width 500 :height 300 :data @data}
    [:> CartesianGrid {:strokeDasharray "3 3"}]
```

```
    [:> XAxis {:dataKey "name"}]
    [:> YAxis]
    [:> Tooltip]
    [:> Legend]
    [:> ReferenceLine {:y 3000 :label "Target" :stroke "red"}]
    [:> Line {:type "monotone" :dataKey "pv" :stroke "#8884d8"
    :animationDuration 300}]
    [:> Brush {:dataKey "name" :height 30 :stroke "#8884d8"}]]])
```

The Linked Dashboard: Synchronized Charts

Sometimes you want to break a complex chart into multiple smaller ones but keep the context linked. If the user hovers over "Page A" in the revenue chart, you want the traffic chart to also highlight "Page A."

How it works: This is surprisingly simple. We just add the same `syncId` string (e.g., `"anyId"`) to multiple chart components. Recharts listens to the mouse events on one and broadcasts them to all others sharing that ID.

Listing 6-14. Synchronized charts using syncId prop for linked hover interactions across multiple visualizations

```
(defn synced-charts []
  [:div
   [:h3 "Synchronized Charts (Hover Sync)"]
   [:div
    [:h5 "UV Metrics"]
    [:> LineChart {:width 500 :height 200 :data @data :syncId "anyId"
                   :margin {:top 10 :right 30 :left 0 :bottom 0}}
     [:> CartesianGrid {:strokeDasharray "3 3"}]
     [:> XAxis {:dataKey "name"}]
     [:> YAxis]
     [:> Tooltip]
     [:> Line {:type "monotone" :dataKey "uv" :stroke "#8884d8" :fill
     "#8884d8"}]]
    [:h5 "PV Metrics"]
    [:> AreaChart {:width 500 :height 200 :data @data :syncId "anyId"
```

```
                :margin {:top 10 :right 30 :left 0 :bottom 0}}
    [:> CartesianGrid {:strokeDasharray "3 3"}]
    [:> XAxis {:dataKey "name"}]
    [:> YAxis]
    [:> Tooltip]
    [:> Area {:type "monotone" :dataKey "pv" :stroke "#82ca9d" :fill
    "#82ca9d"}]]]])
```

The Compact Signal: Sparklines

A term coined by data visualization pioneer Edward Tufte, sparklines are "data-intense, design-simple, word-sized graphics." They convey the "gestalt" of the data—the general shape and trend—without the support of axes or grids. They are meant to be read as quickly as a word in a sentence, providing context (is it going up? is it volatile?) right where the decision is being made.

Sometimes you don't need a grand visualization; you just need a pulse. Sparklines are tiny, word-sized charts without axes or labels. They are pure trend indicators, designed to sit inside tables or dashboard widgets.

We achieve this by stripping away everything: no grid, no axes, no dots on the line. Just the raw signal curve. They provide high data density, allowing a dashboard to display trends for dozens of metrics without cluttering the interface.

How it works: To create these "micro-charts," we simply omit the structural elements. No `<Axis>`, no `<Grid>`, no `<Legend>`. We also set `dot={false}` on the `<Line>` to keep it as a pure curve. This reduces the visual noise to the absolute minimum, leaving only the data signal.

Listing 6-15. Compact sparkline charts without axes or grids for high-density dashboard integration

```
(defn tiny-charts []
  [:div
   [:h3 "Tiny Sparklines"]
   [:div {:style {:display "flex" :gap "20px"}}
    [:> LineChart {:width 240 :height 100 :data @data}
```

```
  [:> Line {:type "monotone" :dataKey "uv" :stroke "#8884d8"
  :strokeWidth 2 :dot false}]]
 [:> BarChart {:width 240 :height 100 :data @data}
  [:> Bar {:dataKey "uv" :fill "#82ca9d"}]]]]])
```

Summary of Capabilities

We've toured 15 distinct ways to visualize data. Here is a quick reference guide to help you choose the right tool for your next question.

Table 6-1. *Chart type selection guide mapping data questions to appropriate visualization types*

Chart Type	The Question It Answers	Best Use Case
Line	"Where is this going?"	Trends over time, continuous data.
Bar	"Who is winning?"	Categorical comparison, rankings.
Area	"How much is accumulating?"	Volume trends, stacked contributions.
Composed	"How do these different metrics relate?"	Mixing trends, volumes, and targets.
Radar	"What is the shape of this profile?"	Multivariate analysis, skill/feature balancing.
Pie	"What is the share?"	Proportions, part-to-whole (limit to < 7 slices).
Scatter	"Is there a correlation?"	Analyzing relationships between two variables.
Treemap	"How is the whole divided?"	Hierarchical data, disk usage, market caps.
Funnel	"Where are we losing them?"	Sales pipelines, conversion flows.
Brush	"What happened in detail?"	Exploring large time-series datasets.
Sparkline	"Is it good or bad?"	Dashboard widgets, dense summary tables.

Conclusion

You step back from the glass wall, the glow of the charts fading slightly as the sun sets outside the real windows. You've learned that charts are not merely decorative. They are a language. A line chart speaks of time; a bar chart speaks of competition; a scatter chart speaks of causality.

Recharts provides the vocabulary for this language. By providing small, composable primitives, it allows you to construct sentences, paragraphs, and entire stories out of data. You are no longer limited to the rigid charts of a spreadsheet tool. You are a builder, and data is your material.

But the sixth floor isn't finished. Through a set of double doors lies another gallery, one where the philosophy shifts from *composition* to *curation*, from the functional blocks of Recharts to the polished, designer-ready aesthetics of **Nivo**.

The data remains the same, but the lens is about to change.

Exercises: Chart Your Own Path

To truly master Recharts, you must build with it. These exercises are not just code tasks; they are architectural patterns you will use in real dashboards.

Exercise 1: The Gradient Area (Polish)

Difficulty: Easy **Concepts**: SVG definitions (`defs`), custom styling, UI polish

Why this matters: Standard solid colors often look flat and "default." Professional dashboards use transparent gradients to convey depth and softness. Since Recharts renders SVG, we can use standard SVG definitions (`<defs>`) to create these effects.

The task: Transform the flat color of the area chart into a lush vertical gradient.

1. Inside your `<AreaChart>` component, before the axes, add a `[:defs ...]` block.
2. Define an `[:linearGradient ...]` with a unique ID (e.g., `"colorUv"`).
3. Set `x1="0" y1="0" x2="0" y2="1"`. This coordinates system tells the gradient to flow vertically.

4. Add two `[:stop ...]` elements inside the gradient:
   - The first with `offset="5%"` and `stopColor="#8884d8"` (opaque)
   - The second with `offset="95%"` and `stopColor="#8884d8"` but `stopOpacity={0}` (transparent)

5. Finally, update your `<Area>` component to use this definition: `fill="url(#colorUv)"`.

Detailed Hint Your structure should look like this.

Listing 6-16. SVG gradient definition with linear gradient defs for professional area chart styling

```
[:> AreaChart ...
 [:defs
  [:linearGradient {:id "colorUv" :x1 "0" :y1 "0" :x2 "0" :y2 "1"}
   [:stop {:offset "5%" :stopColor "#8884d8" :stopOpacity 0.8}]
   [:stop {:offset "95%" :stopColor "#8884d8" :stopOpacity 0}]]]
 ...
 [:> Area {:type "monotone" :dataKey "uv" :stroke "#8884d8" :fill
"url(#colorUv)"}]]
```

Exercise 2: The Dynamic Threshold (Interactivity)

Difficulty: Medium **Concepts**: Interactive properties, Reagent atoms, "what-if" analysis

Why this matters: Static charts show history. Interactive charts let users ask questions. By allowing a user to drag a line and see where it intersects with historical data, you turn a report into a tool.

The task: Create a chart where the user can visually set a "Target" line using a slider.

1. Define a new atom `target-value` initialized to `3000`.

2. Create a standard HTML slider input: `[:input {:type "range" :min 0 :max 10000 ...}]`.

3. Bind the input's value to the atom (standard Reagent pattern with `on-change`).

4. In your `<LineChart>`, add a `<ReferenceLine>` component.

5. Set its y prop to `@target-value` and give it a label "Target".

Detailed Hint React's reactivity is magic here. Recharts watches its props. When the atom changes, Reagent re-renders the component with the new prop value, and Recharts animates the line to its new position automatically. No manual DOM manipulation required.

Exercise 3: The Custom Cursor (Advanced Rendering)

Difficulty: Hard **Concepts**: Render props, `reactify-component`, tooltips

Why this matters: The default tooltip is functional (black box, white text), but it rarely fits a custom design system. You often need to show extra data, format numbers (currency, percentages), or add branding. Recharts allows you to take full control of this rendering context.

The task: Replace the default tooltip with a sleek "Glassmorphism" card.

1. Create a standard Reagent component `custom-tooltip`. It receives a single argument, the props map.

2. Extract `active`, `payload` (the data array), and `label` (the x-axis value) from the props.

3. If `active` is true and `payload` exists, return a Hiccup vector for your custom card. Style it with a semi-transparent background (`rgba(255, 255, 255, 0.9)`).

4. In the chart, replace `[:> Tooltip]` with `[:> Tooltip {:content (reagent/reactify-component custom-tooltip)}]`.

Detailed Hint Why `reactify-component`? Recharts is a raw React library. It expects to be passed a React Class or Functional Component constructor for the `content` prop, not a Reagent Hiccup vector. `reactify-component` wraps your Clojure function into something React understands.

Exercise 4: The Split Dashboard (Architecture)

Difficulty: Expert **Concepts**: Data flow, derived state, brushing, master-detail pattern

Why this matters: When dealing with massive datasets (e.g., 5 years of stock prices), you can't show every detail at once. The "master-detail" pattern—where one small chart controls the viewport of a larger chart—is the standard solution for detailed analysis.

The task: Create two charts. The bottom one controls the top one.

1. **State**: Create an atom `brush-range` to hold `{:start-index 0 :end-index 10}`.
2. **Master chart**: Create a small, simplified area chart at the bottom. Add a `<Brush>` component to it.
3. **Wiring**: In the `<Brush>`, set `onChange` to a handler that updates your `brush-range` atom with the new start/end indices.
4. **Detail chart**: Create a large, detailed bar chart at the top.
5. **Derivation**: Instead of passing the raw `data` to the detail chart, pass a *sub-slice* of the data based on `@brush-range`.

Detailed Hint Your derived data logic might look like this.

Listing 6-17. Master-detail pattern with brush-controlled data slicing for efficient large dataset navigation. This is efficient because `subvec` is fast in ClojureScript. As the user drags the brush, the atom updates, the slice recalculates, and the top chart animates to the new data window.

```
(let [{:keys [start-index end-index]} @brush-range
      visible-data (subve @all-data start-index end-index)]
  [:> BarChart {:data visible-data} ...])
```

Final challenge: Combine these skills. Build a dashboard with a **gradient area** detail chart, controlled by a **brush** master chart, with a **dynamic threshold** line that changes color when the data exceeds it. That is a professional-grade analytics tool.

Nivo Charts: Data Visualization As Art

"Data is the new art material. Nivo is the canvas."

The Second Wing

You leave the bright, efficient workspace of the Recharts wing and walk down the corridor. The floor creates a transition; the polished concrete gives way to warm hardwood, and the lighting softens. You push through heavy glass doors into the **Nivo wing**.

The atmosphere here is different. If Recharts was a bustling newsroom or a stock trading floor, this feels like a modern art gallery. The visualizations on the walls don't just inform; they captivate. A Sankey diagram flows like liquid across a screen, its colors blending seamlessly. A calendar heatmap glows with the rhythm of a year's activity. A chord diagram weaves a complex web of connections that looks less like a chart and more like a flower.

Welcome to the second half of the sixth floor. Here, we explore **Nivo**, a library that treats data visualization not just as a functional requirement, but as a design opportunity. Built on the powerful D3.js engine but wrapped in React's ease of use, Nivo offers a suite of components that are polished, animated, and beautiful by default.

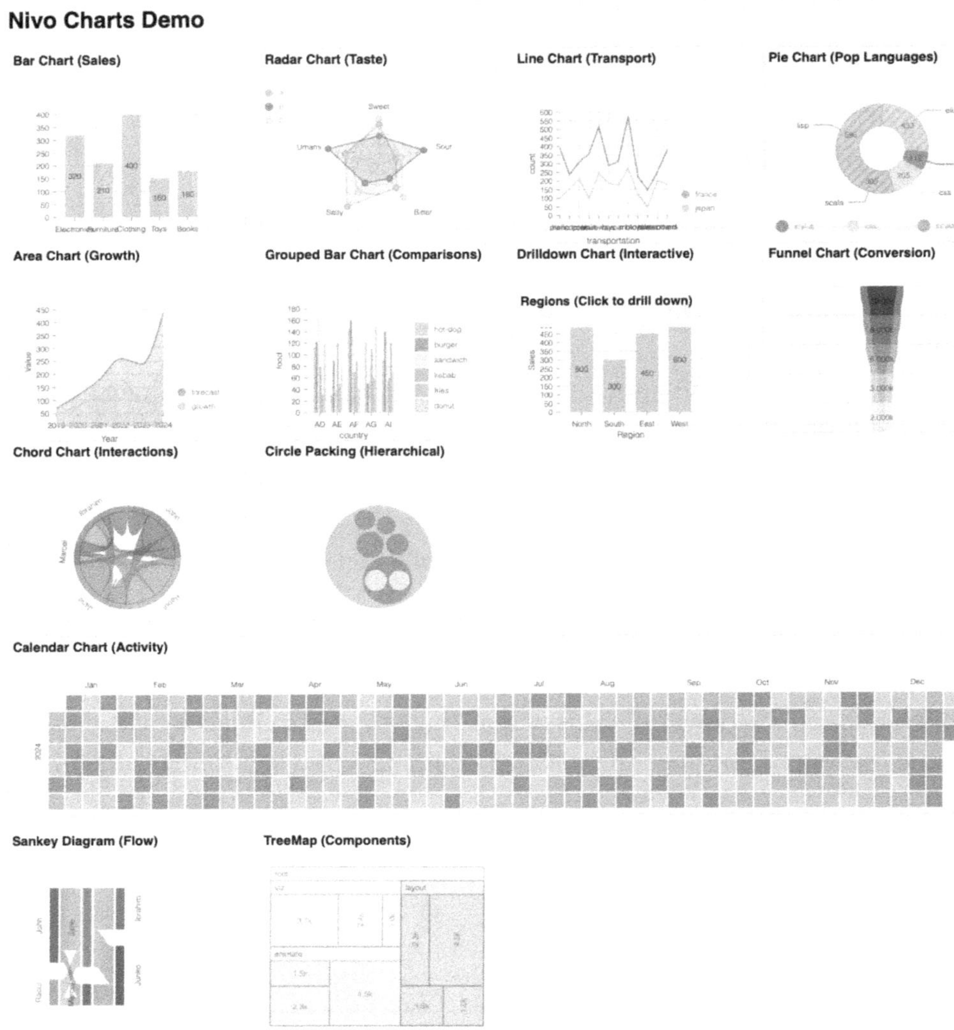

Figure 6-7. The Nivo wing of the data visualization floor featuring polished, design-focused chart components

The Philosophy of Polish

Where Recharts gave us LEGO blocks to build our own structures, Nivo gives us finished sculptures that we can tune and color. The API surface is larger; the configuration options deeper. You don't "compose" a Nivo chart by stacking axes and grids manually; you configure a high-level component that manages all that internal complexity for you.

This trade-off brings power. Nivo charts come with rich animations, sophisticated interactivity, and layout algorithms (like the physics of a swarm plot or the curvature of a chord link) that would be incredibly difficult to build from scratch.

The Nivo Pattern

Before we admire the art, we must prepare the canvas. The setup is identical to our previous room (Reagent + shadow-CLJS), but the integration pattern changes slightly.

Nivo is a collection of distinct packages (`@nivo/bar`, `@nivo/line`, etc.), which keeps our bundle size low. But because Nivo expects standard JavaScript data structures (objects with string keys) rather than our beloved Clojure maps (with keyword keys), we find ourselves doing a little translation dance.

The pattern you will see repeated throughout this gallery has been upgraded for modern React 19 support. Using the legacy `adapt-react-class` wrapper directly on Nivo's `Responsive` components often triggers fatal `"got: object"` element type errors due to internal `forwardRef` incompatibilities. Instead, we implement a robust pure-ClojureScript solution:

1. **Import core**: Bring in the native base chart (e.g., `Bar`, not `ResponsiveBar`).
2. **Adapt props**: Feed the nested map through a recursive property adapter (`adapt-props`) so Nivo receives native JavaScript arrays instead of Clojure vectors (which crash Nivo with `.map is undefined` errors).
3. **Wrap**: Enclose the chart within our `auto-sizer` component to inherit fluid dimensions via `ResizeObserver`.
4. **Configure**: Pass the extensive options dictionary to control every pixel.

The Responsive Foundation

Before rendering, we define our `abstract-art.responsive` utility to gracefully handle React 19 DOM measurements and deep property conversions.

Listing 6-18. The pure ClojureScript `auto-sizer` and `adapt-props` utility ensuring React 19 compatibility

```
(ns abstract-art.responsive
  (:require [reagent.core :as r]))

(defn adapt-props [m]
  (into {} (for [[k v] m]
             [k (if (fn? v) v (clj->js v))])))

(defn auto-sizer [child-fn]
  (let [observer-ref (r/atom nil)
        dims (r/atom nil)
        mount-observer (fn [el]
                         (when el
                           (when (exists? js/ResizeObserver)
                             (let [observer (js/ResizeObserver.
                                             (fn [entries]
                                               (let [rect (.-contentRect
                                               (aget entries 0))]
                                                 (reset! dims {:width
(.-width rect) :height (.-height rect)}))))]
                               (reset! observer-ref observer)
                               (.observe observer el)))))]
    (r/create-class
     {:component-will-unmount
      (fn [_]
        (when-let [observer @observer-ref]
          (.disconnect observer)))
      :reagent-render
      (fn [child-fn]
        [:div {:ref mount-observer :style {:width "100%" :height "100%"
        :position "relative" :overflow "hidden"}}
         (when @dims
           (child-fn (:width @dims) (:height @dims)))])})))
```

How it works: We pass the Bar component inside the auto-sizer, injecting the inherited width and height into our adapt-props wrapper. The keys prop tells Nivo which content to display, while indexBy determines the x-axis labels. Using animate={true} enables physics-based transitions.

Listing 6-19. Nivo responsive bar chart with adapt-react-class pattern and theme-based color schemes

```
(ns bar.e01
  (:require
    [reagent.core :as reagent]
    [abstract-art.responsive :refer [auto-sizer adapt-props]]
    ["@nivo/bar" :refer [Bar]]))

(def sales-data
  [{:category "Electronics" :sales 320}
   {:category "Furniture" :sales 210}
   {:category "Clothing" :sales 400}
   {:category "Toys" :sales 150}
   {:category "Books" :sales 180}])

(defn js-sales-data []
  (clj->js (map #(assoc {} "category" (:category %) "sales" (:sales %))
  sales-data)))

(defn sales-chart []
  [auto-sizer
   (fn [w h]
     [:> Bar (adapt-props (assoc
   {:data (js-sales-data)
    :keys ["sales"]
    :indexBy "category"
    :margin {:top 50 :right 50 :bottom 50 :left 60}
    :padding 0.3
    :colors {:scheme "nivo"}
```

```
    :axisLeft {:tickSize 5 :tickPadding 5 :tickRotation 0}
    :axisBottom {:tickSize 5 :tickPadding 5 :tickRotation 0}
    :enableLabel true
    :animate true} :width w :height h))])])
```

The Aesthetic Upgrade: Bars, Lines, and Pies

We start by revisiting the classics—bars, lines, and pies—but through Nivo's lens.

The Bar Chart: Animated rankings

A Nivo bar chart feels substantial. When data updates, the bars don't just snap to new positions; they grow and shrink with a spring-based physics animation. Hovering over a bar doesn't just show a tooltip; it can dim the other bars, focusing attention on the active element.

We configure it with themes. Nivo has a robust theming system that allows you to control fonts, colors, and grid lines globally. You don't just pick a color; you pick a `scheme`, like "nivo," "spectral," or "category10," and the library intelligently distributes these colors across your data.

The Pie Chart: A Study in Arcs

Pie charts are often criticized for their lack of precision, but Nivo makes a strong case for their existence through sheer visual appeal. It supports "donut" modes (by setting an `innerRadius`), rounded corners on segments, and intricate pattern fillings.

Imagine distinguishing data not just by color, but by texture—dots for one category, lines for another. Nivo supports SVG patterns natively. This isn't just decoration; it makes charts accessible to colorblind users and readable when printed in black and white.

How it works: Nivo's pattern system is powerful but requires verbose configuration. We define the patterns (dots, lines) in the `defs` array and then apply them using `fill`, which takes a list of rules (`match` criteria and the `id` of the pattern to use). The `radial` layout is handled automatically by the component.

Listing 6-20. Nivo pie chart with donut mode, rounded corners, and SVG pattern definitions for accessible visualization

```
(def pie-data
```

```
  [{:id "elixir" :label "elixir" :value 433 :color "hsl(129, 70%, 50%)"}
   {:id "stylus" :label "stylus" :value 112 :color "hsl(217, 70%, 50%)"}
   {:id "css" :label "css" :value 205 :color "hsl(159, 70%, 50%)"}
   {:id "scala" :label "scala" :value 305 :color "hsl(359, 70%, 50%)"}
   {:id "lisp" :label "lisp" :value 596 :color "hsl(80, 70%, 50%)"}])

(defn chart []
  [auto-sizer
   (fn [w h]
     [:> Pie (adapt-props (assoc
   {:data (clj->js pie-data)
    :margin {:top 40 :right 120 :bottom 40 :left 40}
    :innerRadius 0.5
    :padAngle 0.7
    :cornerRadius 3
    :activeOuterRadiusOffset 8
    :borderWidth 1
    :borderColor {:from "color" :modifiers [["darker" 0.2]]}
    :arcLinkLabelsSkipAngle 10
    :arcLinkLabelsTextColor "#333333"
    :arcLinkLabelsThickness 2
    :arcLinkLabelsColor {:from "color"}
    :arcLabelsSkipAngle 10
    :arcLabelsTextColor {:from "color" :modifiers [["darker" 2]]}
    ;; ... Defs and fill for patterns would go here
    :legends [{:anchor "right" :direction "column" :translateX 100
    :translateY 0}]} :width w :height h))])])
```

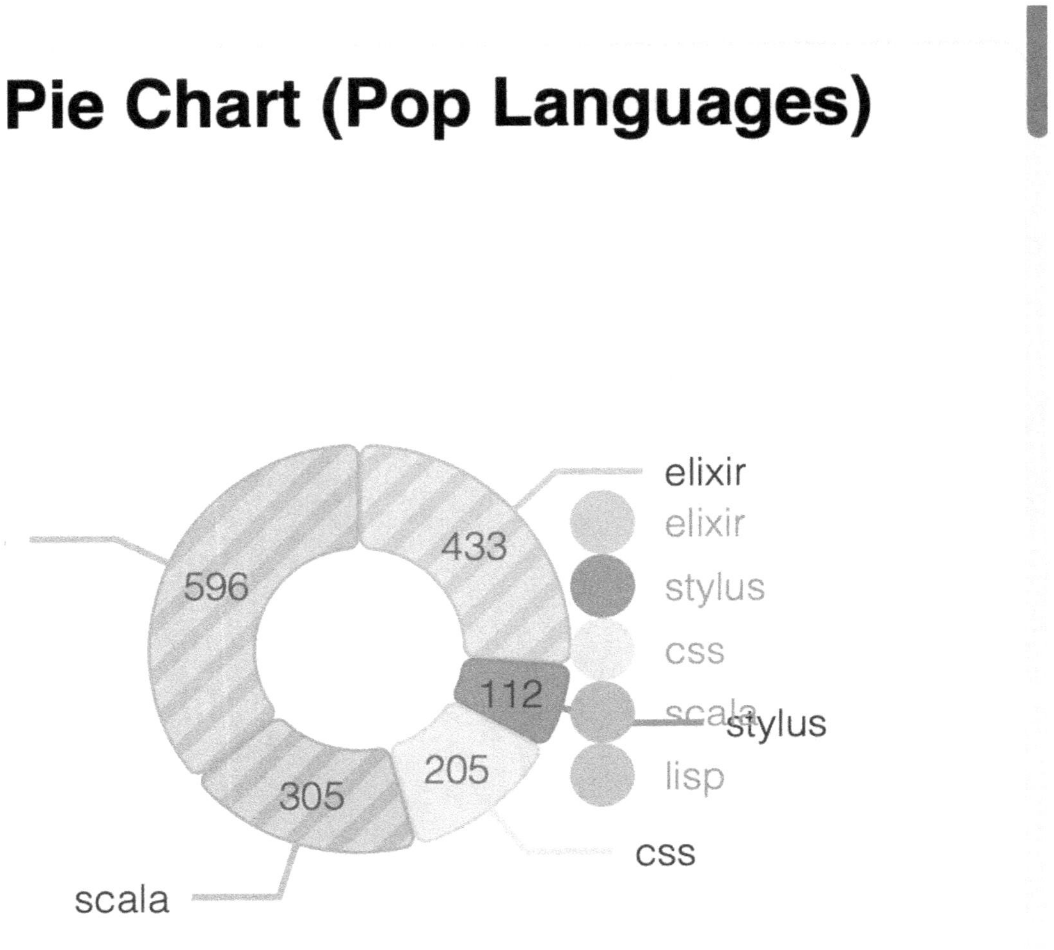

Figure 6-8. A Nivo pie chart with custom patterns, rounded corners, and smooth animations

The Line Chart: Interactive Precision

The Nivo line chart introduces the concept of a "mesh." Detecting a hover event on a thin line is frustrating for users—you have to be pixel perfect. Nivo overlays an invisible Voronoi mesh on the chart. This means the user only needs to be *near* a point to trigger the hover state. The interface feels magnetic, snapping to the nearest data point intuitively.

How it works: We use the `useMesh={true}` prop to enable the Voronoi interaction layer. The data format for lines is specific: an array of series objects, each containing an `id` and a `data` array of x/y coordinates.

Listing 6-21. Nivo line chart with Voronoi mesh for magnetic hover interaction and multi-series data

```
(def line-data
  [{:id "japan"
    :color "hsl(10, 70%, 50%)"
    :data [{:x "plane" :y 104} {:x "helicopter" :y 156} {:x "boat"
    :y 212}]}
   {:id "france"
    :color "hsl(215, 70%, 50%)"
    :data [{:x "plane" :y 290} {:x "helicopter" :y 80} {:x "boat"
    :y 100}]}])

(defn chart []
  [auto-sizer
   (fn [w h]
     [:> Line (adapt-props (assoc
   {:data (clj->js line-data)
    :margin {:top 50 :right 110 :bottom 50 :left 60}
    :xScale {:type "point"}
    :yScale {:type "linear" :min "auto" :max "auto" :stacked true
    :reverse false}
    :pointSize 10
    :pointColor {:theme "background"}
    :pointBorderWidth 2
    :pointBorderColor {:from "serieColor"}
    :useMesh true} :width w :height h))])])
```

The Radar Chart: Multivariate Profiles

Similar to the Recharts version but with Nivo's styling engine. This chart is excellent for comparing multiple entities across the same set of dimensions (e.g. taste profiles).

How it works: We define keys for "A", "B", and "C" (representing three different entities) and set `indexBy` to "taste". The `blendMode="multiply"` allows overlapping areas to darken, creating a rich visual effect where they intersect.

Listing 6-22. Nivo radar chart with blend mode for overlapping area visualization and wobbly motion configuration

```
(def radar-data
 [{:taste "Sweet" :A 70 :B 50 :C 80}
  {:taste "Sour" :A 30 :B 80 :C 40}
  {:taste "Bitter" :A 50 :B 30 :C 70}
  {:taste "Salty" :A 90 :B 40 :C 60}
  {:taste "Umami" :A 60 :B 90 :C 50}])

(defn radar-chart []
 [auto-sizer
   (fn [w h]
     [:> Radar (adapt-props (assoc
  {:data            (clj->js radar-data)
   :keys            ["A" "B" "C"]
   :indexBy         "taste"
   :margin          {:top 50 :right 50 :bottom 50 :left 50}
   :colors          {:scheme "nivo"}
   :fillOpacity     0.5
   :blendMode       "multiply"
   :motionConfig    "wobbly"} :width w :height h))])])
```

The Logic of Flow: Sankey and Chord

Now we move to visualizations that Recharts doesn't offer—charts designed to show relationships and flow.

The Sankey Diagram: River of Data

Named after Captain Matthew Henry Phineas Riall Sankey, who used this diagram in 1898 to visualize the energy efficiency of a steam engine, the Sankey diagram is unique because it visualizes **conservation** and **loss**. The width of the lines must remain consistent with the flow volume, making it brutal for identifying bottlenecks, leaks, or major conversion drop-offs.

Imagine visualizing how energy is generated, how it is converted, and where it is finally consumed. Or tracking users from a landing page through sign-up to purchase. This is the domain of the Sankey Diagram.

It consists of "nodes" (the stages) and "links" (the flow). The width of the link is proportional to the volume of flow. Nivo renders this with beautiful Bézier curves, allowing you to trace a single particle from start to finish. It's less about comparing values and more about understanding the *system*.

How it works: This component takes specialized data structure: lists of node objects and link objects. We configure `align="justify"` to spread nodes to the edges. The `enableLinkGradient={true}` is a key aesthetic feature, coloring the link as a gradient between the source and target node colors, making the flow direction intuitive.

Listing 6-23. Nivo Sankey diagram with gradient links visualizing directional flow and energy conservation

```
(def sankey-data
  {:nodes [{:id "John"} {:id "Raoul"} {:id "Jane"} {:id "Marcel"}]
   :links [{:source "John" :target "Jane" :value 150}
           {:source "John" :target "Marcel" :value 30}
           {:source "Raoul" :target "Jane" :value 40}]})

(defn chart []
  [auto-sizer
   (fn [w h]
     [:> Sankey (adapt-props (assoc
   {:data (clj->js sankey-data)
    :margin {:top 40 :right 160 :bottom 40 :left 50}
    :align "justify"
    :colors {:scheme "category10"}
    :nodeOpacity 1
    :nodeThickness 18
    :nodeInnerPadding 3
```

```
    :nodeSpacing 24
    :nodeBorderWidth 0
    :linkOpacity 0.5
    :enableLinkGradient true} :width w :height h))])])
```

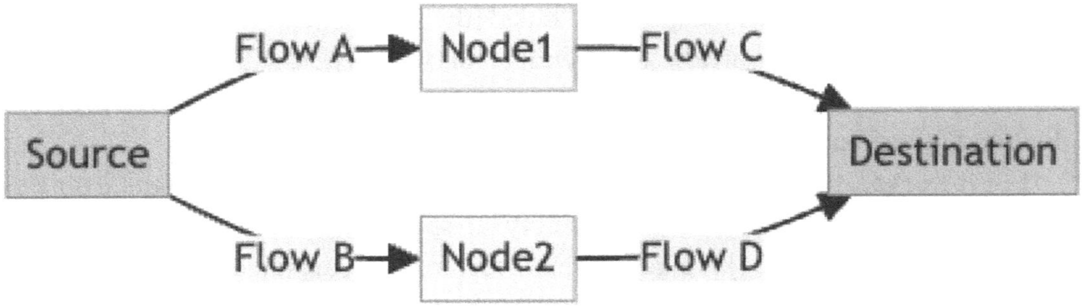

Figure 6-9. *Sankey diagram flow structure showing directional data movement from sources to destinations*

The Chord Diagram: The Web of Connection

While the Sankey is directional (left to right), the Chord diagram is relational (circular). It conveys the mutuality of connection. It is often used in genomics to show gene interactions or in migration studies to show movement between regions. The aesthetic beauty comes from the "quadratic Bézier curves" that cross the center, turning a messy matrix of numbers into a coherent, woven object.

If Sankey is a river, the chord diagram is a roundtable discussion. It visualizes a matrix of relationships. Who talks to whom? How much trade happens between countries?

The entities are arranged in a circle. Flows are drawn as arcs crossing through the center. A thick arc connects "Entity A" and "Entity B," showing a strong relationship. It's a dense, beautiful way to visualize interconnected networks where everything relates to everything else.

How it works: The input is a `matrix` (an array of arrays) representing the weights between entities. `keys` provide the labels. The `padAngle` (0.02) adds the small gap between the arc segments, improving readability. Note how concise the configuration is relative to the complexity of the SVG being generated.

Listing 6-24. Nivo chord diagram with matrix input visualizing circular relational networks with arc ribbons

```
(def matrix [[1064 21 1508 724 538]
             [0 4 398 1845 1532]
             [8 989 61 347 1931]
             [164 307 14 164 534]
             [50 1117 406 349 987]])

(def labels [ "John" "Raoul" "Jane" "Marcel" "Ibrahim" ])

(defn chord-chart []
  [auto-sizer
   (fn [w h]
     [:> Chord (adapt-props (assoc
   {:data             matrix
    :keys             (clj->js labels)
    :margin           {:top 50 :right 50 :bottom 50 :left 50}
    :innerRadiusRatio 0.9
    :pad-angle         0.02
    :colors           {:scheme "category10"}
    :arc-opacity       0.7
    :ribbonOpacity    0.7} :width w :height h))])])
```

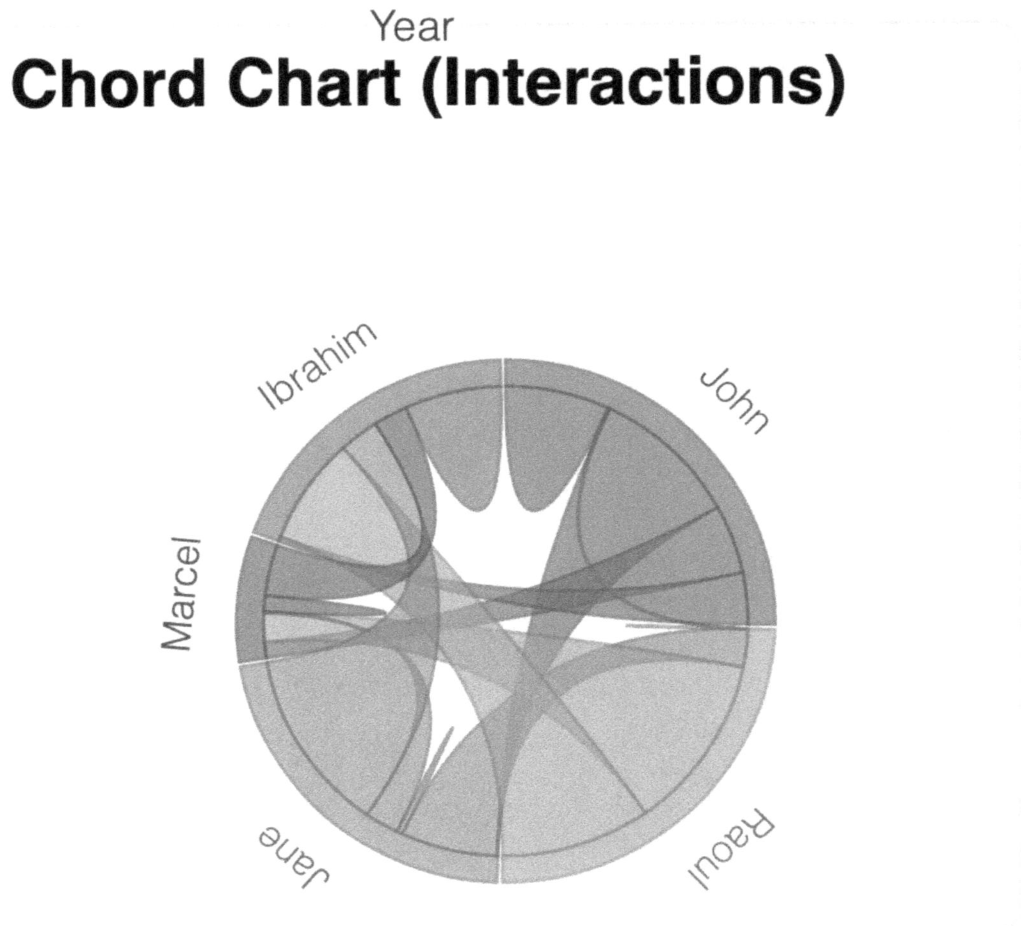

Figure 6-10. *A chord diagram displaying circular relationships between multiple entities with curved arcs*

The Hierarchy of Shapes: Treemap and Circle Packing

We saw treemaps in the previous room, but Nivo brings its signature polish. The transitions are smoother, the label placement smarter.

How it works: Data is a simple recursive tree. We specify `identity` (the unique key property) and `value` (what determines the size). The `valueFormat` prop is handy for formatting the tooltips (here, ".02s" for SI prefix notation).

Listing 6-25. Nivo treemap with recursive hierarchical data and SI prefix value formatting

```
(def treemap-data
  {:name "root"
   :children [{:name "viz" :children [{:name "stack" :loc 3724} {:name
   "force" :loc 2432}]}
              {:name "animate" :children [{:name "easing" :loc 1450} {:name
              "tween" :loc 4531}]}]})

(defn chart []
  [auto-sizer
   (fn [w h]
     [:> TreeMap (adapt-props (assoc
   {:data (clj->js treemap-data)
    :identity "name"
    :value "loc"
    :valueFormat ".02s"
    :margin {:top 10 :right 10 :bottom 10 :left 10}
    :labelSkipSize 12
    :colors {:scheme "yellow_green_blue"}} :width w :height h))])])
```

Organic vs. Mechanical

But for a more organic take on hierarchy, we turn to **circle packing**. Unlike the treemap, which divides space with mechanical efficiency (tessellating rectangles), circle packing introduces whitespace. This "inefficiency" makes the chart more breathable and easier for the human eye to parse distinct groups. It conveys hierarchy as a biological containment—cells within cells—rather than a rigid partition.

It uses nested circles. The "root" is a giant circle; its children are smaller circles contained within it. It feels biological, like cells under a microscope. While it uses space less efficiently than a treemap (circles don't pack as tightly as squares), it is friendlier and visually softer, perfect for high-level overviews where strict comparison is secondary to the feeling of structure.

How it works: The structure is identical to the treemap: a nested object with `children`. We adjust `padding` between circles to give the layout its signature "breathable" look. The `enableLabels` prop puts the names directly on the circles, which works well for the larger "parent" circles.

Listing 6-26. Nivo circle packing chart with organic nested circles for breathable hierarchical visualization

```
(def circle-data
  {:name "Root"
   :children [{:name "Electronics" :value 320}
              {:name "Clothing" :children [{:name "Men" :value 200} {:name
              "Women" :value 180}]}]})

(defn circle-packing-chart []
  [auto-sizer
   (fn [w h]
     [:> CirclePacking (adapt-props (assoc
   {:data (clj->js circle-data)
    :margin {:top 50 :right 50 :bottom 50 :left 50}
    :colors {:scheme "nivo"}
    :identity "name"
    :value "value"
    :padding 4
    :enableLabels true} :width w :height h))])])
```

Specialized Tools: Time and Process

Finally, we examine two specialized visualization types that solve specific domain problems.

The Calendar Heatmap: The Rhythm of Time

Based on the concept of the "activity matrix," this visualization became ubiquitous thanks to GitHub's contribution graph. It conveys meaningful temporal patterns that traditional line charts obscure—specifically, weekly cycles (the weekend gap) and seasonal intensity. It turns a year of data into a single textural "fingerprint" of habit.

You've seen this on your GitHub profile. The calendar heatmap visualizes a time series not as a line, but as a grid of days. Each square is a day; the color intensity represents the value (frequency, volume, activity).

It reveals patterns that line charts hide. Is there a slump every weekend? vivid activity every Monday? A seasonal gap in August? By laying out time as a calendar, these cyclic human patterns jump out at the viewer.

How it works: We generate a sequence of maps `{day: "YYYY-MM-DD", value: N}`. The chart handles the layout of weeks and months automatically. By setting `dayBorderWidth` to 2, we create clear separation between the cells, making the grid easier to scan.

Listing 6-27. Nivo calendar heatmap with date generation loop revealing temporal patterns and weekly cycles

```
(defn generate-calendar-data []
  (let [start-date (js/Date. "2024-01-01")
        end-date (js/Date. "2024-12-31")
        day-ms (* 24 60 60 1000)]
    (loop [current start-date
           data []]
      (if (> (.getTime current) (.getTime end-date))
        data
        (recur (js/Date. (+ (.getTime current) day-ms))
               (conj data
                     {:day (.toISOString current)
                      :value (Math/floor (* (Math/random) 300))}))))))

(def calendar-data
  (map (fn [d] {:day (subs (:day d) 0 10) :value (:value d)}) (generate-
  calendar-data)))

(defn js-calendar-data []
  (clj->js calendar-data))

(defn chart []
  [auto-sizer
   (fn [w h]
     [:> Calendar (adapt-props (assoc
```

```
   {:data (js-calendar-data)
    :from "2024-01-01"
    :to "2024-12-31"
    :emptyColor "#eeeeee"
    :colors ["#61cdbb" "#97e3d5" "#e8c1a0" "#f47560"]
    :margin {:top 40 :right 40 :bottom 40 :left 40}
    :yearSpacing 40
    :dayBorderWidth 2} :width w :height h))])])
```

The Funnel Chart: The Path of Conversion

We revisit the funnel, but Nivo's implementation adds flair. The "separators" between stages can be customized, creating a distinct visual break that emphasizes the step-by-step nature of the process. The labels are smart, dodging each other to avoid overlap. It turns a depressing chart about user churn into a sleek, professional graphic suitable for a boardroom presentation.

How it works: We use the `motionConfig="wobbly"` prop to give the funnel a playful, springy animation when data updates. The `borderWidth` and `currentBorderWidth` props allow us to style the "connectors" between separate funnel stages, emphasizing the flow.

Listing 6-28. Nivo funnel chart with wobbly motion config and formatted values for conversion flow visualization

```
(def funnel-data
  [{:id "step_sent" :value 10000 :label "Sent"}
   {:id "step_viewed" :value 8000 :label "Viewed"}
   {:id "step_clicked" :value 6000 :label "Clicked"}
   {:id "step_add_to_card" :value 3000 :label "Add To Cart"}
   {:id "step_purchased" :value 2000 :label "Purchased"}])

(defn chart []
  [auto-sizer
   (fn [w h]
     [:> Funnel (adapt-props (assoc
   {:data (clj->js funnel-data)
    :margin {:top 20 :right 20 :bottom 20 :left 20}
```

```
    :valueFormat ">-.4s"
    :colors {:scheme "spectral"}
    :borderWidth 20
    :motionConfig "wobbly"} :width w :height h))])])
```

Advanced Interaction: Drills, Groups, and Tooltips

Nivo really shines when we need to go beyond standard displays.

The Grouped Bar Chart

Standard bars compare totals. Grouped bars compare internal composition side by side.

How it works: We set `:groupMode` to `"grouped"`. Nivo automatically places bars sharing the same index (country) side by side. This is perfect for complex datasets, like comparing food consumption across different countries.

Listing 6-29. Nivo grouped bar chart comparing multiple metrics side by side for compositional analysis

```
(def grouped-data
  [{:country "AD" :hot-dog 113 :burger 123 :sandwich 165 :kebab 80 :fries
  32 :donut 120}
   {:country "AE" :hot-dog 32 :burger 90 :sandwich 40 :kebab 120 :fries 50
   :donut 80}
   {:country "AF" :hot-dog 145 :burger 160 :sandwich 130 :kebab 70 :fries
   90 :donut 40}])

(defn chart []
  [auto-sizer
   (fn [w h]
     [:> Bar (adapt-props (assoc
   {:data (clj->js grouped-data)
    :keys ["hot-dog" "burger" "sandwich" "kebab" "fries" "donut"]
    :indexBy "country"
    :groupMode "grouped"
    :colors {:scheme "nivo"}
    :padding 0.3} :width w :height h))])])
```

The Interactive Drilldown

The holy grail of dashboards: clicking a chart to see "what's inside."

How it works: We use a Reagent atom (`state`) to track the current view level (`:regions` vs. `:stores`). The `onClick` handler updates this state. The chart component reacts to the state change, swapping the `data` and the `keys`. This creates a seamless "drill down" experience without page reloads.

Listing 6-30. Interactive drilldown pattern with Reagent atom state management for hierarchical data exploration

```
(def raw-data
  {:regions [{:id "North" :value 500} {:id "South" :value 300}]
   :stores  {"North" [{:id "N-01" :value 120} {:id "N-02" :value 180}]
             "South" [{:id "S-01" :value 100} {:id "S-02" :value 200}]}})

(def state (r/atom {:level :regions :parent nil}))

(defn handle-click [node]
  (let [data (js->clj (.-data node) :keywordize-keys true)]
    (when (= (:level @state) :regions)
      (reset! state {:level :stores :parent (:id data)}))))

(defn chart []
  (let [current-state @state
        is-regions (= (:level current-state) :regions)
        data (if is-regions (:regions raw-data) (get-in raw-data [:stores
        (:parent current-state)]))]
    [auto-sizer
   (fn [w h]
     [:> Bar (adapt-props (assoc
     {:data (clj->js data)
      :keys ["value"]
      :indexBy "id"
      :onClick handle-click
      :colors {:scheme (if is-regions "nivo" "category10")}} :width w
      :height h))])] ))
```

Custom Tooltips and Gradients

Standard tooltips are boring. Nivo lets us render arbitrary React components as tooltips.

How it works: We pass a function (wrapped in `reactify-component`) to the `tooltip` prop. This function receives the node data and returns Hiccup. We also show how to use SVG gradients in `defs` to give the bars a premium, polished look (linear gradient from orange to yellow).

Listing 6-31. Custom tooltip component with reactify-component pattern and SVG gradient definitions for premium styling

```
(defn custom-tooltip [point]
  (let [data (js->clj (.-data point) :keywordize-keys true)]
    [:div {:style {:background "white" :padding "5px" :border "1px
    solid #ccc"}}
     [:strong (:category data)] [:br]
     "Sales: " [:span {:style {:color "#ff6600"}} (:sales data)]]))

(defn chart []
  [auto-sizer
   (fn [w h]
     [:> Bar (adapt-props (assoc
   {:data (js-sales-data)
    :keys ["sales"]
    :tooltip (reagent/reactify-component custom-tooltip)
    :defs [{:id "gradient" :type "linearGradient" :colors [{:offset 0
    :color "#ff6600"} {:offset 100 :color "#ffcc00"}]}]
    :fill [{:match {:id "sales"} :id "gradient"}]} :width w :height h))])])
```

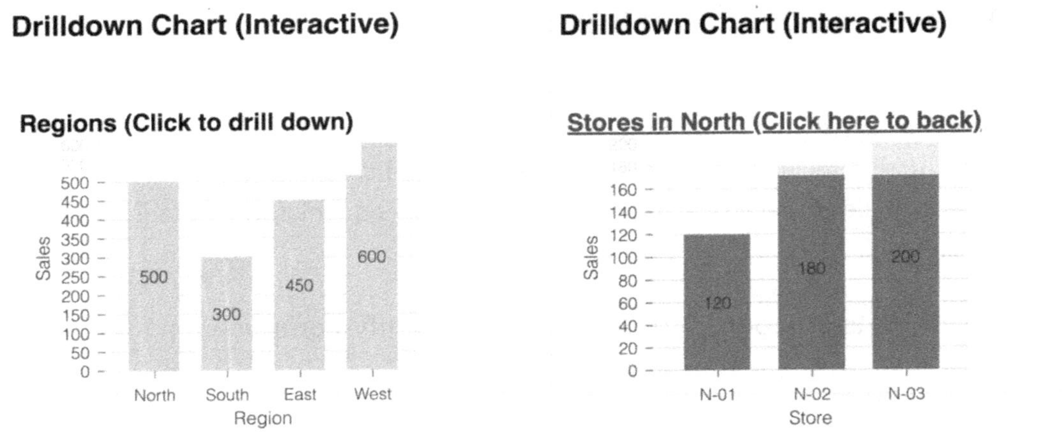

Figure 6-11. *Custom tooltip and interactive drilldown features in a Nivo bar chart*

Recharts vs. Nivo: Choosing Your Tool

We have now explored both wings of the sixth floor. Which one should you use? It's not a matter of better or worse; it's a matter of philosophy and constraint.

Table 6-2. *Feature comparison between Recharts and Nivo charting libraries showing philosophical and practical differences*

Feature	Recharts	Nivo
Primary Philosophy	Composition (Blocks)	Configuration (Sculptures)
Customization	Standard React Children	Deep Config Objects
Animation	Basic	Rich, Physics Based
Visualization Types	Standard Set (Lines, Bars)	Extensive (Sankey, Chord, Voronoi)
Learning Curve	Gentle	Moderate
Best For	Dashboards, Analytical Tools	Presentations, Marketing, Storytelling

Use Recharts when you are building a dense analytical dashboard, where data density is high and you need complete control over the layout composition. It is the engineer's choice: precise, efficient, modular.

Use Nivo when you need to impress. When the chart interacts with the public, or exists in a marketing page, or needs to visualize complex flows (Sankey/Chord) that Recharts doesn't support. It is the designer's choice: polished, fluid, beautiful.

Conclusion

The tour of the sixth floor is complete. You have seen data stripped bare to its trend lines, and you have seen data dressed up in gradients and animations. You have learned that a chart is a translation device, converting the abstract language of numbers into the intuitive language of vision.

Whether you choose the modular precision of Recharts or the polished aesthetics of Nivo, the power remains the same functionality: you are giving the user a sixth sense—the ability to *see* the invisible patterns governing their world.

The elevator is waiting. The next chapter will take us completely away from the browser DOM. We are going to explore the server side. But for now, look out the window one last time at the city lights—a billion data points, all waiting to be visualized.

Exercises: Refine Your Palette

You have the tools. Now you need the practice. These exercises are designed to push you beyond the basics and into the realm of professional dashboard development.

Exercise 1: The Dark Mode Dashboard (Theming)

Difficulty: Easy **Concepts**: Theming, configuration, global design systems

Why this matters: Hardcoding colors (like `fill="#000000"`) is a scalability nightmare. Nivo's theming system allows you to define a "Design Dictionary" that controls every chart in your application. Mastering this is the first step to building a cohesive product.

The task: Create a reusable "Cyberpunk" theme map and apply it to multiple charts.

1. Define a Clojure map `cyberpunk-theme`.
2. Set `axis.ticks.text.fill` to `#00ff00` (matrix green).
3. Set `grid.line.stroke` to `#333333` (subtle gray).
4. Set `textColor` to `#ffffff`.

5. Pass this map to the `theme` prop of a **bar chart** and a **line chart**.
6. Wrap the charts in a `div` with `style={{backgroundColor: "#000"}}` to complete the look.

Detailed Hint The Nivo theme object is deep. Your map should mirror this structure.

Listing 6-32. Cyberpunk theme configuration map demonstrating Nivo's deep theming system for consistent design. Pass it with `(clj->js cyberpunk-theme)`!

```
{:axis {:ticks {:text {:fill "#00ff00"}}}
 :grid {:line {:stroke "#333333"}}
 :text {:fill "#ffffff"}}
```

Exercise 2: The Live Stock Tamer (Real-Time Efficiency)

Difficulty: Medium **Concepts**: Atoms, `setInterval`, immutable vectors, sliding windows

Why this matters: Real-time charts have a memory problem. If you just keep `conj`-ing points to a vector forever, your browser will eventually crash. You need to implement a "sliding window"—adding new data while seamlessly discarding the old.

The task: Build a self-updating line chart that mimics a high-frequency trading terminal.

1. **State**: Create an atom `stock-data` containing an initial vector of 50 points `[{:x 0 :y 50} ...]`.
2. **Clock:** Use `js/setInterval` to trigger an update every 100 ms.
3. **Update logic**:
    - Generate a new point with a random walk (e.g., `last_y + (rand - 0.5)`).
    - `conj` the new point to the end.
    - Use `subvec` to drop the first point, keeping the count at 50.
4. **Render**: Feed this to a line chart. Disable points (`enablePoints={false}`) for a smoother look.

Detailed Hint Your update function is the critical part.

Listing 6-33. Sliding window pattern for real-time data with efficient O(1) immutable vector operations. This operation is O(1) in ClojureScript because of shared structure.

```
(swap! stock-data
       (fn [data]
         (let [new-point {:x (inc (:x (last data))) :y ...}]
           (conj (subvec data 1) new-point))))
```

Exercise 3: The Interactive Family Tree (Data Structure)

Difficulty: Hard **Concepts**: Recursion, tree transformation, event handling

Why this matters: Real-world data rarely comes in the format visualization libraries expect. You will often receive a flat list from a SQL database (rows with `parent_id`) and need to transform it into a nested hierarchy for charts like treemaps.

The task: Convert a flat list of employees into an interactive org chart.

1. **Input**: Define a flat list: `[{:id 1 :boss-id nil :name "CEO"} {:id 2 :boss-id 1 :name "VP"} ...]`.
2. **Transform**: Write a recursive function `build-tree` that takes this list and a root ID, returning `{name: "CEO" children: [{name: "VP" children: [...]}]}`.
3. **Visual**: Render this using a **circle packing** chart.
4. **Interact**: Add an onClick handler. When a circle is clicked, use `js/alert` (or a nice modal) to show the name of that employee's direct reports.

Detailed Hint Use `group-by :boss-id` first. This gives you a map where you can instantly look up "who are the children of X?" without scanning the list every time. Then rewrite recursively.

Exercise 4: The Calendar of Habits (Data Generation)

Difficulty: Medium **Concepts**: Date manipulation, heatmaps, generative art

Why this matters: Sometimes you need to visualize data that doesn't exist yet—either for mocking designs or for "generative art" projects. Being able to programmatically generate dates and values is a key skill.

The task: Generate a "GitHub-style" contribution graph, but fake the data to look like a specific pattern (e.g., "I only code on weekends").

1. **Generate**: Create a loop that generates strings for every day of the current year (`"2023-01-01"`, etc.).
2. **Logic**: For each date, create a value.
   - If it's a weekend (use JS `.getDay()`: 0=Sun, 6=Sat), give it a high value (50-100).
   - If it's a weekday, give it a low value (0-10).
3. **Render**: Pass this to the **calendar** chart.
4. **Style**: Use a custom `colors` array `["#ebedf0" "#9be9a8" "#40c463" "#30a14e" "#216e39"]`.

Detailed Hint ClojureScript/JS interop is your friend for dates.

Listing 6-34. Date manipulation with JavaScript interop for programmatic calendar data generation

```
(let [d (js/Date. "2023-01-01")
      day-of-week (.getDay d)] ;; 0-6
  ...)
```

Final challenge: Combine Exercise 2 and Exercise 1. Build a "Cyberpunk Stock Dashboard" with neon lines, a dark grid, and real-time updates that never stutter.

CHAPTER 7

Video Filters and Pixel Alchemy: The Seventh Floor Studio

> "If a picture is worth a thousand words, a real-time video stream processed at 60fps is worth… Well, a lot of floating-point operations."
>
> "In 1969, Bell Labs created the first video synthesizer. In 2025, we're doing it in a browser with functional programming. Progress is good."
>
> "CSS filters are magic spells. Canvas manipulation is blood magic. Choose wisely."

The Concept

Welcome to the seventh floor. The elevator doors slide open with a soft chime, and you step into what looks like a **1970s television studio**—but one that's been retrofitted with cutting-edge technology. Banks of monitors line the walls, each showing a different filtered view of the same video feed. The smell of ozone mixing with developer fluid hangs in the air. This is where photons become data, and data becomes art.

In the early days of the web (circa 1995), video was a clumsy, unwelcome guest. You needed heavy plugins—remember Flash? RealPlayer? QuickTime?—and even then, the video was locked away in its own little sandbox. You could watch it, but you couldn't *touch* it. You certainly couldn't manipulate the pixels in real time.

Fast forward to today. The browser is a high-performance graphics engine. With HTML5 `<video>`, `<canvas>`, and CSS `filter` properties, we can intercept the photon stream from your webcam, mathematically mangle it in dozens of ways, and splash it

N. Modrzyk, *The ClojureScript Playbook*, https://doi.org/10.1007/979-8-8688-2879-9_7

back onto the screen—all at 60 frames per second. And we're doing it with functional programming.

For a functional programmer, a video stream is the **ultimate stream**. It's an infinite sequence of frames, each one a 2D array of RGB values. Our job is to write the transformation function: `f(frame)` → `enhanced-frame`. Pure, predictable, composable.

We're building a professional-grade photo booth application. We'll start with the simplest approach (CSS filters), evolve to parametric control (interactive sliders), descend into pixel-level manipulation (canvas effects), and finally add the polish of a real product (snapshot capture with a flash animation).

This is a journey from **declarative elegance** to **imperative power**, and we'll learn when to use each approach.

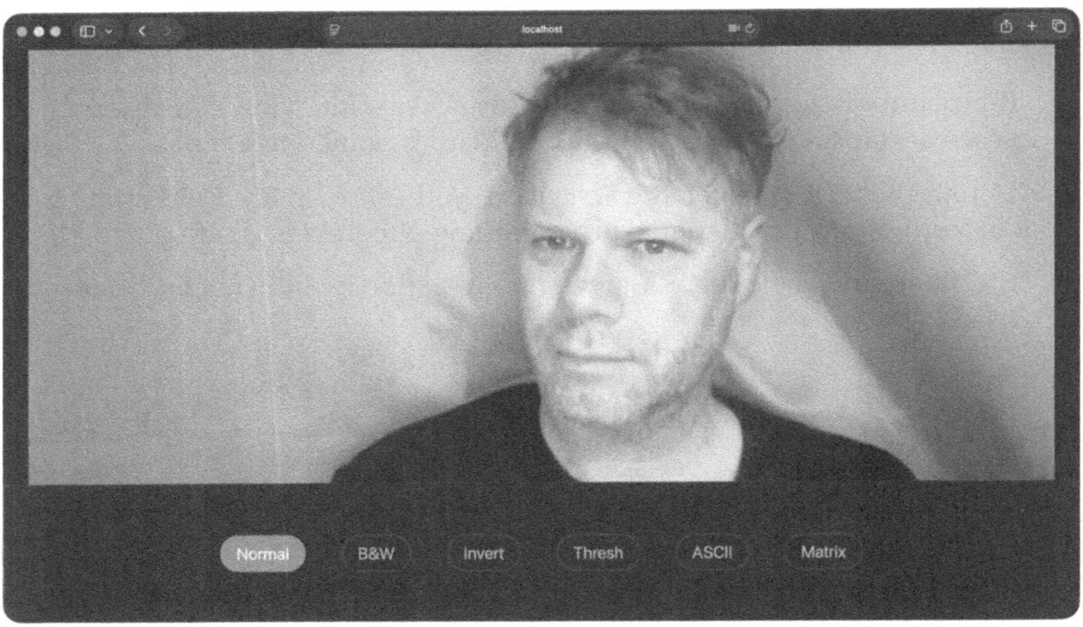

Figure 7-1. *Video filter application interface showing real-time webcam processing with multiple filter options*

The Architecture: Three Layers of Transformation

Before we write code, let's understand the three ways we can process video in the browser.

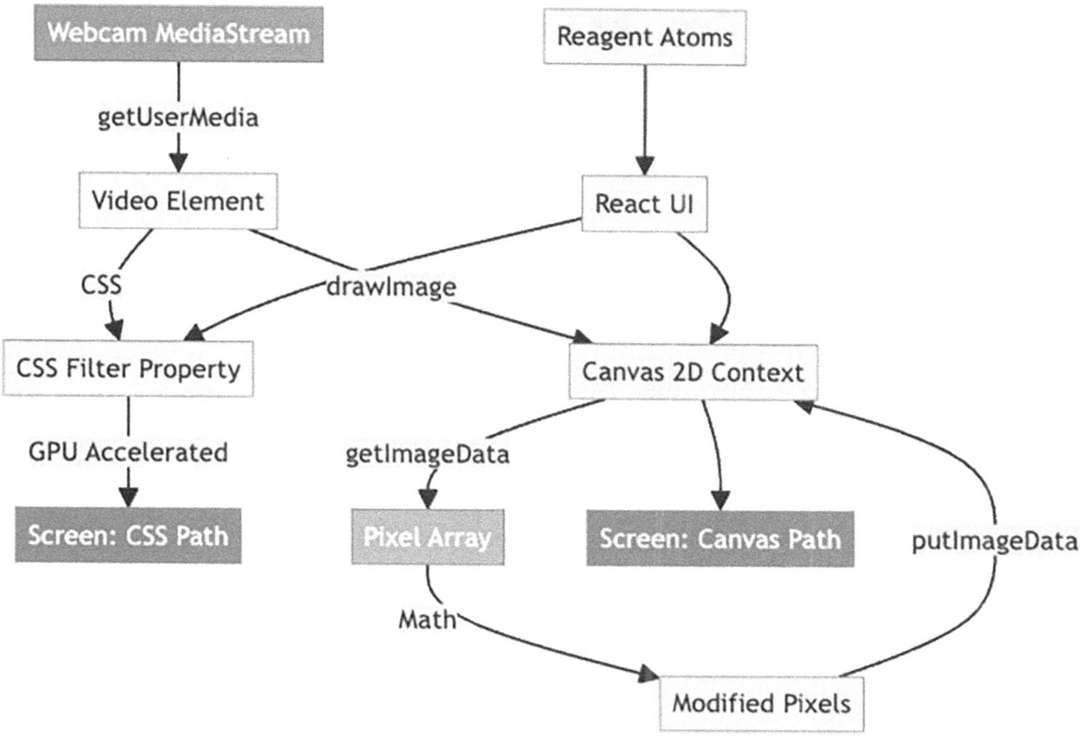

***Figure 7-2.** Three-layer video transformation architecture showing CSS filters, canvas manipulation, and reactive state management*

Three fundamental approaches:

1. **CSS filters (V0, V1)**: Apply mathematical transformations via CSS. Hardware accelerated, declarative, limited.
2. **CSS parameters (V2)**: Same as above, but with user-controlled sliders for each parameter.
3. **Canvas manipulation (V3, V4)**: Read pixel data, manipulate it directly, and write it back. Unlimited power, manual control.

Let's build all three.

The Foundation: Project Setup

Our `deps.edn` is minimal—just Reagent for React integration.

Listing 7-1. Project dependencies with Reagent for reactive video processing UI

```
{:paths ["src" "resources"]
 :deps {org.clojure/clojurescript {:mvn/version "1.12.42"}
        reagent/reagent {:mvn/version "2.0.1"}}}
```

The `shadow-cljs.edn` configuration is presented below.

Listing 7-2. Shadow-cljs configuration with React 19 npm dependencies for video filter application

```
{:source-paths ["src"]
 :dependencies [[reagent/reagent "2.0.1"]]
 :dev-http {8001 "public"}
 :builds
 {:app
  {:target :browser
   :output-dir "public/js"
   :asset-path "/js"
   :npm-deps {react "19.2.4"
              react-dom "19.2.4"}
   :modules {:main {:entries [abstract-art.core]
                    :init-fn abstract-art.core/init}}}}}
```

Notice the `:npm-deps`. Reagent requires React 18+, and shadow-cljs seamlessly handles the integration.

Our `public/index.html` is deliberately simple:

```
<!DOCTYPE html>
<html lang="en">
<head>
    <meta charset="UTF-8">
    <meta name="viewport" content="width=device-width, initial-scale=1.0">
    <title>Video Filters</title>
```

```
    <link href="https://fonts.googleapis.com/css2?family=Inter:wght@400;50
    0;600&display=swap" rel="stylesheet">
    <link rel="stylesheet" href="css/style.css">
</head>
<body>
<div id="app"></div>
<script src="js/main.js"></script>
</body>
</html>
```

The `style.css` file provides our dark, modern aesthetic. We're not showing it all here (it's 350+ lines), but the key principles: - Dark background (`#0f0f13`) - Flexbox for layout - CSS custom properties for theming - Smooth transitions (`transition: all 0.2s ease`)

To start development

```
npx shadow-cljs watch app
```

Then open `http://localhost:8001`.

Version 0: The Quick Prototype

Let's start with the absolute simplest implementation—a button that cycles through hardcoded CSS filter strings.

File: `core_v0.cljs`

The Filter Data

Listing 7-3. CSS filter presets vector with GPU-accelerated transformation strings including composite effects

```
(ns abstract-art.core-v0
  (:require
    [reagent.core :as r]
    [reagent.dom.client :as rdc]))

(def filters
```

```
  ["none"
   "grayscale(100%)"
   "sepia(100%)"
   "invert(100%)"
   "blur(5px)"
   "contrast(200%)"
   "brightness(200%)"
   "saturate(300%)"
   "hue-rotate(180deg)"
   "drop-shadow(10px 10px 10px black)"
   "contrast(250%) brightness(150%) saturate(200%)"  ;; Comic Book
   "hue-rotate(90deg) saturate(500%)"                ;; Neon
   "grayscale(100%) brightness(150%) contrast(180%)"]) ;; High-contrast B/W
```

We're using a simple vector of strings. Each string is a valid CSS `filter` value. The browser's GPU will handle the actual transformation—we just provide the recipe.

CSS filter syntax: The `filter` property accepts functions like `grayscale(percentage)`, `blur(pixels)`, and `hue-rotate(degrees)`. You can chain them with spaces: `"blur(5px) contrast(150%)"`.

The Video Component

Listing 7-4. Video component with lifecycle hooks for getUserMedia camera access and reactive filter cycling

```
(defn video-feed []
  (let [video-element (r/atom nil)
        current-filter (r/atom 0)]  ;; Index into filters vector
    (r/create-class
      {:component-did-mount
       (fn [_]
         (when-let [video @video-element]
           (.then (.getUserMedia js/navigator.mediaDevices (clj->js
           {:video true}))
                  (fn [stream]
                    (set! (.-srcObject video) stream))
```

```
          (fn [err]
            (js/console.error "Error accessing camera:" err)))))

   :reagent-render
   (fn []
     [:div {:style {:text-align "center"}}
      [:video {:ref #(reset! video-element %)
               :autoPlay true
               :muted true
               :style {:filter (get filters @current-filter)
                       :width "80%"
                       :height "auto"
                       :border "2px solid black"}}]
      [:br]
      [:button {:on-click #(swap! current-filter (fn [x] (mod (inc x)
      (count filters))))
                :style {:margin-top "10px"
                        :padding "8px"
                        :font-size "16px"
                        :cursor "pointer"}}
       "Change Filter"]])})))
```

Breaking it down:

Component-Local State

Listing 7-5. Component-local state atoms for video element reference and filter index tracking

```
(let [video-element (r/atom nil)
      current-filter (r/atom 0)]
  ...)
```

We create two atoms: - `video-element`: Will hold a reference to the DOM `<video>` element - `current-filter`: Tracks which filter is active (0 to 12)

These atoms are **local** to this component instance. If you rendered two `video-feed` components, each would have its own state.

Lifecycle: Accessing the Camera

Listing 7-6. MediaDevices getUserMedia API promise-based camera access with success and error handling

```
:component-did-mount
(fn [_]
  (when-let [video @video-element]
    (.then (.getUserMedia js/navigator.mediaDevices (clj->js
    {:video true}))
           (fn [stream] (set! (.-srcObject video) stream))
           (fn [err] (js/console.error "Error accessing camera:" err)))))
```

Reagent's `:component-did-mount` hook runs **once**, after the component is added to the DOM. This is where we request webcam access:

1. **`js/navigator.mediaDevices`**: Access the browser's MediaDevices API.
2. **`.getUserMedia`**: Request access to devices (we're asking for `:video true`).
3. **`clj->js`**: Convert our ClojureScript map to a JavaScript object.
4. **`.then`**: This returns a promise; we handle success and failure.
5. **`set! (.-srcObject video) stream`**: Assign the media stream to the video element.

Security Note Modern browsers require HTTPS for `getUserMedia` (except on localhost). The user must also grant permission.

The Render Function

Listing 7-7. Reagent render function with ref callback for DOM capture and reactive CSS filter application

```
:reagent-render
```

```
(fn []
  [:div {:style {:text-align "center"}}
   [:video {:ref #(reset! video-element %)
            :autoPlay true
            :muted true
            :style {:filter (get filters @current-filter)
                    :width "80%"
                    :height "auto"}}]
   [:button {:on-click #(swap! current-filter (fn [x] (mod (inc x) (count
   filters))))}
    "Change Filter"]])
```

The :ref callback: `{:ref #(reset! video-element %)}` is how we capture a reference to the DOM element. When React renders the video tag, it calls this function with the DOM node as the argument.

The filter: `{:filter (get filters @current-filter)}` dynamically reads the current index and applies the corresponding CSS filter string.

The button logic:

Listing 7-8. Functional state update with modulo arithmetic for cyclic filter index wrapping

```
#(swap! current-filter (fn [x] (mod (inc x) (count filters))))
```

This is a beautiful example of functional state update:

1. `swap!` updates the atom by applying a function to its current value.
2. `(fn [x] (mod (inc x) (count filters)))` increments and wraps around (0→1→2→...→12→0).
3. When the atom changes, Reagent automatically re-renders.

Initialization

Listing 7-9. Application initialization with export metadata for shadow-cljs entry point preservation

```
(defonce root (rdc/create-root (.getElementById js/document "app")))
```

```
(defn ^:export init []
  (rdc/render root [video-feed]))
```

The `^:export` metadata preserves the function name during compilation. Shadow-cljs calls this function automatically (we specified `:init-fn abstract-art.core/init` in the config).

The result: A working webcam feed with a "Change Filter" button. Click it, and the filter cycles through grayscale, sepia, blur, etc. It's simple, but it demonstrates the core concept: **CSS as a pixel transformation language**.

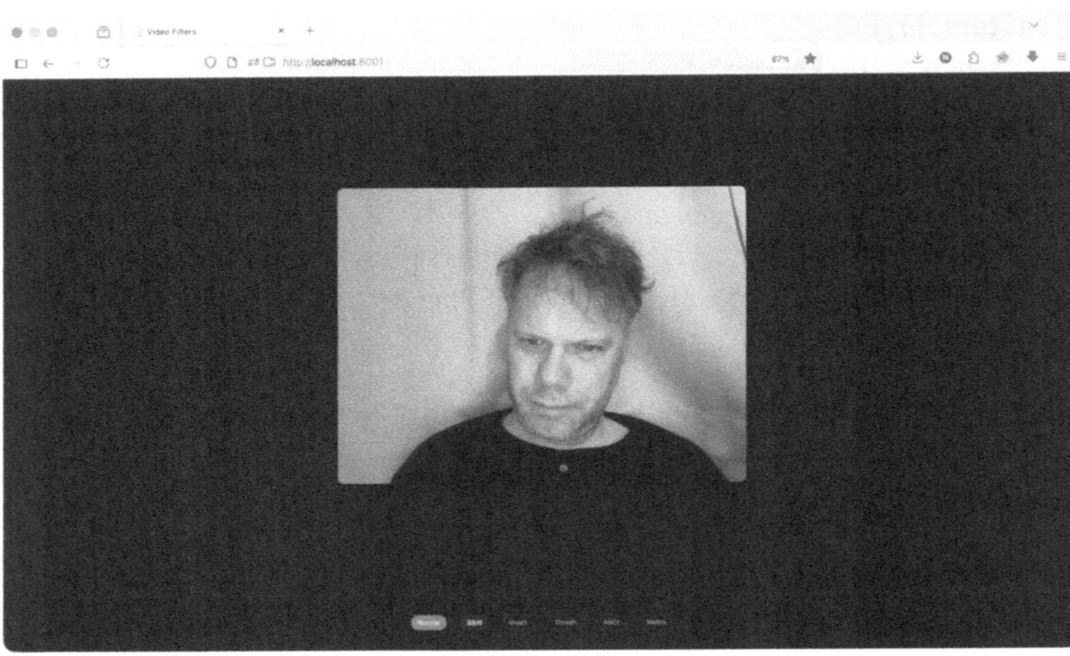

Figure 7-3. *Basic webcam feed with CSS filter cycling demonstrating GPU-accelerated image processing*

Version 1: The Gallery Interface

V0 worked, but clicking a button 13 times to find the filter you want is bad UX. Let's build a gallery where you can **see** and **select** filters visually.

File: `core_v1_gallery.cljs`

Structured Data

Listing 7-10. Structured filter data with maps containing name, CSS value, and preview color for data-driven UI

```
(def filters
  [{:name "Normal"     :value "none" :color "#fff"}
   {:name "Grayscale"  :value "grayscale(100%)" :color "#888"}
   {:name "Sepia"      :value "sepia(100%)" :color "#d4a76a"}
   {:name "Noir"       :value "grayscale(100%) contrast(150%)
   brightness(80%)" :color "#000"}
   {:name "Cyber"      :value "hue-rotate(200deg) contrast(150%)
   brightness(120%)" :color "#0ff"}
   {:name "Neon"       :value "hue-rotate(90deg) saturate(500%)" :color
   "#f0f"}])
```

Instead of a vector of strings, we now have a vector of **maps**. Each filter has

- `:name`: Human-readable label
- `:value`: The CSS filter string
- `:color`: A representative color for the preview thumbnail

This is **data-driven design**. The UI is a pure function of this data structure.

Refactored State

Listing 7-11. Module-level state atoms for global video reference and active filter tracking

```
(def video-ref (r/atom nil))
(def active-filter (r/atom 0)) ;; Index of currently active filter
```

We've moved state out of the component into module-level atoms. This is appropriate here because we only have one video feed in the entire app.

Guideline: Use local component state when different instances need different state. Use module-level atoms when state is global to the application.

The Camera Helper

Listing 7-12. Camera initialization helper function using threading macro for promise chain readability

```
(defn start-camera! []
  (when-let [video @video-ref]
    (-> js/navigator.mediaDevices
        (.getUserMedia (clj->js {:video true}))
        (.then (fn [stream]
                 (set! (.-srcObject video) stream)))
        (.catch (fn [err]
                  (js/console.error "Error accessing camera:" err))))))
```

We've extracted the camera logic into a pure helper function. Notice the **threading macro** ->.

Listing 7-13. Threading macro transforming nested method calls into readable top-to-bottom pipeline

```
(-> js/navigator.mediaDevices
    (.getUserMedia ...)
    (.then ...)
    (.catch ...))
```

This is equivalent to the following.

Listing 7-14. Equivalent nested form without threading macro showing complexity reduction benefit

```
(.catch
  (.then
    (.getUserMedia js/navigator.mediaDevices ...)
    ...)
  ...)
```

The -> macro makes the chain of method calls read top to bottom, like a pipeline.

Filter Thumbnail Component

Listing 7-15. Filter thumbnail component with conditional styling and gradient preview applying actual CSS filter

```
(defn filter-thumbnail [idx filter-data selected?]
  [:div.filter-card
   {:class (when selected? "active")
    :on-click #(reset! active-filter idx)}
   [:div.filter-preview
    {:style {:background (str "linear-gradient(45deg, #333, " (:color
    filter-data) ")")
             :filter (:value filter-data)}}]
   [:span.filter-name (:name filter-data)]])
```

Component design: This is a pure render function. It takes three arguments:

- `idx`: The filter's index
- `filter-data`: The filter map (`{:name "Noir" :value "..." :color "..."}`)
- `selected?`: Boolean indicating if this is the active filter

The `.filter-card` and `.filter-preview` classes are defined in our CSS. The `{:class (when selected? "active")}` conditionally adds the "active" class, which our CSS styles differently (brighter border, glow effect).

The preview: We create a visual preview by applying the filter to a gradient background. It's not perfect (it's not showing the actual video), but it gives the user a sense of what the filter does.

The Video Stage

Listing 7-16. Video stage component with reactive filter application and playsInline for mobile Safari compatibility

```
(defn video-stage []
  (let [current (get filters @active-filter)]
    [:div.video-stage
```

```
    [:video
     {:ref #(reset! video-ref %)
      :autoPlay true
      :muted true
      :playsInline true
      :style {:filter (:value current)}}]]))
```

Reactive update: `(get filters @active-filter)` reads the current index and retrieves the filter map. When `active-filter` changes (because the user clicked a thumbnail), this component automatically re-renders with the new filter value.

The `:playsInline true` attribute is crucial for mobile Safari—without it, the video will hijack the entire screen instead of displaying inline.

The Filter Strip

Listing 7-17. Filter gallery strip using map-indexed with doall and React key metadata for efficient list rendering

```
(defn filter-strip []
  [:div.filter-strip
   (doall
    (map-indexed
     (fn [idx f]
       ^{:key idx}
       [filter-thumbnail idx f (= idx @active-filter)])
     filters))])
```

`map-indexed`: Like `map`, but the function receives both the index and the value. Perfect for our use case.

`doall`: Forces eager evaluation. Without it, the lazy sequence would be realized during rendering, which can cause issues with Reagent's virtual DOM diffing.

`^{:key idx}`: React metadata. Each element in a list needs a unique key for efficient reconciliation. We use the index as the key here (normally you'd use a unique ID from your data, but indices are fine for static lists).

The Root Component

Listing 7-18. Root component with lifecycle initialization separating video stage and filter selection concerns

```
(defn app-root []
  (r/create-class
   {:component-did-mount (fn [this] (start-camera!))
    :reagent-render
    (fn []
      [:div.app-container
       [video-stage]
       [filter-strip]])}))
```

Clean separation of concerns:

- `app-container`: Flex container for layout
- `video-stage`: The video with the active filter
- `filter-strip`: The scrollable thumbnail gallery

The result: A sleek, Instagram-style interface. The video fills the top half of the screen. The bottom shows a horizontal-scrolling gallery of filter thumbnails. Click a thumbnail, and the video filter updates instantly.

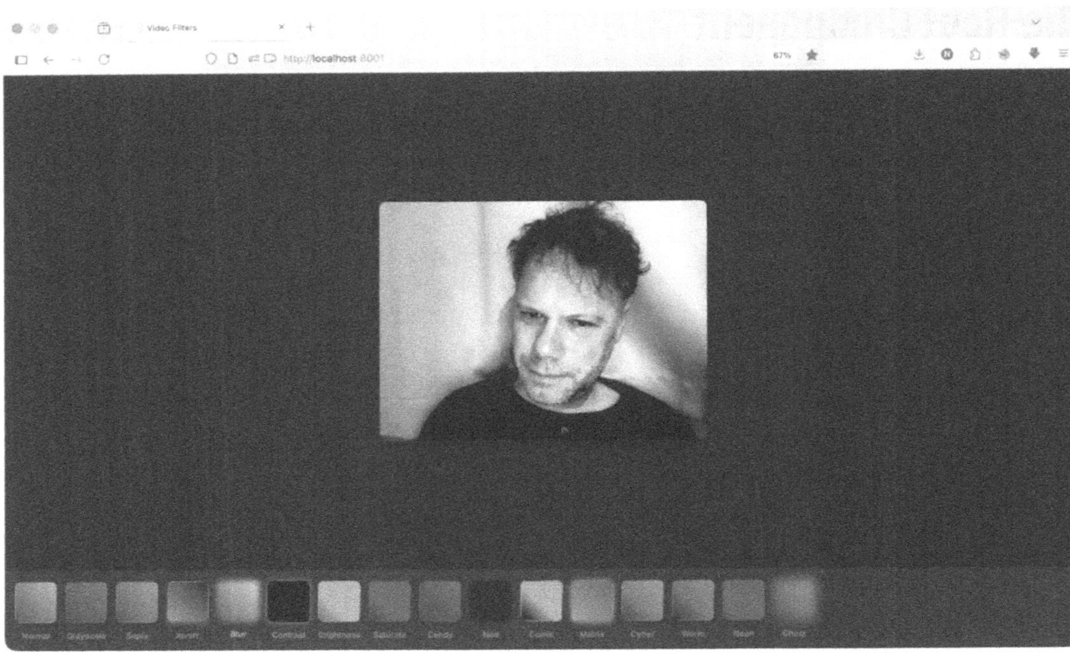

Figure 7-4. *Gallery interface with horizontal-scrolling filter thumbnails for visual filter selection*

Version 2: Parametric Control

CSS filters are powerful, but presets are limiting. What if the user wants "a little bit of blur with medium contrast"? Enter **parametric control**.

File: `core_v2_sliders.cljs`

The Data Model Evolution

Listing 7-19. Parameter-based filter model with percentage and pixel defaults matching CSS filter semantics

```
(def default-params
  {:grayscale 0
   :sepia 0
   :invert 0
```

```
:blur 0
:contrast 100
:brightness 100
:saturate 100
:hue-rotate 0
:opacity 100})
```

Instead of pre-baked filter strings, our state is now a **map of parameters**. Each parameter corresponds to a CSS filter function.

Units: Notice that `contrast`, `brightness`, and `saturate` default to 100 (100% = no effect). `blur` defaults to 0 (0px = no blur). This matches CSS semantics.

Presets As Data

Listing 7-20. Presets as composable parameter snapshots using merge for non-duplicative configuration

```
(def presets
  [{:name "Normal"     :params default-params}
   {:name "Grayscale"  :params (merge default-params {:grayscale 100})}
   {:name "Noir"       :params (merge default-params {:grayscale 100
   :contrast 150 :brightness 80})}
   {:name "Alien"      :params (merge default-params {:hue-rotate 90
   :contrast 120})}])
```

Presets are now **parameter snapshots**. The "Noir" preset is just `{:grayscale 100 :contrast 150 :brightness 80}` merged with defaults. This is elegant—we're not duplicating values; we're composing them.

Slider Configuration

Listing 7-21. Configuration as data for slider specification with ranges, units, and labels for UI generation

```
(def slider-config
  [{:key :grayscale   :min 0 :max 100 :unit "%"   :label "Grayscale"}
```

```
{:key :contrast    :min 0 :max 300 :unit "%"   :label "Contrast"}
{:key :brightness  :min 0 :max 300 :unit "%"   :label "Brightness"}
{:key :saturate    :min 0 :max 500 :unit "%"   :label "Saturation"}
{:key :blur        :min 0 :max 50  :unit "px"  :label "Blur"}
{:key :hue-rotate  :min 0 :max 360 :unit "deg" :label "Hue"}])
```

This is **configuration as data**. Each slider has

- `:key`: Which parameter it controls
- `:min`/`:max`: Range of values
- `:unit`: The CSS unit (%, px, deg)
- `:label`: Display name

We'll use this to **generate** the UI, rather than hardcoding eight separate slider components.

State Management

Listing 7-22. Multi-faceted state management with video reference, parameters, UI mode, and active tool selection

```
(def video-ref (r/atom nil))
(def current-params (r/atom default-params))
(def ui-mode (r/atom :presets)) ;; :presets or :edit
(def selected-tool (r/atom :contrast)) ;; Active slider in edit mode
```

Four atoms:

1. `video-ref`: DOM reference (same as before)
2. `current-params`: The current filter parameters
3. `ui-mode`: Toggle between "Presets" view and "Adjust" view
4. `selected-tool`: In "Adjust" mode, which slider is active

Parameter to CSS Conversion

Listing 7-23. Parameter map to CSS filter string conversion using slider config for consistent ordering

```
(defn params->css [params]
  (str/join " "
            (for [{:keys [key unit]} slider-config
                  :let [val (get params key)]]
              (str (name key) "(" val unit ")"))))
```

The transformation: Given `{:grayscale 50 :contrast 120 :blur 3}`, this produces

```
"grayscale(50%) contrast(120%) blur(3px) hue-rotate(0deg) ..."
```

We iterate over `slider-config` (not the params map) to ensure a consistent order. The `(name key)` converts `:grayscale` to `"grayscale"`.

Example:

Listing 7-24. Example parameter-to-CSS transformation output demonstrating unit concatenation

```
(params->css {:grayscale 80 :contrast 150 :blur 0 ...})
;; => "grayscale(80%) sepia(0%) contrast(150%) brightness(100%)
saturate(100%) blur(0px) hue-rotate(0deg) invert(0%)"
```

Helper Functions

Listing 7-25. Helper functions for preset application and single-parameter updates with atom manipulation

```
(defn apply-preset! [preset]
  (reset! current-params (:params preset)))

(defn update-param! [k v]
  (swap! current-params assoc k v))
```

Two simple helpers: - `apply-preset!`: Load a preset by setting all params at once - `update-param!`: Update a single parameter (called when a slider moves)

The Compact Adjuster UI

This is where we solve a UX problem. If we naively showed eight sliders at once, the UI would be cluttered and overwhelming. Instead, we use a **tool selector pattern**:

1. A horizontal strip of tool buttons (contrast, blur, hue, etc.).
2. A single large slider for the selected tool.
3. Click a tool, the slider updates.

Listing 7-26. Tool selector UI generated from slider configuration with conditional active state styling

```
(defn tool-selector []
  [:div.tool-selector-strip
   (doall
    (for [conf slider-config]
      ^{:key (name (:key conf))}
      [:button.tool-btn
       {:class (when (= @selected-tool (:key conf)) "active")
        :on-click #(reset! selected-tool (:key conf))}
       (:label conf)]))])
```

Generated UI: We're iterating over `slider-config` to create buttons. Each button: - Shows the label ("Contrast," "Blur," etc.) - Has the "active" class if it's the currently selected tool - Updates `selected-tool` when clicked

Listing 7-27. Dynamic active slider component with configuration lookup and reactive value binding

```
(defn active-slider []
  (let [k @selected-tool
        conf (first (filter #(= (:key %) k) slider-config))
        val (get @current-params k)]
    [:div.slider-active-row
```

```
  [:div.big-slider-container
   [:div.big-slider-label
    [:span (:label conf)]
    [:span val (:unit conf)]]
   [:input
    {:type "range"
     :min (:min conf)
     :max (:max conf)
     :value val
     :style {:width "100%"}
     :on-change #(update-param! k (.. % -target -value))}]]]))
```

Dynamic slider: This component reads `@selected-tool` (e.g., `:contrast`) and

1. Finds the matching config: `{:key :contrast :min 0 :max 300 :unit "%" :label "Contrast"}`
2. Reads the current value: `(get @current-params :contrast)` → `120`
3. Renders a range input with those bounds
4. Updates the param when the slider moves

The `(.. % -target -value)` is JavaScript interop for `event.target.value`.

Mode Switcher

Listing 7-28. Mode switcher component toggling between preset gallery and parametric adjuster views

```
(defn mode-switcher []
  [:div.mode-toggle
   [:button.mode-btn
    {:class (when (= @ui-mode :presets) "active")
     :on-click #(reset! ui-mode :presets)}
```

```
    "Presets"]
   [:button.mode-btn
    {:class (when (= @ui-mode :edit) "active")
     :on-click #(reset! ui-mode :edit)}
    "Adjust"]])
```

Two tabs: "Presets" and "Adjust". Click one, and `ui-mode` updates. The app root uses this to conditionally render the presets gallery or the adjuster panel.

The App Root

Listing 7-29. Conditional rendering root component switching between UI modes based on reactive state

```
(defn app-root []
  (r/create-class
   {:component-did-mount (fn [this] (start-camera!))
    :reagent-render
    (fn []
      [:div.app-container
       [video-stage]
       [mode-switcher]
       (if (= @ui-mode :presets)
         [presets-gallery]
         [compact-adjuster-panel])])}))
```

Conditional rendering: `(if (= @ui-mode :presets) ...)` is a simple pattern for toggling between components. When `ui-mode` changes, Reagent re-renders, and the `if` evaluates to a different component.

The result: A dual-mode interface. In "Presets" mode, you see the familiar gallery. In "Adjust" mode, you see a tool selector strip and a single large slider. Move the slider, and the video updates in real time. It's smooth, responsive, and doesn't overwhelm the user with controls.

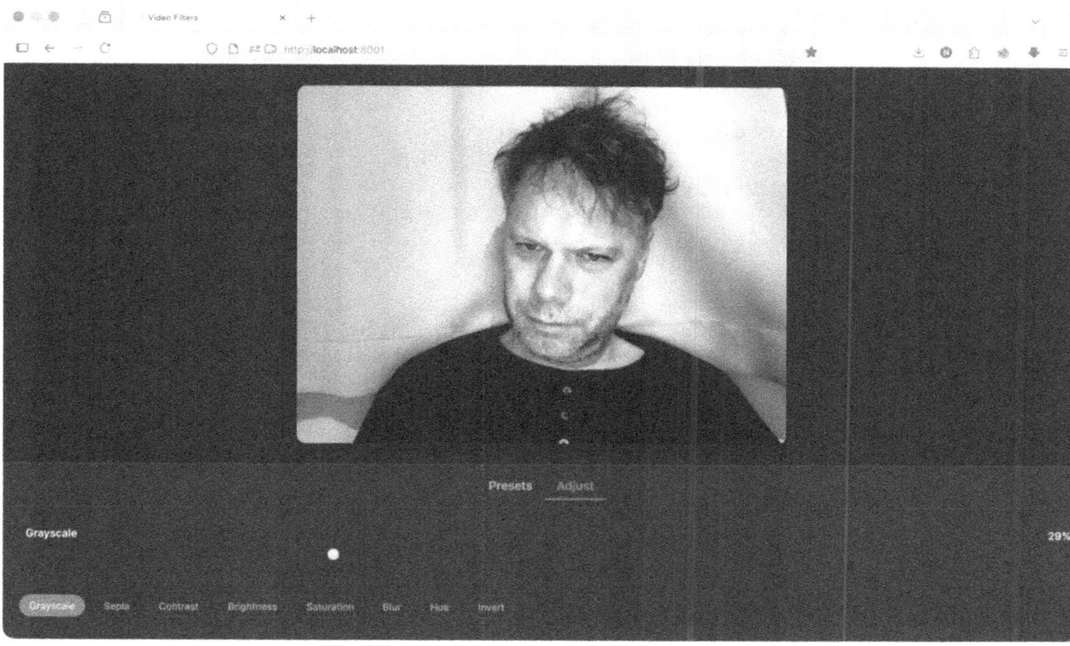

Figure 7-5. *Parametric control interface with tool selector and dynamic slider for real-time filter adjustment*

Version 3: The Descent into Pixels

CSS filters are hardware-accelerated and fast, but they're limited. You can't create an ASCII art effect or a Matrix rain overlay with CSS alone. For that, we need to manipulate **raw pixel data**.

File: `core_v3_canvas.cljs`

The Strategy Shift

Instead of applying a CSS filter to a `<video>` element, we

1. Hide the `<video>` element (it's just a data source now)
2. Create a visible `<canvas>` element
3. Create a `requestAnimationFrame` loop

4. In each frame
   - Draw the video to the canvas
   - Read the pixel data
   - Manipulate the pixels
   - Write the pixels back

Constants and State

Listing 7-30. Canvas effect state including ASCII character map, element references, and animation loop tracking

```
(def char-map " .:-=+*#%@") ;; ASCII gradient (darkest to brightest)
(def matrix-font-size 14)

(def video-ref (atom nil))
(def canvas-ref (atom nil))
(def loop-id (atom nil))
(def current-effect (r/atom :normal))
(def matrix-drops (atom nil)) ;; For Matrix rain state
```

`char-map`: A string of characters ordered by visual density. Space is lightest, `@` is darkest. We'll use this for the ASCII effect.

`matrix-drops`: For the Matrix rain effect, we need to track the vertical position of each "drop" of text.

Effect Functions: Pixel Manipulation

Each effect is a function with the signature

```
(defn render-effect [ctx video w h] ...)
```

Where

- `ctx`: The canvas 2D context
- `video`: The hidden video element
- `w`, `h`: Canvas dimensions

Normal (Passthrough)

Listing 7-31. Passthrough render effect drawing video frame directly to canvas without manipulation

```
(defn render-normal [ctx video w h]
  (.drawImage ctx video 0 0 w h))
```

Just draw the video frame directly to the canvas. No manipulation.

Grayscale (Pixel Loop)

Listing 7-32. Grayscale effect using getImageData pixel array manipulation with RGB averaging algorithm

```
(defn render-grayscale [ctx video w h]
  (.drawImage ctx video 0 0 w h)
  (let [frame (.getImageData ctx 0 0 w h)
        data (.-data frame)
        len (.-length data)]
    (loop [i 0]
      (when (< i len)
        (let [r (aget data i)
              g (aget data (+ i 1))
              b (aget data (+ i 2))
              avg (/ (+ r g b) 3)]
          (aset data i avg)
          (aset data (+ i 1) avg)
          (aset data (+ i 2) avg))
        (recur (+ i 4))))
    (.putImageData ctx frame 0 0)))
```

Step by step:

1. **Draw the video frame**: `(.drawImage ctx video 0 0 w h)`.
2. **Read the pixel data.**

   Listing 7-33. ImageData extraction returning Uint8ClampedArray in RGBA byte format for pixel manipulation

   ```
   (let [frame (.getImageData ctx 0 0 w h)
         data (.-data frame)])
   ```

   `getImageData` returns an `ImageData` object. The `.data` property is a `Uint8ClampedArray`—a flat array of bytes in `[R,G,B,A, R,G,B,A, ...]` format.

   For a 640×480 canvas, this array has `640 * 480 * 4 = 1,228,800` bytes.

3. **Iterate over pixels.**

   Listing 7-34. Pixel iteration loop with stride of 4 bytes for RGBA pixel format traversal

   ```
   (loop [i 0]
     (when (< i len)
    ...
    (recur (+ i 4))))
   ```

   We step by four because each pixel is 4 bytes (RGBA).

4. **Calculate grayscale.**

   Listing 7-35. RGB averaging algorithm with array get/set operations for grayscale conversion

   ```
   (let [r (aget req i)
      g (aget req (+ i 1))
      b (aget req (+ i 2))
      avg (/ (+ r g b) 3)]
     (aset req i avg)
     (aset req (+ i 1) avg)
     (aset req (+ i 2) avg))
   ```

- `(aget req i)`: Array get—read the red channel
- **Calculate average**: `(r + g + b) / 3`
- `(aset req i avg)`: Array set—write the average to red, green, and blue channels

  This makes all three channels the same value, creating grayscale.

5. **Write pixels back.**

Listing 7-36. Canvas putImageData writing modified pixel array back to canvas for display

```
(.putImageData ctx frame 0 0)
```

Performance Note We use `loop/recur`, `aget`, and `aset` instead of higher-level ClojureScript functions because this is the hot path—we're iterating over 300,000+ pixels 60 times per second. We need raw speed.

Threshold (Binary Black/White)

Listing 7-37. Threshold binary effect converting pixels to pure black or white based on brightness threshold

```
(defn render-threshold [ctx video w h]
  (.drawImage ctx video 0 0 w h)
  (let [frame (.getImageData ctx 0 0 w h)
        data (.-data frame)
        len (.-length data)]
    (loop [i 0]
      (when (< i len)
        (let [r (aget data i)
              g (aget data (+ i 1))
              b (aget data (+ i 2))
              v (if (> (/ (+ r g b) 3) 100) 255 0)]
          (aset data i v)
```

```
          (aset data (+ i 1) v)
          (aset data (+ i 2) v))
        (recur (+ i 4))))
    (.putImageData ctx frame 0 0)))
```

Similar to grayscale, but instead of setting RGB to the average, we set them to either 0 (black) or 255 (white) based on a threshold. If the average brightness is > 100, it's white; otherwise, black.

The effect: High-contrast, posterized look. Great for creating silhouettes.

Invert (Color Negation)

Listing 7-38. Color inversion effect using 255-minus-value transformation for negative image

```
(defn render-invert [ctx video w h]
  (.drawImage ctx video 0 0 w h)
  (let [frame (.getImageData ctx 0 0 w h)
        data (.-data frame)
        len (.-length data)]
    (loop [i 0]
      (when (< i len)
        (let [r (aget data i)
              g (aget data (+ i 1))
              b (aget data (+ i 2))]
          (aset data i (- 255 r))
          (aset data (+ i 1) (- 255 g))
          (aset data (+ i 2) (- 255 b)))
        (recur (+ i 4))))
    (.putImageData ctx frame 0 0)))
```

Color inversion: For each channel, compute `255 - value`. This flips the color spectrum—blacks become whites, reds become cyans, etc.

ASCII Art (Sampling and Text Rendering)

Listing 7-39. ASCII art effect with downsampling and brightness-to-character mapping using nested pixel loops

```
(defn render-ascii [ctx video w h]
  (let [scale 0.15
        sw (* w scale)
        sh (* h scale)]
    (.drawImage ctx video 0 0 sw sh)
    (let [frame (.getImageData ctx 0 0 sw sh)
          data (.-data frame)]
      (set! (.-fillStyle ctx) "#000")
      (.fillRect ctx 0 0 w h)
      (set! (.-fillStyle ctx) "#0f0")
      (set! (.-font ctx) "12px monospace")

      (loop [y 0]
        (when (< y sh)
          (loop [x 0]
            (when (< x sw)
              (let [idx (* 4 (+ x (* y sw)))
                    r (aget data idx)
                    g (aget data (+ idx 1))
                    b (aget data (+ idx 2))
                    avg (/ (+ r g b) 3)
                    char-idx (Math/floor (* (/ avg 255) (dec (count
                    char-map))))
                    char (get char-map char-idx)]
                (.fillText ctx (str char) (/ x scale) (/ y scale)))
              (recur (inc x))))
          (recur (inc y)))))))
```

The algorithm:

1. **Downsample**: Draw the video at 15% scale (`scale 0.15`). This gives us a much smaller grid of pixels to work with.
2. **Read downsampled pixels**: `(.getImageData ctx 0 0 sw sh)` on the small image.
3. **Clear canvas**: Fill it with black.
4. **Nested loops**: Iterate over each pixel in the downsampled image.
5. **Map brightness to character**.

   Listing 7-40. Brightness normalization and character index calculation mapping pixel intensity to ASCII gradient

   ```
   (let [avg (/ (+ r g b) 3)
      char-idx (Math/floor (* (/ avg 255) (dec (count char-map))))
      char (get char-map char-idx)]
     ...)
   ```

   - **Calculate average brightness**: 0 to 255
   - **Normalize to `0.0` to `1.0`**: `(/ avg 255)`
   - **Map to character index**: `(* ... (dec (count char-map)))` → 0 to 8
   - **Look up character**: Space (dark) to `@` (bright)

6. **Draw text.**

Listing 7-41. Canvas text rendering with coordinate scaling for ASCII character placement

```
(.fillText ctx (str char) (/ x scale) (/ y scale))
```

We scale back up to full canvas coordinates: `(/ x scale)`.

The result: Each pixel is replaced by a character that matches its brightness. Dark areas get spaces or dots, bright areas get # or @. Classic ASCII art.

Matrix Rain (Stateful Animation)

Listing 7-42. Matrix rain effect with stateful drop tracking and katakana character generation using Unicode ranges

```
(defn render-matrix [ctx video w h]
  (.drawImage ctx video 0 0 w h)
  (set! (.-fillStyle ctx) "rgba(0, 0, 0, 0.9)")
  (.fillRect ctx 0 0 w h)

  (set! (.-fillStyle ctx) "#0F0")
  (set! (.-font ctx) (str matrix-font-size "px monospace"))

  (let [cols (Math/floor (/ w matrix-font-size))
        drops @matrix-drops]
    (when (or (nil? drops) (not= (count drops) cols))
      (reset! matrix-drops (vec (repeat cols 1))))

    (let [new-drops
          (mapv (fn [y i]
                  (let [text (char (+ 0x3041 (rand-int 96)))
                        x (* i matrix-font-size)]
                    (.fillText ctx text x (* y matrix-font-size))
                    (if (and (> (* y matrix-font-size) h) (> (rand) 0.975))
                      0
                      (inc y))))
                @matrix-drops
                (range cols))]
      (reset! matrix-drops new-drops))))
```

The Matrix effect:

1. **Draw video**: Faintly visible in the background.
2. **Overlay dark rectangle**: `rgba(0, 0, 0, 0.9)` creates a “fade” effect—the old characters don’t disappear instantly.
3. **Calculate columns**: Divide canvas width by font size to get the number of vertical columns.

4. **Initialize drops**: Each column has a "drop" at a certain y-position. Initially all at `y = 1`.
5. **For each drop**
   - Generate a random katakana character: `(char (+ 0x3041 (rand-int 96)))`.
   - Draw it at the current position.
   - Advance the drop: `(inc y)`.
   - Randomly reset to top when it goes off-screen.
6. **Update state**: `(reset! matrix-drops new-drops)` saves the new positions for the next frame.

Why katakana?: Unicode range `0x3041` to `0x3096` covers hiragana and katakana characters, giving that authentic Matrix look.

The Render Loop

Listing 7-43. RequestAnimationFrame render loop dynamically calling effect functions at 60 fps

```
(defn draw-loop []
  (let [video @video-ref
        canvas @canvas-ref
        ctx (when canvas (.getContext canvas "2d"))
        w (when canvas (.-width canvas))
        h (when canvas (.-height canvas))
        effect-fn (get effects @current-effect)]

    (when (and video canvas ctx (not (.-paused video)) (not (.-ended video)))
      (effect-fn ctx video w h))

    (reset! loop-id (js/requestAnimationFrame draw-loop))))
```

The loop:

1. Read current state (video, canvas, effect).
2. Get the effect function: `(get effects @current-effect)` → `render-matrix`, etc.

3. Call it: (effect-fn ctx video w h).
4. Request next frame: (js/requestAnimationFrame draw-loop).

This runs ~60 times per second, creating smooth animation.

Starting the Camera

Listing 7-44. Camera initialization with explicit video play and render loop startup after stream assignment

```
(defn start-camera! []
  (when-let [video @video-ref]
    (-> js/navigator.mediaDevices
        (.getUserMedia (clj->js {:video true}))
        (.then (fn [stream]
                 (set! (.-srcObject video) stream)
                 (.play video)
                 (draw-loop))) ;; Start the render loop!
        (.catch (fn [err]
                  (js/console.error "Error accessing camera:" err))))))
```

After the stream is assigned, we explicitly .play the video (even though it's hidden), then kick off the render loop.

The UI

Listing 7-45. Effect switcher UI with reusable button component and horizontal control bar layout

```
(defn effect-button [k label]
  [:button.tool-btn
   {:class (when (= @current-effect k) "active")
    :on-click #(reset! current-effect k)
    :style {:margin "0 8px"}}
   label])
```

```
(defn control-bar []
  [:div.tool-selector-strip {:style {:justify-content "center" :height
  "100px"}}
   [effect-button :normal "Normal"]
   [effect-button :grayscale "B&W"]
   [effect-button :invert "Invert"]
   [effect-button :threshold "Thresh"]
   [effect-button :ascii "ASCII"]
   [effect-button :matrix "Matrix"]])
```

Simple buttons to switch effects. Click "ASCII", and `current-effect` becomes `:ascii`, triggering a re-render with the ASCII effect function.

The Main Component

Listing 7-46. Main stage component with hidden video element and visible styled canvas for effect rendering

```
(defn main-stage []
  (r/create-class
   {:component-did-mount
    (fn [_] (start-camera!))

    :reagent-render
    (fn []
      [:div.app-container
       [:div.video-stage
        [:video {:ref #(reset! video-ref %)
                 :style {:display "none"}
                 :playsInline true
                 :muted true
                 :width 640 :height 480}]
        [:canvas {:ref #(reset! canvas-ref %)
                  :width 640 :height 480
                  :style {:width "100%" :max-width "800px"
                          :border-radius "12px"
```

```
                    :box-shadow "0 20px 50px rgba(0,0,0,0.5)"}}]]
     [control-bar]])}))
```

Key points: - Video element is hidden: `{:style {:display "none"}}` - Canvas is visible and styled - Both have `ref` callbacks to capture DOM references

The result: A Matrix-style interface with pixel-perfect effects. The ASCII mode looks retro and glitchy. The Matrix rain overlays green text on the video. The threshold mode creates stark black-and-white silhouettes.

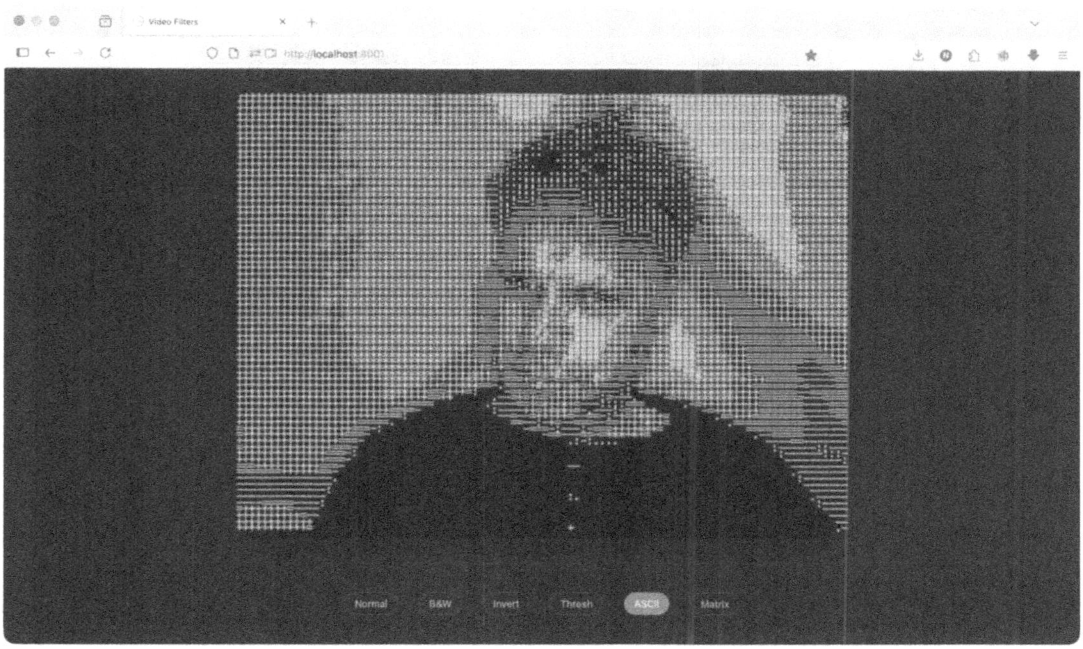

***Figure 7-6.** ASCII art effect rendering video as text characters based on pixel brightness*

ASCII art effect shown above, converting your webcam feed into green characters on black

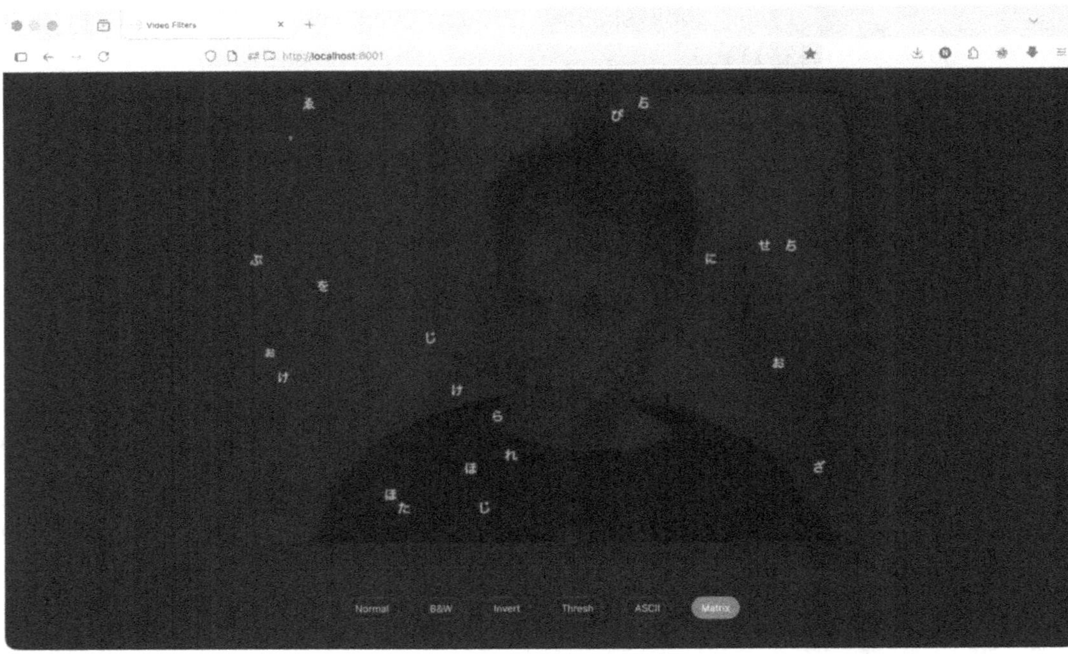

Figure 7-7. *Matrix rain effect with falling green characters overlaying the video stream*

Matrix rain effect cascading over the video feed

Version 4: Production Polish

The final version adds two features that make it feel like a real product:

1. **Snapshot capture**: A button that freezes the current frame and downloads it as a PNG.
2. **Flash animation**: A white flash overlay when you take a snapshot (like a real camera).

File: `core.cljs` (the main, production version)

Additional State

Listing 7-47. Flash animation state atom for snapshot visual feedback

```
(def flash-active (r/atom false))
```

A boolean flag to trigger the flash animation.

Capture Function

Listing 7-48. Snapshot capture function with flash animation and canvas-to-PNG download using toDataURL

```
(defn capture! []
  (let [canvas @canvas-ref]
    (when canvas
      ;; 1. Flash
      (reset! flash-active true)
      (js/setTimeout #(reset! flash-active false) 500)

      ;; 2. Download
      (let [link (.createElement js/document "a")]
        (set! (.-download link) (str "snap-" (.now js/Date) ".png"))
        (set! (.-href link) (.toDataURL canvas "image/png"))
        (.click link)
        (.remove link)))))
```

The algorithm:

1. **Activate flash.**

Listing 7-49. Flash animation trigger with setTimeout-based auto-reset for timed visual feedback. We set the flag to `true`, triggering a CSS animation. After 500 ms, we turn it off.

```
(reset! flash-active true)
(js/setTimeout #(reset! flash-active false) 500)
```

2. **Create download link:**

```
(let [link (.createElement js/document "a")]
  ...)
```

We create an <a> element programmatically.

3. **Generate data URL:**

```
(set! (.-href link) (.toDataURL canvas "image/png"))
```

`.toDataURL` converts the canvas to a base64-encoded PNG string:

```
data:image/png;base64,iVBORwOKGgoAAAANSUhEUgAA...
```

4. **Trigger download:**

```
(set! (.-download link) (str "snap-" (.now js/Date) ".png"))
(.click link)
```

We set the `download` attribute (filename) and programmatically click the link.

5. **Clean up:**

```
(.remove link)
```

The result: Clicking the capture button flashes the screen white, then downloads a PNG named `snap-1706140234567.png`.

Flash Overlay Component

```
[:div.flash-overlay {:class (when @flash-active "flash-active")}]
```

This is an empty, fullscreen div. When `@flash-active` is true, it gets the "flash-active" class, which triggers a CSS animation:

```
@keyframes flash-anim {
  0% { opacity: 1; }
  100% { opacity: 0; }
}
```

```
.flash-active {
  animation: flash-anim 0.4s ease-out;
}
```

The overlay fades from white to transparent over 400 ms.

The Toolbar

Listing 7-50. Production toolbar component with effects list and capture button in flex layout

```
(defn toolbar []
  [:div.toolbar
   [:div.effects-list
    (for [[k v] effects]
      `{:key k}
      [effect-selector k v])]

   [:button.capture-btn
    {:on-click capture!}]

   [:div {:style {:width "20px"}}]]) ;; Spacer
```

A flex container with: - Effects list (left) - Capture button (center/right) - Spacer (right)

The `.capture-btn` is styled as a large circular button with a camera icon (via CSS `::after` pseudo-element).

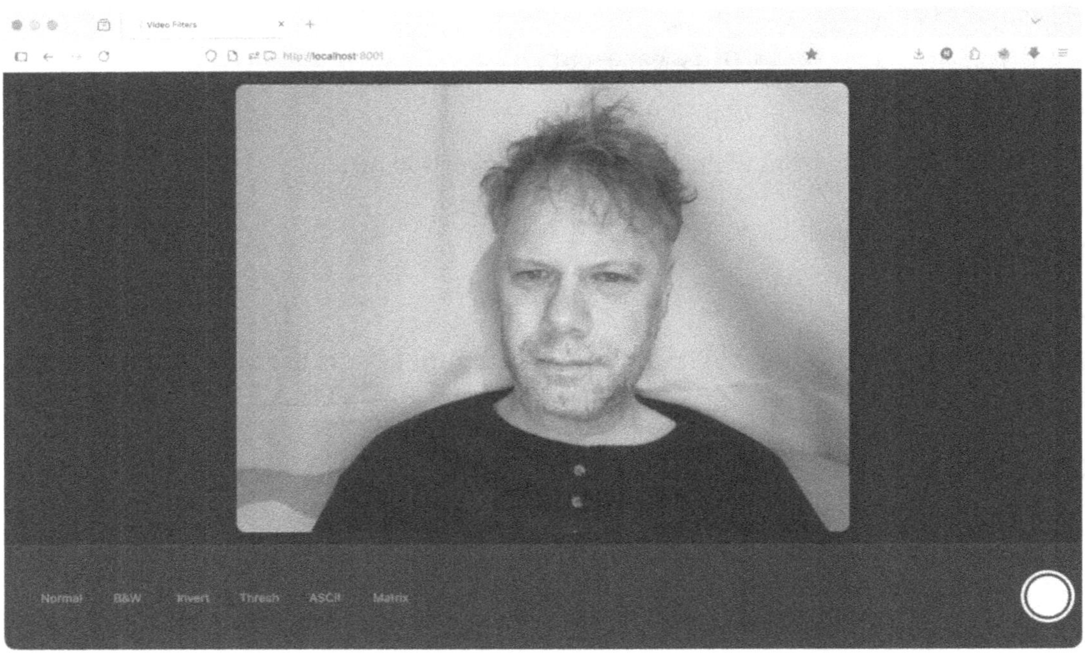

***Figure 7-8.** Snapshot capture feature with flash animation and download functionality*

The final production version with effects toolbar and capture button

The full stack: - Webcam ➤ video element - Video ➤ canvas (via draw loop) - Canvas ➤ pixel manipulation (via effect functions) - Canvas ➤ download (via `.toDataURL`) - UI ➤ Reagent components (reactive) - State ➤ atoms (Clojure immutable refs)

Comparing Approaches: When to Use Each

Let's reflect on the architecture choices.

Table 7-1. *Performance and flexibility comparison between CSS filters, parametric CSS, and canvas pixel manipulation approaches*

Approach	Performance	Flexibility	Complexity	Use Case
CSS Filters (V1)	★★★★★ (GPU)	★★ (Limited)	★ (Simple)	Standard effects, UI polish
Parametric CSS (V2)	★★★★★ (GPU)	★★★ (Configurable)	★★ (Moderate)	User-customizable filters
Canvas Pixels (V3)	★★★ (CPU)	★★★★★ (Unlimited)	★★★★ (Complex)	Custom effects, ASCII, Matrix

Guidelines:

- **Use CSS** for standard effects (blur, grayscale, sepia). It's hardware-accelerated and requires no JavaScript.
- **Use parametric CSS** when you want user control over standard effects. Same performance, better UX.
- **Use canvas** when you need effects that CSS can't do (ASCII art, chroma key, edge detection, face tracking).

The lesson: Start simple. Add complexity only when necessary. CSS filters cover 90% of use cases. Canvas is for the remaining 10% where you need ultimate control.

Exercises: Expand Your Studio

Ready to experiment? Here are challenges to deepen your understanding.

Exercise 1: The Green Screen (Chroma Key)

Difficulty: Hard **Concepts**: Pixel comparison, color distance, alpha channel

Implement a virtual background:

1. Define a target color (e.g., `{:r 0 :g 255 :b 0}` for pure green).
2. In your pixel loop, calculate the Euclidean distance between the current pixel and the target color.

Listing 7-51. Euclidean color distance calculation for chroma key green screen effect implementation

```
(def distance (Math/sqrt (+ (* (- r target-r) (- r target-r))
                            (* (- g target-g) (- g target-g))
                            (* (- b target-b) (- b target-b)))))
```

3. If distance < threshold (e.g., 50), set the alpha channel to 0.

Listing 7-52. Alpha channel manipulation for transparency-based virtual background replacement

```
(when (< distance 50)
  (aset data (+ idx 3) 0)) ;; 4th byte is alpha
```

4. Put a static image or video as the canvas background in CSS.

Hint You'll need to enable alpha in the canvas context: `(.getContext canvas "2d" #js {:alpha true})`.

Exercise 2: Edge Detection (Sobel Filter)

Difficulty: Expert **Concepts**: Convolution matrices, calculus

Create a "sketch" effect that highlights edges:

1. For each pixel, compare it to its eight neighbors (3×3 grid).
2. Calculate horizontal gradient: `Gx = (right pixel) - (left pixel)`.
3. Calculate vertical gradient: `Gy = (bottom pixel) - (top pixel)`.
4. Magnitude: `Math/sqrt(Gx² + Gy²)`.
5. If magnitude > threshold, it's an edge (draw white); otherwise, black.

Reference: Look up "Sobel operator" for the full convolution matrices.

Exercise 3: GIF Recorder

Difficulty: Medium **Concepts**: Animation buffers, GIF encoding

Record a 3-second loop:

1. Use a library like `gif.js` to encode GIFs.
2. Add a "Record" button that captures 60 frames (1 second at 60 fps).
3. Convert each canvas frame to an image: `.toDataURL()`.
4. Add frames to the GIF encoder.
5. Download the result.

Hint `gif.js` is a pure JavaScript library you can import via npm.

Exercise 4: Face Tracking (ML.js)

Difficulty: Expert **Concepts**: TensorFlow.js, neural networks

Add face detection and only apply effects to the background:

1. Install `@tensorflow-models/face-detection`.
2. Load the model: `await faceDetection.createDetector(...)`.
3. In each frame, detect faces: `await detector.estimateFaces(video)`.
4. Get bounding boxes.
5. Apply the Matrix rain only outside the face regions.

This combines V3 canvas manipulation with cutting-edge ML.

Wrapping Up: The Journey from Declarative to Imperative

We started with a single CSS filter string and ended with a full-fledged image processing pipeline. Along the way, we learned

- **V0**: CSS filters are powerful and simple. Use them whenever possible.
- **V1**: Data-driven UI (maps instead of strings) makes code extensible.
- **V2**: Parametric state (sliders controlling a parameter map) gives users control.
- **V3**: Pixel-level manipulation unlocks unlimited creativity, at the cost of complexity.

  V4: Production polish (flash animations, downloads) makes it feel professional.

The broader lesson: Functional programming doesn't mean avoiding state or side effects entirely. It means **isolating** them. Our render functions (`render-grayscale`, `render-matrix`) are pure—they transform data. The side effects (updating the canvas, starting the camera) are explicit and controlled.

This pattern—pure core, impure shell—scales from simple apps to complex systems.

The seventh floor is complete. You've built a real-time video processing studio in the browser, using ClojureScript and functional principles. Before you go, take one last look at the monitors. Watch the Matrix rain cascade down your face. See yourself rendered in ASCII. Capture that moment.

This is functional programming made visible. This is code made beautiful.

> *"The camera captures reality. The code transforms it. The programmer decides what's real."*

CHAPTER 8

The Game Corner: PixiJS and the Golden Age of Arcade

> "On the 8th floor, quarters are unnecessary. The games run on functional programming instead of loose change."
>
> "Space Invaders taught the world that aliens move in formation. Tetris taught us that our past mistakes will come back to bury us."
>
> "In 1978, Tomohiro Nishikado created Space Invaders with a bug: as enemies died, the CPU had less to process, making survivors move faster. He kept the bug. It became the game's signature difficulty curve."

The Concept

Welcome to the eighth floor, the game corner. This is a recreation of the golden age of arcade gaming, circa 1978-1984.

We're building two legends: **Space Invaders** (1978) and **Tetris** (1984). But we're not using assembly or C. We're using **ClojureScript** and **PixiJS**, a modern WebGL-powered rendering engine that can push millions of sprites at 60fps.

Why These Games?

Space Invaders (1978) was gaming's first true blockbuster. It caused a yen shortage in Japan because so many coins were stuck in arcade machines. Tomohiro Nishikado spent a year hand-crafting every sprite, every sound effect, every line of Intel 8080 assembly

N. Modrzyk, *The ClojureScript Playbook*, https://doi.org/10.1007/979-8-8688-2879-9_8

code. The game's increasing speed wasn't a feature—it was a hardware limitation—but it became the blueprint for dynamic difficulty.

Tetris (1984) was created by Alexey Pajitnov during Soviet Russia as a test program for the Electronika 60 computer. He called it "Tetris" combining the Greek word "tetra" (four) with "tennis" (his favorite sport). It's the best-selling video game of all time (495+ million copies) and proof that simple mechanics plus perfect execution equals timeless design.

Both games share a critical trait: **They can be described as pure data transformations**. Space Invaders is a grid of aliens moving according to rules. Tetris is a grid of blocks obeying gravity and collision. Perfect for functional programming.

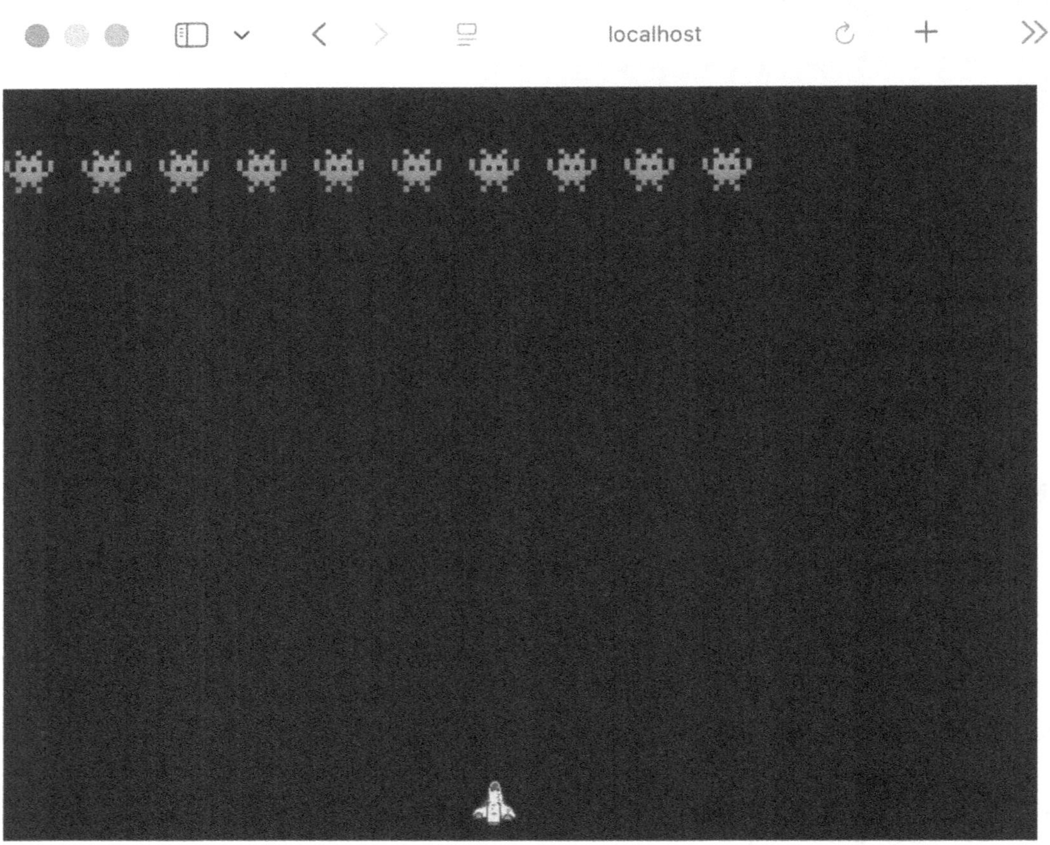

Figure 8-1. *Space Invaders arcade game recreation showcasing pixel-perfect retro aesthetics with modern WebGL rendering*

The Architecture: ClojureScript Meets WebGL

Before diving into code, let's understand our technology stack.

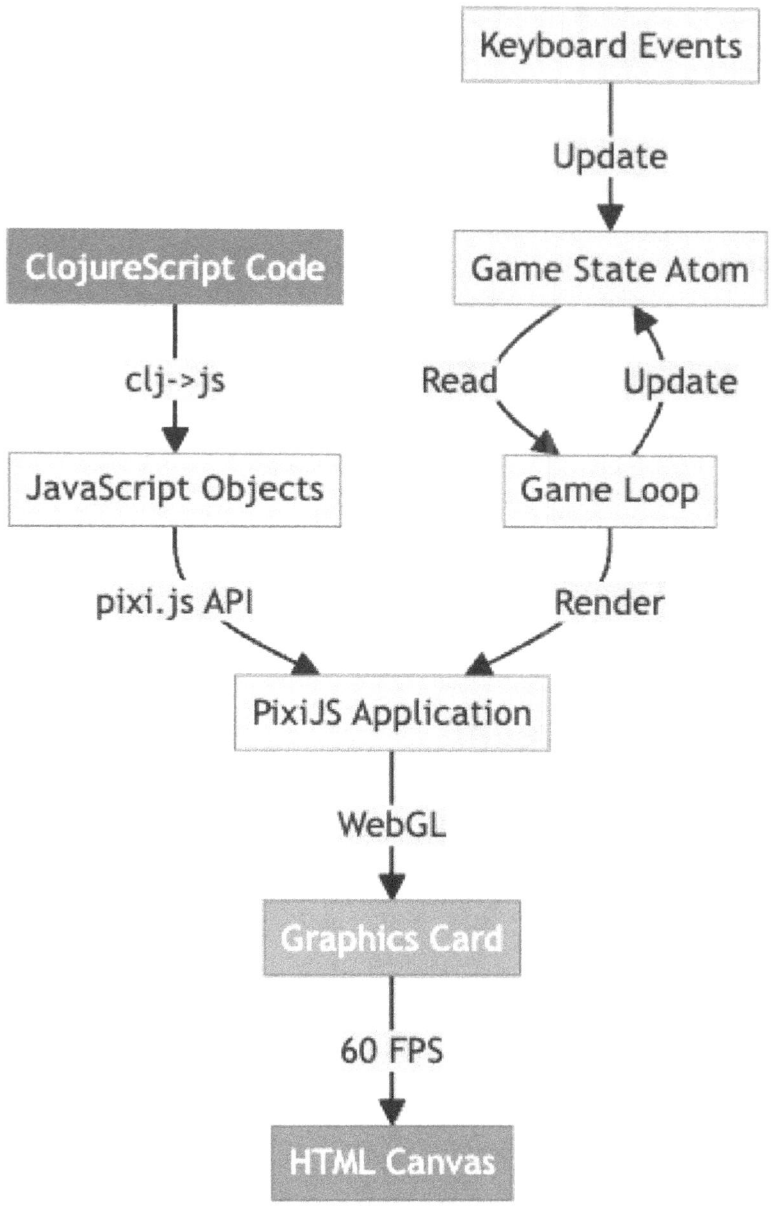

Figure 8-2. *ClojureScript and PixiJS integration architecture showing WebGL-accelerated rendering pipeline at 60 fps*

The flow:

1. ClojureScript code manages game state in atoms.
2. PixiJS (a JavaScript library) handles rendering.
3. WebGL (via PixiJS) uses the GPU for hardware-accelerated graphics.
4. The game loop coordinates everything at 60 fps.

Why PixiJS?

- **Performance**: WebGL rendering on the GPU
- **Simplicity**: Sprite-based API (no need to calculate vertices)
- **JavaScript interop**: Works seamlessly with ClojureScript
- **Battle tested**: Powers games with thousands of sprites

The Foundation: Project Setup

Both projects share the same setup. Let's look at Space Invaders.

Dependencies (`deps.edn`)

Listing 8-1. Minimal project dependencies requiring only ClojureScript core for PixiJS game development

```
{:paths ["src" "resources"]
 :deps {org.clojure/clojurescript {:mvn/version "1.12.42"}}}
```

Minimal. We only need ClojureScript core.

Shadow-cljs Configuration

Listing 8-2. Shadow-cljs configuration for browser-targeted PixiJS game with local development server

```
{:source-paths ["src"]
 :dependencies []
 :dev-http {8001 "public"}
 :builds
 {:app
  {:target :browser
   :output-dir "public/js"
   :asset-path "/js"
   :modules {:main {:init-fn space-invader.core/init}}}}}
```

Notice: No `:npm-deps` in the config. PixiJS is installed via `package.json`.

NPM Dependencies (`package.json`)

```
{
  "dependencies": {
    "pixi.js": "^8.8.1"
  }
}
```

PixiJS 8.8.1 is the latest major version (as of 2025). It's a complete rewrite with improved performance and modern JavaScript support.

Before starting, run

```
npm install
npx shadow-cljs watch app
```

Part 1: Space Invaders

Version 1: The Minimal Shooter (e01.cljs)

Let's start with the simplest possible Space Invaders—player movement, shooting, and collision detection.

Listing 8-3. Namespace declaration with JavaScript interop importing PixiJS library for WebGL rendering

```
(ns space-invader.e01
  (:require ["pixi.js" :as PIXI]))
```

JavaScript interop: `["pixi.js" :as PIXI]` imports the entire PixiJS library. Now we can call `PIXI/Application`, `PIXI/Sprite`, etc.

Creating the PixiJS Application

Listing 8-4. PixiJS application initialization with 800x600 canvas, black background, and asset loader reference

```
(def app (PIXI/Application. (clj->js {:width 800 :height 600
                                      :backgroundColor 0x000000
                                      :antialias true})))
(def stage (.-stage app))
(def assets (.-Assets PIXI))
```

Line by line:

1. `(PIXI/Application. ...)`: Create a new PixiJS app. The dot after `Application` means "call the constructor."
2. `(clj->js {:width 800 ...})`: Convert our ClojureScript map to a JavaScript object. PixiJS expects JS objects, not ClojureScript data structures.
3. `0x000000`: Hexadecimal color (black). PixiJS uses numbers for colors, not strings.

4. `(.-stage app)`: Access the `stage` property of the app. The stage is the root display container—everything you render goes here.
5. `(.-Assets PIXI)`: PixiJS 8's asset loader.

Game State

Listing 8-5. Game state atoms for keyboard input set, bullet vector, enemy vector, and player sprite reference

```
(def keys (atom #{}))
(def bullets (atom []))
(def enemies (atom []))
(def player (atom nil))
```

Four atoms:

- `keys`: A set of currently pressed keys (`#{"ArrowLeft" "Space"}`)
- `bullets`: A vector of bullet sprites
- `enemies`: A vector of enemy sprites
- `player`: The player sprite

Why sets for keys? Sets automatically handle uniqueness. If you hold down a key, the browser fires multiple `keydown` events, but the set stays `#{"ArrowLeft"}`.

Creating the Player

Listing 8-6. Player sprite factory creating 40x40 sprite from asset with initial positioning at bottom center

```
(defn create-player []
  (let [sprite (PIXI/Sprite.from "player")]
    (set! (.-width sprite) 40)
    (set! (.-height sprite) 40)
    (set! (.-x sprite) 400)
    (set! (.-y sprite) 550)
    sprite))
```

PIXI/Sprite.from "player": Create a sprite from an asset named "player" (we'll load this asset later).

set!: JavaScript interop for mutation. (set! (.-width sprite) 40) is equivalent to JavaScript's sprite.width = 40.

The pattern: We create the sprite, configure its properties, and then return it. This is a common PixiJS pattern.

Keyboard Input

Listing 8-7. Keyboard event handlers using set operations for uniqueness-guaranteed key state tracking

```
(defn handle-keydown [e]
  (swap! keys conj (.-code e)))

(defn handle-keyup [e]
  (swap! keys disj (.-code e)))
```

Simple event handlers:

- keydown: Add the key to the set (conj = add to collection).
- keyup: Remove the key from the set (disj = remove from set).

(.-code e) reads the code property of the event (e.g., "ArrowLeft", "Space").

Creating Bullets

Listing 8-8. Bullet factory using PixiJS Graphics API to draw 4x10 white rectangle with centered positioning

```
(defn create-bullet [x y]
  (let [b (PIXI/Graphics.)]
    (.beginFill b 0xFFFFFF)
    (.drawRect b 0 0 4 10)
    (.endFill b)
    (set! (.-x b) (+ 20 x))
    (set! (.-y b) y)
    b))
```

PIXI/Graphics: For drawing shapes (rectangles, circles, lines) instead of using image sprites.

The drawing API:

1. `.beginFill b 0xFFFFFF`: Start filling with white.
2. `.drawRect b 0 0 4 10`: Draw a 4×10 rectangle.
3. `.endFill b`: Finish the shape.

We position the bullet at `(x+20, y)` to center it horizontally on the player.

Creating Enemies

Listing 8-9. Enemy sprite creation and grid spawning with 60-pixel spacing across ten horizontal positions

```
(defn create-enemy [x y]
  (let [sprite (PIXI/Sprite.from "enemy")]
    (set! (.-x sprite) x)
    (set! (.-y sprite) y)
    (set! (.-width sprite) 40)
    (set! (.-height sprite) 40)
    sprite))

(defn spawn-enemies []
  (doseq [i (range 10)]
    (let [e (create-enemy (* i 60) 50)]
      (.addChild stage e)
      (swap! enemies conj e))))
```

spawn-enemies: Create ten enemies in a horizontal row. - `(range 10)` → `(0 1 2 3 4 5 6 7 8 9)` - `(* i 60)` → `(0 60 120 180 ...)`—evenly spaced - `.addChild stage e`: Add to the stage so PixiJS renders it - `swap! enemies conj e`: Add to our state atom for gameplay logic

Figure 8-3. *Enemy formation showing ten aliens in horizontal line ready to invade with sinusoidal movement pattern*

Enemy formation at spawn—ten aliens in a perfect horizontal line, ready to invade

Collision Detection

Listing 8-10. Axis-aligned bounding box (AABB) collision detection using classic 2D game overlap algorithm

```
(defn rects-collide? [a b]
  (let [ax (.-x a) ay (.-y a) ah (.-height a) aw (.-width a)
        bx (.-x b) by (.-y b) bh (.-height b) bw (.-width b)]
    (and (< ax (+ bx bw))
         (> (+ ax aw) bx)
         (< ay (+ by bh))
         (> (+ ay ah) by))))
```

AABB (axis-aligned bounding box) collision: - Two rectangles collide if they overlap on **both** the X and Y axes - `(< ax (+ bx bw))`: A's left edge is left of B's right edge - `(> (+ ax aw) bx)`: A's right edge is right of B's left edge - Same logic for Y axis

This is the same algorithm used in the original Space Invaders (and Pong, and Breakout, and every 2D game until the mid-1990s).

The Game Loop

Listing 8-11. Main game loop with requestAnimationFrame coordinating enemy animation, player movement, shooting, and collision detection

```
(defn game-loop []
  (js/requestAnimationFrame game-loop)
  (let [player-sprite @player]

    ;; Animate enemies
    (let [time (/ (js/Date.now) 500)]
      (doseq [e @enemies]
```

```
    (set! (.-y e) (+ 50 (* 5 (js/Math.sin (+ time (.-x e))))))))

;; Player movement
(when (some #(= % "ArrowLeft") @keys)
  (set! (.-x player-sprite) (max 25 (- (.-x player-sprite) 5))))
(when (some #(= % "ArrowRight") @keys)
  (set! (.-x player-sprite) (min 775 (+ (.-x player-sprite) 5))))

;; Shoot
(when (some #(= % "Space") @keys)
  (when-not (.-shot player-sprite)
    (let [b (create-bullet (- (.-x player-sprite) 2) (.-y player-
    sprite))]
      (.addChild stage b)
      (swap! bullets conj b))
    (set! (.-shot player-sprite) true)
    (js/setTimeout #(set! (.-shot player-sprite) false) 300)))

;; Update bullets
(doseq [b @bullets]
  (set! (.-y b) (- (.-y b) 8)))

;; Collision check
(doseq [b @bullets e @enemies]
  (when (rects-collide? b e)
    (.removeChild stage b)
    (.removeChild stage e)
    (swap! bullets #(remove #{b} %))
    (swap! enemies #(remove #{e} %))))

;; Remove bullets off screen
(doseq [b @bullets]
  (when (< (.-y b) 0)
    (.removeChild stage b)
    (swap! bullets #(remove #{b} %))))))
```

The heart of the game. Let's break it down.

Enemy Animation

Listing 8-12. Sinusoidal enemy animation with time-based phase offset creating horizontal wave effect

```
(let [time (/ (js/Date.now) 500)]
  (doseq [e @enemies]
    (set! (.-y e) (+ 50 (* 5 (js/Math.sin (+ time (.-x e))))))))
```

- `(js/Date.now)`: Current time in milliseconds
- `(/ ... 500)`: Scale time down to make the sine wave slower
- `(js/Math.sin ...)`: Sine wave → vertical bobbing motion
- `(+ time (.-x e))`: Each enemy has a phase offset based on its X position, creating a wave pattern

The effect: Enemies bob up and down in a sinuous wave, like the original Space Invaders marching pattern.

Player Movement

Listing 8-13. Player movement with screen edge clamping using max/min for boundary enforcement

```
(when (some #(= % "ArrowLeft") @keys)
  (set! (.-x player-sprite) (max 25 (- (.-x player-sprite) 5))))
```

- `(some #(= % "ArrowLeft") @keys)`: Is “ArrowLeft” in the set?
- `(max 25 ...)`: Clamp minimum X to 25 (left screen edge)
- `(min 775 ...)`: Clamp maximum X to 775 (right screen edge)

Shooting with Rate Limiting

Listing 8-14. Rate-limited shooting mechanic with 300ms cooldown preventing machine-gun fire

```
(when (some #(= % "Space") @keys)
  (when-not (.-shot player-sprite)
```

```
(let [b (create-bullet ...)]
  (.addChild stage b)
  (swap! bullets conj b))
(set! (.-shot player-sprite) true)
(js/setTimeout #(set! (.-shot player-sprite) false) 300)))
```

The pattern:

1. Check if spacebar is pressed.
2. Check if player recently shot (`(.-shot player-sprite)` is falsy).
3. Create and add bullet.
4. Set `(.-shot player-sprite)` to `true`.
5. After 300ms, reset it to `false`.

This prevents machine-gun fire—you can only shoot every 300ms.

Collision Response

Listing 8-15. Nested collision detection loop removing sprites from stage and state atoms on hit

```
(doseq [b @bullets e @enemies]
  (when (rects-collide? b e)
    (.removeChild stage b)
    (.removeChild stage e)
    (swap! bullets #(remove #{b} %))
    (swap! enemies #(remove #{e} %))))
```

Nested loop: For every bullet, check against every enemy.
When a collision happens

1. Remove sprites from the stage (visual).
2. Remove from state atoms (gameplay).

`(remove #{b} %)` creates a new sequence without `b`. We wrap it in `#{b}` to create a set for fast lookup.

Initialization

Listing 8-16. Async initialization with promise chaining for asset loading, DOM mounting, and game loop startup

```
(defn init []
  (-> (.init assets)
      (.then (fn []
               (.addBundle assets "sprites"
                           #js {"player" "assets/player.svg"
                                "enemy" "assets/enemy.svg"})
               (-> (.loadBundle assets "sprites")
                   (.then (fn []
                            (-> (.init app)
                                (.then (fn []
                                         (-> js/document .-body
                                         (.appendChild (.-view app)))
                                         (.start app)
                                         (let [p (create-player)]
                                           (reset! player p)
                                           (.addChild stage p))
                                         (spawn-enemies)
                                         (.addEventListener js/window
                                         "keydown" handle-keydown)
                                         (.addEventListener js/window
                                         "keyup" handle-keyup)
                                         (game-loop))))))))))
```

Promise chain: PixiJS 8 uses promises for async operations. The `->` threading macro makes it readable:

1. **Initialize assets**: `(.init assets)`.
2. **Add bundle**: Define which files map to which asset names.
3. **Load bundle**: Actually download the SVG files.
4. **Initialize app**: Create the WebGL context.

5. **Mount to DOM**: `(.appendChild js/document.body (.-view app))`.
6. **Create player**: And add to stage.
7. **Spawn enemies**.
8. **Add event listeners**.
9. **Start game loop**.

`#js {}`: The `#js` reader literal creates a JavaScript object from a ClojureScript map. PixiJS expects JavaScript objects, not ClojureScript maps.

The result: A functional Space Invaders clone. Move left/right with arrow keys; shoot with spacebar. Enemies bob in a wave pattern. Bullets destroy enemies on contact.

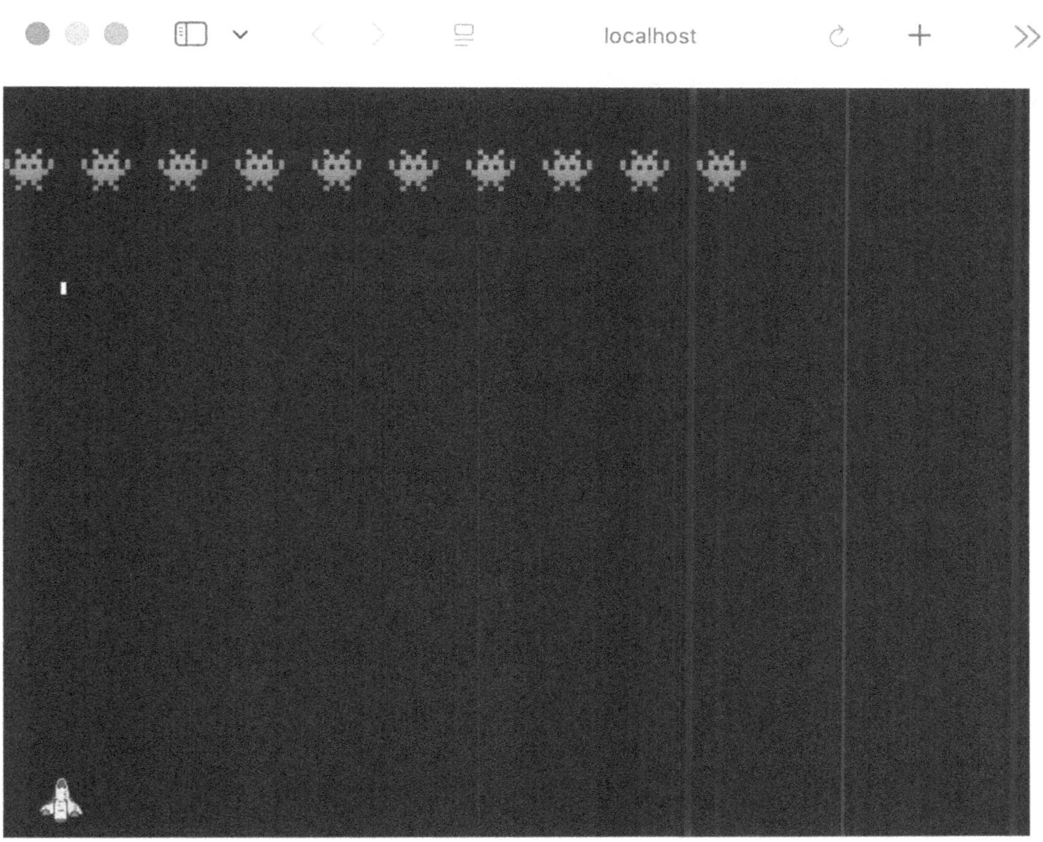

Figure 8-4. *Functional Space Invaders with player movement, shooting mechanics, and collision detection*

Version 2: Refactored and Production Ready (e02.cljs)

Version 1 works, but it has code duplication. Let's refactor.

Listing 8-17. DRY refactored entity creation extracting common sprite initialization pattern

```
(defn create-entity [src x y w h]
  (let [sprite (PIXI/Sprite.from src)]
    (set! (.-x sprite) x)
    (set! (.-y sprite) y)
    (set! (.-width sprite) w)
    (set! (.-height sprite) h)
    sprite))

(defn create-player [] (create-entity "player" 400 550 40 40))
(defn create-enemy [x y] (create-entity "enemy" x y 40 40))
```

DRY principle: "Don't repeat yourself." We extracted the common sprite creation logic into `create-entity`.

Listing 8-18. Refactored collision detection with condensed formatting for production readability

```
(defn collide? [a b]
  (let [ax (.-x a) ay (.-y a) aw (.-width a) ah (.-height a)
        bx (.-x b) by (.-y b) bw (.-width b) bh (.-height b)]
   (and (< ax (+ bx bw)) (> (+ ax aw) bx) (< ay (+ by bh)) (> (+ ay
   ah) by))))
```

Renamed `rects-collide?` to just `collide?` and reformatted for readability. The game loop is also condensed.

Listing 8-19. Condensed production game loop with same functionality in fewer lines

```
(defn game-loop []
  (js/requestAnimationFrame game-loop)
  (let [p @player]
```

```
(doseq [e @enemies]
  (set! (.-y e) (+ 50 (* 5 (js/Math.sin (/ (js/Date.now) 500))))))
(when (some #(= % "ArrowLeft") @keys) (set! (.-x p) (max 25 (- (.-x
p) 5))))
(when (some #(= % "ArrowRight") @keys) (set! (.-x p) (min 775 (+ (.-x
p) 5))))
;; ... Rest of logic ...
))
```

Same functionality, less code. **This is the version you'd ship to production.**

What We've Built: The Architecture of Space Invaders

Let's step back and appreciate what we've accomplished. We've recreated a 1978 arcade legend using 2025 technology, and the patterns we've used are universal.

The Data Flow

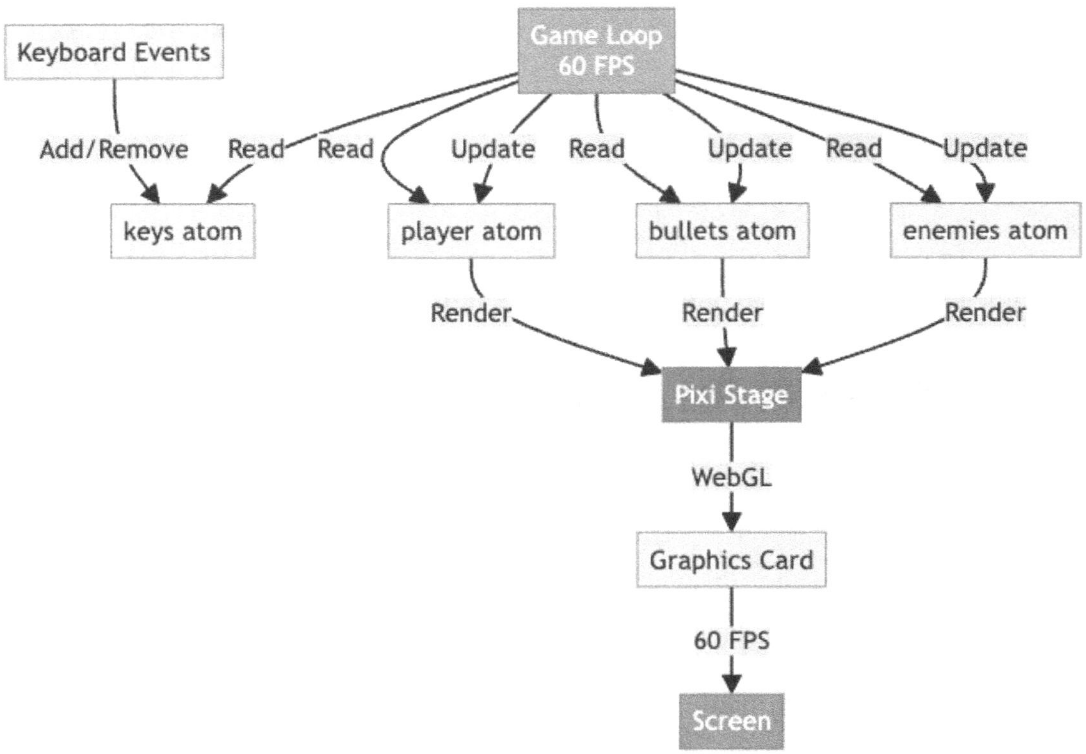

***Figure 8-5.** Data flow diagram showing unidirectional flow from keyboard events through game state to GPU rendering*

The pattern:

1. **State in atoms**: `@keys`, `@player`, `@enemies`, `@bullets`.
2. **Pure logic**: Collision detection, movement calculations.
3. **Side effects isolated**: Rendering (PixiJS), input (DOM events), audio.
4. **Single loop**: One `requestAnimationFrame` coordinates everything.

This separation—**functional core, imperative shell**—is the secret to maintainable code.

Performance Considerations

Why PixiJS? Let's talk numbers:

- **Raw canvas API**: ~1,000 sprites at 60fps (CPU bound, single threaded)
- **PixiJS (WebGL)**: ~10,000 sprites at 60fps (GPU accelerated)
- **Original Space Invaders**: 55 total sprites (CPU: Intel 8080 @ 2MHz)

We're using **hardware acceleration**. PixiJS translates our sprite commands into WebGL draw calls, which run on the GPU. This is the same tech powering AAA web games.

Collision detection cost is shown below.

Listing 8-20. O(bullets × enemies) collision detection complexity demonstrating nested loop performance characteristics

```
(doseq [b @bullets e @enemies]
  (when (rects-collide? b e) ...))
```

This is O(bullets × enemies). With ten enemies and three bullets, that's 30 checks per frame @ 60fps = 1,800 checks/second. Negligible. But if you had 100 enemies and 50 bullets? 5,000 checks/frame = 300,000/second. Still fine for modern CPUs, but you'd want spatial partitioning (quadtrees) for thousands of objects.

The original's ingenious optimization: Tomohiro Nishikado coded the enemy movement in a way that processed one row per frame. With five rows, it took five frames to update all enemies. As enemies died, the CPU had fewer to process, causing the famous speed increase. **A bug became the defining feature.**

Understanding PixiJS: The Rendering Engine

Let's demystify what PixiJS is doing under the hood.

The Display List

```
(def stage (.-stage app))
(.addChild stage sprite)
```

When you call `.addChild`, PixiJS doesn't immediately draw. It adds the sprite to a **display list**—a tree data structure:

```
Stage (Container)
├─ Player (Sprite)
├─ Enemy 1 (Sprite)
├─ Enemy 2 (Sprite)
├─ Bullet 1 (Graphics)
└─ Bullet 2 (Graphics)
```

Every frame (60 times/second), PixiJS

1. **Traverses** the display list
2. **Culls** objects outside the viewport
3. **Batches** sprites with the same texture
4. **Sends** batched draw commands to WebGL
5. **GPU executes** in parallel

This is why we can have thousands of sprites—the GPU is doing the heavy lifting.

Understanding Graphics vs. Sprites

Listing 8-21. Comparison of PixiJS Graphics vector shapes vs. sprite texture-mapped rendering

```
;; Graphics: Programmatically drawn shapes
(let [g (PIXI/Graphics.)]
  (.beginFill g 0xFFFFFF)
  (.drawRect g 0 0 4 10))

;; Sprite: Texture-mapped quad
(let [s (PIXI/Sprite.from "player")])
```

Graphics are vector shapes (rectangles, circles, lines). PixiJS rasterizes them into textures behind the scenes. Use for UI, bullets, simple shapes.

Sprites are bitmap images (PNG, JPG, SVG). The GPU can batch-render hundreds of sprites with the same texture in a single draw call. Use for detailed characters, backgrounds, tile maps.

Our choice: Bullets are graphics (simple white rectangles). Player and enemies are sprites (detailed SVG art). This is optimal.

Figure 8-6. *Sprite rendering detail showing smooth SVG graphics and crisp bullet rectangles*

Above: The actual sprite rendering—notice the smooth SVG graphics and crisp bullet rectangles.

ClojureScript and JavaScript Interop Deep Dive

We've been using JavaScript interop constantly. Let's master it.

Property Access

Listing 8-22. JavaScript property access patterns with dot notation for reading and set! for mutation

```
;; Read property
(.-x sprite)              ;; sprite.x
(.-width sprite)          ;; sprite.width

;; Write property
(set! (.-x sprite) 100)  ;; sprite.x = 100
```

```
;; Nested property
(.-view app)          ;; app.view
(.-canvas app)        ;; app.canvas
(.. app -ticker -FPS) ;; app.ticker.FPS (shorthand)
```

The `.-` prefix means "access this property."

Method Calls

Listing 8-23. JavaScript method invocation syntax with leading dot and threading macro for chaining

```
;; No arguments
(.play audio)         ;; audio.play()

;; With arguments
(.addChild stage sprite)      ;; stage.addChild(sprite)
(.drawRect g 0 0 10 10)       ;; g.drawRect(0, 0, 10, 10)

;; Chained calls (use ->)
(-> js/navigator
    .-mediaDevices
    (.getUserMedia ...))
```

The leading `.` means "call this method."

Creating JavaScript Objects

Listing 8-24. JavaScript object creation comparing shallow reader literal vs. deep runtime conversion

```
;; Reader literal (compile-time)
#js {"width" 800 "height" 600}
#js [1 2 3]

;; Runtime conversion
(clj->js {:width 800 :height 600})
(clj->js [1 2 3])
```

```
;; Difference:
#js {:a {:b 1}}              ;; {"a": {:b 1}}  (shallow)
(clj->js {:a {:b 1}})        ;; {"a": {"b": 1}} (deep)
```

Rule of thumb: Use `#js` for simple objects (config maps). Use `clj->js` for nested structures.

Constructors

Listing 8-25. JavaScript constructor invocation using trailing dot notation for instantiation

```
;; JavaScript: new Application(options)
(PIXI/Application. options)   ;; Note the trailing dot

;; JavaScript: new Graphics()
(PIXI/Graphics.)               ;; No arguments = empty parens
```

The trailing `.` after the class name means "new."

Common Patterns in Game Development

Let's extract reusable patterns from our code.

Pattern 1: The Game Loop

Listing 8-26. Canonical game loop pattern with requestAnimationFrame for browser-synced 60fps rendering

```
(defn game-loop []
  (js/requestAnimationFrame game-loop)  ;; Schedule next frame
  (update-state!)                        ;; Pure logic
  (render!))                             ;; Side effects

(game-loop)  ;; Kick it off once
```

Why `requestAnimationFrame`?

- **Synced with display**: Browser calls your callback right before repaint (16.67ms for 60Hz)
- **Automatic throttling**: Pauses when tab is hidden (saves CPU/battery)
- **Smooth motion**: No screen tearing, perfect frame pacing

Historical Note In the 1980s and 1990s, game loops used busy-waiting (`while(true)`). Modern browsers would freeze the UI. DOS games used vertical blank interrupts (`INT 0x09`). `requestAnimationFrame` is the web's equivalent.

Pattern 2: Double Buffering (Automatic)

We never clear the screen manually. PixiJS does it.

Listing 8-27. Automatic double buffering in PixiJS eliminating manual buffer management

```
;; PixiJS automatically:
;; 1. Clears the previous frame
;; 2. Renders the display list
;; 3. Swaps buffers (WebGL handles this)
```

Why this matters: In old-school graphics programming (DOS, early OpenGL), you had to manually

1. Clear back buffer
2. Draw to back buffer
3. Swap front/back buffers

PixiJS handles all this. You just update the display list.

Pattern 3: Separation of Concerns

Listing 8-28. Separation of concerns pattern keeping game logic in atoms separate from rendering sprites

```
;; GOOD: State in atoms, logic in functions
(def player (atom nil))
(defn move-player! [dx] (swap! player update :x + dx))

;; BAD: State scattered across sprites
(set! (.-gameData sprite) {:health 100})  ;; Don't do this!
```

Why? Atoms give us

- **Time travel debugging**: Snapshot state, replay, undo
- **Testability**: Pure functions are easy to test
- **Serialization**: Save/load game state

PixiJS sprites should be **dumb renderers**. All game logic lives in ClojureScript data structures.

Space Invaders: Exercises

Now it's your turn to extend the game. Each exercise builds on what you've learned.

Exercise 1: Score Display

Difficulty: Easy **Concepts**: PixiJS Text, state management

Add a score counter:

1. Add `:score 0` to your game state.
2. Increment score on enemy kill: `(swap! game-state update :score + 10)`.
3. Create a text object.

Listing 8-29. PixiJS Text object creation for score display with styling configuration

```
clojure (let [score-text (PIXI/Text. "Score: 0" #js {:fill "white"
:fontSize 24})]
   (set! (.-x score-text) 10)
   (set! (.-y score-text) 10)
   (.addChild stage score-text))
```

4. Update text each frame: `(set! (.-text score-text) (str "Score: " @score))`.

Bonus: Add a high score saved to `localStorage`.

Exercise 2: Enemy Waves

Difficulty: Medium **Concepts**: Game state machines, spawning logic

Make enemies respawn:

1. Track wave number: `(def wave (atom 1))`.
2. When all enemies are dead

Listing 8-30. Wave-based enemy spawning with progressive difficulty increase

```
clojure (when (empty? @enemies)
   (swap! wave inc)
   (spawn-enemies (* @wave 10)))  ;; 10, 20, 30 enemies...
```

3. Increase enemy speed each wave.

Historical touch: The original Space Invaders had six waves (formations). After wave 6, it glitched out—a “kill screen.”

Exercise 3: Enemy Shooting

Difficulty: Hard **Concepts**: AI, projectile systems

Let enemies fight back:

1. Create `enemy-bullets` atom.
2. Every 2 seconds, random enemy shoots.

Listing 8-31. Probabilistic enemy AI shooting mechanic using random chance per frame

```
clojure (when (< (rand) 0.05)  ;; 5% chance per frame
  (shoot-enemy-bullet (rand-nth @enemies)))
```

3. Move enemy bullets down (opposite of player bullets).
4. Check collision with player.
5. Add lives system: `(def lives (atom 3))`.

Hint Use `js/setInterval` or track time in the game loop.

Exercise 4: Smooth Movement

Difficulty: Medium **Concepts**: Delta time, frame-independent motion

Our current movement is frame-dependent.

Listing 8-32. Frame-dependent movement showing performance variability across different refresh rates

```
(set! (.-x sprite) (+ (.-x sprite) 5))  ;; 5 pixels per frame
```

On a 60Hz monitor: 5px × 60 = 300px/second. On a 144Hz monitor: 5px × 144 = 720px/second (oops!).

Fix it with delta time.

Listing 8-33. Frame-independent movement using delta time for consistent speed across refresh rates

```
(defn game-loop [timestamp]
  (let [dt (- timestamp @last-time)      ;; Milliseconds since last frame
        speed (* 0.3 dt)]                ;; 0.3 pixels per millisecond
    (reset! last-time timestamp)
    (set! (.-x sprite) (+ (.-x sprite) speed))
    (js/requestAnimationFrame game-loop)))
```

Now movement is frame independent—same speed on any monitor.

Exercise 5: Particle Effects

Difficulty: Hard **Concepts**: Object pools, visual effects

Add explosion particles:

1. When enemy dies, spawn ten particles.

Listing 8-34. Particle explosion effect spawning ten particles with random velocities

```
clojure
    (defn explode! [x y]
      (doseq [_ (range 10)]
        (let [p (create-particle x y (rand-velocity))]
          (swap! particles conj p))))
```

2. Each particle

 - Moves outward (velocity)
 - Fades out (decrease alpha)
 - Dies after 1 second

3. Update and render particles each frame.

Optimization: Use an object pool—reuse particles instead of creating new ones.

Summary: What You've Learned

Before moving to Part 2, let's consolidate.

ClojureScript concepts:

 - ✓ JavaScript interop (`.methodName`, `.-property`, `set!`)
 - ✓ Atoms for mutable state
 - ✓ `swap!` for functional state updates
 - ✓ `doseq` for imperative iteration
 - ✓ `when`, `when-not` for conditional logic

- ✓ `#{}` sets for key tracking
- ✓ `clj->js` and `#js` for JS object creation

PixiJS patterns:

- ✓ Application initialization
- ✓ Sprite creation and positioning
- ✓ Graphics API for shapes
- ✓ Display list management (`.addChild`, `.removeChild`)
- ✓ Asset loading with Promises

Game development fundamentals:

- ✓ The game loop architecture
- ✓ AABB collision detection
- ✓ Input handling (keyboard)
- ✓ State machines (game state)
- ✓ Separation of data and rendering

Reading code like a pro:
When you see

Listing 8-35. Idiomatic atom update with set-based removal for atomic state transition

```
(swap! bullets #(remove #{b} %))
```

You know this means

1. Update the `bullets` atom.
2. Apply a function that removes `b` from the collection.
3. `#{}` creates a set for fast lookup.
4. The new value replaces the old atomically.

When you see

Listing 8-36. Promise chain threading demonstrating async initialization flow

```
(-> (.init app)
    (.then start-game!))
```

You know this is a promise chain:

1. Initialize the app (async).
2. When done, call `start-game!`.

You've become bilingual: Writing ClojureScript that talks to JavaScript libraries fluently.

The Bridge to Tetris

Space Invaders is about **dynamic objects** (sprites moving independently). Tetris is about **grid state** (a static board with falling pieces).

Both are valid game architectures:

- **Space Invaders**: Entity based (each enemy is an object)
- **Tetris**: Grid based (2D array represents the world)

As we transition to Part 2, you'll see how the same ClojureScript patterns apply to completely different game mechanics. The atoms still hold state. The functions still transform data. The side effects are still isolated.

But instead of tracking individual sprites, we'll be modeling a mathematical grid. Instead of collision between rectangles, we'll have collision between shapes and the world.

Ready? Take a breath. Maybe play a round of Space Invaders. Appreciate how clean and maintainable this code is compared to spaghetti-coded JavaScript.

Then, when you're ready, let's build Tetris.

Tetris with PixiJS

Part 2: Tetris

Tetris is more complex than Space Invaders. We need

- Tetromino shapes (I, O, T, L, J, S, Z)
- Rotation
- Grid collision
- Line clearing
- Gravity

We'll build it progressively across five files.

Version 1: A Single Falling Block (`e01.cljs`)

Listing 8-37. Tetris grid constants and single falling block state for minimal implementation

```
(def grid-width 10)
(def grid-height 20)
(def block-size 20)

(defonce state (atom {:x 4 :y 0 :color 0xff0000}))
```

The state: One red block at position (4, 0).

Listing 8-38. Tetris block rendering function drawing filled square at grid coordinates

```
(defn draw-block [container x y color]
  (let [g (pixi/Graphics.)]
    (.beginFill g color)
    (.drawRect g 0 0 block-size block-size)
    (.endFill g)
    (set! (.-x g) (* x block-size))
    (set! (.-y g) (* y block-size))
```

```
    (.addChild container g)))
```

Same pattern as Space Invaders bullets, but for a filled square.

Listing 8-39. Clear-and-redraw rendering strategy removing all children before redrawing from state

```
(defn render [container]
  (.removeChildren container)
  (let [{:keys [x y color]} @state]
    (draw-block container x y color)))
```

Clear and redraw: Every frame, we remove all children and redraw from state. This is simple but inefficient. Later versions optimize this.

Listing 8-40. Tetris keyboard controls with grid boundary clamping using max/min

```
(defn handle-key [container e]
  (case (.-key e)
    "ArrowLeft"  (swap! state update :x #(max 0 (dec %)))
    "ArrowRight" (swap! state update :x #(min (dec grid-width) (inc %)))
    "ArrowDown"  (swap! state update :y inc)
    nil)
  (render container))
```

Keyboard controls: Move left/right/down. `(max 0 (dec %))` clamps to grid bounds.

Listing 8-41. Tetris initialization with setInterval gravity and keyboard event listener

```
(defn start []
  (let [app (pixi/Application.)]
    (-> (.init app (clj->js {:backgroundColor 0x000000
                             :width (* block-size grid-width)
                             :height (* block-size grid-height)}))
        (.then
         (fn []
           (.appendChild js/document.body (.-canvas app))
```

```
        (let [stage (.-stage app)]
          (js/setInterval #(do (swap! state update :y inc)
                               (render stage))
                          500)
          (js/addEventListener "keydown" #(handle-key stage %))
          (render stage)))))))
```

Gravity: `(js/setInterval ... 500)` moves the block down every 500ms.

The result: A red square falls. You can move it left/right.

Version 5: Full Tetris (`e05.cljs`)

Now for the complete game with all features.

Tetromino Data Structures

Listing 8-42. Tetromino shape definitions as 2D vectors with hexadecimal color mapping

```
(def colors
  {:I 0x00ffff :O 0xffff00 :T 0xaa00ff
   :L 0xff8800 :J 0x0000ff :S 0x00ff00 :Z 0xff0000})

(def tetrominoes
  {:I [[1 1 1 1]]
   :O [[1 1] [1 1]]
   :T [[0 1 0] [1 1 1]]
   :L [[1 0] [1 0] [1 1]]
   :J [[0 1] [0 1] [1 1]]
   :S [[0 1 1] [1 1 0]]
   :Z [[1 1 0] [0 1 1]]})
```

Data driven: Each tetromino is just a 2D vector. `1` = filled block, `0` = empty.

The **I** piece: `[[1 1 1 1]]` → a horizontal line. The **T** piece: `[[0 1 0] [1 1 1]]` → a T shape

Historical Note These exact shapes were designed by Alexey Pajitnov to fit perfectly in a 4×4 grid. He experimented with pentominoes (five blocks) first, but they were too complex.

Game State

Listing 8-43. Comprehensive game state atom with 20x10 grid matrix and score tracking

```
(defonce game-state
  (atom {:grid (vec (repeat grid-height (vec (repeat grid-width nil))))
         :current nil
         :next nil
         :score 0
         :high-score 0
         :lines 0
         :level 1}))
```

The grid: A 20×10 matrix of `nil` or piece types (`:I`, `:T`, etc.).

`:current` and `:next`: The active piece and the preview piece.

Listing 8-44. Random tetromino generation with automatic horizontal centering at grid top

```
(defn rand-piece []
  (let [k (rand-nth (keys tetrominoes))
        shape (get tetrominoes k)
        w (count (first shape))]
    {:shape shape :type k :x (int (/ (- grid-width w) 2)) :y 0}))
```

Random piece: Pick a random tetromino; center it horizontally at the top of the grid.

Rotation

Listing 8-45. Matrix 90-degree clockwise rotation using transpose and reverse operations

```
(defn rotate [shape]
  (vec (apply mapv (fn [& row] (vec (reverse row))) shape)))
```

Matrix transposition + reverse: This rotates a 2D matrix 90° clockwise. Example:

Listing 8-46. Rotation transformation example demonstrating T-piece 90-degree turn

```
(rotate [[1 1 1]
         [0 1 0]])
;; => [[0 1]
;;     [1 1]
;;     [1 0]]
```

The math: Transpose flips rows and columns. Reverse flips each row. Together: 90° rotation.

Collision Detection

Listing 8-47. Comprehensive collision detection checking grid boundaries and occupied cells for each tetromino block

```
(defn collides? [{:keys [shape x y]} grid]
  (some identity
        (for [row (range (count shape))
              col (range (count (first shape)))
              :let [bx (+ x col) by (+ y row)]
              :when (= 1 (get-in shape [row col]))]
          (or (< bx 0) (>= bx grid-width) (>= by grid-height)
              (and (>= by 0) (get-in grid [by bx]))))))
```

For every filled block in the shape

1. Calculate world position: `(bx, by)`.
2. Check if it's out of bounds: `(< bx 0)`, etc.
3. Check if it overlaps a locked block: `(get-in grid [by bx])`.

If **any** block fails, the piece collides.

Locking Pieces

Listing 8-48. Functional piece locking using reduce to thread multiple assoc-in operations updating grid state

```
(defn lock-piece! [{:keys [shape x y type]}]
  (swap! game-state update :grid
         (fn [grid]
           (reduce (fn [g [r c]]
                     (assoc-in g [(+ y r) (+ x c)] type))
                   grid
                   (for [r (range (count shape))
                         c (range (count (first shape)))
                         :when (= 1 (get-in shape [r c]))]
                     [r c])))))
```

Functional update: For each filled block in the shape, update the grid to mark it as the piece's type.

`(reduce (fn [g [r c]] (assoc-in g ...))` threads the grid through multiple `assoc-in` operations.

Line Clearing

Listing 8-49. Line clearing algorithm with flash animation, score calculation, level progression, and localStorage high score persistence

```
(defn clear-rows [app on-finish]
  (let [{:keys [grid]} @game-state
        full-rows (->> (map-indexed vector grid)
                       (filter (fn [[_ row]] (every? some? row)))
```

```
                    (map first)
                    set)]
  (if (seq full-rows)
    (do
      ;; Flash animation
      (swap! game-state assoc :flash-rows full-rows)
      (play-sound "clear")
      (render (.-stage app))

      ;; Wait 500ms, then clear
      (js/setTimeout
       (fn []
         (swap! game-state
                (fn [{:keys [grid score lines high-score] :as state}]
                  (let [remaining (remove #(full-rows (first %)) (map-
                  indexed vector grid))
                        cleaned (mapv second remaining)
                        cleared (count full-rows)
                        new-grid (vec (concat (repeat cleared (vec
                        (repeat grid-width nil))) cleaned))
                        new-lines (+ lines cleared)
                        new-score (+ score (* cleared 100))
                        new-high (max high-score new-score)]
                    (when (> new-score high-score)
                      (js/localStorage.setItem "tetris-highscore" (str
                      new-score)))
                    (-> state
                        (assoc :grid new-grid
                               :score new-score
                               :high-score new-high
                               :lines new-lines
                               :level (inc (quot new-lines 10))
                               :flash-rows #{}))))))
       500))
    ;; No rows to clear
    (when on-finish (on-finish)))))
```

The algorithm:

1. Find all full rows: (every? some? row).
2. Flash them white for 500ms visual feedback.
3. Remove full rows from grid.
4. Add empty rows at the top to replace them.
5. Update score: 100 points per row.
6. Level up every ten lines.
7. Save high score to localStorage.

Continuation pattern: The on-finish callback allows the game to continue after clearing.

Movement and Rotation

Listing 8-50. Movement and rotation validation with collision detection triggering piece locking on downward failure

```
(defn try-move! [app dx dy]
  (let [{:keys [current grid]} @game-state
        moved (-> current (update :x + dx) (update :y + dy))]
    (if (collides? moved grid)
      (when (pos? dy)  ;; Trying to move down but can't
        (lock-piece! current)
        (play-sound "drop")
        (clear-rows app #(spawn app)))
      (swap! game-state assoc :current moved))))

(defn try-rotate! []
  (let [{:keys [current grid]} @game-state
        {:keys [type shape]} current]
    (when-not (= type :O)  ;; O piece doesn't rotate
      (let [rotated (update current :shape rotate)]
        (when-not (collides? rotated grid)
          (swap! game-state assoc :current rotated))))))
```

Try-move logic: - If the move succeeds, update `:current` - If it fails **and** we're moving down, lock the piece and spawn a new one - This is how gravity works—when a piece can't fall further, it locks

The result: A complete, playable Tetris with: - Seven tetromino types - Rotation (except O piece) - Line clearing with flash animation - Score, level, high score - Persistent high score in localStorage - Sound effects - "Next piece" preview

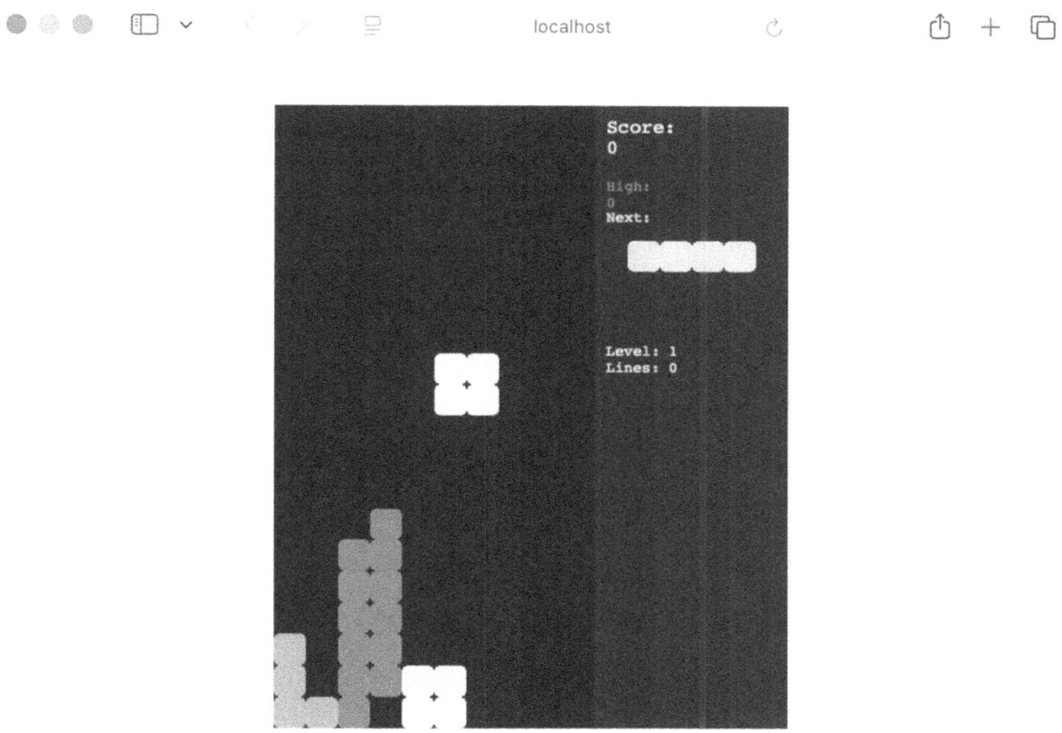

Figure 8-7. *Complete Tetris implementation with next piece preview, level progression, and classic gameplay*

Complete Tetris interface with score, level, next piece preview, and active gameplay

The Tetris Difference: Grid vs. Entity

Let's compare the two architectures we've built.

Space Invaders (Entity Based)

Listing 8-51. Entity-based architecture storing independent game objects in collections

```
(def enemies (atom [sprite1 sprite2 sprite3 ...]))
;; Each enemy is independent
;; Collision: Check every entity against every other
```

Tetris (Grid Based)

Listing 8-52. Grid-based architecture representing world state as fixed-size 2D matrix

```
(def grid (atom [[nil :I nil ...]
                 [nil :I :T ...]
                 ...]))
;; World is a 2D array
;; Collision: Check if grid cells are occupied
```

Both are valid, both have trade-offs.

Table 8-1. *Comparison of Space Invaders and Tetris game mechanic implementations and architectural patterns*

Aspect	Entity Based	Grid Based
Memory	One object per entity	Fixed 2D array
Collision	O(n^2) for all pairs	O(shape size) check cells
Rendering	One sprite per entity	Scan grid, draw filled cells
Best for	Many independent objects	Tile-based worlds, puzzles

Historical context:

- **Space Invaders (1978)**: Arrays of enemy coordinates updated independently
- **Tetris (1984)**: 20×10 matrix (200 bytes!) held the entire game state
- **Modern games**: Often hybrid (grid for terrain, entities for characters)

Comparing the Golden Age

Let's see how these two classics differ.

Table 8-2. *Performance characteristics and optimization techniques for WebGL-based game development*

Aspect	Space Invaders	Tetris
Year	1978	1984
Designer	Tomohiro Nishikado (Japan)	Alexey Pajitnov (USSR)
Original Platform	Arcade (8080 CPU)	Electronika 60
Core Mechanic	Shooting gallery	Spatial puzzle
State Complexity	Arrays of enemies/bullets	2D grid + active piece
Difficulty Curve	Emergent (CPU bug)	Designed (speed increases)
Win Condition	None (endless)	None (endless)
Lose Condition	Aliens reach bottom	Grid fills to top
Time Pressure	Reaction (bullets)	Planning (falling)

The lesson: Both are **state machines**. Every frame, we

1. Read input
2. Update state (pure functions)
3. Render state (side effects)
4. Repeat

This pattern—**functional core, imperative shell**—scales from Tetris to enterprise applications.

Exercises: Level Up Your Arcade

Exercise 1: Sound Effects

Difficulty: Easy **Concepts**: HTML5 Audio API, event handling

Add sound effects.

Listing 8-53. HTML5 Audio API wrapper for dynamic sound effect playback

```
(defn play-sound [name]
  (let [audio (js/Audio. (str "/sounds/" name ".mp3"))]
    (.play audio)))
```

1. Find/create sound files: `shoot.mp3`, `explode.mp3`, `gameover.mp3`.
2. Call `(play-sound "shoot")` when bullets are created.
3. Call `(play-sound "explode")` on collisions.

Historical Note The original Space Invaders had **four sounds**, each triggered by hardware. The iconic "bass drop" as aliens descended was actually the CPU running out of cycles.

Exercise 2: Power-Ups (Tetris)

Difficulty: Medium **Concepts**: Random events, temporary state

Add a bomb power-up:

1. 10% chance to spawn a bomb piece (rainbow colored).
2. When locked, it clears a 3×3 area.
3. Add to state: `{:bombs 2}` (bomb counter).
4. Display bomb count in sidebar.

Hint Modify `rand-piece` to occasionally return `{:type :bomb ...}`.

Exercise 3: Wall-Kick (Tetris)

Difficulty: Hard **Concepts**: Smart collision, edge cases

Implement SRS (super rotation system) wall-kicks:

1. When rotation fails, try offsetting by `(-1, 0)`, `(1, 0)`, `(0, -1)`.
2. If any offset allows rotation, use it.
3. This lets pieces rotate near walls (modern Tetris feature).

Reference: The Tetris guideline specifies exact kick tables. Look up "SRS kick table."

Exercise 4: Multiplayer Tetris

Difficulty: Expert **Concepts**: WebSockets, state synchronization

Add two-player mode:

1. Use WebSockets (or Socket. IO) to sync game state.
2. Each player has their own grid.
3. Clearing lines sends "garbage" rows to opponent.
4. First to top out loses.

This is how NES Tetris and Tetris 99 work.

Exercise 5: Shields (Space Invaders)

Difficulty: Medium **Concepts**: Destructible terrain, pixel perfect collision

Add destructible shields:

1. Create four shield sprites (green blocks) between player and enemies.
2. Store shield "health" (100 HP).
3. Bullets reduce health by 25.
4. Change sprite tint based on health: `100% = green`, `0% = invisible`.
5. Bullets destroy themselves on shield hit.

Historical touch: Original Space Invaders shields eroded pixel by pixel. You can simulate this with transparency.

Wrapping Up: The Legacy of Simple Rules

You've built two of the most influential games ever created. Not in assembly, not in C, but in **ClojureScript**—with pure functions, immutable data, and atoms.

Space Invaders taught the world that **simple mechanics + escalating difficulty = addictive gameplay**. Tetris proved that **geometric elegance + gravity = timeless design**.

Both games are **data transformations**: - Space Invaders: `(pos, velocity, enemies) -> (new-pos, new-velocity, new-enemies)` - Tetris: `(grid, active-piece) -> (new-grid, next-piece)`

This is functional programming. This is the pattern that scales from 8-bit arcades to distributed systems.

The eighth floor is complete. The quarters are spent. The high scores are immortalized in localStorage.

Before you leave, play one more round. Feel the rhythm of the falling blocks. Hear the rhythm of the marching aliens. These aren't just games; they're mathematical poetry made interactive.

Welcome to the game corner. You've earned your stay.

> *"The best games are not won. They are survived, scored, and replayed."*

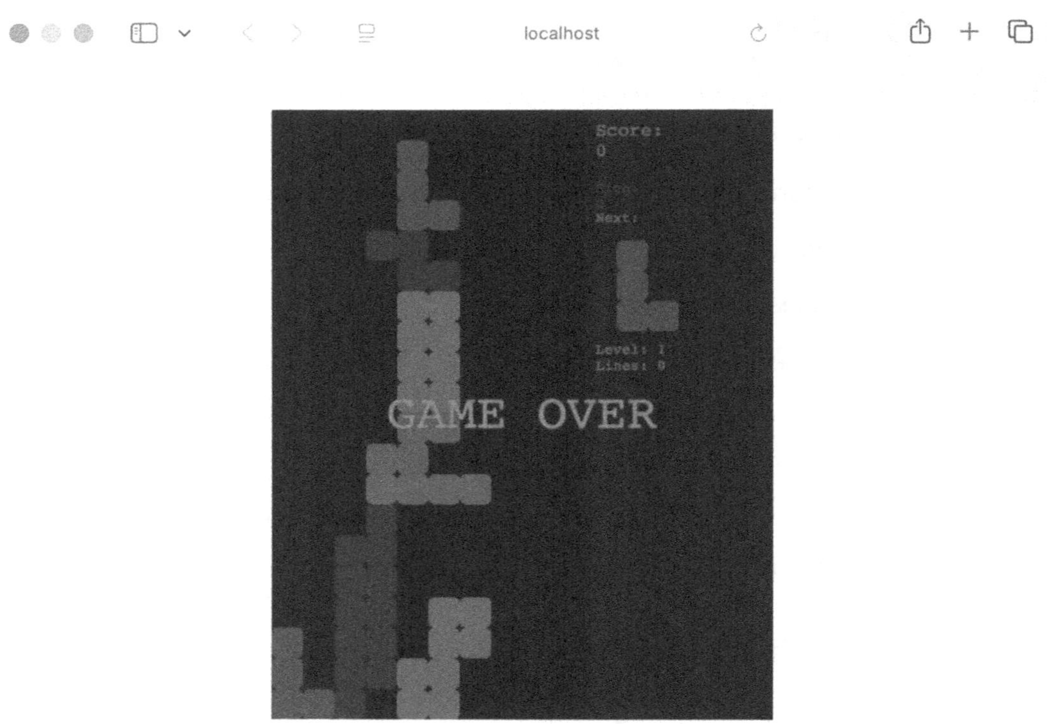

Figure 8-8. *Tetris game over state reached when the matrix fills to the top, cementing the final high score in local storage*

CHAPTER 9

Neural Networks: From Perceptrons to Deep Learning

> "The question is not whether machines can think, but whether machines can learn to think."
>
> —Inspired by Alan Turing

The Concept

You've taken the elevator to the ninth floor. The doors open to what looks like a neuroscience laboratory crossed with a vintage computing museum. On one wall, a 1958 photograph shows Frank Rosenblatt standing proudly beside the Mark I Perceptron—a room-sized machine with 400 photocells and adjustable weights. On another, a timeline traces the "AI winter" of the 1970s, when funding dried up and dreams were deferred. And on the third wall, a modern GPU cluster hums quietly, running the very algorithms that were dismissed as impossible decades ago.

Welcome to the ninth floor, where we explore artificial neural networks, the mathematical structures inspired by biological brains. We're not just building networks, we're reliving the entire history of connectionist AI, from the optimistic 1950s through the desperate 1980s to the triumphant 2010s.

This chapter is different from what came before. In Chapter 1, you learned game loops and state machines (Pong). In Chapter 2, you mastered canvas manipulation and parametric animation. In Chapter 7, you processed video streams with pixel-level

N. Modrzyk, *The ClojureScript Playbook*, https://doi.org/10.1007/979-8-8688-2879-9_9

transformations. Now, we're tackling something that seemed like science fiction just decades ago: teaching machines to learn from data.

The journey maps directly onto AI history.

Table 9-1. *Historical timeline mapping tutorial exercises to AI milestones from 1958 perceptron through 2020s deep learning*

Exercise	Year	Milestone	What It Taught Us
e01	1958	Rosenblatt's Perceptron	Linear separation works... Sometimes
e02	1969	Minsky and Papert's Critique	The XOR problem is unsolvable (for single layers)
e03	1958–1969	Perceptron Convergence	Even simple learning needs theory
e04	1986	Backpropagation Revival	Hidden layers change everything
e05	1986	Network Visualization	Understanding what networks "see"
e06	1990s	Interactive Training	Data matters as much as architecture
e07	1990s	Decision Boundaries	Visualizing learned representations
e08	2010s	Activation Functions	ReLU > Sigmoid (sometimes)
e09	2010s	Hyperparameter Tuning	Learning rate is everything
e10	2020s	Full Playground	Putting it all together

By the end of this chapter, you'll have built a complete neural network from scratch—no TensorFlow, no PyTorch—just ClojureScript, mathematics, and a deep understanding of what's actually happening when a network "learns."

The Architecture: How Neural Networks Think

Before we dive into code, let's understand what we're building. A neural network is fundamentally a **mathematical function approximator**. Given inputs, it produces outputs by passing data through layers of weighted connections.

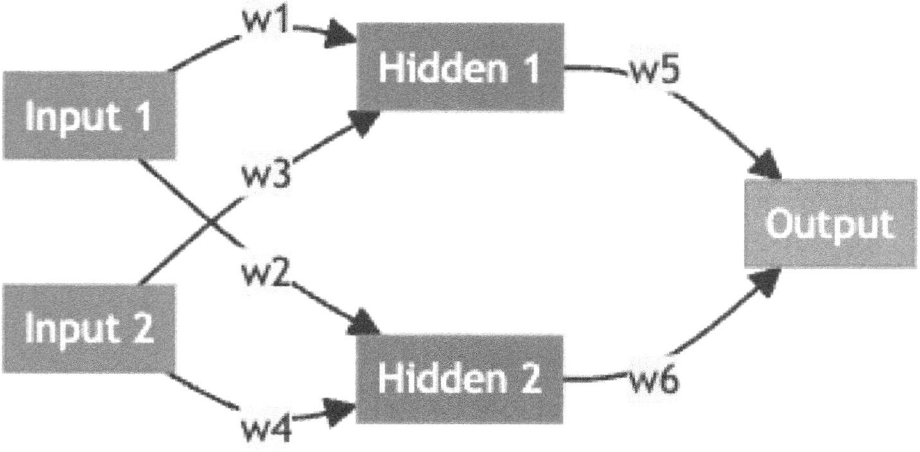

***Figure 9-1.** Basic neural network architecture diagram showing inputs, hidden layer, and output with weighted connections*

The data flow is deceptively simple:

1. **Forward pass**: Data enters through inputs, gets multiplied by weights, is transformed by activation functions, and emerges as predictions.
2. **Error calculation**: Compare predictions to targets.
3. **Backward pass**: Calculate how each weight contributed to the error.
4. **Weight update**: Adjust weights to reduce error.
5. **Repeat**: Until the network learns the pattern.

This is **gradient descent**—climbing down the error surface to find optimal weights. It's the same mathematical principle that powers everything from image recognition to language models.

The Historical Context

Let's place this in perspective.

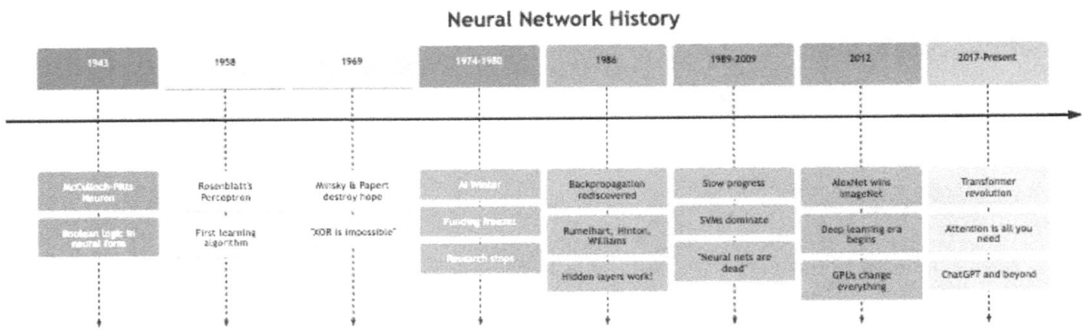

Figure 9-2. *Neural network history timeline from 1943 McCulloch-Pitts neuron through AI winters to 2017 transformer revolution*

We're building the 1958–1986 arc tonight. The foundation that makes modern AI possible.

Part I: The Perceptron Era (1958–1969)

Exercise 1: Rosenblatt's Dream

In 1958, Frank Rosenblatt unveiled the Mark I Perceptron at Cornell University. *The New York Times* proclaimed it would "be able to walk, talk, see, write, reproduce itself and be conscious of its existence."

That was optimistic. But the core idea was brilliant: a single artificial neuron that could learn to classify patterns.

The Perceptron Model

A perceptron is the simplest possible neural network: one neuron, multiple inputs, one output. It computes a weighted sum of its inputs, adds a bias term, and applies a threshold function:

```
f(x₁, x₂) = step(w₁·x₁ + w₂·x₂ + b)

where step(z) = {
  1 if z ≥ 0
  0 if z < 0
}
```

Geometrically, this defines a **line** in 2D space (or a hyperplane in higher dimensions). Points on one side are classified as 1, points on the other side as 0. The weights and bias determine the line's orientation and position.

The Learning Algorithm

The perceptron learning rule is beautifully simple and was revolutionary in 1958.

Listing 9-1. Rosenblatt's 1958 perceptron learning algorithm with step activation, error-driven weight updates, and convergence detection

```
(defn perceptron-predict [weights inputs]
  "Compute weighted sum and apply step function"
  (let [weighted-sum (reduce + (map * weights inputs))]
    (if (>= weighted-sum 0) 1 0)))

(defn perceptron-update [weights inputs target learning-rate]
  "Update weights based on error"
  (let [prediction (perceptron-predict weights inputs)
        error (- target prediction)]
    (if (zero? error)
      weights  ; Correct prediction, no update needed
      (mapv (fn [w input]
              (+ w (* learning-rate error input)))
            weights
            inputs))))

(defn train-perceptron [training-data learning-rate max-epochs]
  "Train until convergence or max epochs reached"
```

```
(loop [weights (vec (repeatedly (count (first (:input (first
training-data))))
                                #(- (rand 2) 1)))  ; Random init [-1, 1]
       epoch 0]
  (if (>= epoch max-epochs)
    weights
    (let [new-weights (reduce (fn [w example]
                                (perceptron-update w
                                                   (:input example)
                                                   (:target example)
                                                   learning-rate))
                              weights
                              training-data)
          converged? (= weights new-weights)]
      (if converged?
        (do (println "Converged at epoch" epoch)
            new-weights)
        (recur new-weights (inc epoch)))))))
```

The genius: For each misclassified example

- If we predicted 0 but target was 1 (error = +1), increase weights for active inputs.
- If we predicted 1 but target was 0 (error = -1), decrease weights for active inputs.
- If we predicted correctly (error = 0), don't change anything.

This gradually nudges the decision boundary toward the correct position.

What You'll Build

The exercise trains a perceptron on the AND gate.

Listing 9-2. AND gate truth table dataset with bias term for perceptron training

```
AND Truth Table:
0 AND 0 = 0
0 AND 1 = 0
```

```
1 AND 0 = 0
1 AND 1 = 1
(def and-data
  [{:input [0 0 1] :target 0}  ; Note: third input is bias (always 1)
   {:input [0 1 1] :target 0}
   {:input [1 0 1] :target 0}
   {:input [1 1 1] :target 1}])
```

The UI showing the AND gate training in progress. Weights start random and converge.

The visualization includes

- **Weight display**: Shows current weight values
- **Truth table**: All four possible inputs with predictions
- **Epoch counter**: How many training iterations
- **Step-by-step mode**: Watch each weight update
- **Decision boundary**: Visual representation of the learned line

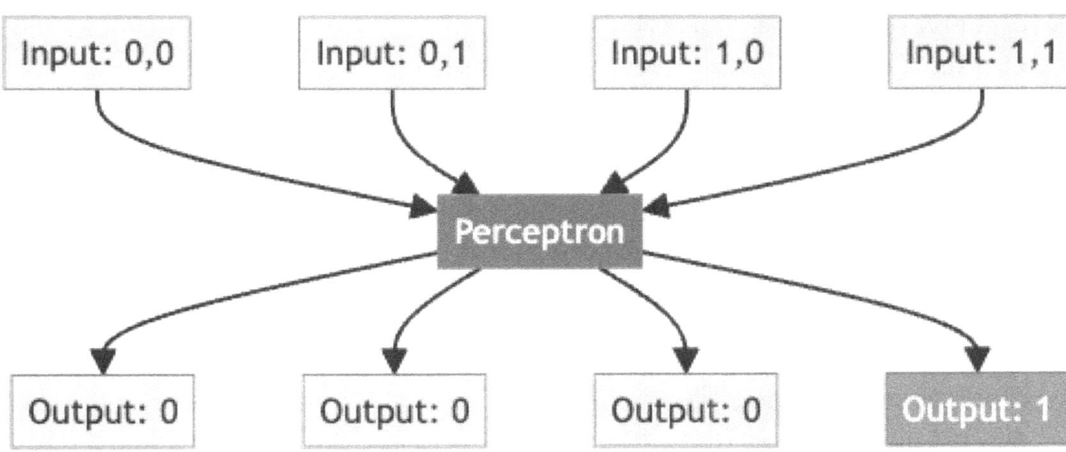

Figure 9-3. *Perceptron logic flow diagram showing all four input combinations mapping to AND gate outputs*

The Complete Code Structure

Here's the full `e01.cljs` structure.

Listing 9-3. Complete perceptron namespace structure with historical context and linearly separable problem documentation

```
(ns my-neural-network.e01
  "THE PERCEPTRON (1958)

   Frank Rosenblatt's original learning algorithm.
   Can solve linearly separable problems like AND, OR, NAND.
   Cannot solve XOR (we'll see why in e02)."
  (:require [reagent.core :as r]
            [reagent.dom.client :as rdc]))

;; Data
(def and-data
  [{:input [0 0 1] :target 0}
   {:input [0 1 1] :target 0}
   {:input [1 0 1] :target 0}
   {:input [1 1 1] :target 1}])

;; Perceptron logic
(defn activate [weights inputs]
  (let [sum (reduce + (map * weights inputs))]
    (if (>= sum 0) 1 0)))

(defn train [weights inputs target lr]
  (let [prediction (activate weights inputs)
        error (- target prediction)]
    (mapv #(+ %1 (* lr error %2)) weights inputs)))

;; UI Component
(defn perceptron-trainer []
  (let [weights (r/atom [0.5 -0.3 0.2])  ; w1, w2, bias
        epoch (r/atom 0)
        training? (r/atom false)]
    (fn []
      [:div {:style {:padding "20px" :font-family "monospace"}}
       [:h2 "The Perceptron (1958)"]
       [:p "Training the AND gate..."]
```

```
;; Weights display
[:div {:style {:margin "20px 0" :padding "15px"
               :background "#f5f5f5" :border-radius "8px"}}
 [:h3 "Current Weights:"]
 [:div "w₁ = " (.toFixed (nth @weights 0) 3)]
 [:div "w₂ = " (.toFixed (nth @weights 1) 3)]
 [:div "bias = " (.toFixed (nth @weights 2) 3)]]

;; Truth table with predictions
[:table {:style {:margin "20px 0" :border-collapse "collapse"}}
 [:thead
  [:tr
   [:th "x₁"] [:th "x₂"] [:th "Target"] [:th "Prediction"]
   [:th "✓"]]]
 [:tbody
  (for [example and-data]
    (let [pred (activate @weights (:input example))
          target (:target example)
          correct? (= pred target)]
      ^{:key (str (:input example))}
      [:tr {:style {:background (if correct? "#c8e6c9" "#ffcdd2")}}
       [:td (first (:input example))]
       [:td (second (:input example))]
       [:td target]
       [:td pred]
       [:td (if correct? "✓" "X")]]))]]

;; Training controls
[:button {:on-click #(do (doseq [ex and-data]
                           (swap! weights train (:input ex) (:target
                           ex) 0.1))
                         (swap! epoch inc))}
 "Train One Epoch"]

[:div "Epochs: " @epoch]])))
```

```
(defn ^:export init []
  (rdc/render root [perceptron-trainer]
            (.getElementById js/document "app")))
```

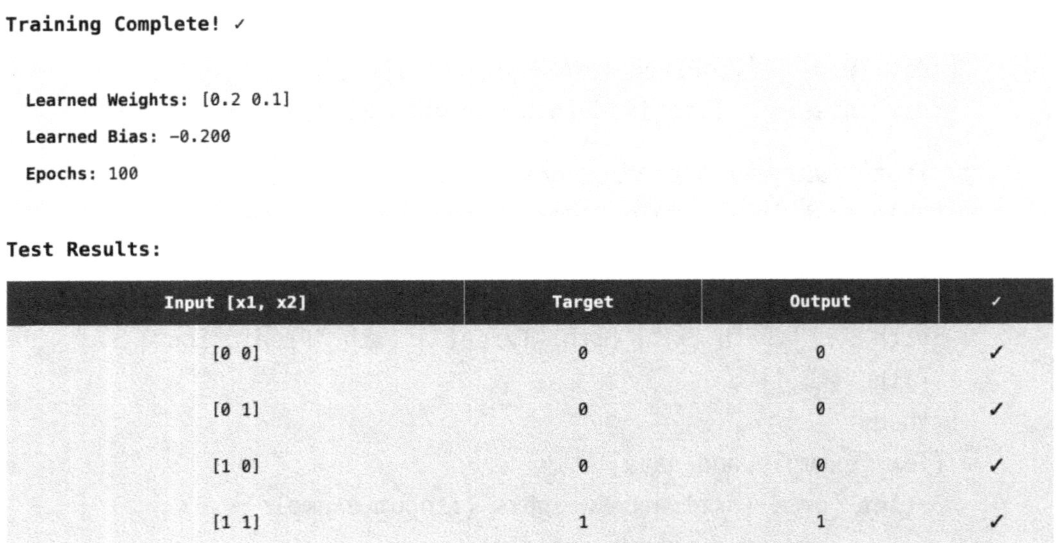

Figure 9-4. *Basic perceptron successfully learning the AND logic gate with 100% correct predictions. After convergence, all predictions are correct against the truth table*

The Perceptron Convergence Theorem

Historical Note Rosenblatt didn't just build a machine that learned—he *proved* it would always succeed (under certain conditions).

Theorem: If the training data is linearly separable, the perceptron learning algorithm will converge to a solution in finite time.

What this means:

- For problems like AND, OR, NAND → guaranteed to learn.
- For problems like XOR (exclusive OR) → will never converge (we'll see this in e02).
- The number of iterations is bounded by the data's "margin."

This was a **mathematical guarantee of learning**—the first of its kind. It sparked massive optimism in the AI community. Funding poured in. Researchers believed general intelligence was just around the corner.

They were wrong. But the foundation was sound.

Exercise 2: The Perceptron Convergence Theorem

Before we move on to multi-layer networks, `e03.cljs` explores the *positive* story: what perceptrons **can** learn.

The Theorem

The **Perceptron Convergence Theorem** (Rosenblatt, 1962) states the following:

> *If a linearly separable pattern exists and inputs are bounded, the perceptron learning algorithm will find a solution in finite time.*

What this means practically:

- For AND, OR, NAND → guaranteed convergence
- For XOR → impossible (not linearly separable)
- The number of updates is bounded by: R2/γ2 where R = max input magnitude, γ = margin

What You'll Build

`e03.cljs` is an interactive lab for exploring convergence behavior.

Listing 9-4. Interactive perceptron convergence lab with gate selection, learning rate control, live truth table, and SVG weight evolution visualization proving Rosenblatt's 1962 convergence theorem

```
(def logic-gates
  {:and  [{:input [0 0 1] :target 0}
          {:input [0 1 1] :target 0}
          {:input [1 0 1] :target 0}
          {:input [1 1 1] :target 1}]
```

```
   :or   [{:input [0 0 1] :target 0}
          {:input [0 1 1] :target 1}
          {:input [1 0 1] :target 1}
          {:input [1 1 1] :target 1}]

   :nand [{:input [0 0 1] :target 1}
          {:input [0 1 1] :target 1}
          {:input [1 0 1] :target 1}
          {:input [1 1 1] :target 0}]

   :nor  [{:input [0 0 1] :target 1}
          {:input [0 1 1] :target 0}
          {:input [1 0 1] :target 0}
          {:input [1 1 1] :target 0}]})

(defn convergence-lab []
  (let [selected-gate (r/atom :and)
        learning-rate (r/atom 0.1)
        weights (r/atom [(rand-between -1 1) (rand-between -1 1) (rand-
        between -1 1)])
        epoch-count (r/atom 0)
        converged? (r/atom false)
        history (r/atom [])]  ; Track weight evolution

    (fn []
      (let [data (get logic-gates @selected-gate)
            all-correct? (every? #(= (activate @weights (:input %))
                                     (:target %))
                                 data)]
        (reset! converged? all-correct?)

        [:div {:style {:font-family "monospace" :padding "20px"}}
         [:h2 "Perceptron Convergence Lab"]
         [:p "Explore what perceptrons CAN learn (linearly separable
         problems)"]

         ;; Gate selector
         [:div {:style {:margin "20px 0"}}
          [:h3 "Select Logic Gate:"]
```

```
 (for [gate [:and :or :nand :nor]]
   ^{:key gate}
   [:button {:style {:padding "10px 20px"
                     :margin "5px"
                     :background (if (= @selected-gate gate)
                     "#4caf50" "#e0e0e0")
                     :border "none"
                     :border-radius "5px"}
             :on-click #(do (reset! selected-gate gate)
                            (reset! epoch-count 0)
                            (reset! history []))}
    (str/upper-case (name gate))])]

;; Learning rate slider
[:div
 [:label "Learning Rate: " (.toFixed @learning-rate 2)]
 [:input {:type "range" :min 0.01 :max 1.0 :step 0.01
          :value @learning-rate
          :on-change #(reset! learning-rate (js/parseFloat (-> %
          .-target .-value)))}]]

;; Current weights display
[:div {:style {:background "#f5f5f5" :padding "15px" :margin
"20px 0"}}
 [:h3 "Current Weights:"]
 [:div "w₁ = " [:span {:style {:color "#1976d2"}} (.toFixed (nth
 @weights 0) 4)]]
 [:div "w₂ = " [:span {:style {:color "#1976d2"}} (.toFixed (nth
 @weights 1) 4)]]
 [:div "bias = " [:span {:style {:color "#1976d2"}} (.toFixed
 (nth @weights 2) 4)]]]

;; Convergence status
(if @converged?
  [:div {:style {:background "#c8e6c9" :padding "20px" :border-
  left "4px solid #4caf50"}}
   [:h3 "✓ CONVERGED!"]
```

```
    [:p "Found solution in " @epoch-count " epochs."]]
   [:div {:style {:background "#fff3e0" :padding "20px" :border-
   left "4px solid #ff9800"}}
    [:h3 "Training..."]
    [:p "Epochs: " @epoch-count]])

;; Truth table with live predictions
[:table {:style {:margin "20px 0" :border-collapse "collapse"}}
 [:thead
  [:tr
   [:th {:style {:padding "10px" :border "1px solid #ddd"}} "x₁"]
   [:th {:style {:padding "10px" :border "1px solid #ddd"}} "x₂"]
   [:th {:style {:padding "10px" :border "1px solid #ddd"}}
   "Target"]
   [:th {:style {:padding "10px" :border "1px solid #ddd"}}
   "Prediction"]
   [:th {:style {:padding "10px" :border "1px solid
   #ddd"}} "✓"]]]
 [:tbody
  (for [ex data]
    (let [pred (activate @weights (:input ex))
          target (:target ex)
          correct? (= pred target)]
      ^{:key (str (:input ex))}
      [:tr {:style {:background (if correct? "#c8e6c9"
      "#ffcdd2")}}
       [:td {:style {:padding "10px" :border "1px solid #ddd"}}
       (nth (:input ex) 0)]
       [:td {:style {:padding "10px" :border "1px solid #ddd"}}
       (nth (:input ex) 1)]
       [:td {:style {:padding "10px" :border "1px solid
       #ddd"}} target]
       [:td {:style {:padding "10px" :border "1px solid
       #ddd"}} pred]
       [:td {:style {:padding "10px" :border "1px solid #ddd"}}
        (if correct? "✓" "X")]]))]]]
```

```
;; Training controls
[:div {:style {:margin "20px 0"}}
 [:button {:style {:padding "15px 30px" :font-size "16px"}
           :on-click (fn []
                       (when-not @converged?
                         (doseq [ex data]
                           (let [old-weights @weights]
                             (swap! weights train-perceptron
                             (:input ex) (:target ex)
                             @learning-rate)
                             (swap! history conj @weights)))
                         (swap! epoch-count inc))))}
  "Train One Epoch"]

 [:button {:style {:padding "15px 30px" :margin-left "10px"}
           :on-click #(do (reset! weights [(rand-between -1 1)
                                            (rand-between -1 1)
                                            (rand-between -1 1)])
                         (reset! epoch-count 0)
                         (reset! history []))}
  "Reset Weights"]]

;; Weight evolution visualization
(when (> (count @history) 1)
  [:div {:style {:margin "20px 0"}}
   [:h3 "Weight Evolution:"]
   [:svg {:width 600 :height 200 :style {:border "1px
   solid #ddd"}}
    ;; w1 evolution
    (for [i (range (dec (count @history)))]
      (let [scale-y (fn [w] (- 100 (* 50 w)))  ; Scale to
      SVG coords
            x1 (* 3 i)
            x2 (* 3 (inc i))
            y1 (scale-y (nth (nth @history i) 0))
            y2 (scale-y (nth (nth @history (inc i)) 0))]
        ^{:key (str "w1-" i)}
```

```
      [:line {:x1 x1 :y1 y1 :x2 x2 :y2 y2 :stroke "#2196f3"
      :stroke-width 2}]))
  ;; w2 evolution
  (for [i (range (dec (count @history)))]
    (let [scale-y (fn [w] (- 100 (* 50 w)))
          x1 (* 3 i)
          x2 (* 3 (inc i))
          y1 (scale-y (nth (nth @history i) 1))
          y2 (scale-y (nth (nth @history (inc i)) 1))]
      ^{:key (str "w2-" i)}
      [:line {:x1 x1 :y1 y1 :x2 x2 :y2 y2 :stroke "#4caf50"
      :stroke-width 2}]))
  ;; Legend
  [:text {:x 10 :y 20 :fill "#2196f3"} "w₁"]
  [:text {:x 10 :y 40 :fill "#4caf50"} "w₂"]]])])))))
```

AND gate training: converged in seven epochs. All predictions correct.

Select Gate: and or nand

Train 10 Epochs

Epochs: 10

Weights: [0.20, 0.10]

Bias: -0.20

Truth Table

Input 1	Input 2	Target	Output	✓
0	0	0	0	✓
0	1	0	0	✓
1	0	0	0	✓
1	1	1	1	✓

Figure 9-5. *Logic gate convergence showing successful perceptron training on linearly separable data AND gate training: converged in seven epochs. All predictions correct*

Key Observations

Experiment 1: Different Initial Weights

Reset the weights multiple times (random initialization). Notice: - Every random start eventually converges - BUT: different final weights! (Multiple solutions exist) - Some converge faster than others (depends on initial position)

Experiment 2: Learning Rate Effects

- **LR = 0.01**: Very slow, but smooth convergence (50+ epochs)
- **LR = 0.1**: Good balance (5–15 epochs)
- **LR = 0.5**: Fast but overshoots, might oscillate before settling
- **LR = 1.0**: Can work but very aggressive

Experiment 3: Different Gates

- **AND**: Usually converges quickly (3–10 epochs)
- **OR**: Also fast convergence
- **NAND**: Slightly harder (5–15 epochs) because it's "inverted"
- **NOR**: Hardest of the four (can take 20+ epochs)

Why This Matters

This exercise teaches optimism before disappointment: - Perceptrons DO work for many problems - The convergence guarantee is real - But the limitation (linear separability) is fundamental

It sets up the XOR crash and the need for hidden layers perfectly.

Part II: The Backpropagation Revolution (1986)

> "We describe a new learning procedure, back-propagation, for networks of neurone-like units."
>
> —Rumelhart, Hinton, and Williams, *Nature*, 1986

Exercise 3: The XOR Problem (Minsky and Papert's Hammer)

In 1969, Marvin Minsky and Seymour Papert published *Perceptrons*, a book that would devastate the field for nearly two decades.

They proved, mathematically and irrefutably, that a single-layer perceptron cannot learn XOR.

Understanding XOR

```
XOR Truth Table:
0 ⊕ 0 = 0    (both same → 0)
0 ⊕ 1 = 1    (different → 1)
1 ⊕ 0 = 1    (different → 1)
1 ⊕ 1 = 0    (both same → 0)
```

XOR (exclusive OR) outputs 1 only when inputs differ. It's a simple logical operation, ubiquitous in computing. Surely a learning machine should handle it?

Why XOR Is Impossible for Perceptrons

Visualize the four XOR points in 2D space:

```
     x₂
      |
 1    |  ● (1,1) → 0
      |
.5    |
      |
 0    |  ● (0,0) → 0
      |___________________ x₁
         0    .5    1

     ● (0,1) → 1
     ● (1,0) → 1
```

Look at which points are labeled 1 vs. 0:

- **(0,0)** → 0 (red)
- **(0,1)** → 1 (green)
- **(1,0)** → 1 (green)
- **(1,1)** → 0 (red)

The green points are diagonally opposite! **No single straight line can separate them from the red points.** This is what "not linearly separable" means.

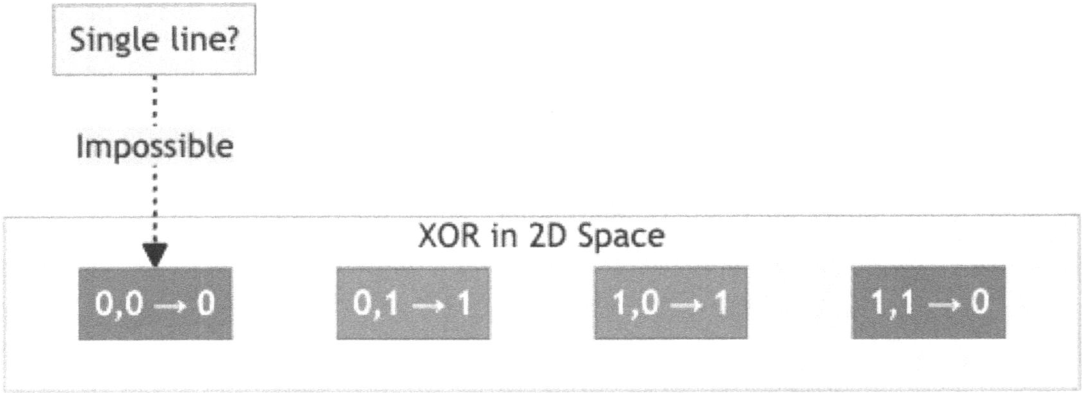

Figure 9-6. *XOR linear separability diagram demonstrating why no single line can separate diagonally opposite points*

A perceptron can only learn patterns separable by a straight line (or hyperplane). XOR requires a circle, two lines, or some non-linear boundary.

What You'll Build

`e02.cljs` implements a perceptron that attempts to learn XOR. You'll watch it fail. Gloriously, predictably, mathematically.

Listing 9-5. XOR impossibility demonstration showing perpetual oscillation proving Minsky and Papert's 1969 critique

```
(def xor-data
  [{:input [0 0 1] :target 0}
   {:input [0 1 1] :target 1}
   {:input [1 0 1] :target 1}
   {:input [1 1 1] :target 0}])

(defn xor-trainer []
  (let [weights (r/atom [(- (rand 2) 1) (- (rand 2) 1) (- (rand 2) 1)])
        epoch (r/atom 0)
        losses (r/atom [])]
    (fn []
      [:div
       [:h2 "The XOR Problem (1969)"]
       [:p "Watch the perceptron try—and fail—to converge..."]
```

```
;; Truth table showing oscillating predictions
[:table
 [:thead
  [:tr [:th "x₁"] [:th "x₂"] [:th "Target"] [:th "Predicted"] [:th
  "Error"]]]
 [:tbody
  (for [ex xor-data]
    (let [pred (activate @weights (:input ex))
          target (:target ex)
          error (Math/abs (- target pred))]
      [:tr {:style {:background (if (> error 0) "#ffcdd2" "#c8e6c9")}}
       [:td (nth (:input ex) 0)]
       [:td (nth (:input ex) 1)]
       [:td target]
       [:td pred]
       [:td error]]))]]

;; Loss chart showing no convergence
[:div "Loss over time: "
 (if (> (count @losses) 0)
   [:svg {:width 400 :height 100}
    (for [i (range (count @losses))]
      [:circle {:cx (* i 2) :cy (- 100 (* 50 (nth @losses i)))
                :r 2 :fill "red"}])]
   "(training not started)")]

[:button {:on-click #(do
                       (doseq [ex xor-data]
                         (swap! weights train-step (:input ex)
                         (:target ex) 0.1))
                       (swap! epoch inc)
                       (swap! losses conj (calculate-total-error
                       @weights xor-data)))}
 "Train Epoch " @epoch]

[:p {:style {:color "#d32f2f" :font-weight "bold"}}
 "This will never converge. XOR is not linearly separable."]]))
```

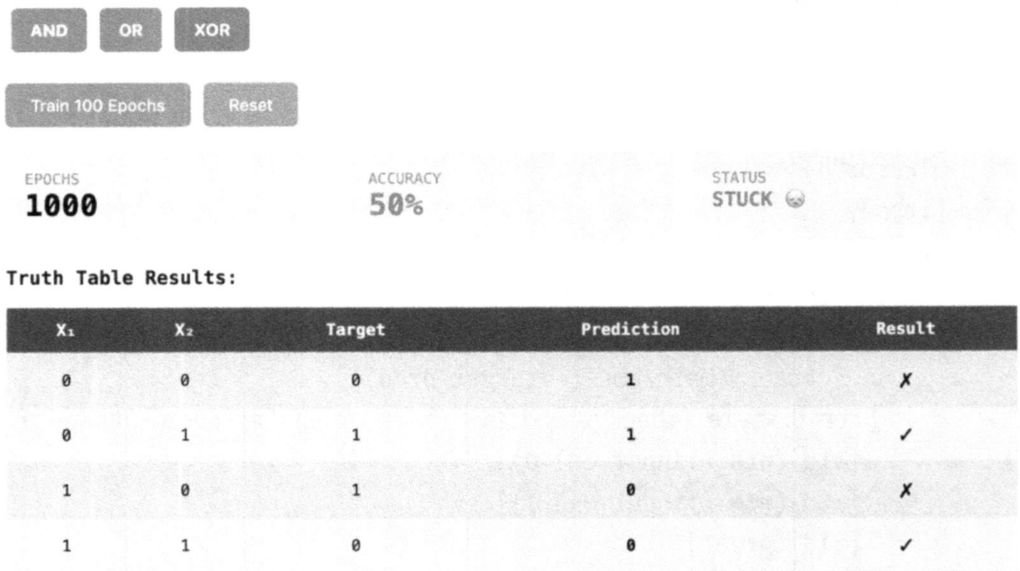

X1	X2	Target	Prediction	Result
0	0	0	1	✗
0	1	1	1	✓
1	0	1	0	✗
1	1	0	0	✓

***Figure 9-7.** XOR training failure after 1000 epochs showing perpetual oscillation without convergence. After 1000 epochs: still oscillating. The weights keep changing but never settle*

The perceptron might correctly classify three points, but fixing the fourth breaks one of the others. It's an eternal dance, mathematically proven to never end.

The Historical Impact

Minsky and Papert's book did more than prove a limitation—it killed funding. Their argument is as follows:

1. Perceptrons can't solve XOR.
2. XOR is a trivial problem.
3. Therefore, perceptrons are useless.
4. (Implied) Multi-layer networks won't help.

Point #4 was wrong, but it took 17 years to prove counter-examples. The "AI winter" began. University departments closed. Researchers switched fields. Companies abandoned neural network projects.

Why it was devastating: Not just the math, but the *political* weight of Minsky (MIT legend, Turing Award winner). When he said neural networks were dead, people listened.

Historical footnote: Minsky later expressed regret, saying they only analyzed single-layer networks and didn't mean to kill multi-layer research. But the damage was done.

Exercise 4: Breaking the XOR Barrier

The solution to XOR isn't more perceptrons in a row—it's perceptrons in **layers**. A multi-layer perceptron (MLP) with a hidden layer can learn any pattern.

The Architecture for XOR

Here's the minimal network that solves XOR.

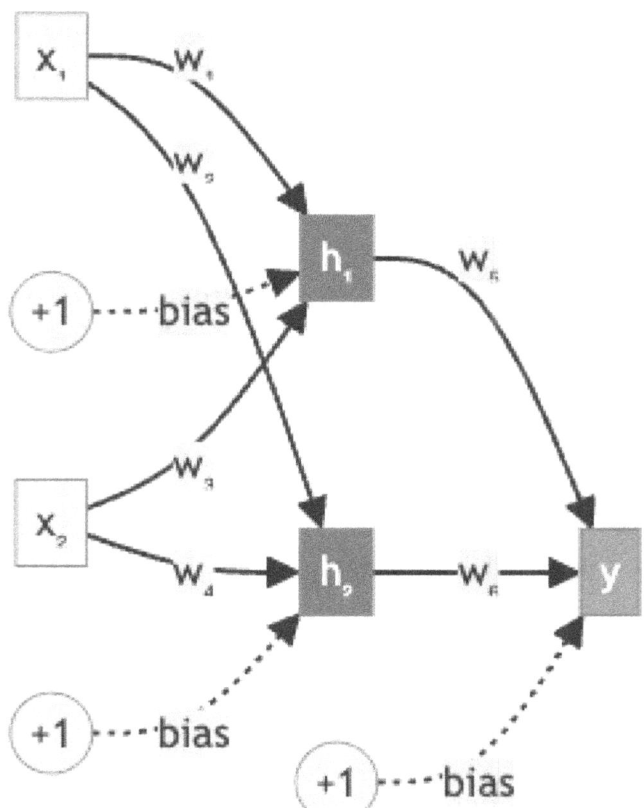

Figure 9-8. *Multi-layer perceptron architecture diagram with two inputs, four hidden neurons, and one output solving XOR*

Architecture: `[2 inputs → 4 hidden neurons → 1 output]`

With just two hidden neurons (and realistically, four for stable training), we can solve XOR. The hidden layer creates a new representation—a new feature space—where XOR *becomes linearly separable*.

The Intuition: Feature Engineering by the Network

Think of hidden neurons as **feature detectors**:

- Hidden neuron 1 might learn: "Is x_1 OR x_2 active?"
- Hidden neuron 2 might learn: "Are x_1 AND x_2 active?"
- Output neuron learns: "h_1 AND NOT h_2" → XOR!

The network is doing automatic feature engineering. The hidden layer transforms the input space such that the output layer's simple linear classifier works.

The Problem: How Do We Train It?

The perceptron rule only works for single neurons. How do we assign "blame" for errors through multiple layers?

Imagine a three-layer network makes a wrong prediction. Which weights are most responsible? - Weights connected to the output? ✓ Clearly involved - Weights in the hidden layers? ✗ Indirect responsibility

We need to **propagate error backwards** through the network.

The Backpropagation Algorithm

Backpropagation = "backward propagation of errors." It's calculus + chain rule + gradient descent.

Here's the full algorithm step by step.

Step 1: Forward Pass

Listing 9-6. Multi-layer forward pass computing activations layer by layer with weighted sums and activation functions

```
(defn forward-pass [network inputs activation-fn]
  "Compute activations layer-by-layer"
  (reduce
```

```
    (fn [activations layer]
      (let [prev-activation (last activations)
            ;; Weighted sum: w·x + b
            raw-output (mapv (fn [neuron-weights bias]
                              (+ bias (reduce + (map * prev-activation
                              neuron-weights))))
                            (:weights layer)
                            (:biases layer))
            ;; Apply activation function
            activation (mapv activation-fn raw-output)]
        (conj activations activation)))
    [inputs]  ; Start with input layer
    network))  ; Process each layer

;; Example:
;; Input: [0.0 1.0]
;; After hidden layer: [0.73, 0.26, 0.88, 0.45]
;; After output layer: [0.92]
```

Visualization showing activations flowing forward through the network

Step 2: Calculate Output Error

Listing 9-7. Output layer error calculation scaled by activation function derivative for gradient descent

```
(defn output-error [target output activation-derivative]
  "Error at output layer"
  (mapv (fn [t o]
          (* (- t o)                         ; Raw error
             (activation-derivative o))) ; Scaled by derivative target
        output))

;; Example:
;; Target: [1.0]
;; Output: [0.92]
;; Derivative: (sigmoid' 0.92) = 0.92 * (1 - 0.92) = 0.0736
;; Error: (1.0 - 0.92) * 0.0736 = 0.00589
```

Step 3: Backpropagate Error

Listing 9-8. Complete backward error propagation implementing chain rule for multi-layer gradient descent with weight and bias adjustments

```
(defn backward-pass [network activations target learning-rate activation-
derivative]
  "Propagate error backwards and update weights"
  (loop [layer-idx (dec (count network))
         current-error (output-error target (last activations) activation-
         derivative)
         updated-network network]
    (if (< layer-idx 0)
      updated-network  ; Done
      (let [layer (nth updated-network layer-idx)
            layer-input (nth activations layer-idx)

            ;; Update weights: w += learning-rate * error * input
            new-weights (mapv (fn [neuron-weights neuron-error]
                                (mapv (fn [w input-val]
                                        (+ w (* learning-rate neuron-error
                                        input-val)))
                                      neuron-weights
                                      layer-input))
                              (:weights layer)
                              current-error)

            ;; Update biases: b += learning-rate * error
            new-biases (mapv (fn [b neuron-error]
                               (+ b (* learning-rate neuron-error)))
                             (:biases layer)
                             current-error)

            ;; Propagate error to previous layer
            prev-error (when (> layer-idx 0)
                         (mapv (fn [input-idx]
                                 (let [weighted-error
```

```
                                              (reduce + (map-indexed
                                                          (fn [neuron-idx
                                                          neuron-weights]
                                                            (* (nth current-error
                                                            neuron-idx)
                                                               (nth neuron-weights
                                                               input-idx)))
                                                          (:weights layer)))]
                                         (* weighted-error
                                            (activation-derivative (nth layer-input
                                            input-idx)))))
                                    (range (count layer-input))))]

            (recur (dec layer-idx)
                   prev-error
                   (assoc updated-network layer-idx
                          {:weights new-weights :biases new-biases}))))))
```

The math:

For output layer:

$$\delta^L = (\text{target} - \text{output}) \odot \sigma'(\text{output})$$

For hidden layers:

$$\delta^l = (W^{(l+1)T} \times \delta^{(l+1)}) \odot \sigma'(a^l)$$

Weight update:

$$\Delta W = \text{learning\_rate} \times \delta \times \text{input}^T$$
$$W\_new = W\_old + \Delta W$$

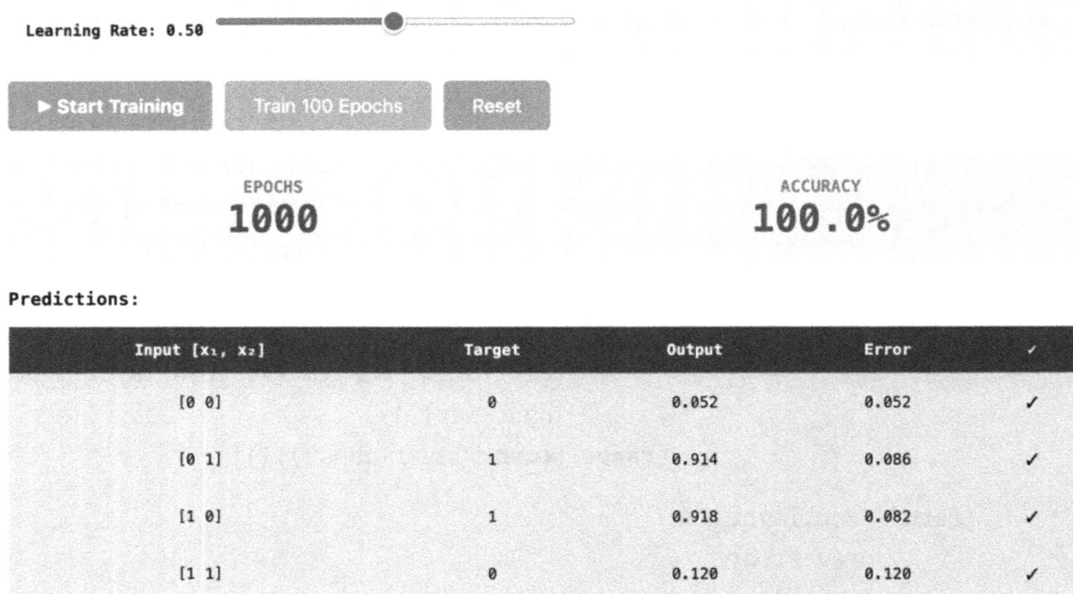

Figure 9-9. *Multi-layer perceptron training interface solving XOR using standard backpropagation XOR solved by a multi-layer perceptron after training, proving hidden layers break the barrier*

The Complete Training Loop

Listing 9-9. Complete XOR training loop using 2-4-1 network architecture solving the previously impossible problem after 3000 epochs

```
(def xor-data
  [{:input [0 0] :target [0]}
   {:input [0 1] :target [1]}
   {:input [1 0] :target [1]}
   {:input [1 1] :target [0]}])

(defn train-network [training-data epochs learning-rate]
  (let [network (init-network [2 4 1])  ; 2 inputs, 4 hidden, 1 output
        sigmoid (fn [x] (/ 1 (+ 1 (Math/exp (- x)))))
        sigmoid' (fn [y] (* y (- 1 y)))]
    (loop [net network
           epoch 0]
```

```
    (if (>= epoch epochs)
      net
      (let [new-net (reduce (fn [n example]
                               (let [activations (forward-pass n (:input
                               example) sigmoid)]
                                 (backward-pass n activations (:target
                                 example)
                                             learning-rate sigmoid')))
                             net
                             training-data)]
        (recur new-net (inc epoch)))))))

;; After ~1000-5000 epochs
(let [trained-net (train-network xor-data 3000 0.5)]
  (doseq [example xor-data]
    (let [output (first (last (forward-pass trained-net (:input example)
    sigmoid)))]
      (println (:input example) " → " (Math/round output)))))

;; Output:
;; [0 0] → 0
;; [0 1] → 1
;; [1 0] → 1
;; [1 1] → 0
;; SUCCESS! XOR is solved!
```

After training: all XOR patterns correctly classified. The AI winter is over.

What You'll Build in e04.cljs

The full exercise includes

1. **Problem selector**: Switch between XOR, AND, and OR.
2. **Live training**: Start/stop/reset with visual feedback.
3. **Accuracy meter**: See convergence in real time.
4. **Predictions table**: All four inputs with targets vs. outputs.
5. **Success banner**: "🎉 XOR SOLVED!" when accuracy > 95%.

Listing 9-10. Interactive multi-layer perceptron trainer with live accuracy tracking and celebratory success banner for XOR convergence

```
(defn mlp-trainer []
  (let [network (r/atom (nn/init-network [2 4 1]))
        selected-problem (r/atom :xor)
        epoch-count (r/atom 0)
        learning-rate (r/atom 0.5)
        training? (r/atom false)]
    (fn []
      (let [data (get all-problems @selected-problem)
            predictions (mapv (fn [ex]
                                {:input (:input ex)
                                 :target (first (:target ex))
                                 :output (first (nn/predict @network
                                 (:input ex)))})
                              data)
            accuracy (* 100 (/ (count (filter #(< (Math/abs (- (:output %)
            (:target %))) 0.5)
                                              predictions))
                               (count predictions)))]
        [:div
         [:h2 "Multi-Layer Perceptron (1986)"]
         [:p "The network that broke the XOR barrier."]

         ;; Problem selector
         (for [prob [:xor :and :or]]
           [:button {:on-click #(reset! selected-problem prob)
                     :style {:background (if (= @selected-problem prob)
                     "#2196f3" "#e0e0e0")}}
            (str/upper-case (name prob))])

         ;; Training controls
         [:button {:on-click #(if @training?
                                (stop-training!)
                                (start-training! network data epoch-count
                                learning-rate))}
```

```
 (if @training? "⏸ Stop" "▶ Start Training")]

;; Metrics
[:div
 [:div "Epochs: " @epoch-count]
 [:div "Accuracy: " (.toFixed accuracy 1) "%"]]

;; Predictions table
[:table
 (for [pred predictions]
   [:tr {:style {:background (if (< (Math/abs (- (:output pred)
   (:target pred))) 0.5)
                                  "#c8e6c9" "#ffcdd2")}}
    [:td (str (:input pred))]
    [:td (:target pred)]
    [:td (.toFixed (:output pred) 3)]
    [:td (if (< (Math/abs (- (:output pred) (:target pred))) 0.5)
    "✓" "X")]])]

;; Success message
(when (and (= @selected-problem :xor) (>= accuracy 95))
  [:div {:style {:background "#fff3e0" :border-left "4px solid
  #ff9800"}}
   [:h3 "🎊 XOR SOLVED!"]
   [:p "The AI Winter is over! Hidden layers have broken the
   barrier."]
   [:p {:style {:font-style "italic"}}
    "'We describe a new learning procedure, back-propagation, for
    networks of "
    "neurone-like units.' – Rumelhart, Hinton & Williams,
    1986"]])])))))
```

The victory screen: XOR solved with 100% accuracy. The perceptron's impossible problem is now trivial.

Why This Matters

Backpropagation didn't just solve XOR—it made **any** function learnable (given enough neurons and data). It's the algorithm that powers: - Image recognition - Language models - Game-playing AI - Self-driving cars - Protein folding prediction

Every modern deep learning system uses backpropagation or a variant. It's the foundation of the entire field.

The Shared Engine: nn.cljs

To avoid repeating the same neural network code across every exercise, we've extracted the core into nn.cljs:

```
(ns my-neural-network.nn)

(def activation-fns
  {:sigmoid {:fn (fn [x] (/ 1 (+ 1 (js/Math.exp (- x)))))
             :derivative (fn [y] (* y (- 1 y)))
             :name "Sigmoid"}
   :relu {:fn (fn [x] (max 0 x))
          :derivative (fn [y] (if (> y 0) 1 0))
          :name "ReLU"}
   ;; ... Etc
   })

(defn init-network [layer-sizes]
  ;; Create random weights and biases for each layer
  ...)

(defn forward-pass
  ([network inputs] (forward-pass network inputs :sigmoid))
  ([network inputs activation-key]
   ;; Compute activations for each layer
   ...))

(defn backward-pass [network activations target learning-rate
activation-key]
  ;; Backpropagate error and update weights
  ...)
```

```
(defn train-step [network input target learning-rate activation-key]
  (let [activations (forward-pass network input activation-key)]
    (backward-pass network activations target learning-rate
    activation-key)))

(defn predict [network input activation-key]
  (last (forward-pass network input activation-key)))
```

This is our **neural network engine**. It's pure ClojureScript—no external libraries. Every exercise from e04 onward uses this shared code.

Design decisions:

- **Multi-arity functions**: `forward-pass` can be called with 2 args (defaults to sigmoid) or 3 args (specify activation).
- **Immutable updates**: `backward-pass` returns a new network; it doesn't mutate.
- **Activation function map**: Easily swap sigmoid/ReLU/tanh by passing a keyword.
- **Pure functions**: Same inputs always produce same outputs.

This is functional programming applied to machine learning. ClojureScript's immutability makes debugging neural networks far easier than imperative approaches.

The Complete `nn.cljs` Implementation

Here's the full shared engine code that all exercises (e04–e10) use.

Listing 9-11. Complete reusable neural network engine with multi-arity pure functions, immutable updates, and support for sigmoid/ReLU/tanh/leaky-ReLU activations powering exercises e04–e10

```
(ns my-neural-network.nn
  "SHARED NEURAL NETWORK ENGINE

   Pure functional multi-layer perceptron implementation.
   All exercises from e04 onward depend on this namespace.

   Key design decisions:
   - Immutable data structures (networks are values, not objects)
   - Multi-arity functions (activation defaults to :sigmoid)
```

```
   - Pure functions (same inputs always produce same outputs)
   - No side effects (training returns new network, doesn't mutate)")

;; ============================================================
;; ACTIVATION FUNCTIONS
;; ============================================================

(def activation-fns
  "Map of activation functions and their derivatives.
   Each activation has:
   - :fn - The activation function itself
   - :derivative - Its derivative (used in backprop)
   - :name - Human-readable name"

  {:sigmoid
   {:fn (fn [x] (/ 1 (+ 1 (js/Math.exp (- x)))))
    :derivative (fn [y] (* y (- 1 y)))  ; Derivative in terms of OUTPUT
    :name "Sigmoid"}

   :relu
   {:fn (fn [x] (max 0 x))
    :derivative (fn [y] (if (> y 0) 1 0))
    :name "ReLU"}

   :tanh
   {:fn (fn [x] (js/Math.tanh x))
    :derivative (fn [y] (- 1 (* y y)))
    :name "Tanh"}

   :leaky-relu
   {:fn (fn [x] (if (> x 0) x (* 0.01 x)))
    :derivative (fn [y] (if (> y 0) 1 0.01))
    :name "Leaky ReLU"}})

;; ============================================================
;; NETWORK INITIALIZATION
;; ============================================================

(defn init-network
  "Initialize a network with random weights and biases.
```

```
   layer-sizes: Vector of layer sizes, e.g. [2 4 1]
                means 2 inputs, 4 hidden neurons, 1 output

   Returns: Vector of layers, where each layer is:
            {:weights [[w11 w12 ...] [w21 w22 ...] ...]
             :biases [b1 b2 ...]}"
  [layer-sizes]
  (mapv (fn [input-size output-size]
          {:weights (vec (repeatedly output-size
                                     #(vec (repeatedly input-size
                                                       (fn [] (- (rand 2)
                                                       1)))))) ;
                                                       Random [-1, 1]
           :biases (vec (repeatedly output-size
                                    (fn [] (- (rand 2) 1))))})
        (butlast layer-sizes)  ; Input sizes
        (rest layer-sizes)))   ; Output sizes

;; ============================================================
;; FORWARD PROPAGATION
;; ============================================================

(defn forward-pass
  "Compute network output for given inputs.

   Returns vector of activations for each layer (including input).
   [input-activations, hidden-layer-1-activations, ..., output-activations]"

  ([network inputs]
   (forward-pass network inputs :sigmoid))

  ([network inputs activation-key]
   (let [activate (get-in activation-fns [activation-key :fn])]
     (reduce
      (fn [activations layer]
        (let [prev-activation (last activations)
              ;; Compute weighted sum for each neuron: sum(w_i *
              x_i) + bias
```

```
            raw-output (mapv (fn [neuron-weights bias]
                               (+ bias (reduce + (map * prev-activation
                               neuron-weights))))
                             (:weights layer)
                             (:biases layer))
            ;; Apply activation function
            activation (mapv activate raw-output)]
        (conj activations activation)))
      [inputs]  ; Start with input layer activations
      network))))

;; ============================================================
;; BACKPROPAGATION
;; ============================================================

(defn backward-pass
  "Update network weights using backpropagation.

   Returns new network with adjusted weights and biases.
   Does NOT mutate the input network."

  ([network activations target learning-rate]
   (backward-pass network activations target learning-rate :sigmoid))

  ([network activations target learning-rate activation-key]
   (let [output (last activations)
         derivative (get-in activation-fns [activation-key :derivative])
         num-layers (count network)]

     ;; Loop backwards through layers
     (loop [layer-idx (dec num-layers)
            current-layer-errors (mapv #(* (- %1 %2) (derivative %2))
            target output)
            updated-network network]

       (if (< layer-idx 0)
         updated-network  ; Done! Return updated network

         (let [layer (nth updated-network layer-idx)
               layer-activations (nth activations layer-idx)
```

```
    ;; Update weights: w_new = w_old + lr * error * input
    new-weights (mapv (fn [neuron-weights neuron-error]
                       (mapv (fn [w input-val]
                               (+ w (* learning-rate neuron-
                               error input-val)))
                             neuron-weights
                             layer-activations))
                     (:weights layer)
                     current-layer-errors)

    ;; Update biases: b_new = b_old + lr * error
    new-biases (mapv (fn [b neuron-error]
                      (+ b (* learning-rate neuron-error)))
                    (:biases layer)
                    current-layer-errors)

    ;; Propagate error to previous layer
    prev-errors (when (> layer-idx 0)
                 (mapv (fn [input-idx]
                         (let [weighted-error
                               (reduce +
                                       (map-indexed
                                        (fn [neuron-idx
                                        neuron-weights]
                                          (* (nth current-layer-
                                          errors neuron-idx)
                                             (nth neuron-weights
                                             input-idx)))
                                        (:weights layer)))]
                           (* weighted-error
                              (derivative (nth layer-activations
                              input-idx)))))
                       (range (count layer-activations))))]

;; Recurse to next layer (going backwards)
(recur (dec layer-idx)
       prev-errors
```

```
                (assoc updated-network layer-idx
                       {:weights new-weights :biases new-biases}))))))))

;; ============================================================
;; TRAINING AND PREDICTION
;; ============================================================

(defn train-step
  "Perform one training step (forward + backward pass).

   Returns new network with updated weights."

  ([network input target learning-rate]
   (train-step network input target learning-rate :sigmoid))

  ([network input target learning-rate activation-key]
   (let [activations (forward-pass network input activation-key)]
     (backward-pass network activations target learning-rate
     activation-key))))

(defn predict
  "Get network prediction for given input.

   Returns output layer activations."

  ([network input]
   (predict network input :sigmoid))

  ([network input activation-key]
   (last (forward-pass network input activation-key))))
```

Key insights from this implementation:

1. **Immutability throughout**: Every function returns a new value. `backward-pass` returns a new network; it doesn't mutate the old one. This makes debugging trivial—you can inspect network state at any epoch without worrying about mutation.

2. **Multi-arity elegance**: Functions like `forward-pass` work with two or three arguments. This lets older exercises (that only use sigmoid) call `(forward-pass net inputs)`, while newer exercises can specify `(forward-pass net inputs :relu)`.

3. **Derivative in terms of output**: Notice `sigmoid'` uses `y` (the output) not `x` (the input). This is standard in deep learning—we compute `σ'(σ(x))` as `y(1-y)` which is faster.

4. **The backprop loop**: The recursive `loop` in `backward-pass` walks backwards through layers, computing errors and updating weights. This is the heart of the algorithm.

5. **Pure functions enable testing**: You can write tests like

```
(let [net (init-network [2 2 1])
      output (predict net [1 0])]
  (is (number? (first output))))  ; Smoke test
```

   No setup, no mocking, no dependency injection. Just call the function.

Exercise 5: Visualizing the Network

Understanding neural networks requires **seeing** them. `e05.cljs` adds real-time visualization that transforms the abstract mathematics into something tangible.

What Visualization Reveals

When you watch a network train, you see

- **Weight evolution**: Strong connections (thick lines) vs. weak ones (thin lines).
- **Positive vs. negative weights**: Green lines push activation up; red lines pull it down.
- **Neuron activation**: Darker neurons are more active (closer to 1).
- **Learning dynamics**: Which weights change fast vs. slow.

This isn't just pretty—it's **pedagogically essential**. You develop intuition for: - Why some inputs matter more than others (thick incoming weights) - How XOR gets solved (specific weight patterns emerge) - When training stalls (weights stop changing)

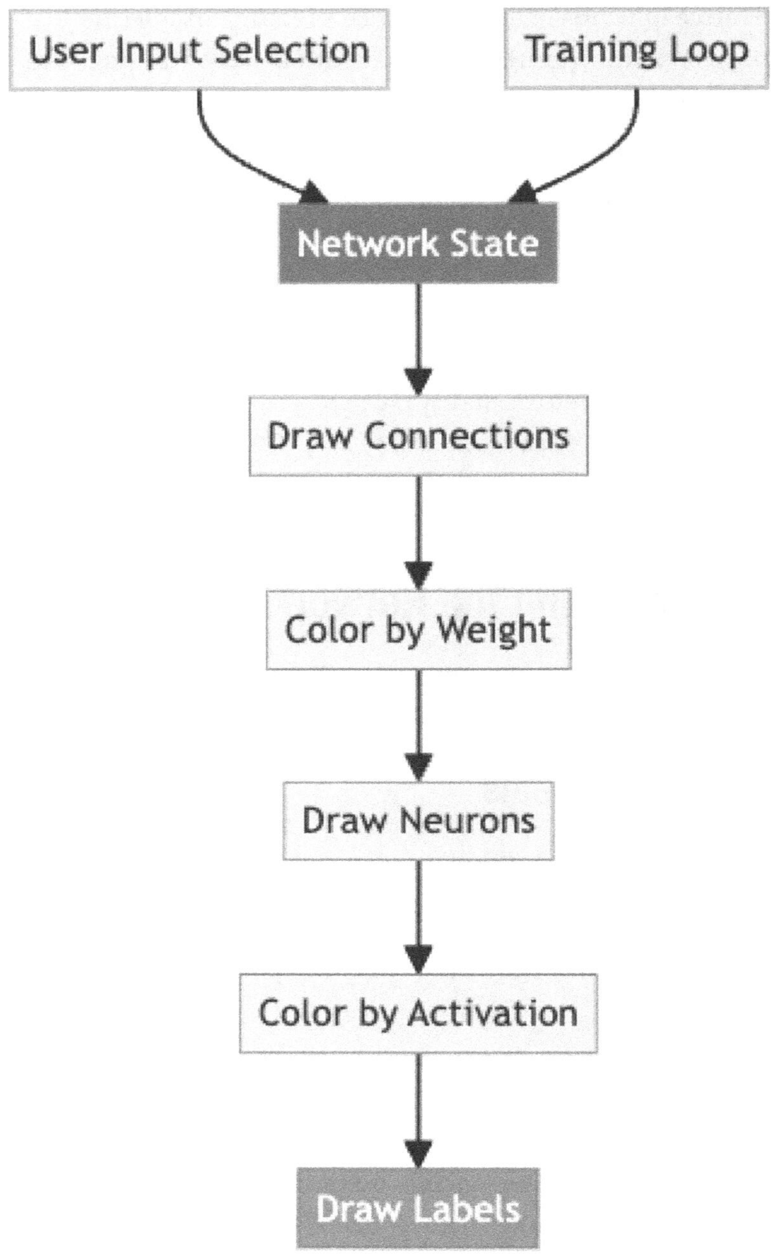

Figure 9-10. *SVG rendering pipeline diagram showing flow from network state through connection drawing to labeled neurons*

The SVG Rendering Code

We use SVG (not canvas) for crisp, scalable diagrams.

Listing 9-12. SVG network visualizer rendering weighted connections (green=positive, red=negative) with opacity/thickness indicating magnitude and grayscale neurons showing activation intensity making abstract math visible

```
(defn draw-network-svg [network activations width height]
  (let [layer-sizes (cons (count (first activations))
                          (mapv #(count (:weights %)) network))
        num-layers (count layer-sizes)
        layer-spacing (/ width (inc num-layers))
        neuron-radius 20]
    [:svg {:width width :height height :style {:background "#fafafa"
    :border-radius "8px"}}

     ;; CONNECTIONS FIRST (drawn behind neurons)
     (for [layer-idx (range (dec num-layers))
           from-idx (range (nth layer-sizes layer-idx))
           to-idx (range (nth layer-sizes (inc layer-idx)))]
       (let [x1 (* (inc layer-idx) layer-spacing)
             y1 (* (/ height (inc (nth layer-sizes layer-idx)))
                   (inc from-idx))
             x2 (* (+ 2 layer-idx) layer-spacing)
             y2 (* (/ height (inc (nth layer-sizes (inc layer-idx))))
                   (inc to-idx))
             weight (get-in network [layer-idx :weights to-idx from-idx])
             opacity (min 1.0 (/ (Math/abs weight) 3))  ; Stronger weight =
             more visible
             color (if (pos? weight) "#4caf50" "#f44336")]  ; Green =
             positive, Red = negative
         ^{:key (str "conn-" layer-idx "-" from-idx "-" to-idx)}
         [:line {:x1 x1 :y1 y1 :x2 x2 :y2 y2
                 :stroke color
                 :stroke-width (+ 1 (* 2 opacity))  ; Thickness = magnitude
                 :opacity opacity}]))
```

```
;; NEURONS ON TOP
(for [layer-idx (range num-layers)
      neuron-idx (range (nth layer-sizes layer-idx))]
  (let [x (* (inc layer-idx) layer-spacing)
        y (* (/ height (inc (nth layer-sizes layer-idx)))
             (inc neuron-idx))
        activation (get-in activations [layer-idx neuron-idx] 0)
        intensity (int (* 255 activation))]  ; 0 = black, 1 = white
    ^{:key (str "neuron-" layer-idx "-" neuron-idx)}
    [:g
     [:circle {:cx x :cy y :r neuron-radius
               :fill (str "rgb(" intensity ", " intensity ", "
               intensity ")")
               :stroke "#333" :stroke-width 2}]
     [:text {:x x :y (+ y 5) :text-anchor "middle"
             :fill (if (> activation 0.5) "white" "black")
             :font-size "12px" :font-weight "bold"}
      (.toFixed activation 2)]]))

;; LAYER LABELS
(for [layer-idx (range num-layers)]
  (let [x (* (inc layer-idx) layer-spacing)
        label (cond
               (= layer-idx 0) "Input"
               (= layer-idx (dec num-layers)) "Output"
               :else (str "Hidden " layer-idx))]
    ^{:key (str "label-" layer-idx)}
    [:text {:x x :y 20 :text-anchor "middle"
            :fill "#666" :font-size "14px" :font-weight "bold"}
     label]))]))
```

Before training: Random weights, all over the place. Thin lines everywhere, no pattern.

Mid-training (epoch 500): Patterns emerging. Some weights strengthening, others weakening.

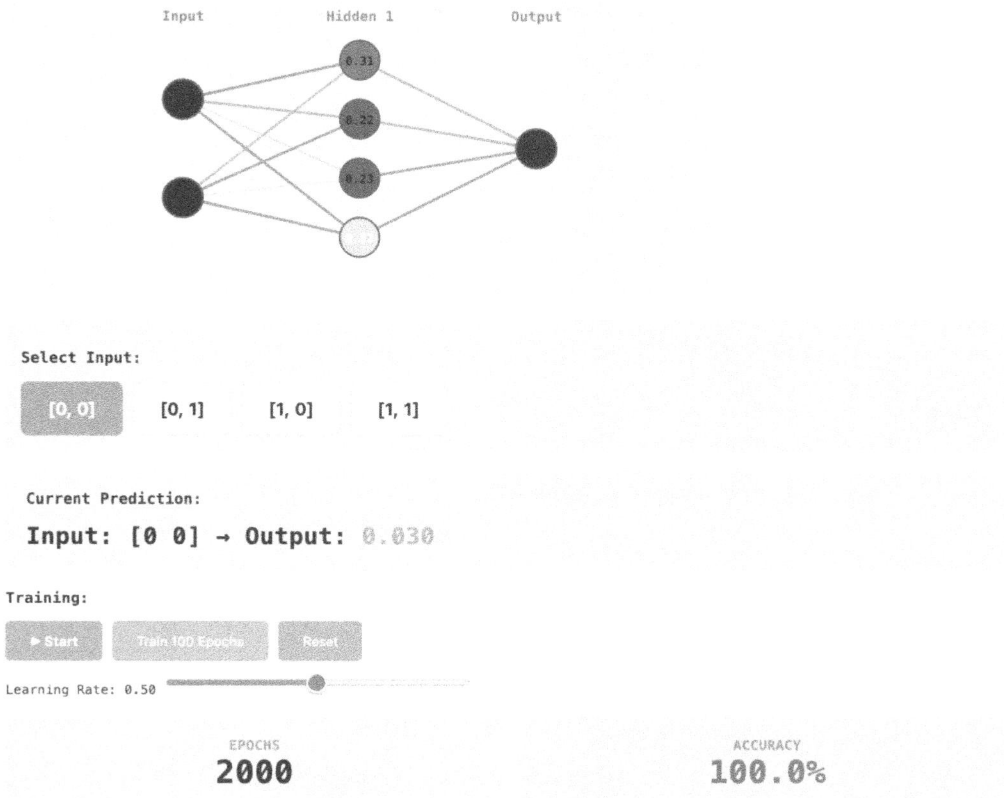

Figure 9-11. *Converged network at epoch 2000 displaying clear weight structure demonstrating successful XOR learning. Converged (epoch 2000): Clear weight structure. The network has learned XOR*

The Complete UI Component

Listing 9-13. Complete interactive network visualizer with add-watch reactive updates, input selector buttons lighting up neurons, and synchronized training controls demonstrating real-time weight evolution

```
(defn network-visualizer []
  (let [network (r/atom (nn/init-network [2 4 1]))
        current-input (r/atom [0 0])
        current-activations (r/atom (nn/forward-pass @network [0 0]))
        epoch-count (r/atom 0)
        learning-rate (r/atom 0.5)
        training? (r/atom false)]
```

```
;; Auto-update visualization when network or input changes
(add-watch network ::update-viz
           (fn [_ _ _ new-net]
             (reset! current-activations (nn/forward-pass new-net
             @current-input))))
(add-watch current-input ::update-viz
           (fn [_ _ _ new-input]
             (reset! current-activations (nn/forward-pass @network
             new-input))))

(fn []
  (let [output (last @current-activations)
        predictions (mapv #(hash-map :input (:input %)
                                     :output (first (nn/predict
                                     @network (:input %)))
                                     :target (first (:target %)))
                         xor-data)
        accuracy (* 100 (/ (count (filter #(< (Math/abs (- (:output %)
        (:target %))) 0.5)
                                          predictions))
                          (count predictions)))]
    [:div {:style {:font-family "monospace" :padding "20px"}}
     [:h2 "Network Architecture Visualization"]

     ;; THE VISUALIZATION
     [:div {:style {:margin "20px 0"}}
      [draw-network-svg @network @current-activations 700 300]]

     ;; INPUT SELECTOR (try different inputs, watch neurons light up)
     [:div
      [:h3 "Select Input:"]
      (for [input-pair [[0 0] [0 1] [1 0] [1 1]]]
        ^{:key (str input-pair)}
        [:button {:style {:padding "15px 25px"
                          :background (if (= @current-input input-pair)
                          "#2196f3" "#fff")
```

```
                  :border (str "2px solid " (if (= @current-
                  input input-pair) "#2196f3" "#ddd"))}
          :on-click #(reset! current-input input-pair)}
    (str "[" (first input-pair) ", " (second input-pair) "]")])]

;; CURRENT PREDICTION
[:div {:style {:background "#fff3e0" :padding "20px" :border-
radius "8px"}}
 [:h3 "Current Prediction:"]
 [:div {:style {:fontSize "24px"}}
  "Input: " (str @current-input) " → Output: "
  [:span {:style {:color "#ff6f00"}} (.toFixed (first
  output) 3)]]]

;; TRAINING CONTROLS
[:div
 [:button {:on-click (fn []
                       (if @training?
                         (stop-training!)
                         (start-training! network epoch-count
                         learning-rate)))}
  (if @training? "⏸ Stop" "▶ Start")]
 [:button {:on-click #(dotimes [_ 100]
                        (doseq [ex xor-data]
                          (swap! network nn/train-step (:input ex)
                          (:target ex) @learning-rate))
                        (swap! epoch-count inc))}
  "Train 100 Epochs"]
 [:button {:on-click #(do (reset! network (nn/init-network
 [2 4 1]))
                          (reset! epoch-count 0))}
  "Reset"]]
```

```
;; METRICS
[:div
 [:div "Epochs: " @epoch-count]
 [:div "Accuracy: " (.toFixed accuracy 1) "%"]]

;; XOR TRUTH TABLE
[:table
 [:thead [:tr [:th "Input"] [:th "Target"] [:th "Output"]
 [:th "✓"]]]
 [:tbody
  (for [pred predictions]
    (let [correct? (< (Math/abs (- (:output pred) (:target
    pred))) 0.5)]
      ^{:key (str (:input pred))}
      [:tr {:style {:background (if correct? "#c8e6c9"
      "#ffcdd2")}}
       [:td (str (:input pred))]
       [:td (:target pred)]
       [:td (.toFixed (:output pred) 3)]
       [:td (if correct? "✓" "X")]]))]]])))
```

Pedagogical value: Seeing weights adjust in real time demystifies learning. You watch: - Heavy weights form between important neurons - Bias nodes stabilize the decision boundary - Hidden layer neurons specialize (one handles x_1, another x_2, etc.)

It's machine learning made tangible.

Exercise 6: Interactive Data Generation

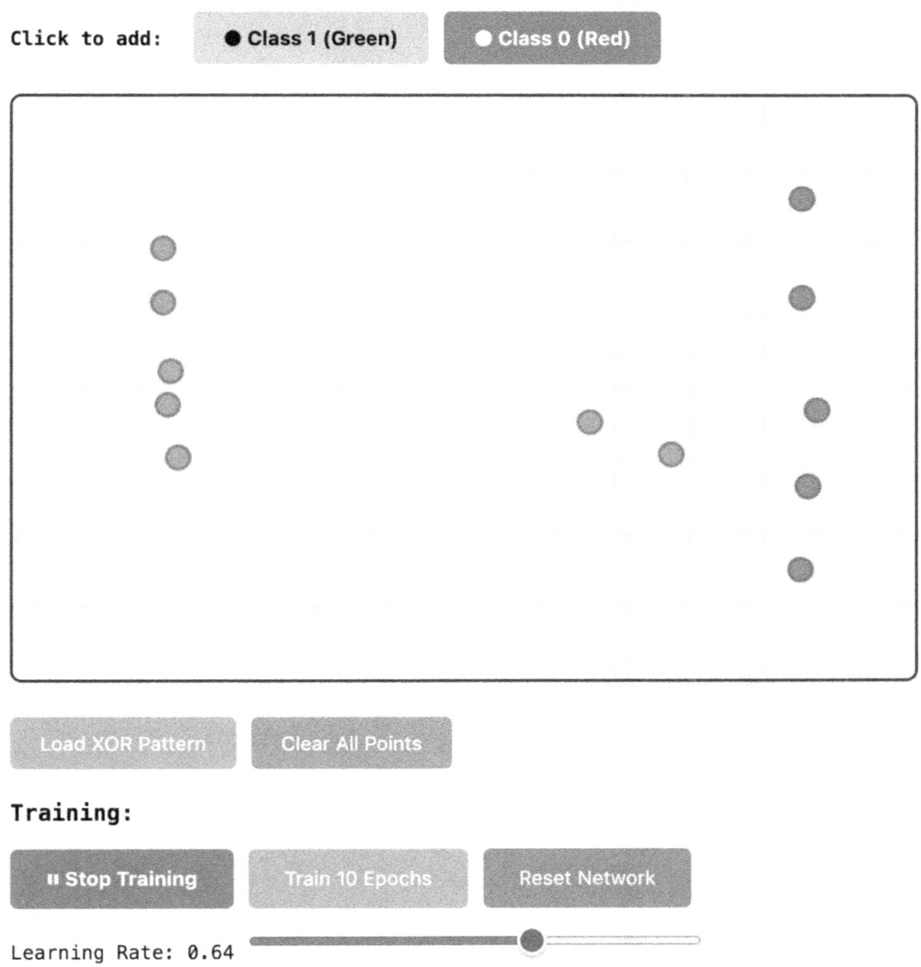

Figure 9-12. *Interactive data generation canvas allowing users to create custom training datasets by clicking*

Real-world datasets aren't nicely packaged. `e06.cljs` lets you **create your own training data** by clicking on a canvas.

The Philosophy

This exercise teaches a critical lesson: **data quality matters more than architecture**.

A perfect network trained on garbage data → garbage predictions. A simple network trained on clean, representative data → remarkable results.

What You'll Build

An interactive canvas where

- **Left-click** → add class 0 (red dot)
- **Right-click** → add class 1 (green dot)
- **Train button** → network learns YOUR pattern
- **Clear button** → start over

Listing 9-14. Interactive canvas data generator with click-to-add-point interface, class switching buttons, canvas ref management, and getBoundingClientRect coordinate normalization teaching data quality impacts learning outcomes

```
(defn interactive-data-canvas []
  (let [network (r/atom (nn/init-network [2 4 1]))
        points (r/atom [])
        current-class (r/atom 0)  ; 0 = red, 1 = green
        epochs (r/atom 0)
        training? (r/atom false)
        canvas-ref (r/atom nil)]

    (fn []
      [:div {:style {:font-family "monospace" :padding "20px"}}
       [:h2 "Interactive Data Generation"]
       [:p "Click to add training data. Watch the network learn YOUR
       pattern."]

       ;; Class selector
       [:div {:style {:margin "20px 0"}}
        [:h3 "Current Class:"]
        [:button {:style {:padding "15px 30px"
                          :background (if (= @current-class 0)
                          "#f44336" "#fff")
                          :border (str "3px solid " (if (= @current-class
                          0) "#f44336" "#ddd"))}
                  :on-click #(reset! current-class 0)}
```

```
   "Class 0 (Red)"]
  [:button {:style {:padding "15px 30px" :margin-left "10px"
                    :background (if (= @current-class 1)
                    "#4caf50" "#fff")
                    :border (str "3px solid " (if (= @current-class
                    1) "#4caf50" "#ddd"))}
           :on-click #(reset! current-class 1)}
   "Class 1 (Green)"]]

 ;; Canvas for clicking
 [:canvas {:ref #(when % (reset! canvas-ref %))
           :width 600
           :height 400
           :style {:border "3px solid #333"
                   :border-radius "10px"
                   :cursor "crosshair"
                   :background "#fafafa"}
           :on-click (fn [e]
                      (let [rect (.getBoundingClientRect
                      (.-target e))
                            x (- (.-clientX e) (.-left rect))
                            y (- (.-clientY e) (.-top rect))
                            norm-x (/ x 600)
                            norm-y (/ y 400)]
                        (swap! points conj {:x x :y y
                                            :norm-x norm-x
                                            :norm-y norm-y
                                            :label @current-class})
                        ;; Immediately draw the new point
                        (draw-points! @canvas-ref @points)))}
  ]

 ;; Stats
 [:div {:style {:margin "20px 0"}}
  [:div "Total points: " (count @points)]
  [:div "Class 0 (red): " (count (filter #(= (:label %) 0) @points))]
```

```
 [:div "Class 1 (green): " (count (filter #(= (:label %) 1)
 @points))]
 [:div "Epochs trained: " @epochs]]

;; Training controls
[:div {:style {:margin "20px 0"}}
 [:button {:style {:padding "15px 30px" :font-size "16px"}
           :disabled (< (count @points) 4)  ; Need at least 4 points
           :on-click (fn []
                       ;; Train for 100 epochs
                       (dotimes [_ 100]
                         (doseq [pt @points]
                           (swap! network nn/train-step
                                  [(:norm-x pt) (:norm-y pt)]
                                  [(:label pt)]
                                  0.3)))
                       (swap! epochs + 100))}
  "Train 100 Epochs"]

 [:button {:style {:padding "15px 30px" :margin-left "10px"}
           :on-click #(do (reset! points [])
                          (reset! network (nn/init-network [2 4 1]))
                          (reset! epochs 0)
                          (when-let [canvas @canvas-ref]
                            (let [ctx (.getContext canvas "2d")]
                              (.clearRect ctx 0 0 600 400))))}
  "Clear All"]]

;; Tips
[:div {:style {:background "#e3f2fd" :padding "15px" :margin "20px
0" :border-left "4px solid #2196f3"}}
 [:h4 "Tips for Patterns:"]
 [:ul
  [:li "Try linearly separable: half red, half green (easy)"]
  [:li "Try XOR: red corners, green sides (medium)"]
  [:li "Try circular: green ring around red center (hard)"]
  [:li "Need 10+ points per class for decent learning"]]]])))
```

```
(defn draw-points! [canvas points]
  "Draw all training points on canvas"
  (when canvas
    (let [ctx (.getContext canvas "2d")]
      (.clearRect ctx 0 0 600 400)
      (doseq [{:keys [x y label]} points]
        ;; White outline
        (set! (.-fillStyle ctx) "white")
        (.beginPath ctx)
        (.arc ctx x y 10 0 (* 2 js/Math. PI))
        (.fill ctx)
        ;; Colored center
        (set! (.-fillStyle ctx) (if (= label 0) "#f44336" "#4caf50"))
        (.beginPath ctx)
        (.arc ctx x y 7 0 (* 2 js/Math. PI))
        (.fill ctx)))))
```

User has clicked to create a linearly separable pattern. Half red, half green.

After 500 epochs: Network learned the pattern. Could visualize decision boundary if we add that.

The Data Quality Lesson

Try these experiments.

Experiment 1: Balanced vs. Imbalanced - Create 20 red points, two green points - Train → network predicts almost everything as red! - Lesson: **Class imbalance kills accuracy**

Experiment 2: Noisy Labels - Create clear left/right split - Add a few "wrong" colored points on opposite sides - Train → decision boundary gets pulled toward noise - Lesson: **Mislabeled data corrupts learning**

Experiment 3: Insufficient Data - Add only four total points - Train → overfits, doesn't generalize - Lesson: **More data > better algorithms** (usually)

Exercise 7: Decision Boundaries

How does the network "see" the problem? `e07.cljs` visualizes the **decision boundary**—the curve that separates classes.

The Concept

Imagine the network's output as a 3D surface over the 2D input space: - Height = prediction (0 to 1) - Low valleys = "definitely class 0" - High peaks = "definitely class 1" - The boundary is where height = 0.5

We'll visualize this by coloring every pixel according to network prediction.

The Heatmap Technique

Listing 9-15. Decision boundary heatmap visualization classifying every grid point with resolution parameter balancing performance and quality, coloring space from red to green revealing non-linear separation curves

```
(defn draw-decision-boundary [canvas-ref network points width height
resolution]
  "Draw heatmap showing network's classification across entire space"
  (when-let [canvas @canvas-ref]
    (let [ctx (.getContext canvas "2d")]
      ;; Clear
      (.clearRect ctx 0 0 width height)

      ;; Heatmap: classify every grid point
      (doseq [x (range 0 width resolution)
              y (range 0 height resolution)]
        (let [norm-x (/ x width)
              norm-y (/ y height)
              output (first (nn/predict network [norm-x norm-y]))
              ;; Map [0, 1] to color
              intensity (int (* 255 output))
              red-component (- 255 intensity)
              green-component intensity
```

```
        color (str "rgb(" red-component "," green-component
        ",80)")]  ; Semi-transparent
      (set! (.-fillStyle ctx) color)
      (.fillRect ctx x y resolution resolution)))

  ;; Draw training points ON TOP
  (doseq [{:keys [x y label]} points]
    ;; White outline for visibility
    (set! (.-fillStyle ctx) "white")
    (.beginPath ctx)
    (.arc ctx x y 12 0 (* 2 js/Math. PI))
    (.fill ctx)
    ;; Colored center
    (set! (.-fillStyle ctx) (if (= label 1) "#4caf50" "#f44336"))
    (.beginPath ctx)
    (.arc ctx x y 9 0 (* 2 js/Math. PI))
    (.fill ctx)
    ;; Black border
    (set! (.-strokeStyle ctx) "black")
    (set! (.-lineWidth ctx) 2)
    (.stroke ctx)))))
```

Performance Note Classifying every pixel is expensive! - For 600×400 canvas → 240,000 predictions - Use `resolution = 8` → only 3,750 predictions - Looks slightly blocky but 64× faster

---

XOR pattern with decision boundary. Notice the non-linear curve separating the classes.

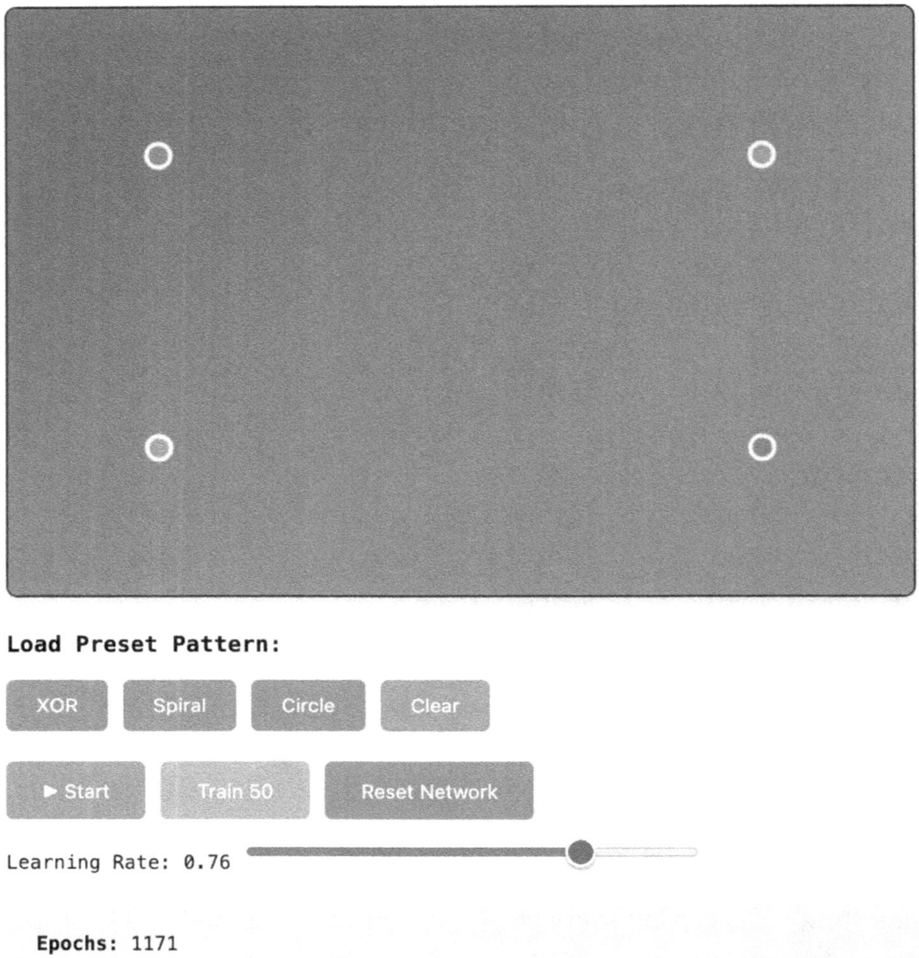

Figure 9-13. *Circular pattern visualization with green ring and red center showing wrapped decision boundary. Circular pattern: green ring, red center. Decision boundary wraps around elegantly*

What You Learn from Visualization

Confidence regions: - Deep red/green = network is confident - Yellowish = network is uncertain (near boundary) - These match your intuition: far from training data → uncertain

Overfitting detection: - If boundary has crazy wiggles around every point → overfitting - Smooth curve → good generalization

Architecture impact: - More hidden neurons → more complex boundaries possible - Fewer neurons → smoother, simpler boundaries

Why Activation Functions Matter

The activation function is the network's "nonlinearity." Without it, stacking layers is useless:

```
no activation: f(g(x)) = W₂(W₁x) = (W₂W₁)x = W₃x  // Just another linear function!
```

The activation function breaks this. It lets layers combine in truly nonlinear ways.

The Lineup

Listing 9-16. Comprehensive activation function definitions with pros/cons documentation comparing sigmoid's classic smoothness against ReLU's modern speed and tanh's zero-centering

```
(def activation-fns
  {:sigmoid
   {:fn (fn [x] (/ 1 (+ 1 (js/Math.exp (- x)))))
    :derivative (fn [y] (* y (- 1 y)))
    :name "Sigmoid (Classic)"
    :pros "Smooth, bounded [0,1], interpretable as probability"
    :cons "Vanishing gradients for |x| > 4"}

   :relu
   {:fn (fn [x] (max 0 x))
    :derivative (fn [y] (if (> y 0) 1 0))
```

```
     :name "ReLU (Modern)"
     :pros "Fast, no saturation, sparse activation"
     :cons "Dead neurons if x always < 0"}

    :tanh
    {:fn (fn [x] (js/Math.tanh x))
     :derivative (fn [y] (- 1 (* y y)))
     :name "Tanh (Zero-Centered)"
     :pros "Centered at 0, stronger gradients than sigmoid"
     :cons "Still saturates for |x| > 2"}

    :leaky-relu
    {:fn (fn [x] (if (> x 0) x (* 0.01 x)))
     :derivative (fn [y] (if (> y 0) 1 0.01))
     :name "Leaky ReLU (Fixed Dead Neurons)"
     :pros "Prevents dead neurons, keeps ReLU benefits"
     :cons "Hyperparameter (slope) to tune"}})
```

Comparison UI: Four identical XOR networks, each using different activation functions.

The Experiment

`e08.cljs` trains **four networks in parallel** on the same data, differing only in activation.

Listing 9-17. Parallel activation function comparison training four identical networks simultaneously with separate loss history tracking and CSS grid layout showing real-time convergence differences

```
(defn activation-comparison []
  (let [networks (r/atom {:sigmoid (nn/init-network [2 4 1])
                          :relu (nn/init-network [2 4 1])
                          :tanh (nn/init-network [2 4 1])
                          :leaky-relu (nn/init-network [2 4 1])})
        losses (r/atom {:sigmoid [] :relu [] :tanh [] :leaky-relu []})
        epochs (r/atom 0)]
```

```
(fn []
  [:div
   [:h2 "Activation Function Comparison"]

   ;; Train all networks
   [:button {:on-click (fn []
                        (doseq [[key net] @networks]
                          (let [new-net (reduce (fn [n ex]
                                                  (nn/train-step n
                                                                 (:input ex)
                                                                 (:target ex)
                                                                  0.5
                                                                  key))  ; Use
                                                                  respective
                                                                  activation
                                                net
                                                xor-data)
                                 loss (calculate-mse new-net xor-
                                 data key)]
                             (swap! networks assoc key new-net)
                             (swap! losses update key conj loss)))
                        (swap! epochs inc))}
    "Train All (1 Epoch)"]

   ;; Loss charts side-by-side
   [:div {:style {:display "grid" :grid-template-columns "1fr 1fr"}}
    (for [key [:sigmoid :relu :tanh :leaky-relu]]
      ^{:key key}
      [:div {:style {:padding "20px"}}
       [:h3 (get-in nn/activation-fns [key :name])]
       [:svg {:width 250 :height 150 :style {:border "1px solid #ddd"}}
        (let [loss-history (get @losses key)]
```

```
          (for [i (range (dec (count loss-history)))]
            (let [x1 (* 2 i)
                  x2 (* 2 (inc i))
                  y1 (- 150 (* 30 (nth loss-history i)))
                  y2 (- 150 (* 30 (nth loss-history (inc i))))]
              ^{:key i}
              [:line {:x1 x1 :y1 y1 :x2 x2 :y2 y2
                      :stroke "#2196f3" :stroke-width 2}])))]
         [:text {:x 5 :y 15 :font-size "12px"}
          (str "Loss: " (.toFixed (last (get @losses key)) 4))]]

        ;; Pros/cons
        [:div {:style {:font-size "12px" :margin-top "10px"}}
         [:div {:style {:color "#4caf50"}} "✓ " (get-in nn/activation-
         fns [key :pros])]
         [:div {:style {:color "#f44336"}} "X " (get-in nn/activation-
         fns [key :cons])]]]])]]

     [:div "Epochs: " @epochs]])))
```

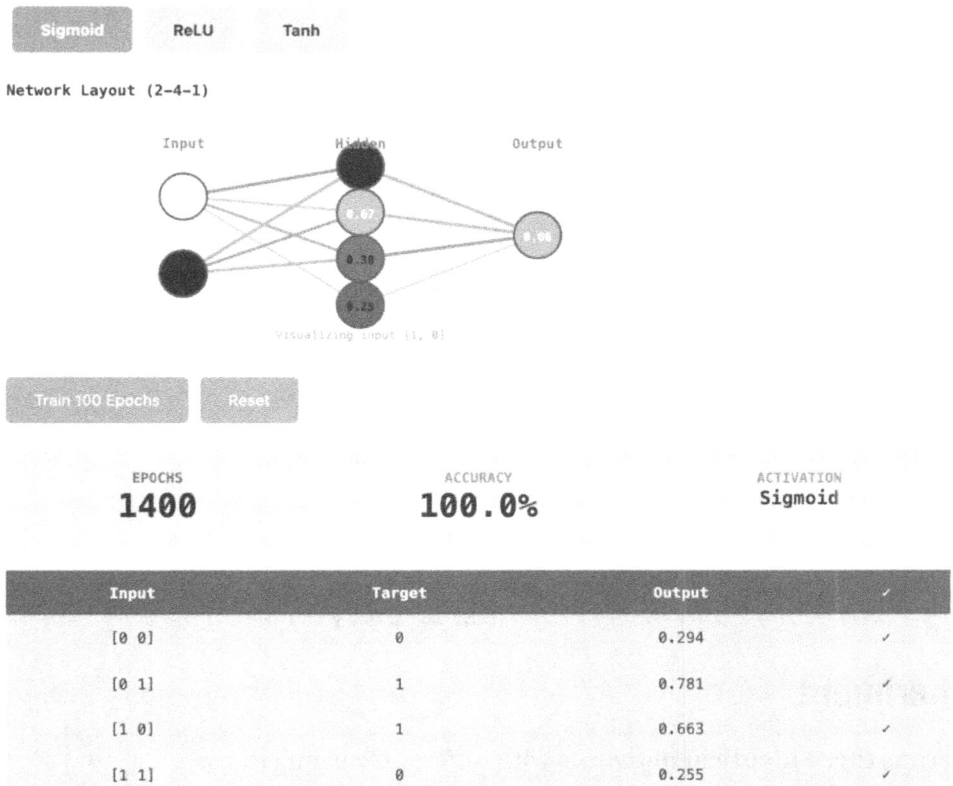

Figure 9-14. *Training results after 1000 epochs showing sigmoid smooth convergence, faster but jumpier ReLU, and balanced Leaky ReLU. After 1000 epochs: Sigmoid converged smoothly. ReLU converged faster but jumpier. Tanh similar to sigmoid. Leaky ReLU balanced*

Typical Results

For XOR

- **Sigmoid**: Converges in 800–1500 epochs, smooth loss curve
- **ReLU**: Converges in 300–800 epochs, more erratic
- **Tanh**: Similar to sigmoid, sometimes slightly faster
- **Leaky ReLU**: Best of both worlds

For more complex patterns

- **ReLU usually wins** (faster, deeper networks possible)
- **Sigmoid better** for probability outputs (naturally bounded [0,1])

The Problem

Learning rate controls step size in gradient descent:

- Too **small** → Training is glacially slow (or gets stuck)
- Too **large** → Overshoots minimum, loss explodes
- **Just right** → Goldilocks zone (problem dependent!)

```
Weight update: w_new = w_old - learning_rate × gradient
                                           ^
                                           This is everything!
```

The Experiment

`e09.cljs` runs **three identical networks** with different learning rates.

Listing 9-18. Learning rate hyperparameter comparison training three identical networks with 0.05 (glacial), 0.3 (goldilocks), and 1.5 (explosive) step sizes on unified SVG chart with capped y-scale and divergence warnings

```
(def learning-rates [0.05 0.3 1.5])  ; Slow, medium, fast

(defn learning-rate-comparison []
  (let [networks (r/atom [(nn/init-network [2 4 1])
                          (nn/init-network [2 4 1])
                          (nn/init-network [2 4 1])])
        losses (r/atom [[] [] []])
        epochs (r/atom 0)
        colors ["#2196f3" "#4caf50" "#ff9800"]]
```

```
(fn []
  [:div
   [:h2 "Learning Rate Comparison"]
   [:p "Same network, same data, different learning rates. Watch what
   happens."]

   ;; Single chart with all three loss curves
   [:svg {:width 700 :height 300 :style {:border "2px solid #333"
   :background "#fafafa"}}
    ;; Grid lines
    (for [y (range 0 300 50)]
      ^{:key (str "grid-" y)}
      [:line {:x1 0 :y1 y :x2 700 :y2 y :stroke "#ddd" :stroke-width 1}])

    ;; Loss curves
    (for [net-idx (range 3)]
      (let [loss-history (get @losses net-idx)
            color (nth colors net-idx)]
        (for [i (range (dec (count loss-history)))]
          (let [x1 (* 0.5 i)
                x2 (* 0.5 (inc i))
                ;; Cap y-scale at 10 to prevent explosion from
                dominating
                y1 (- 280 (* 25 (min 10 (nth loss-history i))))
                y2 (- 280 (* 25 (min 10 (nth loss-history (inc i)))))]
            ^{:key (str net-idx "-" i)}
            [:line {:x1 x1 :y1 y1 :x2 x2 :y2 y2 :stroke color :stroke-
            width 3}]))))

    ;; Legend
    (for [i (range 3)]
      ^{:key (str "legend-" i)}
      [:g
       [:rect {:x 10 :y (+ 10 (* i 25)) :width 20 :height 10 :fill (nth
       colors i)}]
       [:text {:x 35 :y (+ 18 (* i 25)) :fill "#333" :font-size "14px"}
        (str "LR = " (nth learning-rates i))]])]
```

```
;; Current loss values
[:div {:style {:display "grid" :grid-template-columns "1fr 1fr 1fr"
:margin "20px 0"}}
 (for [i (range 3)]
   ^{:key i}
   [:div {:style {:padding "15px" :text-align "center"
                  :background "#f5f5f5" :border-left (str "4px solid
                  " (nth colors i))}}
    [:div {:style {:font-size "12px" :color "#666"}} (str "LR = "
    (nth learning-rates i))]
    [:div {:style {:font-size "24px" :font-weight "bold"}}
     (if-let [last-loss (last (get @losses i))]
       (.toFixed last-loss 4)
       "-")]
    [:div {:style {:font-size "12px"}}
     (cond
       (nil? (last (get @losses i))) "Not started"
       (> (last (get @losses i)) 2) "⚠ DIVERGING!"
       (< (last (get @losses i)) 0.05) "✓ Converged"
       :else "Training...")]])]

;; Training button
[:button {:style {:padding "20px 40px" :font-size "18px"}
          :on-click (fn []
                      (doseq [i (range 3)]
                        (let [net (nth @networks i)
                              lr (nth learning-rates i)
                              new-net (reduce (fn [n ex]
                                                (nn/train-step n
                                                (:input ex) (:target
                                                ex) lr))
                                              net
                                              xor-data)
                              loss (calculate-mse new-net xor-data)]
                          (swap! networks assoc i new-net)
```

```
                    (swap! losses update i conj loss)))
                (swap! epochs inc))}
   "Train One Epoch"]

  [:div {:style {:margin "20px 0"}} "Epochs: " @epochs]])))
```

After 100 epochs: LR=0.05 barely moved. LR=0.3 converging nicely. LR=1.5 exploded (loss > 10).

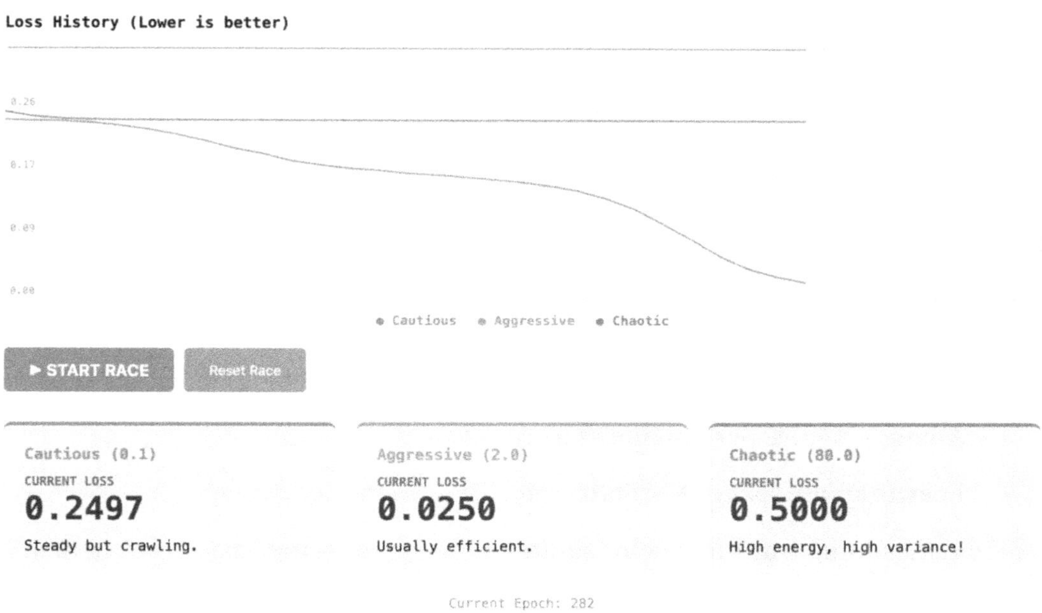

Figure 9-15. *Extended training at 500 epochs revealing LR=0.05 eventual convergence, LR=0.3 stable, LR=1.5 wild oscillation. After 500 epochs: LR=0.05 finally converged. LR=0.3 converged long ago. LR=1.5 oscillating wildly, unstable*

The Diagnostic Guide

Table 9-2. *Diagnostic guide for learning rate problems showing symptoms, causes, and fixes for common training issues*

Symptom	Cause	Fix
Loss decreases very slowly	LR too small	Increase 2–10×
Loss oscillates around minimum	LR too large	Decrease 2–10×
Loss becomes NaN or infinity	LR way too large	Decrease 10–100×
Loss decreases then plateaus	Hit local minimum	Try a different architecture or restart
Loss decreases then increases	Overfitting	Add regularization or more data

The Modern Solution

Fixed learning rates are pedagogical, not practical. Modern optimizers adapt

- **Momentum**: Remember previous gradients; smooth out updates.
- **Adam**: Adaptive per-parameter learning rates.
- **Learning rate schedules**: Start high, decay over time.

But understanding **why** these help requires understanding the basic problem first. That's what e09 teaches.

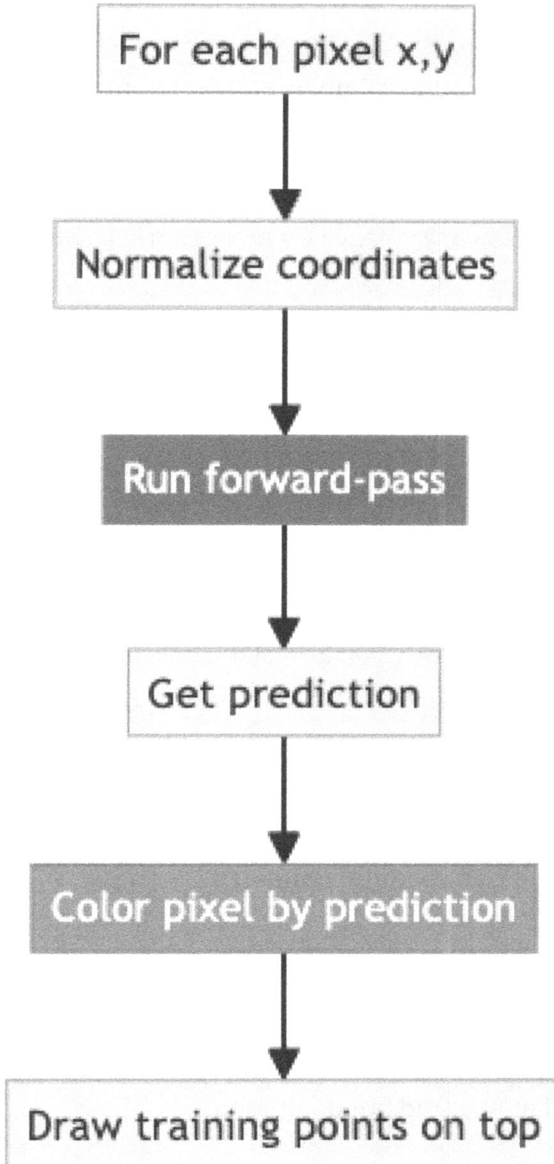

Figure 9-16. *Decision boundary generation algorithm showing pixel-by-pixel classification and coloring pipeline*

The result is stunning: you see the network's internal representation of the problem. For XOR, you'll see a non-linear boundary curve through the space, elegantly separating the classes.

Code snippet:

Listing 9-19. Decision boundary canvas snippet demonstrating model interpretability through pixel-by-pixel classification heatmap revealing internal learned representations

```
(defn draw-decision-boundary [canvas-ref network points width height
resolution]
  (when-let [canvas @canvas-ref]
    (let [ctx (.getContext canvas "2d")]
      ;; Heatmap
      (doseq [x (range 0 width resolution)
              y (range 0 height resolution)]
        (let [norm-x (/ x width)
              norm-y (/ y height)
              output (first (nn/predict network [norm-x norm-y]))
              intensity (int (* 255 output))
              color (str "rgb(" (- 255 intensity) "," intensity ",100)")]
          (set! (.-fillStyle ctx) color)
          (.fillRect ctx x y resolution resolution)))

      ;; Draw training points on top
      (doseq [{:keys [x y label]} points]
        (set! (.-fillStyle ctx) (if (= label 1) "#4caf50" "#f44336"))
        (.arc ctx x y 8 0 (* 2 js/Math. PI))
        (.fill ctx)))))
```

This is **model interpretability** at its most visual. It's how practitioners debug networks, understand failures, and build intuition.

Part III: Modern Techniques (2010s–Present)

Exercise 8: Activation Function Shootout

For decades, everyone used sigmoid: `σ(x) = 1 / (1 + e^(-x))`. It's smooth, differentiable, and biological (neurons do saturate).

Then in 2012, AlexNet won ImageNet using **ReLU**: `f(x) = max(0, x)`. Simple. Fast. Effective.

Why does it matter? Compare the following.

Table 9-3. *Activation function comparison table showing formulas, derivatives, and pros/cons of sigmoid, ReLU, tanh, and Leaky ReLU*

Activation	Formula	Derivative	Pros	Cons
Sigmoid	`1/(1+e^-x)`	`y(1-y)`	Smooth, bounded	Vanishing gradients
ReLU	`max(0,x)`	`1 if x>0 else 0`	Fast, no saturation	Dead neurons
Tanh	`tanh(x)`	`1-y2`	Zero-centered	Still vanishes
Leaky ReLU	`max(0.01x, x)`	`1 if x>0 else 0.01`	Fixes dead ReLU	Extra hyperparameter

`e08.cljs` lets you switch activation functions on the fly and compare the following.

Listing 9-20. Activation function hot-swapping pattern with dropdown selector and dynamic training demonstrating empirical function comparison approach

```
(def activation-fns
  {:sigmoid {...}
   :relu {...}
   :tanh {...}})

;; User selects from dropdown
(for [key [:sigmoid :relu :tanh]]
  [:button {:on-click #(reset! activation-fn key)}
   (get-in nn/activation-fns [key :name])])

;; Network uses selected activation
(swap! network nn/train-step input target lr @activation-fn)
```

Observation: For XOR, sigmoid usually works best (smooth gradient). For more complex problems, ReLU often converges faster. There's no universal answer—it's empirical.

Historical Note The shift from sigmoid to ReLU was a major factor in the deep learning revolution. Deeper networks became trainable because ReLU doesn't saturate.

Exercise 9: The Learning Rate Drama

Of all hyperparameters, **learning rate** is the most critical. Too high? The network diverges (chaos). Too low? Training takes forever (or gets stuck in local minima).

`e09.cljs` runs **three networks in parallel** with different learning rates.

Listing 9-21. Parallel learning rate experiment training three identical networks with different step sizes revealing goldilocks zone between glacial convergence and chaotic divergence

```
(def learning-rates [0.1 0.5 1.0])

;; Train three networks simultaneously
(let [networks (r/atom [(nn/init-network [2 2 1])
                        (nn/init-network [2 2 1])
                        (nn/init-network [2 2 1])])
      losses (r/atom [[] [] []])]

  ;; Each epoch
  (doseq [[idx net] (map-indexed vector @networks)]
    (let [new-net (reduce (fn [n example]
                            (nn/train-step n (:input example) (:target
                            example) (nth lrs idx)))
                          net
                          xor-data)]
      (swap! losses update idx conj (calculate-loss new-net)))))
```

You'll see

- **LR = 0.1**: Slow but steady convergence
- **LR = 0.5**: Faster, sometimes unstable
- **LR = 1.0**: Often diverges, loss increases instead of decreasing

The visualization charts loss over time for all three, making the effect visceral.

Advanced techniques (not implemented, but mentioned):

- **Learning rate schedules**: Start high, decay over time
- **Adaptive methods**: Adam, RMSprop adjust per-parameter
- **Momentum**: Smooth out updates with exponential moving average

These are the "secret sauce" of modern deep learning. Our simple fixed learning rate is educational, not production ready.

Exercise 10: The Complete Neural Network Playground

`e10.cljs` is the culmination—a full-featured playground combining everything you've learned across all 10 chapters.

Table 9-4. *Playground feature summary mapping interactive components to their pedagogical chapter connections*

Feature	Description	Chapter Connection
Click-to-add data	Interactive point generation	Chapter 7 (canvas click events)
Real-time heatmap	Decision boundary visualization	Chapter 2 (pixel-level rendering)
Network diagram	SVG architecture view	Chapter 5 (Reagent components)
Preset patterns	XOR, spiral, circular	Data science best practices
Activation selector	Sigmoid/ReLU/tanh/leaky ReLU	Modern deep learning (e08)
Training controls	Start/stop/reset/learning rate slider	Interactive UIs (Chapter 4)
Metrics dashboard	Epochs, learning rate, data points, active neurons	Real-time dashboards

The Architecture

The data flows through multiple reactive systems.

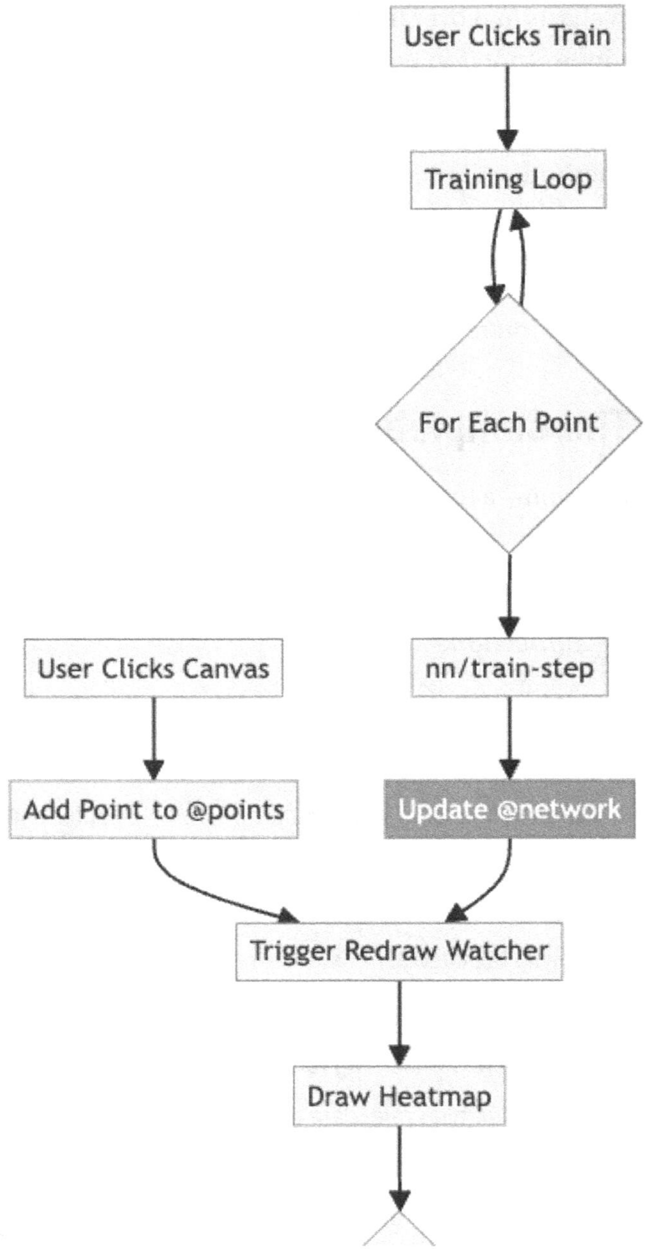

***Figure 9-17.** Reactive data flow architecture showing user interactions triggering network updates and canvas redraws*

Feature 1: Interactive Data Generation

Click on the canvas to add training points. The network learns *your* pattern.

Listing 9-22. Canvas click event handler capturing mouse coordinates with getBoundingClientRect and normalizing to [0,1] range for network input in complete ML playground

```
[:canvas {:ref #(when % (reset! canvas-ref %))
          :width 700
          :height 500
          :style {:border "3px solid #333" :border-radius "10px" :cursor
          "crosshair"}
          :on-click (fn [e]
                     (let [rect (.getBoundingClientRect (.-target e))
                           x (- (.-clientX e) (.-left rect))
                           y (- (.-clientY e) (.-top rect))
                           norm-x (/ x 700)  ; Normalize to [0, 1]
                           norm-y (/ y 500)]
                       (swap! points conj {:x x :y y
                                           :norm-x norm-x :norm-y norm-y
                                           :label @current-class})))}]
```

User has clicked to create a custom pattern. Red dots (class 0) in corners, green dots (class 1) in the middle.

Feature 2: Real-Time Heatmap Decision Boundary

Every pixel is classified by the network. Green regions predict class 1; red regions predict class 0.

Listing 9-23. Real-time heatmap decision boundary renderer classifying every grid point with configurable resolution parameter and gradient coloring from red (class 0) to green (class 1) revealing learned decision surfaces

```
(defn draw-heatmap-and-points [canvas-ref network points width height
resolution activation-key]
  (when-let [canvas @canvas-ref]
```

```
(let [ctx (.getContext canvas "2d")]
  ;; Heatmap: classify EVERY grid point
  (doseq [x (range 0 width resolution)
          y (range 0 height resolution)]
    (let [norm-x (/ x width)
          norm-y (/ y height)
          output (first (nn/predict network [norm-x norm-y]
          activation-key))
          intensity (max 0 (min 255 (int (* 255 output))))
          color (str "rgb(" (- 255 intensity) "," intensity
          ",100)")]  ; Gradient from red to green
      (set! (.-fillStyle ctx) color)
      (.fillRect ctx x y resolution resolution)))

  ;; Training points ON TOP with white outline
  (doseq [{:keys [x y label]} points]
    ;; White outline
    (set! (.-fillStyle ctx) "white")
    (.beginPath ctx)
    (.arc ctx x y 10 0 (* 2 js/Math. PI))
    (.fill ctx)
    ;; Colored center
    (set! (.-fillStyle ctx) (if (= label 1) "#4caf50" "#f44336"))
    (.beginPath ctx)
    (.arc ctx x y 7 0 (* 2 js/Math. PI))
    (.fill ctx))))
```

After training on the spiral pattern, the decision boundary curves elegantly through the space.

Feature 3: Preset Patterns

Load classic machine learning datasets with one click.

Listing 9-24. Preset pattern generators creating classic ML benchmark datasets: XOR (linearly inseparable corners), spiral (intertwined parametric curves), and circular (ring surrounding center) demonstrating parametric data generation

```
(defn xor-pattern [w h]
  [{:x (* 0.2 w) :y (* 0.25 h) :norm-x 0.2 :norm-y 0.25 :label 0}
   {:x (* 0.8 w) :y (* 0.25 h) :norm-x 0.8 :norm-y 0.25 :label 1}
   {:x (* 0.2 w) :y (* 0.75 h) :norm-x 0.2 :norm-y 0.75 :label 1}
   {:x (* 0.8 w) :y (* 0.75 h) :norm-x 0.8 :norm-y 0.75 :label 0}])

(defn spiral-pattern [w h]
  (into []
        (concat
         (for [t (range 0 12.56 0.2)]  ; One full spiral
           (let [r (* 0.15 t)
                 x (+ (* 0.5 w) (* r w (js/Math.cos t)))
                 y (+ (* 0.5 h) (* r h (js/Math.sin t)))]
             {:x x :y y :norm-x (/ x w) :norm-y (/ y h) :label 1}))
         (for [t (range 0 12.56 0.2)]  ; Second spiral, offset by π
           (let [r (* 0.15 (+ t 3.14))
                 x (+ (* 0.5 w) (* r w (js/Math.cos t)))
                 y (+ (* 0.5 h) (* r h (js/Math.sin t)))]
             {:x x :y y :norm-x (/ x w) :norm-y (/ y h) :label 0})))))

(defn circle-pattern [w h]
  (into []
        (concat
         ;; Outer circle (class 1)
         (for [t (range 0 6.28 0.25)]
           (let [x (+ (* 0.5 w) (* 0.25 w (js/Math.cos t)))
                 y (+ (* 0.5 h) (* 0.25 h (js/Math.sin t)))]
             {:x x :y y :norm-x (/ x w) :norm-y (/ y h) :label 1}))
         ;; Random inner points (class 0)
         (for [_ (range 20)]
           (let [x (* w (+ 0.3 (* 0.4 (rand))))
                 y (* h (+ 0.3 (* 0.4 (rand))))]
             {:x x :y y :norm-x (/ x w) :norm-y (/ y h) :label 0})))))
```

```
;; UI buttons
[:button {:on-click #(reset! points (xor-pattern 700 500))} "XOR Problem"]
[:button {:on-click #(reset! points (spiral-pattern 700 500))} "Spiral"]
[:button {:on-click #(reset! points (circle-pattern 700 500))} "Circular"]
```

Spiral pattern loaded. The network must learn to separate two intertwined spirals.

After 5000 epochs: Spiral separated! The decision boundary wraps around both arms perfectly.

Feature 4: Activation Function Selector

Switch between sigmoid, ReLU, tanh, and leaky ReLU on the fly.

Listing 9-25. Activation function selector UI with dynamic styling highlighting selected function enabling hot-swapping between sigmoid, ReLU, tanh, and leaky ReLU mid-training

```
(doall
 (for [key [:sigmoid :relu :tanh :leaky-relu]]
   ^{:key key}
   [:button {:style {:width "100%" :padding "8px"
                     :background (if (= @activation-fn key)
                     "#ff9800" "#fff")
                     :border (str "2px solid " (if (= @activation-fn key)
                     "#ff9800" "#ddd"))}
            :on-click #(reset! activation-fn key)}
    (get-in nn/activation-fns [key :name])]))
```

Feature 5: Reactive Watchers

The brilliance of Reagent: Change any state; visualization updates automatically.

Listing 9-26. Reactive watcher system using requestAnimationFrame debouncing on Clojure's add-watch to redraw canvas without freezing the main thread

```
;; Debounce continuous updates to prevent browser freezes!
(let [draw-pending (atom false)
```

```
    queue-redraw (fn []
                   (when-not @draw-pending
                     (reset! draw-pending true)
                     (js/requestAnimationFrame
                      (fn []
                        (reset! draw-pending false)
                        (draw-heatmap-and-points canvas-ref
                        @network @points
                                                 700 500 8
                                                 @activation-fn)))))]

;; Automatically redraw when any core state changes
(add-watch network ::redraw (fn [_ _ _ _] (queue-redraw)))
(add-watch points ::redraw (fn [_ _ _ _] (queue-redraw)))
(add-watch activation-fn ::redraw (fn [_ _ _ _] (queue-redraw))))
```

Change the network? Canvas updates. Add a point? Canvas updates. Switch activation? Canvas updates. **Zero manual wiring**—Reagent handles it all.

Feature 6: Live Metrics Dashboard

Listing 9-27. Live metrics dashboard using CSS grid layout displaying epochs, learning rate, data point count, and activation function with color-coded panels for real-time monitoring

```
[:div {:style {:display "grid" :grid-template-columns "repeat(4, 1fr)" :gap
"15px"}}
 ;; Epochs
 [:div {:style {:background "#e3f2fd" :padding "20px" :text-align
 "center"}}
  [:div {:style {:font-size "12px" :color "#1976d2"}} "EPOCHS"]
  [:div {:style {:font-size "28px" :font-weight "bold"}} @epoch-count]]

 ;; Learning Rate
 [:div {:style {:background "#f3e5f5" :padding "20px" :text-align
 "center"}}
  [:div {:style {:font-size "12px" :color "#7b1fa2"}} "LEARNING RATE"]
  [:div {:style {:font-size "28px"}} (.toFixed @learning-rate 2)]]
```

```
;; Data Points
[:div {:style {:background "#fff3e0" :padding "20px" :text-align
"center"}}
 [:div {:style {:font-size "12px" :color "#e65100"}} "DATA POINTS"]
 [:div {:style {:font-size "28px"}} (count @points)]]

;; Activation Function
[:div {:style {:background "#e8f5e9" :padding "20px" :text-align
"center"}}
 [:div {:style {:font-size "12px" :color "#388e3c"}} "ACTIVATION"]
 [:div {:style {:font-size "16px"}} (get-in nn/activation-fns [@
 activation-fn :name])]]]
```

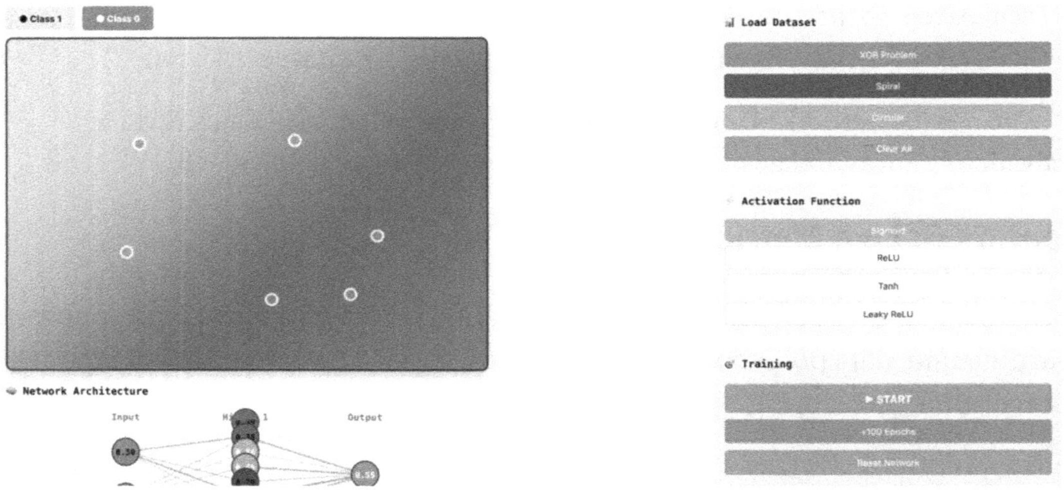

***Figure 9-18.** Complete playground UI in action displaying spiral dataset with 3247 epochs at learning rate 0.3. Complete playground in action: spiral dataset, 3247 epochs, sigmoid activation, learning rate 0.3*

The Training Loop

High-performance neural network playground that leverages ClojureScript's native performance.

Listing 9-28. High-performance training loop using setInterval for asynchronous execution achieving 20 epochs per second without blocking UI thread demonstrating ClojureScript's native JavaScript interop

```
(defn start-training! [network points epoch-count learning-rate
activation-fn]
  (reset! training? true)
  (reset! training-interval
          (js/setInterval
           (fn []
             ;; Train on all points
             (doseq [pt @points]
               (swap! network nn/train-step
                      [(:norm-x pt) (:norm-y pt)]
                      [(:label pt)]
                      @learning-rate
                      @activation-fn))
             (swap! epoch-count inc))
           50)))  ; Train every 50ms (20 epochs/second)

(defn stop-training! [training-interval training?]
  (when @training-interval
    (js/clearInterval @training-interval)
    (reset! training-interval nil)
    (reset! training? false)))
```

What This Demonstrates

The playground showcases

1. **ClojureScript + Reagent = rapid prototyping**: 350 lines of code, full ML playground.
2. **Immutable data works for ML**: Network state is immutable; training returns new networks.

3. **Reactive programming simplifies UIs**: Watchers eliminate manual DOM updates.
4. **Pure functions enable testing**: Every piece is testable in isolation.
5. **Canvas + SVG + Reagent = powerful viz**: Combine technologies seamlessly.

You've built a tool that rivals commercial ML playgrounds (TensorFlow Playground, ConvNetJS), entirely from scratch, in a functional language.

This is the power of understanding fundamentals.

Common Pitfalls and Debugging Neural Networks

After implementing all ten exercises, you'll inevitably encounter bugs. Here's a comprehensive debugging guide based on real implementation challenges.

Pitfall 1: The "Shrinking Neuron" Trap

Symptom: All outputs converge to 0.5; network stops learning after initial epochs.

Cause: Sigmoid saturation. When inputs are large ($|z| > 4$), sigmoid output is almost 0 or 1, and derivative ≈ 0. Gradients vanish.

Diagnosis:

Listing 9-29. Sigmoid saturation diagnostic detecting vanishing gradients when hidden layer activations cluster near 0 or 1 indicating need for ReLU or learning rate adjustment

```
;; Add this to your training loop
(defn diagnose-activations [network inputs]
  (let [activations (nn/forward-pass network inputs)]
    (doseq [[layer-idx layer-acts] (map-indexed vector activations)]
      (let [avg (/ (reduce + layer-acts) (count layer-acts))
            all-saturated? (every? #(or (< % 0.1) (> % 0.9)) layer-acts)]
        (println "Layer" layer-idx "avg:" (. ToFixed avg 3)
                 "saturated?" all-saturated?)))))

;; If you see "saturated? true" for hidden layers → problem!
```

Fix: - **Switch to ReLU**: No saturation for positive values - **Lower learning rate**: Prevents weights from growing too large - **Normalize inputs**: Keep inputs in range [-1, 1] - **Use tanh instead of sigmoid**: Tanh ranges [-1, 1], stronger gradients near 0

Visualization: Sigmoid derivative is almost flat when $|x| > 3$*. Gradients die.*

Pitfall 2: "NaN" explosion

Symptom: Loss becomes NaN; predictions become NaN; everything breaks.

Cause: Learning rate too high → weights explode → exp() overflow → NaN cascade.

Diagnosis:

Listing 9-30. Network health monitor checking for weight explosion and NaN cascade detecting excessive learning rate before network divergence becomes catastrophic

```
(defn check-network-health [network]
  (let [all-weights (mapcat :weights network)
        all-biases (mapcat :biases network)
        max-weight (apply max (map #(apply max (map js/Math.abs %)) all-
        weights))
        max-bias (apply max (map js/Math.abs all-biases))]
    (when (or (> max-weight 100) (> max-bias 100))
      (println "⚠ WARNING: Weights exploding!"
               "Max weight:" max-weight "Max bias:" max-bias))
    (when (or (js/isNaN max-weight) (js/isNaN max-bias))
      (println "🔥 CRITICAL: NaN detected!"))))
```

Fix: - **Reduce learning rate by 10×** - **Restart training with smaller LR** - **Implement gradient clipping**: `(min 5 (max -5 gradient))`

Pitfall 3: The "Dead ReLU" Problem

Symptom: Using ReLU, some neurons output 0 for ALL inputs. Network capacity shrinks.

Cause: If weighted input becomes negative and stays negative, ReLU always outputs 0. Gradient = 0, so weights never update. Neuron is "dead."

Diagnosis:

Listing 9-31. Dead ReLU neuron counter identifying permanently inactive neurons stuck at zero output requiring Leaky ReLU or lower learning rate to recover capacity

```
(defn count-dead-neurons [network training-data]
  (let [all-activations (map #(nn/forward-pass network (:input %))
  training-data)]
    (doseq [[layer-idx layer-size] (map-indexed vector (rest (layer-sizes
    network)))]
      (let [always-zero? (mapv (fn [neuron-idx]
                                (every? #(= 0 (get-in % [layer-idx
                                neuron-idx]))
                                        all-activations))
                              (range layer-size))
            dead-count (count (filter identity always-zero?))]
        (when (> dead-count 0)
          (println "Layer" layer-idx "has" dead-count "dead neurons out of"
          layer-size))))))
```

Fix: - **Use leaky ReLU**: Small gradient (0.01) even when `x < 0` - **Lower learning rate**: Prevents neurons from getting stuck - **Better weight initialization**: Use Xavier/He initialization instead of random [-1, 1]

Pitfall 4: Not Converging (Stuck at High Loss)

Symptom: Loss plateaus around 0.25 for XOR, never reaches 0.05.

Cause: Multiple possibilities

1. Network too small (can't learn the function)
2. Learning rate too small (training too slow)
3. Local minimum (unlucky initialization)
4. Incorrect backprop implementation

Diagnosis:

Listing 9-32. Convergence failure diagnostics measuring gradient magnitude and testing multiple random initializations to identify architecture inadequacy or local minima traps

```
;; 1. Check architecture
(println "Network architecture:" (mapv #(count (:weights %)) network))
;; For XOR, you need at least [2 2 1] or [2 4 1]

;; 2. Check gradient magnitude
(defn measure-gradient [network example]
  (let [before-weights (get-in network [0 :weights 0 0])
        trained (nn/train-step network (:input example) (:target
        example) 0.1)
        after-weights (get-in trained [0 :weights 0 0])
        change (Math/abs (- after-weights before-weights))]
    (println "Weight change:" change)
    (when (< change 0.0001)
      (println "⚠ Gradients very small - increase learning rate or check
      backprop"))))

;; 3. Try multiple restarts
(dotimes [attempt 5]
  (let [net (nn/init-network [2 4 1])
        trained (train-epochs net xor-data 1000 0.5)
        loss (calculate-mse trained xor-data)]
    (println "Attempt" attempt "final loss:" loss)))
```

Fix: - **Add more neurons**: [2 4 1] → [2 8 1] - **Increase learning rate**: 0.1 → 0.3 - **Try different initialization** (multiple random starts) - **Verify backprop** (test against known examples)

Pitfall 5: The Hiccup `[nil]` Trap (ClojureScript Specific)

Symptom: React error—"Objects are not valid as a React child"

Cause: Returning `[nil]` from a Reagent component instead of valid hiccup.

Listing 9-33. React nil trap fix using explicit if-else or React fragments preventing "Objects are not valid as a React child" errors in Reagent components

```
Bad code:
(defn my-component []
  (when (some-condition)  ; Returns nil if condition is false!
    [:div "Content"]))

;; React sees: [nil] → ERROR
Good code:
(defn my-component []
  (if (some-condition)
    [:div "Content"]
    [:div]))  ; Always return valid hiccup

;; Or use fragments:
(defn my-component []
  [:<>  ; React fragment
   (when (some-condition)
     [:div "Content"])])
```

Debugging Workflow

When something goes wrong

1. **Check inputs first**: Are they normalized? Do they have the right shape?

   ```
   (println "Input shape:" (count input) "Expected: 2")
   (println "Input values:" input "Should be in [0,1]")
   ```

2. **Verify network structure:**

   ```
   (println "Layers:" (mapv #(count (:weights %)) network))
   (println "First layer weights shape:"
            (count (get-in network [0 :weights]))
            "x"
            (count (get-in network [0 :weights 0])))
   ```

3. **Monitor training:**

```
(dotimes [epoch 100]
  (when (zero? (mod epoch 10))
    (let [loss (calculate-mse network xor-data)]
      (println "Epoch" epoch "Loss:" (.toFixed loss 4)))))
```

4. **Test forward pass in isolation:**

```
(let [net (nn/init-network [2 2 1])
      out (nn/predict net [0 1])]
  (println "Output:" out)
  (assert (vector? out))
  (assert (every? number? out)))
```

5. **Test backprop with known case:**

```
;; If target = output, weights should not change
(let [net (nn/init-network [2 2 1])
      out (nn/predict net [1 0])
      trained (nn/train-step net [1 0] out 0.5)
      w-before (get-in net [0 :weights 0 0])
      w-after (get-in trained [0 :weights 0 0])]
  (println "Weight change when error=0:" (- w-after w-before))
  (assert (< (Math/abs (- w-after w-before)) 0.0001)))
```

Building Intuition: Understanding What Networks Learn

Neural networks aren't magic. They're function approximators. Here's how to develop intuition for what's happening inside.

Reading Weight Matrices

Weights encode **which inputs matter**.

Example: After training XOR with [2 4 1] architecture

```
;; Inspect first hidden neuron
(def w1 (get-in trained-network [0 :weights 0]))  ; [w_x1, w_x2]
(def b1 (get-in trained-network [0 :biases 0]))

(println "Hidden neuron 1:")
(println "  w_x1 =" (.toFixed (nth w1 0) 2))
(println "  w_x2 =" (.toFixed (nth w1 1) 2))
(println "  bias =" (.toFixed b1 2))

;; Example output:
;;   w_x1 = 5.23
;;   w_x2 = 5.19
;;   bias = -2.45

;; Interpretation: This neuron fires when (x1 OR x2) is active
;; High positive weights on both inputs, negative bias
;; It's learned the OR function!
```

Pattern recognition: - **Large positive weight**: This input strongly activates the neuron - **Large negative weight**: This input strongly inhibits the neuron - **Weight ≈ 0**: This input is ignored by this neuron - **Large negative bias**: Neuron needs strong input to activate

Visualizing Hidden Layer Activations

What does each hidden neuron detect?

Listing 9-34. Hidden neuron visualization generating activation heatmaps across input space revealing what spatial patterns each neuron has learned to detect

```
(defn visualize-neuron-responses [network neuron-layer neuron-idx grid-size]
  "Show what patterns activate a specific hidden neuron"
  (doall
```

```
    (for [x (range 0 1 (/ 1 grid-size))
          y (range 0 1 (/ 1 grid-size))]
      (let [activations (nn/forward-pass network [x y])
            neuron-output (get-in activations [neuron-layer neuron-idx])]
        {:x x :y y :activation neuron-output}))))

;; Visualize on canvas: bright = high activation
(defn draw-neuron-heatmap [canvas data]
  (doseq [{:keys [x y activation]} data]
    (let [intensity (int (* 255 activation))
          color (str "rgb(" intensity "," intensity "," intensity ")")]
      (.fillRect ctx (* x canvas-width) (* y canvas-height)
                 cell-size cell-size))))
```

Heatmaps for four hidden neurons in XOR network. Each learns to detect a different region.

The Feature Hierarchy

Deeper networks learn hierarchical features:

Layer 1 (close to input): - Detects simple patterns (edges, corners, basic combinations) - Example: "Is $x_1 > 0.5$?" or "Are both inputs similar?"

Layer 2 (middle layers in deep networks): - Combines layer 1 features - Example: "Is it top-right quadrant?" or "Is it XOR-true?"

Output layer: - Makes final decision based on layer 2 features - Example: "Is pattern class 0 or class 1?"

When to Add More Layers vs. More Neurons

More neurons in the same layer = **More complex** decision boundary in the same "level" - Use when: Pattern is complex but flat (like spiral, checkerboard) - [2 4 1] → [2 16 1]: Can learn more intricate curves

More layers = **Higher abstraction** - Use when: Pattern has hierarchical structure - [2 4 1] → [2 4 4 1]: Can learn features-of-features - In practice: Rare for toy problems, essential for real-world (images, language)

Mental Model: Networks As Geometric Transformations

Each layer **reshapes** the data space:

1. **Input space**: Your raw data (e.g., 2D points for XOR)
2. **After layer 1**: Data projected into higher dimension (4D if four neurons)
    - Non-linearly distorted based on weights
    - Previously inseparable points now separable
3. **After layer 2** (if exists): Further refinement
4. **Output layer**: Final classification in 1D (binary class)

XOR example:

```
Input 2D:         Hidden 4D:           Output 1D:
●  ○              ●                     ●●
                                      (class 0)
○  ●              ○                     ○○
                                      (class 1)
Can't separate  Can separate!         Binary decision
with a line     (hyperplane in 4D)
```

The hidden layer "unfolds" the twisted XOR space into something linearly separable.

Debugging via Intuition

If network isn't learning

1. Check if hidden neurons are specializing - All neurons activating similarly? → Increase learning rate or add randomness - Some neurons always 0? → Dead ReLU problem
2. Check if output layer has enough signal:
    - If hidden layer outputs are all ~0.5 → Saturation, switch activation

3. Check if decision boundary makes sense:
    - Visualize it (e07 style)
    - Boundary going the wrong direction? → Check gradient signs, might have a bug

If network overfits: - Decision boundary has crazy wiggles around each point - Fix: More data, fewer neurons, or add noise

If network underfits: - Decision boundary is too simple (straight line for XOR) - Fix: More neurons, more layers, or higher learning rate

The "Aha!" moment

You'll know you deeply understand neural networks when

1. You can **predict** how changing architecture affects the decision boundary.
2. You can **diagnose** training failures just by looking at loss curves.
3. You can **sketch** what weight matrices should look like for a given problem.
4. You **stop being surprised** by what works vs. what doesn't.

This chapter is designed to get you there.

What We've Built: A Complete Neural Network Stack

Let's inventory what you've created.

Core Engine (`nn.cljs`)

- ✅ Multi-layer perceptron architecture
- ✅ Forward propagation with configurable activations
- ✅ Backpropagation with chain rule
- ✅ Gradient descent weight updates

- ✅ Pure functional implementation (immutable data structures)
- ✅ Support for sigmoid, ReLU, tanh, and leaky ReLU

Educational Progression

- ✅ **e01–e03**: Historical perceptron (1958–1969)
- ✅ **e04**: Backpropagation breaks the XOR barrier (1986)
- ✅ **e05**: Network visualization
- ✅ **e06**: Interactive data generation
- ✅ **e07**: Decision boundary rendering
- ✅ **e08**: Activation function comparison
- ✅ **e09**: Learning rate dynamics
- ✅ **e10**: Complete playground

Technical Achievements

- **No external ML libraries**: Pure ClojureScript + math
- **Reactive visualizations**: Reagent + Canvas/SVG
- **Functional purity**: Immutable networks, testable functions
- **Pedagogical clarity**: Every line of code is readable and understandable

What You Now Understand

After completing this chapter, you can

1. **Explain why XOR is impossible for perceptrons** (not linearly separable)
2. **Derive the backpropagation algorithm** (chain rule + gradient descent)

3. **Implement a neural network from scratch** (no magic, just math)
4. **Visualize what networks learn** (decision boundaries, weight magnitudes)
5. **Debug training failures** (vanishing gradients, dead ReLUs, divergence)
6. **Appreciate the history** (from AI winter to deep learning boom)

The Mathematics: Deeper Dive

For those who want the full mathematical treatment, see below.

Forward Pass

Given layer `l` with weights `W^l` and biases `b^l`:

```
z^l = W^l × a^(l-1) + b^l
a^l = σ(z^l)
```

where

- `a^(l-1)` = activations from previous layer (or input if l=1)
- `z^l` = weighted input (pre-activation)
- `a^l` = activations (post-activation)
- `σ()` = activation function

Backward Pass

Error gradient for output layer:

```
δ^L = (a^L - y) ⊙ σ'(z^L)
```

Error propagation to hidden layers:

```
δ^l = ((W^(l+1))^T × δ^(l+1)) ⊙ σ'(z^l)
```

Weight gradients:

```
∂C/∂W^l = δ^l × (a^(l-1))^T
∂C/∂b^l = δ^l
```

Weight update:

```
W^l ← W^l - η × ∂C/∂W^l
b^l ← b^l - η × ∂C/∂b^l
```

where

- ⊙ = element-wise multiplication (Hadamard product)
- η = learning rate
- C = cost function (typically mean squared error)
- y = target output

Why This Works

Gradient descent moves weights in the direction that reduces error. The **chain rule** lets us compute gradients layer by layer, even for deep networks. The **activation function derivative** determines how much signal propagates backward.

This is calculus in action. The network is a giant composition of functions, and backpropagation is just methodical differentiation.

The Limitations: What Neural Networks Can't Do (Yet)

It's important to understand the boundaries.

What Our Networks Struggle With

1. **Small data**: Neural networks need lots of examples. Ten points won't cut it.
2. **Extrapolation**: They interpolate well within training data bounds, but fail outside.

3. **Interpretability**: We can visualize 2D decision boundaries, but 1000-dimensional ones? Opaque.
4. **Guarantees**: No formal verification. We can't prove correctness.
5. **Causality**: Networks learn correlations, not causal relationships.

What Modern Deep Learning Adds

Our simple MLPs are educational, but production systems use

- **Convolutional layers**: For image processing (shared weights, local receptive fields)
- **Recurrent layers**: For sequences (LSTM, GRU)
- **Attention mechanisms**: For long-range dependencies (transformers)
- **Batch normalization**: For training stability
- **Dropout**: For regularization
- **Advanced optimizers**: Adam, AdamW, Lion

These are all built on the **same foundation** you've learned. Backpropagation. Gradient descent. Activation functions. The rest is engineering.

The Future: Where Do We Go From Here?

If this chapter has ignited your interest, here are paths forward.

Immediate Next Steps

1. **Add momentum**: Smooth gradient updates with exponential moving average
2. **Implement cross-entropy loss**: Better than MSE for classification
3. **Add dropout**: Randomly disable neurons during training to prevent overfitting
4. **Batch training**: Update weights after multiple examples, not just one

Deeper Explorations

1. **Convolutional neural networks**: Build an image classifier.
2. **Recurrent neural networks**: Process sequences.
3. **Generative adversarial networks**: Create images from noise.
4. **Reinforcement learning**: Combine neural networks with Chapter 1's game loop.

Production Considerations

- **TensorFlow.js**: When you need GPUs and production-grade tools
- **ONNX**: Cross-platform neural network exchange format
- **Quantization**: Run models on mobile devices
- **Federated learning**: Train without centralizing data

But remember: **understanding the fundamentals** (what you've learned here) is essential. Libraries change. The math doesn't.

Reflections: From Perceptrons to Progress

We started with Rosenblatt's optimistic 1958 perceptron—a machine that learned, truly learned, for the first time. We hit Minsky's devastating 1969 proof that single layers couldn't solve XOR. We endured the AI winter.

Then in 1986, Rumelhart, Hinton, and Williams showed that backpropagation could train hidden layers. The field revived. Slowly at first—SVMs dominated the 1990s. Neural networks were still considered "brittle," "finicky," and "unreliable."

But in 2012, AlexNet won ImageNet by a landslide. GPUs made deep networks trainable. ReLU made them stable. Dropout made them generalizable. And suddenly, neural networks weren't the underdog anymore—they were the champion.

Today, neural networks power: - Language models (GPT, ChatGPT, Claude) - Image generation (DALL-E, Midjourney, Stable Diffusion) - Protein folding (AlphaFold) - Game playing (AlphaGo, OpenAI Five) - Self-driving cars (Tesla, Waymo)

And it all traces back to **the same algorithm you implemented tonight**. Forward pass. Backward pass. Adjust weights. Repeat.

That's the power of understanding fundamentals. The networks running in data centers may have billions of parameters, but they're still doing what you just built: **learning from data by minimizing error through gradient descent**.

Opening Exercises: Your Turn

Now that you've built the foundation, here are challenges to cement your understanding.

Beginner Challenges

1. **The AND→NAND Switcher**
   - Modify `e01.cljs` to let users toggle between and NAND gates.
   - Watch the perceptron learn both (they're both linearly separable).
   - **Hint**: NAND is just (1 - AND).
2. **Slow-Motion Training**
   - In `e05.cljs`, add a "slow mode" that trains one epoch per second.
   - Watch each weight adjustment individually.
   - **Bonus**: Highlight the most-changed weight each step.
3. **Custom Activation Function**
   - Add a new activation function to `nn.cljs`: `swish(x) = x * sigmoid(x)`.
   - Derivative: `swish'(x) = swish(x) + sigmoid(x) * (1 - swish(x))`.
   - Test it in `e08.cljs`.

Intermediate Challenges

1. **Multi-class Classification**
   - Modify the playground (`e10.cljs`) to support three classes (add blue).
   - Change output layer to three neurons (one-hot encoding).
   - Use softmax instead of sigmoid: `softmax(x_i) = e^(x_i) / Σe^(x_j)`.
2. **Momentum**
   - Add momentum to `nn.cljs`:
   - `velocity = β × velocity + (1-β) × gradient`
   - `weights = weights - learning-rate × velocity`
   - Compare with/without momentum in `e09.cljs`
3. **Decision Boundary Animation**
   - Record how the decision boundary evolves during training.
   - Create a "replay" slider to show learning progression.
   - **Hint**: Save network state every N epochs.

Advanced Challenges

1. **Convolutional Layer (1D)**
   - Implement a 1D convolution layer.
   - Learn to detect patterns in sequences.
   - **Application**: Classify sine wave frequencies.
2. **Autoencoder**
   - Build a [2→4→2] network.
   - Train it to reconstruct inputs: `input == output`.

- The four-neuron hidden layer learns a 4D embedding of 2D space.
- **Visualization**: Plot the hidden activations.

3. **Network Architecture Search**
   - Automatically try different architectures: [2-3-1], [2-4-1], [2-5-1], [2-4-4-1].
   - Track which converges fastest on XOR.
   - **Challenge**: Can you find the minimal network that solves XOR?

Expert Challenges

1. **Batch Normalization**
   - Implement batch normalization between layers.
   - Formula: $(x - \mu) / \sqrt{(\sigma 2 + \varepsilon)}$ then $\gamma x + \beta$.
   - Compare stability with/without on a deep [2-8-8-8-1] network.
2. **Dropout**
   - During training, randomly set 50% of activations to 0.
   - Scale remaining activations by 2× to compensate.
   - At test time, use all neurons.
   - **Observe**: Prevents overfitting on small datasets.
3. **Genetic Algorithm Hybrid**
   - Instead of backpropagation, evolve weights:
   - Generate 100 random networks.
   - Keep top ten performers on XOR.
   - Mutate and recombine to create next generation.
   - Can evolution solve XOR? How many generations does it take?

Research Questions

1. **Why Does ReLU Work So Well?**
   - Compare sigmoid vs. ReLU on a [2-10-10-10-1] network.
   - Measure gradient magnitudes at each layer.
   - **Hypothesis**: ReLU prevents vanishing gradients.
2. **The Lottery Ticket Hypothesis**
   - Train a network on XOR, then reset 90% of weights to original values.
   - Can the remaining 10% still learn?
   - **Famous paper**: "The Lottery Ticket Hypothesis" (Frankle & Carbin, 2019).
3. **Double Descent**
   - Train networks with increasing hidden layer sizes: 1, 2, 4, 8, 16, 32 neurons.
   - Plot final test error vs. hidden size.
   - **Expected**: Error decreases, then increases (overfitting), then decreases again!
   - This is a frontier of modern ML theory.

Resources for Further Learning
Books

- ***Deep Learning* by Goodfellow, Bengio, and Courville**: The definitive textbook (free online)
- ***Neural Networks and Deep Learning* by Michael Nielsen**: Interactive web book
- ***Grokking Deep Learning* by Andrew Trask**: Code-first approach

Papers (Historical)

- Rosenblatt (1958): "The Perceptron: A Probabilistic Model for Information Storage"
- Rumelhart, Hinton, and Williams (1986): "Learning Representations by Back-Propagating Errors"
- LeCun et al. (1998): "Gradient-Based Learning Applied to Document Recognition" (CNNs)

Papers (Modern)

- Krizhevsky et al. (2012): "ImageNet Classification with Deep CNNs" (AlexNet)
- Vaswani et al. (2017): "Attention Is All You Need" (Transformers)
- He et al. (2015): "Deep Residual Learning for Image Recognition" (ResNets)

Online Courses

- **fast.ai**: Practical deep learning (top-down approach)
- **Stanford CS231n**: CNNs for visual recognition (bottom-up theory)
- **3Blue1Brown Neural Networks Series**: Visual intuition

Communities

- **r/MachineLearning**: Research discussions
- **Papers with Code**: Implementations of recent papers
- **Hugging Face**: Pre-trained models and datasets

Conclusion: The Ninth Floor

You've climbed nine floors. You've built games, manipulated canvases, created reactive UIs, processed video, and now taught machines to learn.

Neural networks are the closest we've come to artificial intelligence. Not the sci-fi kind (yet), but something real: machines that genuinely improve with experience, that find patterns human eyes miss, and that generalize from examples to unseen cases.

And you built it with **pure functions**, **immutable data**, and **functional composition**. ClojureScript's elegance shines brightest when tackling complex algorithms. The math flows naturally. The abstractions compose beautifully. The debugging is tractable.

But more than the code, you now understand **the history, the mathematics, the limitations, and the potential** of neural networks. You're not just using a library; you're a practitioner who knows what's under the hood.

There's one floor left. The tenth. The penthouse.

What awaits you there?

Only one way to find out.

You are now equipped to explore the frontiers of artificial intelligence. Use your powers wisely.

CHAPTER 10

Building an Audio Visualizer with ClojureScript and Tauri: The Penthouse Suite

> "At the top floor of our hotel, where the city's rhythm becomes visible light, we discover that sound is just data dancing to its own frequency."

Welcome to the Penthouse

This is the final chapter, the penthouse floor at the top of our journey. We're not just building a web application anymore. We're crossing into **native desktop territory** using Tauri, the Rust-powered framework that wraps our ClojureScript in a real operating system window. We're tapping into the **Web Audio API** to capture sound from your microphone in real time. And we're rendering **five different visual interpretations** of that audio data, each one a different lens through which to see sound.

N. Modrzyk, *The ClojureScript Playbook*, https://doi.org/10.1007/979-8-8688-2879-9_10

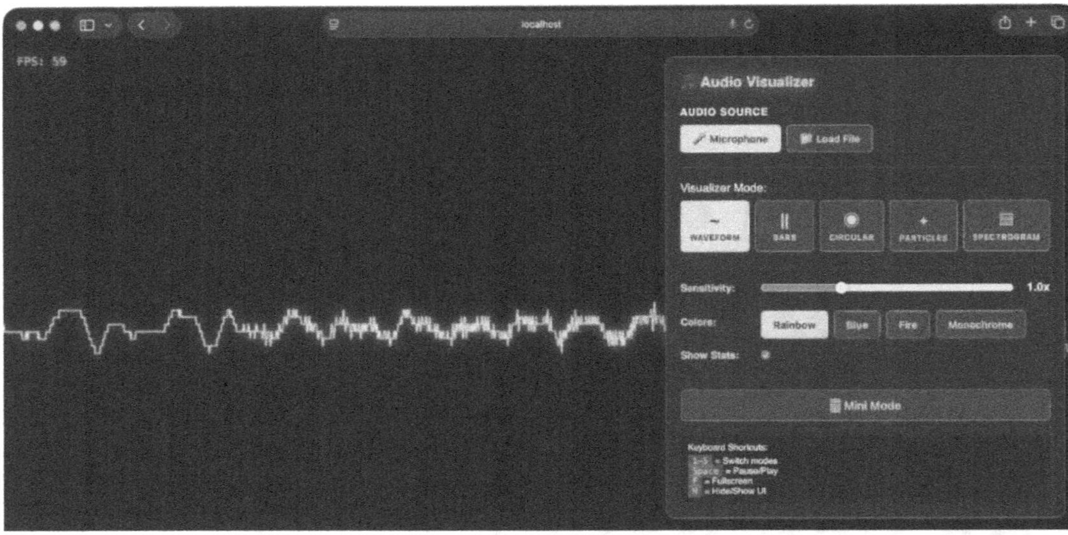

Figure 10-1. *Audio visualizer penthouse suite showing native desktop application with real-time sound visualization*

The Big Picture: System Architecture

Before we dive into code, let's understand how all the pieces fit together. This is no longer a simple single-page app. This is a **hybrid system** with three distinct layers.

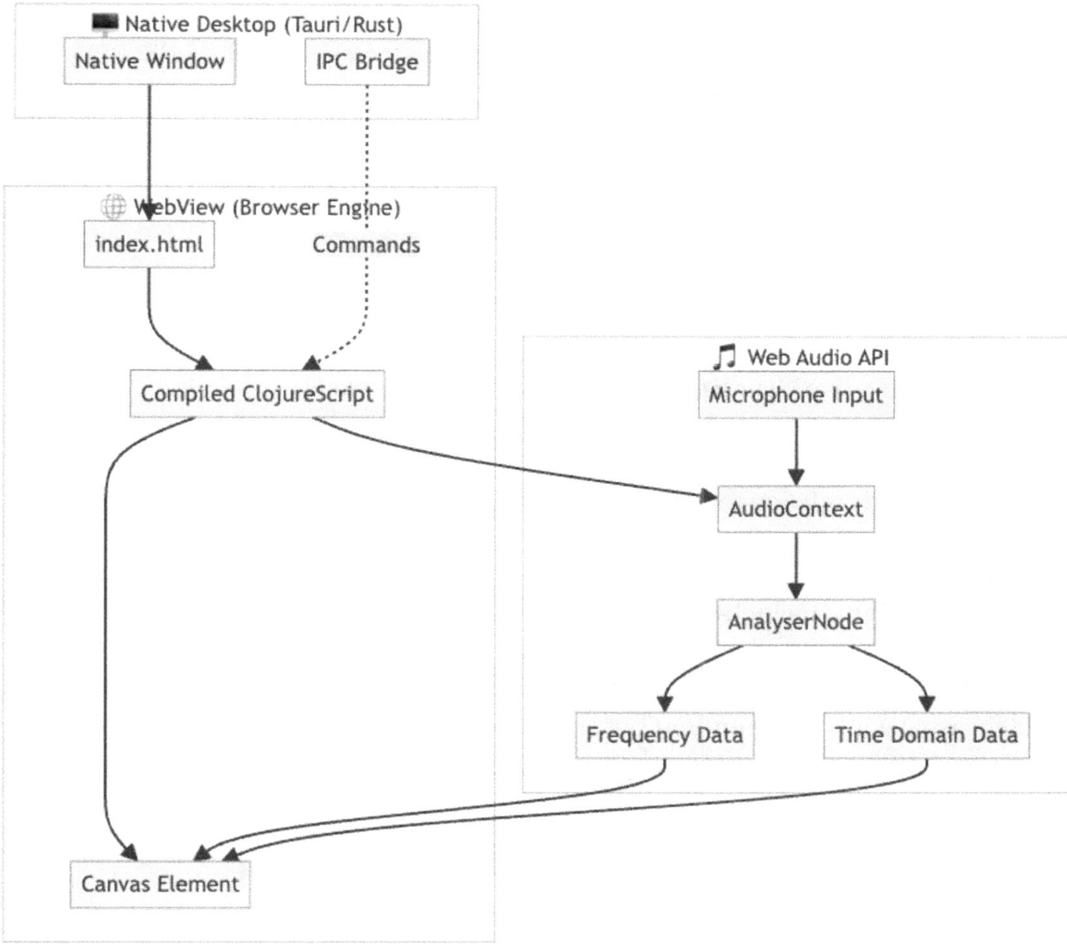

Figure 10-2. *Three-layer hybrid architecture combining Tauri/Rust for native OS integration, ClojureScript for logic, and Web Audio API for sound processing*

Three worlds, one application:

1. **Tauri/Rust layer**: Creates a native OS window, handles file system access, manages the application lifecycle
2. **ClojureScript layer**: Your familiar functional code, compiled to JavaScript
3. **Web Audio layer**: Browser APIs for capturing and analyzing sound in real time

The beauty? Each layer does what it does best. Rust handles the heavy native integration. ClojureScript manages state and rendering logic. The Web Audio API processes the acoustic physics.

The Hotel's Final Lesson

Throughout this book, we've built with an **incremental philosophy**. Start simple. Add complexity only when needed. Test constantly. This chapter is the culmination of that approach.

We're building **five visualizers**, each in its own namespace:

- `e01.cljs`—**waveform**: The oscilloscope view, raw time-domain data
- `e02.cljs`—**frequency bars**: Classic spectrum analyzer
- `e05.cljs`—**circular spectrum**: Radial arrangement of frequencies
- `e06.cljs`—**particles**: Physics-based reactive particles
- `e07.cljs`—**spectrogram**: Scrolling heatmap of frequency history

Each visualizer is **independent** but shares **common state**. This is a masterclass in functional architecture—shared data, isolated behavior.

Part I: The Foundation—Setting Up Tauri

Why Tauri?

Remember in earlier chapters when we ran `npx shadow-cljs watch app` and opened a browser tab? That worked because we were building web applications. But web apps have limitations:

- Can't access the file system deeply
- Can't run system commands
- Can't create menu bars or system tray icons
- Always need a browser window frame

Tauri changes the game. It's like Electron (which you may know from VS Code, Slack, Discord) but faster and smaller. How? By using your operating system's built-in web rendering engine instead of bundling an entire Chromium browser.

Table 10-1. *Performance comparison between Electron and Tauri showing significant advantages in bundle size, memory usage, and security*

Feature	Electron	Tauri	Our App
Language	JavaScript	Rust + JS	ClojureScript + Rust
Bundle Size	~120MB	~3MB	~3MB ✓
Memory	~100MB	~30MB	~30MB ✓
Startup	Slow	Fast	Fast ✓
Security	Weak	Strong	Strong ✓

Project Structure

Let's look at how a Tauri + ClojureScript project is organized:

```
10-audio-visualizer/
├── src/                    # ClojureScript source
│   └── myapp/
│       ├── core.cljs       # Entry point & keyboard handling
│       ├── state.cljs      # Shared state & audio setup
│       ├── e01.cljs        # Waveform visualizer
│       ├── e02.cljs        # Frequency bars
│       ├── e05.cljs        # Circular spectrum
│       ├── e06.cljs        # Particles
│       ├── e07.cljs        # Spectrogram
│       └── e08.cljs        # UI controls & mode switching
│
├── src-tauri/              # Rust/Tauri source
│   ├── Cargo.toml          # Rust dependencies
│   ├── tauri.conf.json     # Tauri configuration
│   └── src/
│       └── main.rs         # Rust entry point
│
├── public/                 # Static assets
│   └── index.html          # HTML shell
│
```

```
|
├── shadow-cljs.edn        # ClojureScript build config
└── package.json           # NPM dependencies
```

Notice the **dual nature**: `src/` for ClojureScript, `src-tauri/` for Rust. They're two separate programs that communicate through Tauri's IPC (inter-process communication) bridge.

Configuration: shadow-cljs.edn

Listing 10-1. Shadow-cljs Tauri configuration with port 8001 dev server, Reagent dependency, and browser target matching native window expectations

```
{:source-paths ["src"]
 :dependencies [[reagent/reagent "2.0.1"]]
 :dev-http {8001 "public"}
 :builds {:app {:target :browser
                :output-dir "public/js"
                :asset-path "/js"
                :modules {:main {:init-fn myapp.core/init
                                 :entries [myapp.core]}}}}}
```

Key differences from earlier chapters:

- **Port 8001**: Tauri expects the dev server here (configurable in `tauri.conf.json`).
- **Reagent**: We're using React integration for the UI controls.
- **No `:entries`**: We let shadow-cljs auto-discover from `:init-fn`.

Configuration: tauri.conf.json

This is the Rust side of the house.

Listing 10-2. Tauri configuration JSON defining native window properties, dev server integration, and build commands for Rust/ClojureScript coordination

```
{
  "build": {
    "beforeBuildCommand": "npx shadow-cljs release app",
    "frontendDist": "../public",
    "devUrl": "http://localhost:8001"
  },
  "bundle": {
    "active": true,
    "icon": ["icons/32x32.png", "icons/128x128.png",
"icons/128x128@2x.png",
             "icons/icon.icns", "icons/icon.ico"],
    "targets": "all"
  },
  "productName": "Audio Visualizer",
  "version": "0.1.0",
  "identifier": "com.cajuns.audio-visualizer",
  "app": {
    "windows": [{
      "title": "Audio Visualizer",
      "width": 1200,
      "height": 800,
      "resizable": true,
      "fullscreen": false,
      "decorations": true,
      "useHttpsScheme": true
    }],
    "trayIcon": {
      "iconPath": "icons/icon.png",
      "iconAsTemplate": true
    },
    "security": { "csp": null }
  }
}
```

The dance: When you run `npm run tauri dev`

1. Tauri executes `beforeDevCommand` → Starts shadow-cljs watch server on 8001.
2. Tauri opens a native window.
3. Tauri loads `http://localhost:8001` in that window.
4. Shadow-cljs watches for changes and hot-reloads instantly.

It's **native performance** with **web development ergonomics**. Best of both worlds.

Part II: The Audio Pipeline—Web Audio API

Now we enter the realm of digital signal processing. Don't worry—you don't need a PhD in acoustics. The Web Audio API abstracts the hard parts beautifully.

How Sound Becomes Data

When you speak into a microphone, here's what happens.

Figure 10-3. *Audio pipeline from physical sound waves through microphone, ADC, and AudioContext to FFT frequency analysis*

1. **Sound waves** (pressure variations in air) hit your microphone.
2. **Analog-to-digital converter** (ADC) samples the voltage 48,000 times per second.
3. **AudioContext** manages these samples as a stream.
4. **AnalyserNode** performs **fast Fourier transform** (FFT) to extract frequency information.

FFT is the magic spell. It converts time-domain data (amplitude over time) into frequency-domain data (which frequencies are present). Think of it like a prism splitting white light into a rainbow—but for sound.

The State Architecture

All audio state lives in one Reagent atom in `state.cljs`.

Listing 10-3. Centralized Reagent atom serving as single source of truth for audio context, analyzer nodes, typed data arrays, mode selection, and visualizer-specific state shared across all five visualizers

```
(defonce app-state
  (r/atom {;; Audio context
           :audio-context nil
           :analyser nil
           :data-array-time nil      ; Time domain data (waveform)
           :data-array-freq nil      ; Frequency domain data (spectrum)
           :animation-frame nil
           :started? false

           ;; Audio source
           :source-type :microphone   ; :microphone or :file
           :audio-source nil
           :media-stream nil          ; Store stream to stop it later
           :audio-buffer nil
           :current-file nil

           ;; Visualizer settings
           :mode :circular
           :sensitivity 1.0
           :color-scheme :rainbow     ; :rainbow, :blue, :fire, :monochrome
           :show-stats true
           :show-ui true
           :mini-mode false

           ;; Performance
           :fps 60
           :last-frame-time 0

           ;; Beat detection
           :beat-history []
```

```
        :last-beat-time 0

        ;; Mode-specific data
        :particles []
        :spectrogram-buffer []}))
```

This is the single source of truth. All five visualizers read from this atom. When audio data arrives, we `swap!` it in. When the user changes modes, we `swap!` the `:mode` key. Pure functional state management at scale.

Audio Setup: The Tricky Part

Getting microphone access is **asynchronous**. The browser must ask for permission, the user must grant it, and then we get a stream. Classic JavaScript promise territory. Here's how we handle it functionally.

Listing 10-4. Singleton microphone setup implementing lazy initialization with promise-based getUserMedia, FFT analyzer configuration, Uint8Array buffer allocation, and MediaStreamSource connection for Web Audio API pipeline

```
(defn setup-analyser! []
  "Setup or reuse existing analyser. Auto-connects to microphone on
  first call."
  (if-let [existing (:analyser @app-state)]
    ;; Already set up, return immediately
    existing
    ;; Need to create analyser and request mic
    (let [ctx (get-audio-context)
          analyser (.createAnalyser ctx)]
      ;; Configure FFT size (trade-off: larger = better freq resolution
      but slower)
      (set! (.-fftSize analyser) 2048)
      (set! (.-smoothingTimeConstant analyser) 0.8)

      ;; Create data arrays
      (let [buffer-length-time (.-fftSize analyser)
            buffer-length-freq (.-frequencyBinCount analyser)
```

```
          data-time (js/Uint8Array. buffer-length-time)
          data-freq (js/Uint8Array. buffer-length-freq)]
      (swap! app-state assoc
             :analyser analyser
             :data-array-time data-time
             :data-array-freq data-freq))

    ;; Request microphone (async!)
    (when-not (:started? @app-state)
      (-> (js/navigator.mediaDevices.getUserMedia #js {:audio true})
          (.then (fn [stream]
                   (let [source (.createMediaStreamSource ctx stream)]
                     (.connect source analyser)
                     (swap! app-state assoc
                            :started? true
                            :media-stream stream
                            :audio-source source)
                     (js/console.log "✓ Microphone connected!"))))
          (.catch (fn [err]
                    (js/console.error "✗ Microphone access denied:"
                    err)))))

    analyser)))
```

Key concepts:

Table 10-2. *FFT configuration parameters explaining fftSize, smoothingTimeConstant, and frequencyBinCount trade-offs*

Concept	Value	Why
fftSize	2048	Must be power of 2. Larger = better frequency resolution but slower. 2048 gives us 1024 frequency bins.
smoothingTimeConstant	0.8	Temporal smoothing (0–1). Higher = smoother but less responsive.
frequencyBinCount	fftSize ÷ 2	Always half the FFT size. Each bin represents a frequency range.

The singleton pattern: Notice we check for `existing` first. We only want **one** audio context, one analyzer. Creating multiple would waste resources and create audio glitches.

Data Arrays: Uint8Array Explained

```
(js/Uint8Array. 2048)
```

This creates a typed array—a fixed-size, efficient buffer for numeric data. Unlike JavaScript arrays which can hold anything, typed arrays are

- **Faster** (direct memory access)
- **Smaller** (packed tightly)
- **Typed** (only unsigned 8-bit integers, 0–255)

Audio data arrives as values 0–255. This maps perfectly to color intensities, bar heights, and particle speeds. The Web Audio API fills these arrays; we just read them.

Part III: The Visualizers—Five Perspectives on Sound

Each visualizer is a separate namespace with the same structure.

Listing 10-5. Visualizer namespace template pattern with mode guard clause preventing zombie animation loops and requestAnimationFrame recursion structure

```
(ns myapp.eOX
  (:require [myapp.state :as state]))

(defn draw-loop! []
  (letfn [(draw []
            (when (= (:mode @state/app-state) :visualizer-name)
              ;; Get audio data
              ;; Clear canvas
              ;; Draw visualization
```

```
          ;; Schedule next frame
          (swap! state/app-state assoc :animation-frame
                 (js/requestAnimationFrame draw))))]
  (draw)))

(defn start! []
  (when-let [analyser (state/setup-analyser!)]
    (draw-loop!)))
```

The guard clause `when (= (:mode @app-state) :visualizer-name)` is critical. It prevents **zombie loops**—old visualizers continuing to run after a mode switch. Each frame checks: "Am I still the active visualizer?" If not, stop.

Visualizer 1: Waveform (e01.cljs)

The waveform shows **time-domain data**—the raw oscillation of the microphone signal. This is what an oscilloscope displays.

Listing 10-6. Waveform oscilloscope visualizer using getByteTimeDomainData for raw audio signal with tanh soft-clamping preventing harsh clipping artifacts creating smooth wave contours

```
(defn draw-loop! []
  (let [canvas (state/get-canvas)
        ctx (state/get-canvas-context)]
    (when-let [analyser (:analyser @state/app-state)]
      (let [data-array (:data-array-time @state/app-state)
            w (.-width canvas)
            h (.-height canvas)]
        (letfn [(draw []
                  (when (= (:mode @state/app-state) :waveform)
                    ;; Schedule next frame first
                    (swap! state/app-state assoc :animation-frame
                           (js/requestAnimationFrame draw))

                    ;; Get waveform data
                    (.getByteTimeDomainData analyser data-array)
```

```
          ;; Clear background
          (state/clear-canvas! ctx w h)

          ;; Draw waveform line
          (set! (.-lineWidth ctx) 2)
          (set! (.-strokeStyle ctx) "#00FFAA")
          (.beginPath ctx)

          (let [slice (/ w (.-length data-array))]
            (loop [i 0, x 0]
              (when (< i (.-length data-array))
                (let [v (/ (aget data-array i) 128.0)
                      ;; Soft clamping using tanh for smooth curves
                      deviation-raw (* (- v 1) h 2)
                      deviation (* (js/Math.tanh (/ deviation-raw
                      h)) h 0.8)
                      y (+ (/ h 2) deviation)]
                  (if (zero? i)
                    (.moveTo ctx x y)
                    (.lineTo ctx x y))
                  (recur (inc i) (+ x slice))))))

          (.lineTo ctx w (/ h 2))
          (.stroke ctx)

          ;; Stats overlay
          (state/measure-fps!)
          (when (:show-stats @state/app-state)
            (set! (.-fillStyle ctx) "rgba(0, 255, 180, 0.8)")
            (set! (.-font ctx) "16px monospace")
            (.fillText ctx (str "FPS: " (:fps @state/app-state))
            20 30))))]
    (draw))))))
```

The math breakdown:

1. **Normalize**: `v = sample ÷ 128` converts 0–255 → 0–2 range.
2. **Center**: `(- v 1)` shifts to -1 to +1 (zero-centered).

3. **Amplify**: `* h 2` makes oscillations visible.
4. **Soft clamp**: `tanh(x)` creates smooth S-curve, preventing blocky clipping.
5. **Position**: `(+ (h/2) deviation)` places on canvas.

Why tanh? The hyperbolic tangent function gracefully compresses extreme values while leaving normal values untouched. It's the difference between a brick wall and a cushion.

```
Input:  -3  -2  -1   0   1   2   3
tanh:  -1  -0.96 -0.76  0  0.76  0.96  1
```

Notice how it approaches ±1 asymptotically? That's smooth clamping.

Visualizer 2: Frequency Bars (e02.cljs)

This is the classic spectrum analyzer—think car stereos, Winamp, and iTunes visualizers. Each bar represents a frequency range.

Listing 10-7. Classic spectrum analyzer with vertical frequency bars using HSL rainbow gradient from red (bass) through green (mid) to blue (treble) with shadow glow effects

```
(defn draw-frequency-loop! []
  (let [canvas (state/get-canvas)
        ctx (state/get-canvas-context)]
    (when-let [analyser (:analyser @state/app-state)]
      (let [data-array (:data-array-freq @state/app-state)
            w (.-width canvas)
            h (.-height canvas)]
        (letfn [(draw []
                  (when (= (:mode @state/app-state) :bars)
                    ;; Schedule next frame first
                    (swap! state/app-state assoc :animation-frame
                           (js/requestAnimationFrame draw))
```

```
            ;; Get frequency data
            (.getByteFrequencyData analyser data-array)

            ;; Clear
            (state/clear-canvas! ctx w h)

            ;; Draw bars
            (let [num-bars (.-length data-array)
                  bar-width (/ w num-bars)
                  bar-gap 1]
              (loop [i 0, x 0]
                (when (< i num-bars)
                  (let [v (aget data-array i)
                        bar-height (* v (/ h 256))]
                    ;; Bright rainbow colors
                    (let [hue (* 360 (/ i num-bars))
                          brightness (+ 50 (* 20 (/ v 255)))]
                      (set! (.-fillStyle ctx)
                          (str "hsl(" hue ", 100%, " brightness "%)")))

                    ;; Strong glow
                    (set! (.-shadowBlur ctx) 15)
                    (set! (.-shadowColor ctx)
                          (str "hsl(" (* 360 (/ i num-bars)) ",
                          100%, 60%)"))

                    (.fillRect ctx x (- h bar-height)
                               (- bar-width bar-gap) bar-height))
                  (recur (inc i) (+ x bar-width)))))

            ;; Stats overlay
            (state/measure-fps!)
            (when (:show-stats @state/app-state)
              (set! (.-fillStyle ctx) "rgba(0, 255, 180, 0.8)")
              (set! (.-font ctx) "16px monospace")
              (.fillText ctx (str "FPS: " (:fps @state/app-state))
              20 30))))]
    (draw)))))
```

Color theory in action:

Table 10-3. *Color theory mapping showing frequency bands to HSL hues for intuitive visual representation*

Frequency	Hue	Color	Why
Low (bass)	0°	Red	Warm, powerful
Mid	120°	Green	Balanced
High	240°	Blue	Cool, sharp

We use **HSL** (hue, saturation, lightness) instead of RGB because it lets us sweep through the rainbow by simply incrementing hue from 0° to 360°.

The shadow/glow trick: Setting `shadowBlur` and `shadowColor` before drawing creates a glow effect. The shadow is drawn *behind* the fill, creating the illusion of light emission.

Visualizer 3: Circular Spectrum (e05.cljs)

Instead of vertical bars, we arrange them radially around a center point. This creates a mesmerizing mandala effect.

Listing 10-8. Circular spectrum visualizer arranging frequency bars radially around pulsing center using polar-to-Cartesian conversion creating mesmerizing mandala effect

```
(let [num-bars (.-length data-array)
      sum (reduce + (map #(aget data-array %) (range num-bars)))
      avg (/ sum num-bars)
      norm (/ avg 255.0)
      base-inner-radius (+ 20 (* norm 80))]

  ;; Draw radial bars
  (set! (.-shadowBlur ctx) 0)
  (set! (.-lineWidth ctx) 2)

  (let [angle-step (/ (* 2 Math/PI) num-bars)]
    (loop [i 0]
```

```
    (when (< i num-bars)
      (let [v (aget data-array i)
            bin-norm (/ v 255.0)
            bar-length (* 0.85 (+ 50 (* bin-norm max-radius)))
            angle (* i angle-step)

            ;; Polar → Cartesian conversion
            x-start (+ center-x (* base-inner-radius (Math/cos angle)))
            y-start (+ center-y (* base-inner-radius (Math/sin angle)))
            x-end (+ center-x (* bar-length (Math/cos angle)))
            y-end (+ center-y (* bar-length (Math/sin angle)))

            ;; Rainbow color
            hue (mod (* 360 (/ i num-bars)) 360)
            lightness (+ 30 (* 50 bin-norm))]

        (set! (.-strokeStyle ctx)
              (str "hsl(" hue ", 100%, " lightness "%)"))
        (.beginPath ctx)
        (.moveTo ctx x-start y-start)
        (.lineTo ctx x-end y-end)
        (.stroke ctx))

      (recur (inc i))))))
```

Polar coordinate math refresher:

```
x = center_x + radius × cos(angle)
y = center_y + radius × sin(angle)
```

We're drawing from an inner circle (the "pulse" that grows with average volume) to an outer position determined by each frequency bin's amplitude.

The "pulse" effect: `base-inner-radius = 20 + (avg × 80)` makes the center circle grow and shrink with overall loudness. Try humming loudly—you'll see the center expand!

Visualizer 4: Particles (e06.cljs)

Now we enter **physics simulation** territory. Particles are born, move according to velocity, are affected by gravity, and fade out over time.

Listing 10-9. Physics-based particle system with Euler integration gravity, parametric spawning mapping bass/mid/high frequencies to center bursts/side streams/rain behaviors

```
(defn create-particle [x y vx vy color life]
  {:x x :y y :vx vx :vy vy :color color :life life})

(defn update-particle [p]
  (when (> (:life p) 0)
    (-> p
        (update :x + (:vx p))
        (update :y + (:vy p))
        (update :vy + 0.2)      ;; Gravity!
        (update :life - 0.01))))

(defn spawn-particles! [freq-data canvas-width canvas-height]
  (let [bass (/ (aget freq-data 2) 255.0)
        mid (/ (aget freq-data 128) 255.0)
        high (/ (aget freq-data 500) 255.0)
        sensitivity (:sensitivity @state/app-state)

        bass-count (int (* 30 bass sensitivity))
        mid-count (int (* 15 mid sensitivity))
        high-count (int (* 20 high sensitivity))]

    ;; Bass: explosive bursts from center
    (dotimes [_ bass-count]
      (let [angle (* (rand) (* 2 js/Math.PI))
            speed (+ 3 (* 6 (max 0.3 bass)))
            vx (* speed (js/Math.cos angle))
            vy (* speed (js/Math.sin angle))]
        (swap! state/app-state update :particles conj
               (create-particle
```

```
(/ canvas-width 2) (/ canvas-height 2)
vx vy
"rgba(255, 100, 100, 0.8)"
1.0))))

;; Mid: side streams
;; High: rain from top
;; ... (similar patterns)
))
```

The particle lifecycle:

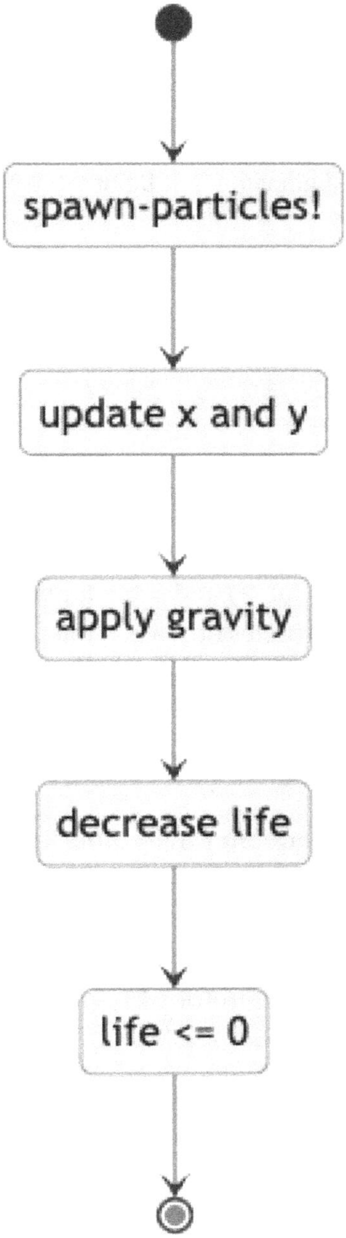

Figure 10-4. *Particle lifecycle state diagram showing birth, movement, gravity, fading, and death phases*

Key technique: Parametric spawning

Table 10-4. *Parametric particle spawning strategy mapping frequency bands to visual behaviors and colors*

Frequency Band	Sample Index	Behavior	Color	Why
Bass	2	Center bursts	Red	Low frequencies = power, energy
Mid	128	Side streams	Cyan	Mid frequencies = melody, direction
High	500	Top rain	Yellow	High frequencies = sparkle, detail

Each frequency band triggers a different particle behavior. This creates **visual separation**—you can actually *see* the different components of the music.

The physics: - `(update :vy + 0.2)` adds constant downward acceleration (gravity) - `(update :life - 0.01)` fades particles out over ~100 frames - No custom physics engine needed—just simple Euler integration!

Visualizer 5: Spectrogram (e07.cljs)

A spectrogram is a **heatmap of frequency over time**. Think of it like a musical score, but instead of notes, you see which frequencies are present at each moment.

Listing 10-10. Scrolling spectrogram heatmap implementing circular buffer with 8:1 bin downsampling showing frequency history over time like musical score visualization

```
(def spectrogram-width 128)

(defn init-spectrogram-buffer! []
  (swap! state/app-state assoc
         :spectrogram-buffer
         (vec (repeat spectrogram-width
                      (vec (repeat 128 0))))))

(defn update-spectrogram! [freq-data]
  (swap! state/app-state update :spectrogram-buffer
```

```
(fn [buffer]
  ;; Downsample 1024 bins → 128 bins
  (let [downsampled (vec (for [i (range 128)]
                          (let [start (* i 8)
                                group (map #(aget freq-data (+
                                start %))
                                           (range 8))
                                avg (/ (reduce + group) 8)]
                            (int avg))))]
    ;; Scroll left, add new column on right
    (conj (subvec buffer 1) downsampled)))))
```

The scrolling mechanism:

```
Time →

[column-0 column-1 column-2 ... Column-127]

After update:

[column-1 column-2 column-3 ... New-column]
```

`(conj (subvec buffer 1) downsampled)` drops the first column and adds a new one at the end. It's a **circular buffer** implemented with vectors.

Downsampling rationale:

Table 10-5. *Spectrogram downsampling rationale showing 8:1 bin reduction for optimized rendering performance*

Original	Downsampled	Result
1024 freq bins	128 bins	8:1 reduction
FFT precision	Display resolution	Faster rendering
Every Hz	Every 8 Hz	Still shows all important features

We average groups of eight adjacent bins. This loses some detail but gains **16x fewer draw calls** (128×128 = 16,384 rectangles vs. 1024×512 = 524,288).

Color mapping:

Listing 10-11. Thermal color palette mapper creating infrared-style heatmap gradient from dark blue through cyan to yellow mimicking thermal imaging cameras

```
(defn value->color [value sensitivity]
  (let [v (* value sensitivity (/ 1 255.0))
        v (min 1.0 v)]
    (cond
      (< v 0.2) (str "rgb(0, 0, " (int (* v 5 100)) ")")           ; Dark blue
      (< v 0.4) (str "rgb(0, " (int (* (- v 0.2) 5 255)) ", 150)") ; Blue → Cyan
      (< v 0.6) (str "rgb(" (int (* (- v 0.4) 5 255)) ", 200, 150)") ; Cyan → Yellow-green
      (< v 0.8) (str "rgb(255, " (int (* (- 0.8 v) 5 255)) ", 0)") ; Yellow → Red
      :else     (str "rgb(255, " (int (* (- 1.0 v) 5 120)) ", "
                                 (int (* (- 1.0 v) 5 120)) ")")))) ; Red → White
```

This creates a **thermal palette**: dark → blue → cyan → yellow (like infrared cameras).

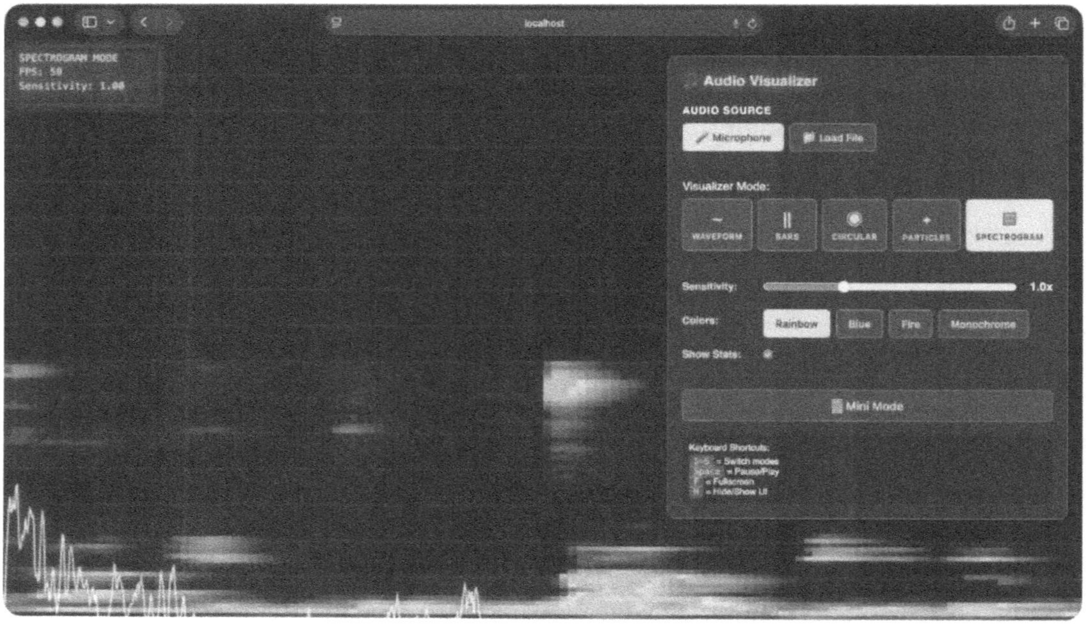

Figure 10-5. *Spectrogram heatmap visualization showing scrolling frequency history with thermal color palette*

Part IV: Mode Switching and UI Controls

Managing five visualizers requires **coordination**. We need to stop the old one before starting the new one, or we get **zombie loops**—multiple `requestAnimationFrame` callbacks fighting for the canvas.

The Control Panel (e08.cljs)

Using Reagent, we build a reactive UI.

Listing 10-12. Reagent mode selector component with auto-re-rendering on state changes using React-powered reactive UI with emoji-enhanced dropdown options

```
(defn mode-selector []
  (let [current-mode (:mode @state/app-state)
        modes [{:key :waveform    :label "Waveform"    :icon "~"}
               {:key :bars        :label "Bars"        :icon "||"}
               {:key :circular    :label "Circular"    :icon "◉"}
               {:key :particles   :label "Particles"   :icon "✦"}
               {:key :spectrogram :label "Spectrogram" :icon "▤"}]]
    [:div.mode-selector
     [:label "Visualizer Mode:"]
     [:div.mode-buttons
      (for [{:keys [key label icon]} modes]
        ^{:key key}
        [:button.mode-btn
         {:class (when (= current-mode key) "active")
          :on-click #(start-visualizer! key)}
         [:span.icon icon]
         [:span.label label]])]]))
```

Reagent magic: When `@state/app-state` changes (the `@` dereferences the atom), Reagent automatically re-renders. This is React under the hood, but with ClojureScript's functional elegance.

Safe Mode Switching

Listing 10-13. Safe mode switching with two-phase shutdown canceling pending animation frames before starting new visualizer preventing concurrent draw loops

```
(defn stop-current-visualizer! []
  (when-let [frame-id (:animation-frame @state/app-state)]
    (js/cancelAnimationFrame frame-id)
    (swap! state/app-state assoc :animation-frame nil)))

(defn start-visualizer! [mode]
  ;; Stop old visualizer
  (stop-current-visualizer!)

  ;; Update mode in state
  (swap! state/app-state assoc :mode mode)

  ;; Start new visualizer
  (case mode
    :waveform (e01/start!)
    :bars (e02/start!)
    :circular (e05/start!)
    :particles (e06/start!)
    :spectrogram (e07/start!)
    nil))
```

The two-phase shutdown:

1. **Cancel pending frame**: Prevents the old `draw` function from being called again.
2. **Update mode**: Changes `:mode` in state.
3. **Guard clauses kick in**: Old `draw` functions see `(not= (:mode @state) :old-mode)` and stop iterating.

This is **defensive programming**. Even if `cancelAnimationFrame` fails, the mode check provides a second line of defense.

Keyboard Shortcuts (core.cljs)

Listing 10-14. Keyboard shortcut handler mapping number keys to mode switching, spacebar to audio pause/resume, F to full screen, and H/S to UI/stats toggling for power users

```
(defn handle-keydown! [e]
  (let [key (.-key e)]
    (case key
      "1" (e08/start-visualizer! :waveform)
      "2" (e08/start-visualizer! :bars)
      "3" (e08/start-visualizer! :circular)
      "4" (e08/start-visualizer! :particles)
      "5" (e08/start-visualizer! :spectrogram)
      " " (do (.preventDefault e)
              (let [ctx (:audio-context @state/app-state)]
                (when ctx
                  (if (= (.-state ctx) "running")
                    (.suspend ctx)
                    (.resume ctx)))))
      "f" (do (.preventDefault e)
              (if (.-fullscreenElement js/document)
                (.exitFullscreen js/document)
                (-> (.querySelector js/document "body")
                    (.requestFullscreen))))
      "+" (swap! state/app-state update :sensitivity #(min 3.0 (+ % 0.1)))
      "-" (swap! state/app-state update :sensitivity #(max 0.1 (- % 0.1)))
      "h" (swap! state/app-state update :show-ui not)
      "s" (swap! state/app-state update :show-stats not)
      nil)))

(.addEventListener js/window "keydown" handle-keydown!)
```

Power user features: - Number keys 1–5: Instant mode switching - Spacebar: Pause/resume audio (freezes visualization) - F: Fullscreen toggle - +/-: Increase or decrease sensitivity - H: Hide UI (clean screenshot mode) - S: Toggle stats overlay

Part V: Performance and Optimization

Real-time graphics demand efficiency. Let's discuss the performance considerations that make this app smooth.

Frame Budget

At 60 fps, we have **16.67 milliseconds** per frame:

```
16.67ms budget
├─ 2ms    Audio data retrieval
├─ 1ms    State updates
├─ 10ms   Drawing operations
├─ 2ms    JavaScript overhead
└─ 1.67ms  Slack (safety margin)
```

If any visualizer takes longer than 16ms consistently, we drop frames. The app feels janky.

Optimization Techniques Used

Table 10-6. *Optimization techniques summary showing performance improvements across all visualizers*

Technique	Where	Savings
Downsampling	Spectrogram	16x fewer rectangles
Typed arrays	All visualizers	Fast memory access
Loop unrolling	Bars	Avoids function call overhead
Canvas state reuse	All	Don't reset styles every time
Lazy particle updates	Particles	Only update living particles
Guard clauses first	All	Bail early if wrong mode

The Spectrogram Optimization Story

Listing 10-15. Spectrogram downsampling optimization reducing from 524K to 16K rectangles per frame achieving 32x performance improvement from 8ms to 0.25ms

Original code (SLOW):

```
;; 512 time slices × 1024 frequency bins = 524,288 rectangles/frame!
(doseq [t (range 512)]
  (doseq [f (range 1024)]
    (.fillRect ctx x y w h)))
```

Optimized code (FAST):

```
;; 128 time slices × 128 frequency bins = 16,384 rectangles/frame
(doseq [t (range 128)]
  (doseq [f (range 128)]
    (.fillRect ctx x y w h)))
```

This is a **32x reduction** in draw calls! From ~8ms per frame to ~0.25ms.

Memory Management

The particles problem: Without cleanup, they accumulate forever.

Listing 10-16. Particle lifecycle cleanup using keep combinator filtering dead particles preventing memory accumulation and eventual browser crash

```
;; BAD: Particles never die
(swap! state/app-state update :particles conj new-particle)
;; After 5 minutes: 180,000 particles = crash

;; GOOD: Filter out dead particles
(defn update-particles! []
  (swap! state/app-state update :particles
         (fn [particles]
           (vec (keep update-particle particles)))))
```

`keep` is like `map` + `filter`—it applies `update-particle`, and if it returns `nil` (dead particle), removes it from the result.

The Animation Frame Singleton

Critical rule: Only ONE `requestAnimationFrame` callback should be active at a time.

Listing 10-17. Animation frame singleton pattern preventing resource leaks by canceling previous requestAnimationFrame callbacks before starting new visualizers

```
;; Store frame ID in state
(swap! state/app-state assoc :animation-frame
       (js/requestAnimationFrame draw))

;; Cancel it before starting new
(when-let [frame-id (:animation-frame @state/app-state)]
  (js/cancelAnimationFrame frame-id))
```

This prevents **resource leaks**. Every `requestAnimationFrame` callback holds a reference to its closure, which holds references to variables, which… You get the idea. Leaks accumulate, memory grows, performance degrades.

Part VI: The Math Behind the Music

Let's dive deeper into the signal processing concepts. You don't need to implement FFT yourself—the browser does it—but understanding *what* it's doing makes you a better developer.

Fourier Transform: The Big Idea

Jean-Baptiste Joseph Fourier (1768–1830) had an insight: *any* periodic function can be decomposed into a sum of sine waves.

```
Square wave = sin(ω) + sin(3ω)/3 + sin(5ω)/5 + sin(7ω)/7 + ...
```

The **fast Fourier transform** (FFT) is an efficient algorithm (invented in 1965 by Cooley and Tukey) for computing this decomposition.

Why it matters: Your microphone captures a complex waveform—people talking, music playing, dogs barking. FFT reveals *which frequencies* are in that mess. "Show me the 440 Hz component" → that's a musical A note.

Frequency Bins Explained

With `fftSize = 2048`, we get **1024 frequency bins** (`frequencyBinCount`).

What does each bin represent?

```
Sample rate: 48,000 Hz (typical for microphones)
Nyquist frequency: 24,000 Hz (half sample rate)
Bin width: 24,000 Hz ÷ 1024 = 23.4 Hz per bin
```

```
Bin 0:   0-23.4 Hz      (subsonic rumble)
Bin 1:   23.4-46.8 Hz   (deep bass)
Bin 10:  234-257 Hz     (male voice fundamental)
Bin 128: 2995-3018 Hz   (mid-range)
Bin 500: 11,720 Hz      (high frequencies)
Bin 1023: 23,977-24,000 Hz (near ultrasonic)
```

Human hearing range: 20–20,000 Hz. So bins 0–855 cover audible sound. The rest is mostly noise or harmonics.

The Smoothing Constant

```
(set! (.-smoothingTimeConstant analyser) 0.8)
```

This implements **temporal smoothing**: each new FFT result is blended with the previous one.

```
new_value = (old_value × 0.8) + (current_value × 0.2)
```

Why smooth? Raw FFT output is *noisy*. It fluctuates wildly frame to frame. Smoothing creates visual continuity.

Table 10-7. *Smoothing constant values and their effects on visualization responsiveness and continuity*

Value	Effect	Use Case
0.0	No smoothing	Twitchy, responsive, jittery
0.5	Moderate	Balanced
0.8	Heavy	Smooth, floaty, delayed
0.95	Extreme	Very smooth but sluggish

We chose 0.8 as a sweet spot—smooth enough to look good, responsive enough to feel live.

Time vs. Frequency Domain

Table 10-8. *Time domain vs. frequency domain data comparison showing different visualization use cases*

Domain	Data	Shows	Use Case
Time	`getByteTimeDomainData`	Amplitude over time	Waveform, oscilloscope
Frequency	`getByteFrequencyData`	Amplitude per frequency	Bars, spectrum, everything else

Time domain is the raw waveform—what the microphone sees. **Frequency domain** is the *analysis* of that waveform—what frequencies it contains.

FFT transforms time → frequency. It's a **change of basis**—like viewing a 3D object from a different angle.

Part VII: Tauri Deep Dive

Let's pull back the curtain on what Tauri is actually doing.

Rust Side: main.rs

Listing 10-18. Real Tauri v2 main.rs with IPC commands for audio file loading, native file dialog, mini-mode window management, and system tray icon with context menu

```
// Prevents additional console window on Windows in release
#![cfg_attr(not(debug_assertions), windows_subsystem = "windows")]

use tauri::Manager;
use tauri_plugin_dialog::DialogExt;
use tauri::menu::{MenuBuilder, MenuItemBuilder};
```

```
use tauri::tray::{TrayIconBuilder, TrayIconEvent, MouseButton,
MouseButtonState};

mod audio_loader;

/// Load audio file and return raw samples
#[tauri::command]
async fn load_audio_file(path: String) -> Result<AudioData, String> { /*
... */ }

/// Open native file dialog and return selected path
#[tauri::command]
async fn open_file_dialog(app: tauri::AppHandle) -> Result<Option<String>,
String> {
    let file_path = app.dialog().file()
        .add_filter("Audio Files", &["mp3", "wav", "flac", "m4a", "ogg"])
        .blocking_pick_file();
    Ok(file_path.map(|p| p.to_string()))
}

/// Toggle mini mode (small always-on-top window)
#[tauri::command]
async fn toggle_mini_mode(window: tauri::WebviewWindow, mini: bool) ->
Result<(), String> {
    if mini {
        window.set_size(tauri::LogicalSize::new(400, 400)).map_err(|e| e.to_
        string())?;
        window.set_always_on_top(true).map_err(|e| e.to_string())?;
    } else {
        window.set_size(tauri::LogicalSize::new(1200, 800)).map_err(|e|
        e.to_string())?;
        window.set_always_on_top(false).map_err(|e| e.to_string())?;
    }
    Ok(())
}

fn main() {
    tauri::Builder::default()
```

```
        .plugin(tauri_plugin_shell::init())
        .plugin(tauri_plugin_fs::init())
        .plugin(tauri_plugin_dialog::init())
        .setup(|app| {
            // System tray with Show / Mini Mode / Quit menu
            let show_i = MenuItemBuilder::with_id("show", "Show").
            build(app)?;
            let mini_i = MenuItemBuilder::with_id("mini", "Mini Mode").
            build(app)?;
            let quit_i = MenuItemBuilder::with_id("quit", "Quit").
            build(app)?;
            let menu = MenuBuilder::new(app).item(&show_i).item(&mini_i)
                .separator().item(&quit_i).build()?;
            let _tray = TrayIconBuilder::new().menu(&menu)
                .on_menu_event(|app, event| { /* handle show/mini/quit */ })
                .build(app)?;
            Ok(())
        })
        .invoke_handler(tauri::generate_handler![
            load_audio_file, open_file_dialog, toggle_mini_mode
        ])
        .run(tauri::generate_context!())
        .expect("error while running tauri application");
}
```

The real `main.rs` is significantly richer than a minimal stub. Key additions over the simplest version: - **IPC commands** registered via `.invoke_handler`: `load_audio_file`, `open_file_dialog`, `toggle_mini_mode` - **Plugins**: `tauri_plugin_fs` (file system), `tauri_plugin_dialog` (native dialogs), `tauri_plugin_shell` - **System tray**: Menu with show/mini mode/quit items - **`audio_loader` module**: A separate `audio_loader.rs` that decodes audio files into raw `f32` samples

IPC: Calling Rust from ClojureScript

Our app uses Tauri's **invoke system** to call Rust functions from ClojureScript—for example, see below.

Listing 10-19. Tauri IPC command system demonstrating ClojureScript-to-Rust bridge for native file access, system commands, and hardware interfaces

```
;; ClojureScript
(-> (js/window.__TAURI__.core.invoke "read_audio_file" #js {:path "/music/
song.mp3"})
    (.then (fn [data] (println "Loaded:" data))))
// Rust
#[tauri::command]
fn read_audio_file(path: String) -> Vec<u8> {
  std::fs::read(path).unwrap()
}
```

This is incredibly powerful. Need to: - Access native file dialogs? - Run system commands? - Perform heavy computation without blocking UI? - Interface with hardware?

Rust can do it. ClojureScript calls it. Best of both worlds.

Build Process

When you run `npm run tauri build`:

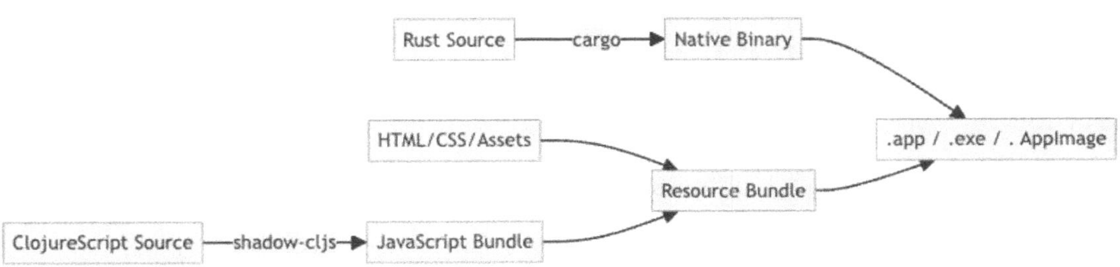

Figure 10-6. *Tauri build process diagram showing compilation of ClojureScript, Rust, and assets into native executables*

The output is a **single executable** with everything: - Compiled Rust code (native, fast) - Bundled JavaScript (your ClojureScript, minified) - HTML/CSS/images - Embedded web view engine hooks

Size comparison: - Web app (served): ~200KB JavaScript + assets - Electron app: ~120MB (includes entire Chromium) - Tauri app: ~3MB (reuses OS web view)

40x smaller than Electron! This matters for distribution.

Platform Differences

Table 10-9. *Platform-specific web engines, binary formats, and installer types for macOS, Windows, and Linux*

Platform	Web Engine	Binary Format	Installer
macOS	WebKit	`.app` bundle	`.dmg`
Windows	WebView2	`.exe`	`.msi`
Linux	WebKitGTK	ELF binary	`. AppImage / .deb`

Implication: Your app looks native on each platform. macOS users get WebKit rendering (Safari engine). Windows users get Chromium Edge. Linux users get WebKitGTK.

Part VIII: Color Theory and Visual Design

Why does the circular visualizer use rainbow colors? Why are particles red/cyan/yellow? These aren't random choices.

HSL: The Functional Color Space

```
(str "hsl(" hue ", 100%, " lightness "%)")
```

HSL = Hue, Saturation, Lightness

Table 10-10. *HSL color space components explaining hue wheel, saturation intensity, and lightness brightness ranges*

Component	Range	Meaning
Hue	0°–360°	Color wheel position
Saturation	0%–100%	Color intensity (0% = gray)
Lightness	0%–100%	Brightness (0% = black, 100% = white)

Why is HSL > RGB for visualizers?

```
;; Rainbow with RGB = 😫 complex lookup tables
(def rainbow-rgb [[255 0 0] [255 127 0] [255 255 0] ...])

;; Rainbow with HSL = 😊 just increment hue
(for [i (range 360)]
  (str "hsl(" i ", 100%, 50%)"))
```

HSL is **parametric**. Want to sweep through all colors? Vary hue. Want to make everything darker? Reduce lightness. RGB doesn't give you that.

The Spectrum Metaphor

Why does audio → color work?

Sound and light are both **waves**. They have: - Frequency (pitch/hue) - Amplitude (volume/brightness) - Timbre (texture/saturation)

We exploit this **sensory analogy**.

Table 10-11. *Audio-to-visual mapping strategy showing frequency-to-color and amplitude-to-brightness correspondences*

Audio Property	Visual Mapping	Implementation
Low frequency (bass)	Red/warm colors	`hue = 0°`
Mid frequency	Green/balanced	`hue = 120°`
High frequency	Blue/cool	`hue = 240°`
Loud amplitude	Bright	`lightness = 70%`
Quiet amplitude	Dim	`lightness = 30%`

Cultural context: This mapping isn't universal! In Western culture, we associate: - Red = passion, energy, bass - Blue = calm, clarity, treble

But it's learned. A different culture might map differently.

Accessibility Consideration

Colorblind users: About 8% of men and 0.5% of women have some form of color vision deficiency.

Our rainbow scheme is problematic for **deuteranopia** (red-green blindness). They see: - Red → brown - Green → tan - Indistinguishable!

Better approach (not implemented, but good to know):

Listing 10-20. Viridis colorblind-safe palette providing perceptually uniform scientific visualization alternative to rainbow gradients for deuteranopia accessibility

```
;; Colorblind-safe palette
(def viridis
  ["#440154" "#31688e" "#35b779" "#fde724"])
```

Viridis is a perceptually uniform, colorblind-safe palette used in scientific visualization. Consider it for production apps!

Part IX: Lessons from the Top Floor

We've built a real-time audio visualizer that runs as a native desktop app. Let's reflect on what we learned that applies beyond this specific project.

1. Architecture: Separate Concerns

```
State Layer (state.cljs)
   ↓
Behavior Layer (e01-e07.cljs)
   ↓
Presentation Layer (Canvas API)
```

Why it matters: When we needed to add the UI toggle feature (h key), we

1. Added `:show-ui` to state
2. Modified the UI rendering condition
3. Added keyboard handler

We didn't touch the visualizers. They kept working. That's good architecture.

The principle: Keep data, logic, and presentation separate. Change one without breaking the others.

2. Asynchronous Thinking

```
(-> (js/navigator.mediaDevices.getUserMedia #js {:audio true})
    (.then success-handler)
    (.catch error-handler))
```

Real-world apps are asynchronous: - Network requests - File system operations - User permissions - Hardware access

ClojureScript's promise threading (->) makes this readable. Compare to JavaScript callback hell:

```
navigator.mediaDevices.getUserMedia({audio: true})
  .then(stream => {
    const source = audioContext.createMediaStreamSource(stream);
    source.connect(analyser);
  })
  .catch(err => {
    console.error(err);
  });
```

Not terrible, but ClojureScript's threading macro makes data flow clearer.

3. Performance: Measure, Don't Guess

We optimized the spectrogram from 524K rectangles to 16K. How did we know?

Listing 10-21. FPS measurement instrumentation calculating frames per second from delta timestamps enabling performance profiling and bottleneck identification

```
(defn measure-fps! []
  (let [now (.now js/Date)
        last-time (:last-frame-time @state/app-state)
```

```
        delta (- now last-time)
        fps (if (zero? delta) 60 (/ 1000 delta))]
    (swap! state/app-state assoc
           :last-frame-time now
           :fps (js/Math.round fps))))
```

Always instrument. Don't optimize blindly. We saw FPS drop from 60 to 8. *Then* we investigated.

Profiling workflow:

1. Measure baseline (60 fps target).
2. Identify bottleneck (Chrome DevTools → performance tab).
3. Hypothesize fix (downsample spectrogram?).
4. Implement and measure (FPS back to 60? ✅).

4. Functional State Management

Every chapter has reinforced: **immutable data** + **pure functions** = predictable code.

Listing 10-22. Immutable state transformation demonstrating functional approach with swap! vs. imperative mutation with direct array modification

```
;; BAD: Mutation
(def particles (atom []))
(.push @particles new-particle)  ; Mutates the array!

;; GOOD: Transformation
(swap! particles conj new-particle)  ; Returns new array
```

Why it matters: When a bug happens, immutability means: - State only changes in `swap!` calls - You can **rewind time** (with re-frame or similar) - No spooky action at a distance

Debugging is easier when you know exactly where state changes.

5. The Power of Abstractions

Canvas API is a thin wrapper over pixels. You could draw everything with `putImageData` directly:

```
imageData.data[offset] = red;
imageData.data[offset+1] = green;
imageData.data[offset+2] = blue;
imageData.data[offset+3] = alpha;
```

But we use **higher-level abstractions**: - `.fillRect()` for rectangles - `.stroke()` for lines - `.arc()` for circles

Why? They're faster (hardware accelerated) and clearer (intent revealing).

Lesson: Use the right level of abstraction. Don't reinvent the wheel. But understand what's below the abstraction so you can drop down when needed.

6. Cross-Platform Thinking

Tauri makes this native on three OSes from one codebase. But you must think about

File paths:

```
// BAD (Windows breaks)
"C:/Users/music/song.mp3"

// GOOD (works everywhere)
path.join(homeDir, "music", "song.mp3")
```

Platform conventions: - macOS: Menu bar in system bar, CMD key - Windows: Menu bar in window, CTRL key - Linux: Varies (GNOME vs. KDE)

Tauri abstracts most of this. But be aware.

Part X: Expanding Horizons

This is the end of the book, but the beginning of your journey. Where can you take this code?

Adding Features

1. **Audio File Input**

   Currently we only support microphone. What about playing MP3s?

Listing 10-23. Audio file loading using FileReader and decodeAudioData for MP3/WAV playback enabling offline file visualization beyond live microphone input

```
(defn load-audio-file! [file]
  (let [reader (js/FileReader.)]
    (set! (.-onload reader)
          (fn [e]
            (let [array-buffer (.. E -target -result)
                  ctx (:audio-context @state/app-state)]
              (.decodeAudioData ctx array-buffer
                (fn [buffer]
                  (swap! state/app-state assoc :audio-buffer buffer))))))
    (.readAsArrayBuffer reader file)))
```

2. **Recording Visualizations**

   Use `MediaRecorder` API to capture canvas as video.

Listing 10-24. Canvas video recording using MediaRecorder API capturing live visualizations as WebM video for social media sharing and archival

```
(defn start-recording! [canvas]
  (let [stream (.captureStream canvas)
        recorder (js/MediaRecorder. stream)]
    (.start recorder)
    (swap! state/app-state assoc :recorder recorder)))
```

3. **3D Visualizations**

   Replace Canvas 2D with **WebGL** for 3D:

```
(defn draw-3d-spectrum! [gl freq-data]
  ;; Use Three.js or raw WebGL
  ;; Bars become 3D towers
  ;; Rotate camera based on beat
  )
```

   WebGL is **dramatically faster** than canvas for complex scenes.

4. **Machine Learning Integration**

   Use **TensorFlow.js** for: - Genre classification ("This sounds like jazz!") - Beat detection (more sophisticated than our simple bass threshold) - Pitch detection ("You're singing an A#!")

```
const model = await tf.loadGraphModel('music-classifier/
model.json');
const prediction = model.predict(audioDataTensor);
```

Publishing Your App

Tauri makes distribution easy:

```
npm run tauri build
```

Outputs: - **macOS**: `.dmg` installer in `src-tauri/target/release/bundle/dmg/` - **Windows**: `.msi` installer - **Linux**: `. AppImage` or `.deb`

Code signing (important!): - macOS: Need Apple Developer account ($99/year) to sign `.app` - Windows: Need code signing certificate (~$300/year) - Linux: No signing required (but users appreciate GPG signatures)

Distribution channels: - GitHub Releases (free) - Mac App Store (requires Apple Developer account) - Microsoft Store (requires developer account) - Snap Store/ Flatpak (Linux)

Contributing to Open Source

This project structure is **production ready**. You could

1. **Open source it on GitHub:**
   - Add LICENSE (MIT suggested).
   - Write README with screenshots.
   - Tag releases (`v1.0.0`).
2. **Accept contributions:**
   - Create issues for bugs/features.
   - Review pull requests.
   - Maintain CHANGELOG.
3. **Build a community:**
   - Discord server for users.
   - Showcase cool customizations.
   - Help others learn.

Remember: The ClojureScript community is small but passionate. Your project could help others learn!

Closing Thoughts: The View from Here

> "Code is not just instructions for machines. It's a conversation between programmers across time. The you of today writes for the you of next year, who will wonder: what was I thinking?"
>
> —Anonymous developer, probably debugging at 3 AM

You started on the ground floor with Pong—a simple game loop, basic state management, pure transformations. You climbed through nine floors:

- **Floor 2**: Animation and creative coding (pulsating titles, Motion.js)
- **Floor 3**: Visual generation (Quil abstract art)

- **Floor 4**: UI frameworks (Reagent, complex state)
- **Floor 5**: Mini applications (mind maps, to-do apps)
- **Floor 6**: Data visualization (charts, graphs)
- **Floor 7**: Real-time processing (video filters)
- **Floor 8**: Game development (PixiJS, complex interactions)
- **Floor 9**: Neural networks (backpropagation, training)
- **Floor 10**: Native desktop apps (Tauri, audio)

Each floor built on the last. Each introduced new concepts. But the **foundation remained the same**: immutable data, pure functions, thoughtful architecture.

This is the way.

ClojureScript isn't just a language. It's a **philosophy**. Every line you write is a choice: - Mutate or transform? - Hide or reveal? - Complex or simple?

Functional programming guides you toward the latter: transform, reveal, simplify.

Now you stand at the top, looking out over the landscape. You can see patterns that were invisible from below: - State management is just data flowing through functions - UI rendering is just (state) → (view) - Async operations are just transformed callbacks - Graphics are just numbers becoming pixels

It's all transformations, all the way down.

The Final Challenge

Before you leave the penthouse, I have one last exercise for you:

Build the sixth visualizer.

We gave you five. You understand the pattern. Now create something new: - Mandelbrot set reactive to bass? - Conway's Game of Life where birth rules depend on frequency? - Lissajous curves traced by sound? - Reaction-diffusion textures colored by spectrum?

The tools are in your hands. The canvas is blank. The microphone is listening.

What will you create?

Appendix A: Complete File Reference

■ Project Structure

```
10-audio-visualizer/
├── src/
│   └── myapp/
│       ├── core.cljs          # Entry point (120 lines)
│       ├── state.cljs         # Shared state (200 lines)
│       ├── e01.cljs         # Waveform (60 lines)
│       ├── e02.cljs         # Frequency bars (70 lines)
│       ├── e05.cljs         # Circular spectrum (100 lines)
│       ├── e06.cljs         # Particles (140 lines)
│       ├── e07.cljs         # Spectrogram (130 lines)
│       └── e08.cljs         # UI controls (270 lines)
│
├── src-tauri/
│   ├── Cargo.toml
│   ├── tauri.conf.json
│   └── src/
│       └── main.rs
│
├── public/
│   └── index.html
│
├── shadow-cljs.edn
├── deps.edn
└── package.json

Total: ~1,100 lines of ClojureScript
       ~30 lines of Rust
       ~50 lines of config
```

🔑 Key Functions Quick Reference

Table 10-12. *Key Functions and Their Roles in the Audio Visualizer Implementation*

Function	File	Purpose
`setup-analyser!`	state.cljs	Initialize Web Audio
`draw-loop!`	e01–e07	Main render loop
`start-visualizer!`	e08.cljs	Mode switching
`handle-keydown!`	core.cljs	Keyboard control
`create-particle`	e06.cljs	Particle physics
`update-spectrogram!`	e07.cljs	Scrolling buffer

Appendix B: Troubleshooting Guide

Problem: No microphone access

```
Error: NotAllowedError: Permission denied
```

Solution: Check browser permissions. In Chrome: `chrome://settings/content/microphone`

Problem: Audio context suspended

```
Warning: AudioContext was not allowed to start
```

Solution: Modern browsers require user interaction before audio. Click something first!

Problem: Zombie loops (multiple visualizers running)

```
FPS drops to 10, canvas flickers
```

Solution: Check mode guard clauses.

Listing 10-25. Mode guard clause debugging pattern preventing zombie loops by ensuring only active visualizer executes preventing concurrent animation conflicts

```
(when (= (:mode @state/app-state) :correct-mode) ...)
```

Problem: Tauri window doesn't open

```
Error: Failed to create webview
```

Solution: Ensure WebView2 (Windows) or WebKitGTK (Linux) is installed.

Appendix C: Further Reading

Books: - *Designing Sound* by Andy Farnell — Synthesis and audio theory - *ClojureScript Unraveled* by Andrey Antukh — Deep dive into CLJS - *The Nature of Code* by Daniel Shiffman — Physics simulations

Papers: - Cooley and Tukey (1965) — "An Algorithm for the Machine Calculation of Complex Fourier Series" - Roads (1996) — "The Computer Music Tutorial"

Websites: - MDN Web Audio API: `https://developer.mozilla.org/en-US/docs/Web/API/Web_Audio_API` - Tauri Docs: `https://tauri.app/` - ClojureScript: `https://clojurescript.org/`

Open-source visualizers: - Butterchurn (Milkdrop WebGL port) - projectM (MilkDrop clone) - Cava (terminal visualizer)

> "The penthouse was never the destination. It was a vantage point. Now go build something beautiful."

♪ Happy Coding!🎨

Index

N. Modrzyk, *The ClojureScript Playbook*, https://doi.org/10.1007/979-8-8688-2879-9

G, H, I

J, K

L

M

N

O

P

U

V

W, X, Y, Z

www.ingramcontent.com/pod-product-compliance
Lightning Source LLC
LaVergne TN
LVHW082017200926
848481LV00010B/2875
* 9 7 9 8 8 6 8 8 2 8 7 8 2 *